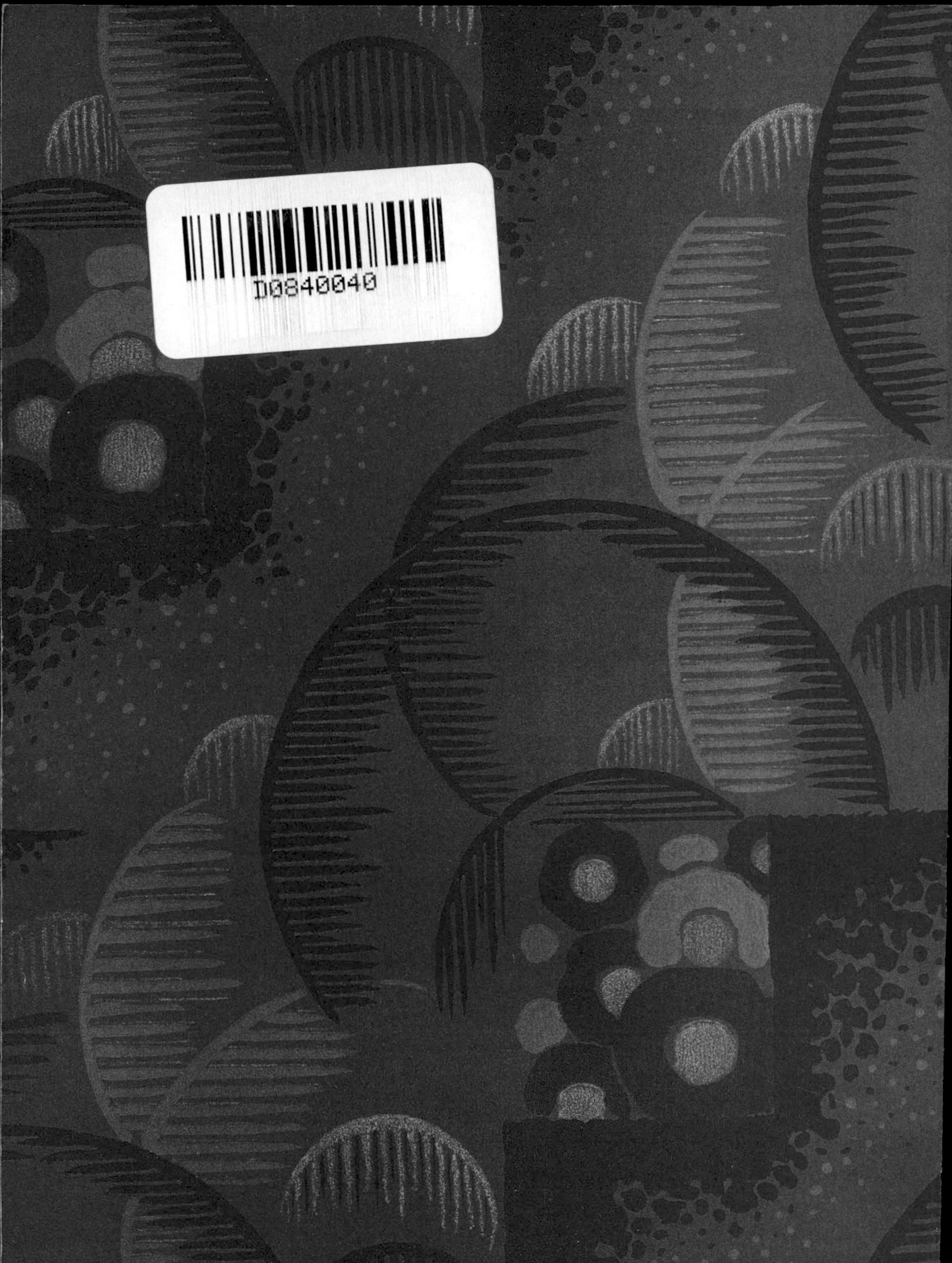

NATSUME ONO made her professional debut in 2003
with the webcomic *La Quinta Camera*. Her subsequent
works *not simple*, *Ristorante Paradiso*, *Gente* and *House
of Five Leaves* (*Saraiya Goyou*) met with both critical and
popular acclaim. Both *Ristorante Paradiso* and *House of
Five Leaves* have been adapted into TV anime series.

House of Five Leaves

さらい屋五葉

7 第七集

NATSUME ONO

HOUSE OF さらい屋 五葉 FIVE LEAVES

THE STORY THUS FAR

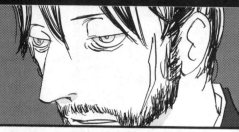

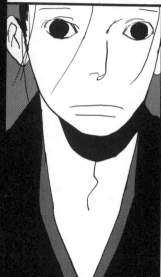

As a member of Bakuro.

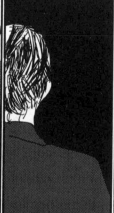

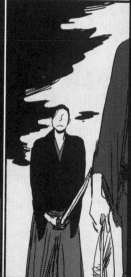

MASANOSUKE, an impoverished *ronin*, fell in with a group of kidnappers calling themselves the "**FIVE LEAVES**." Gradually, the bonds of friendship grew between them, but **YAICHI**, pursued by members of his old gang, begins to distance himself from the crew. As the Five Leaves prepare for their last job, Masa learns that Yaichi himself had been a kidnapping victim. The ronin then goes to see **GOINKYO** and asks about Yaichi's past, about the time when he was known as "Sei the Drifter."

お絹 OKINU
Ume's daughter. One of the few people who know about the existence of the Five Leaves.

仁 JIN (The man with the scar)
One of Yaichi's former superiors, now pursuing him.

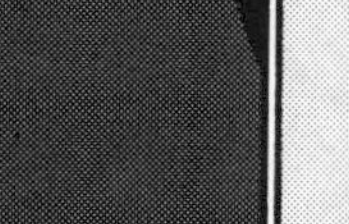

立花 TACHIBANA
Works under Yagi. A regular at Ume's establishment.

ご隠居 GOINKYO (Soji the Saint)
An ex-gang boss who sometimes lends the Five Leaves a hand.

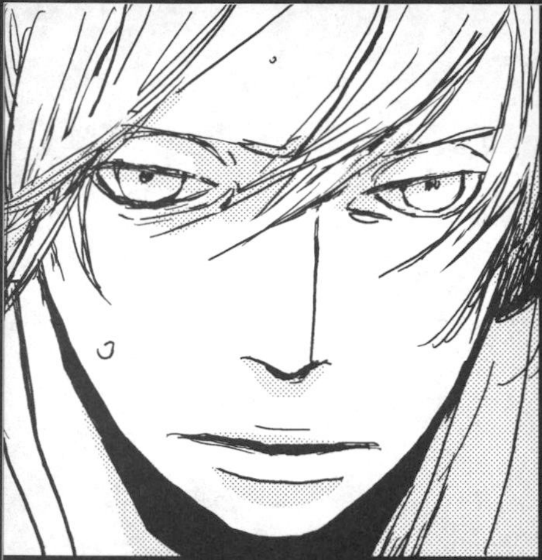

弥一 **YAICHI**

The leader of the Five Leaves, a kidnapping crew. Once known as "Sei the Drifter," he ran with the Bakuro no Kuhei gang and is now being pursued by them. He was finally tracked down by Jin, but Masa saved him during the confrontation.

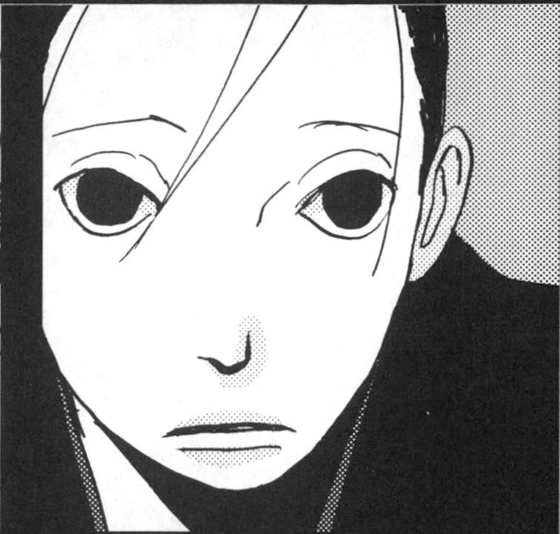

秋津政之助 **AKITSU MASANOSUKE**

A *ronin* striving to become a samurai retainer again. A skilled swordsman, he cannot exhibit his talents in front of people due to his timid nature. In need of money to service his brother's debt back home. Concerned about his brother's precarious situation, at the same time he's fiercely curious about Yaichi's true identity.

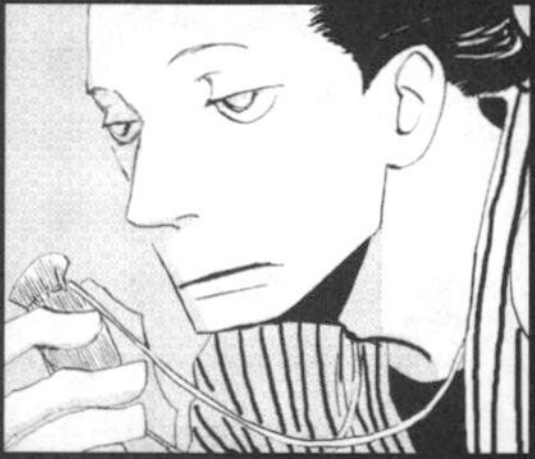

松吉 **MATSUKICHI**

A member of the Five Leaves, he's a silent man who serves as the gang's spy. An ornament craftsman, he used to work solo as a thief but is loyal to Yaichi for saving his life.

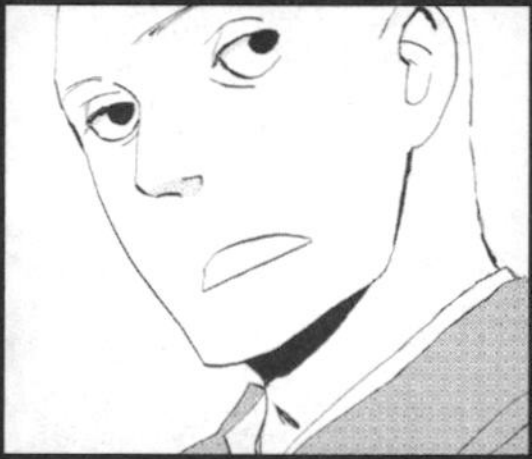

梅造 **UMEZO**

A member of the Five Leaves and owner of the *izakaya* where the crew gathers. An ex-thief, he loves his daughter and has feelings for Otake.

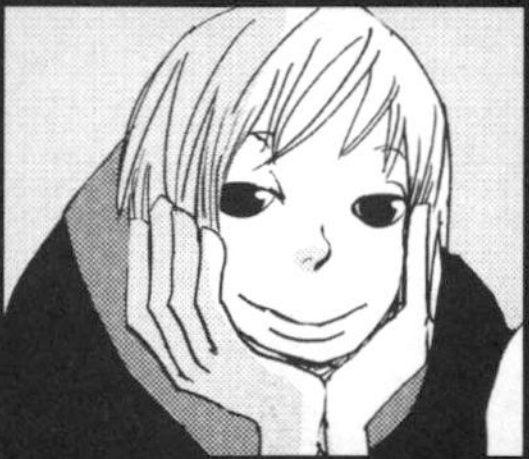

銀太 **GINTA**

An intermediary with ties to the *Machikata*. In need of money to reopen his master's store, which was robbed by bandits.

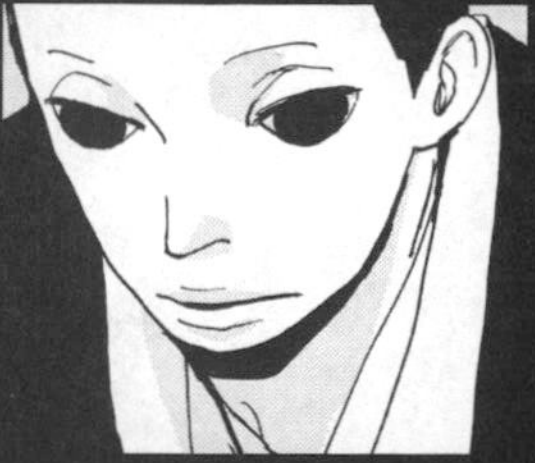

文之助 **BUNNOSUKE**

Masa's younger brother, he assumed the role of head of their family. Sent to Edo on his lord's order, he's scheming to secure a promotion via bribery.

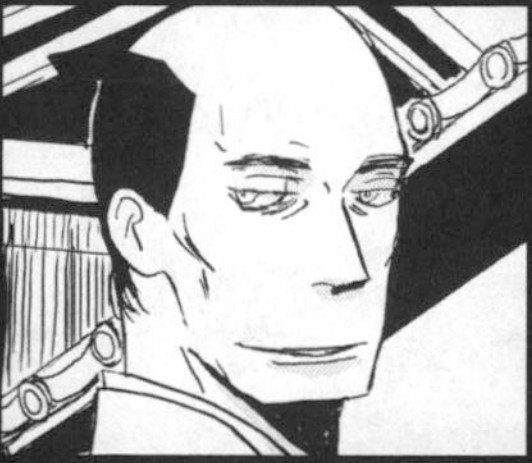

八木平左衛門 **YAGI HEIZAEMON**

A superintendant of the *Machikata*. Realizes that Yaichi is the legitimate heir of his neighboring family but is now using their dead servant's name.

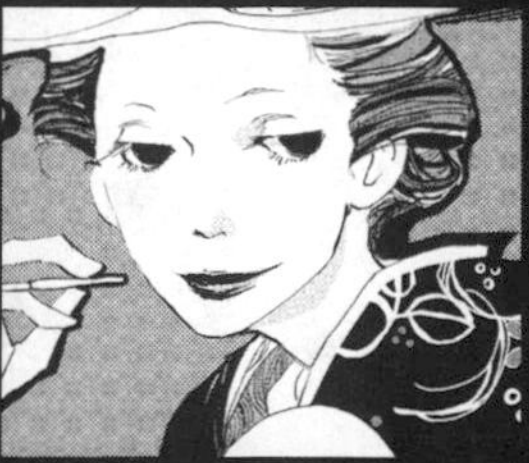

おたけ **OTAKE**

A member of the Five Leaves, she used to work in a brothel but was freed by Yaichi. She lives next to Masa in the rowhouse. She has a fondness for sake.

House of Five Leaves

TABLE OF CONTENTS

7 第七集

Chapter Forty-Three The Drifter (Part One)

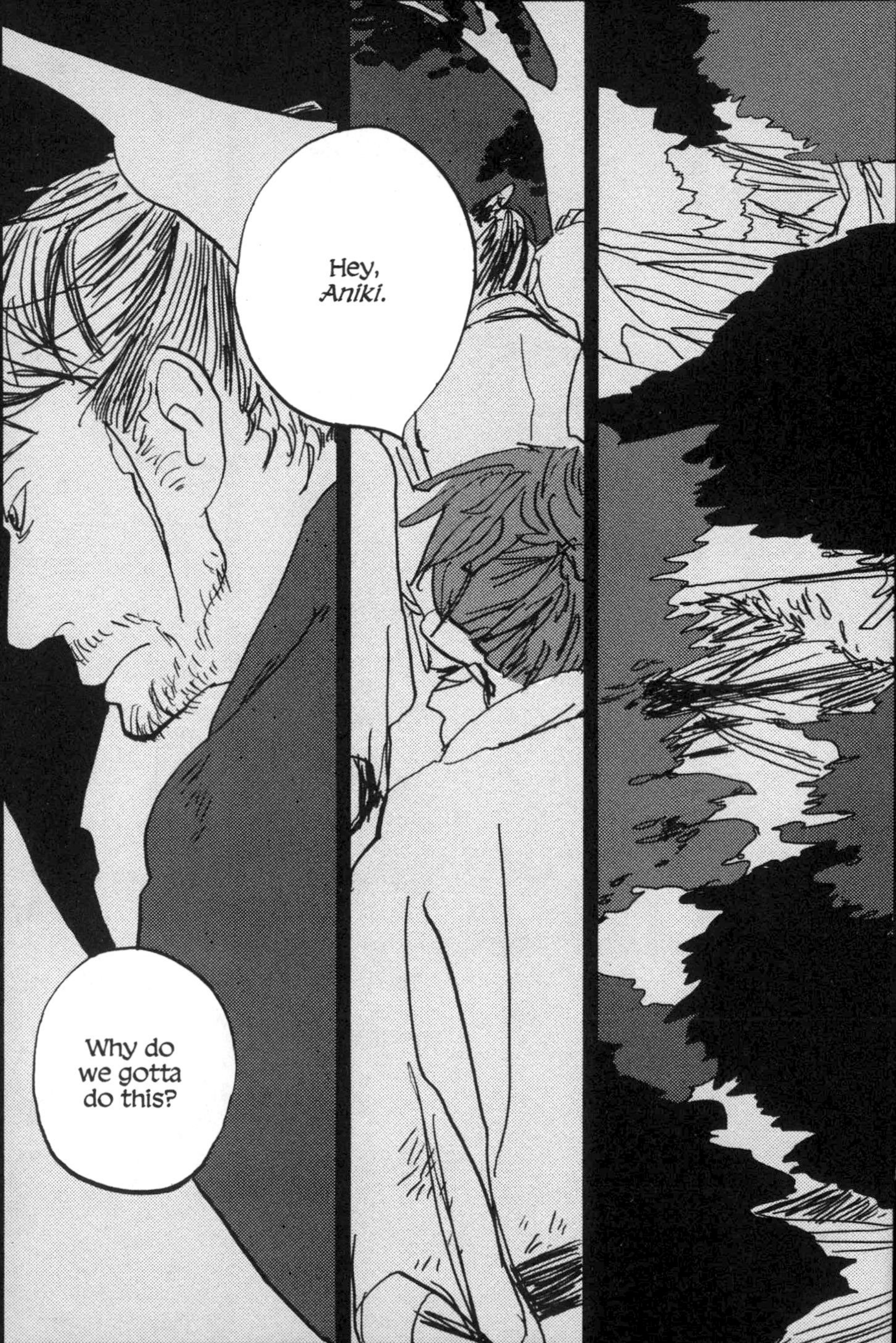
Hey, *Aniki.*
Why do we gotta do this?

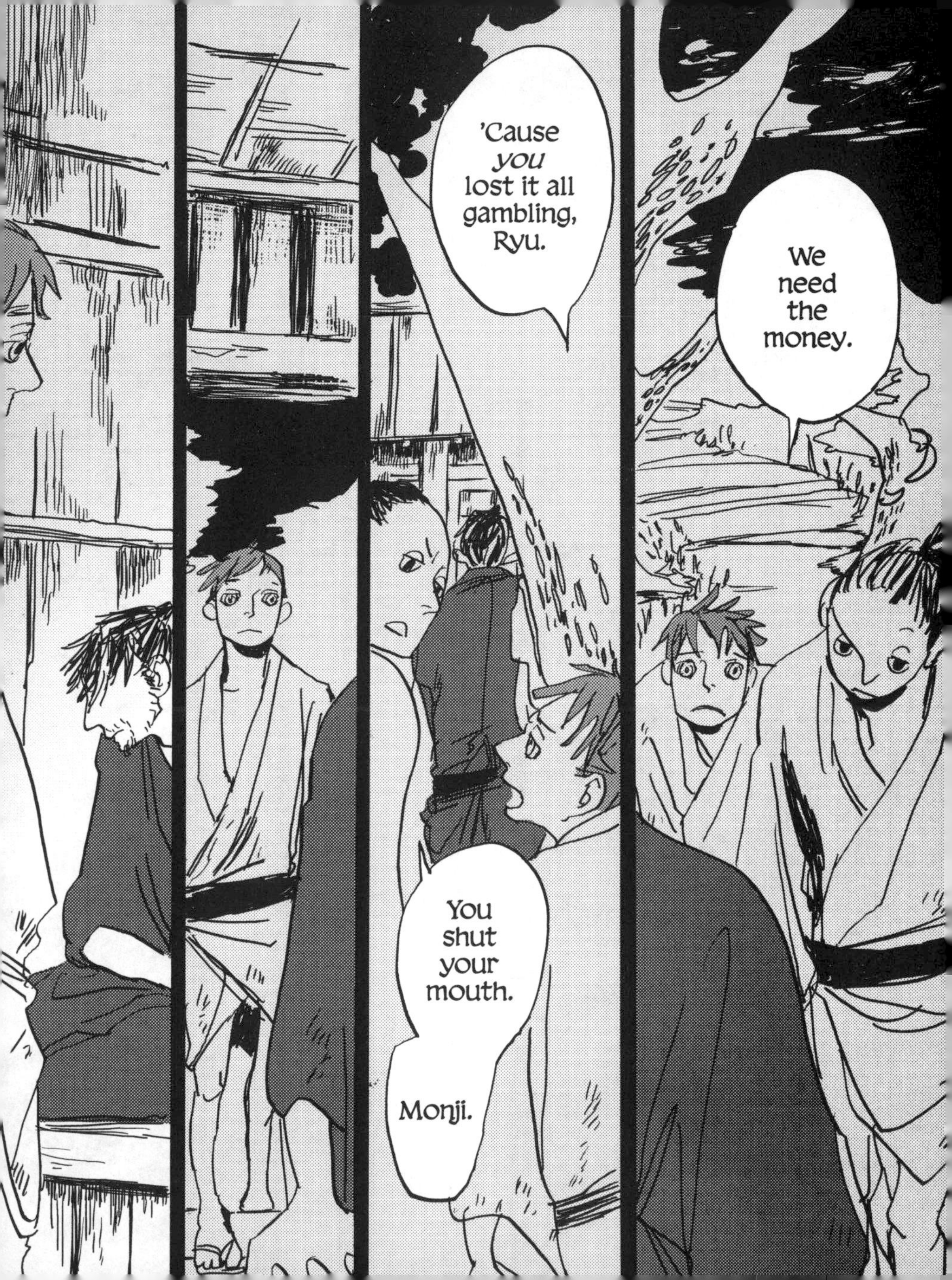
We need the money.
'Cause *you* lost it all gambling, Ryu.
You shut your mouth.
Monji.

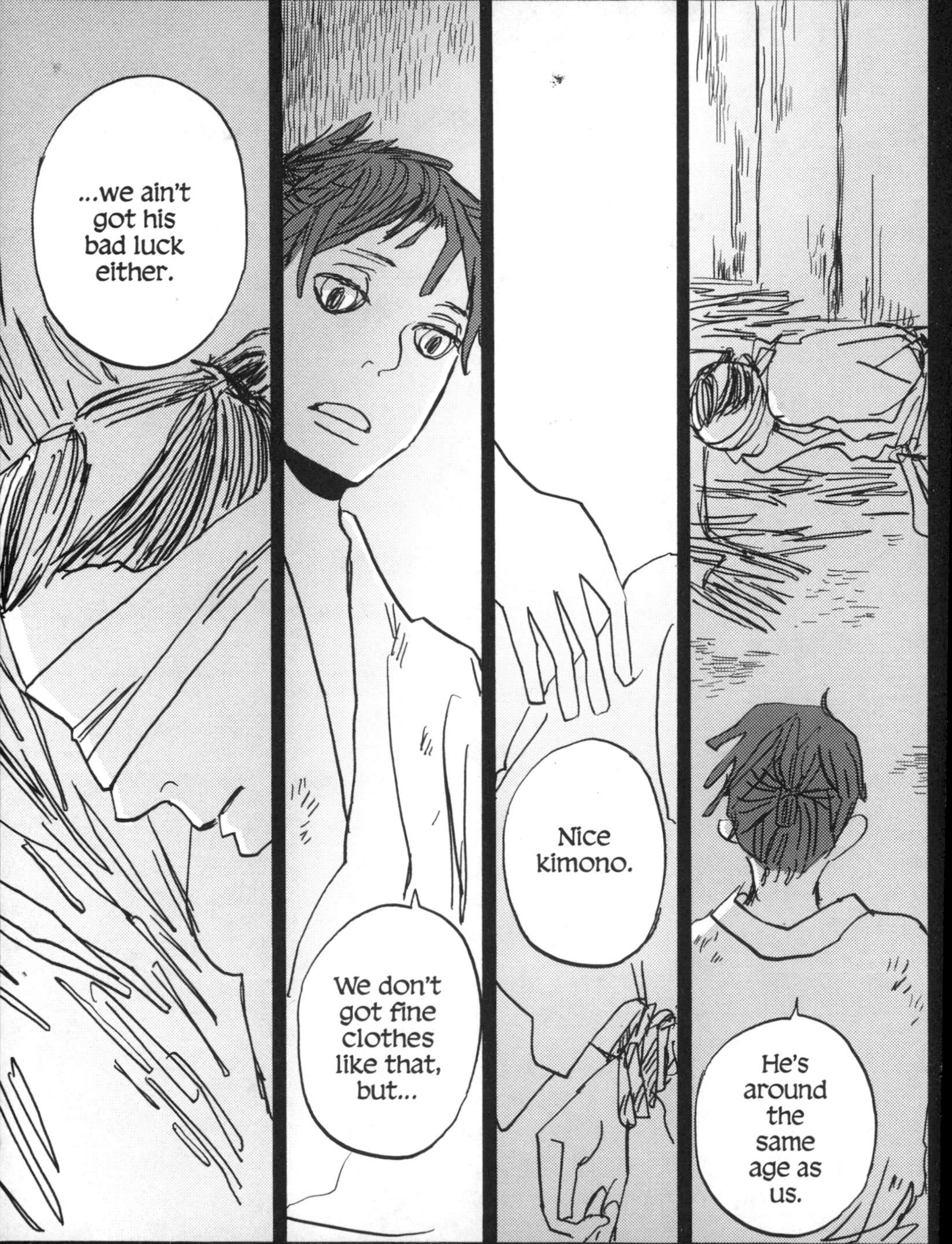
He's around the same age as us.
Nice kimono.
We don't got fine clothes like that, but...
...we ain't got his bad luck either.

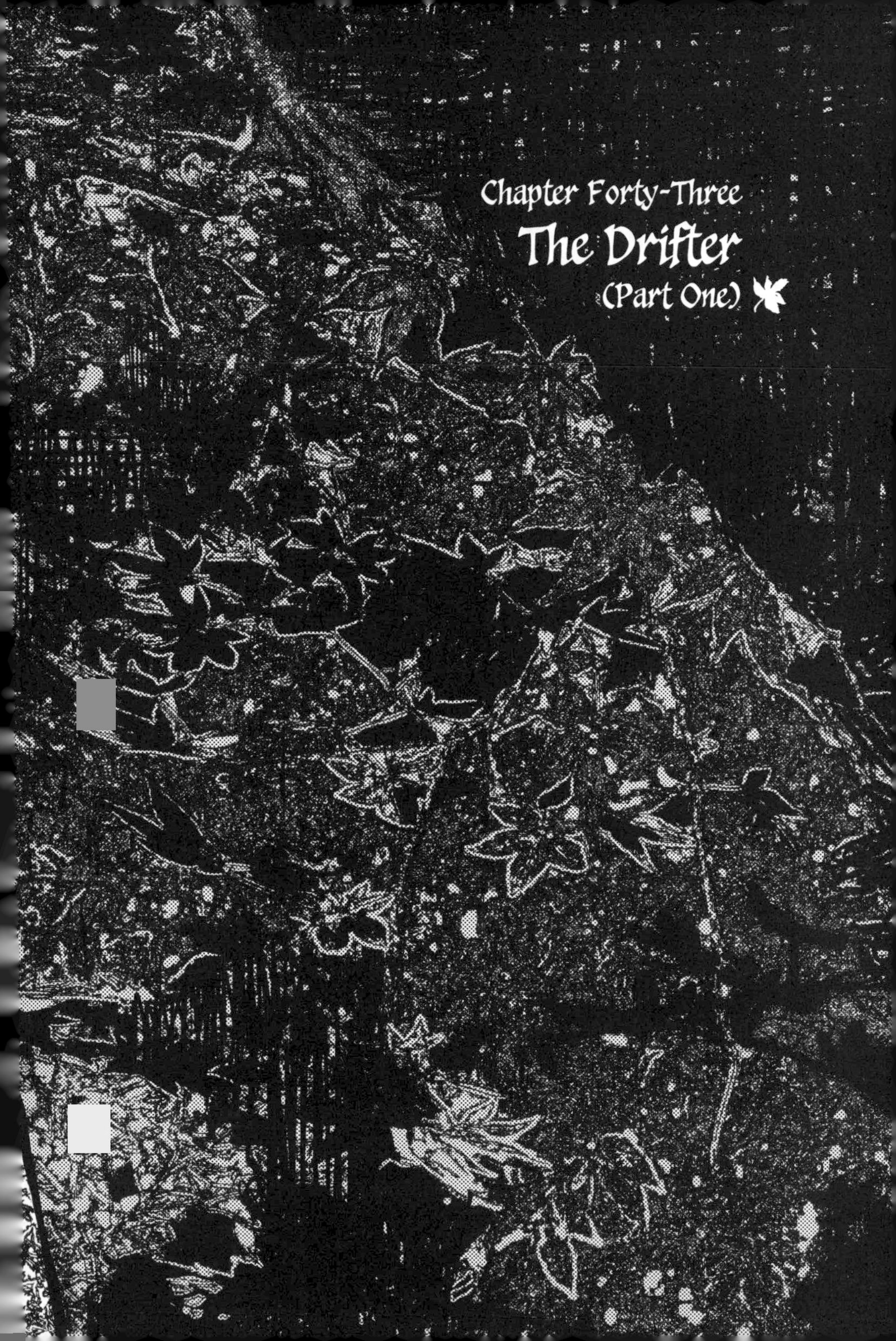
Chapter Forty-Three
The Drifter
(Part One)

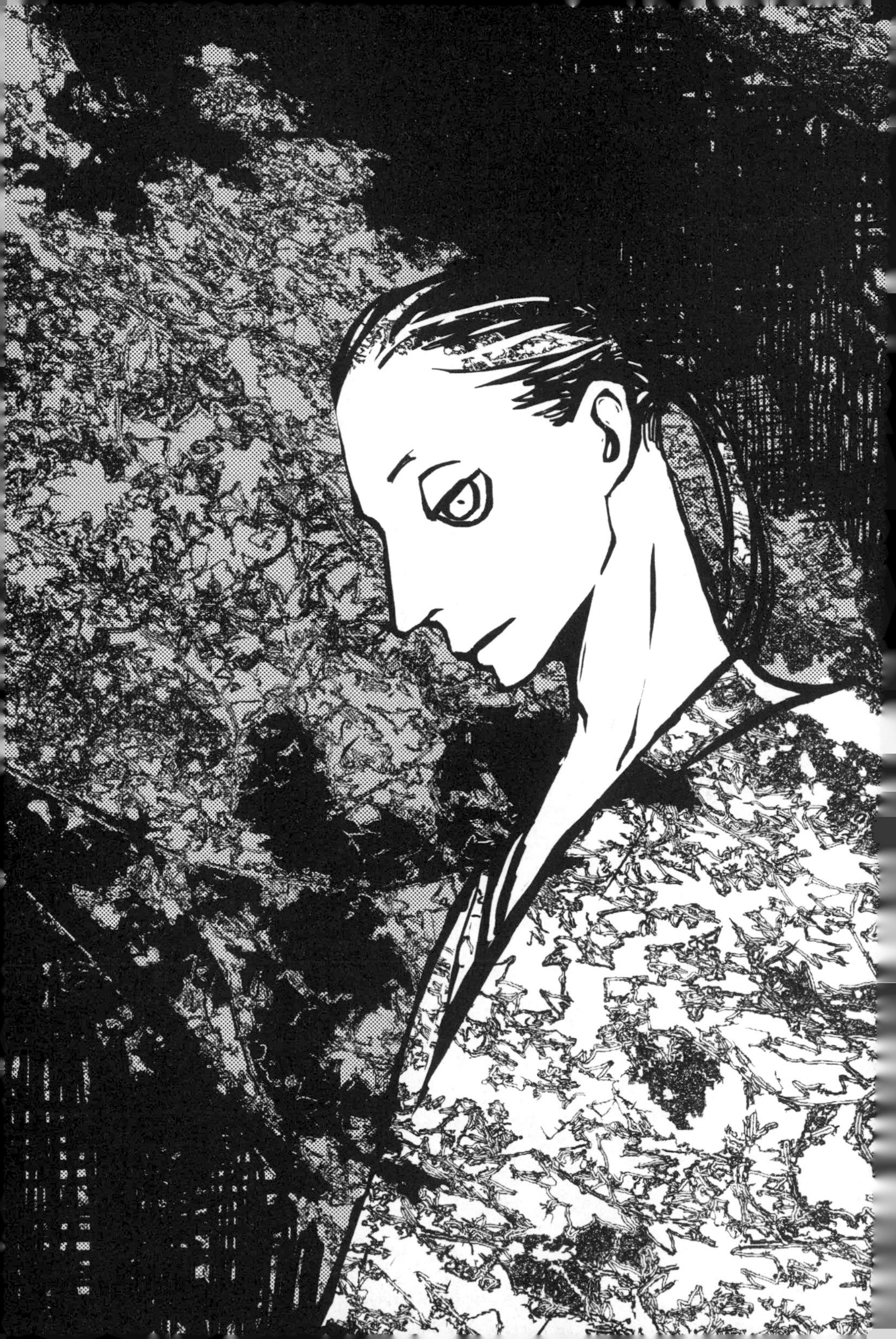

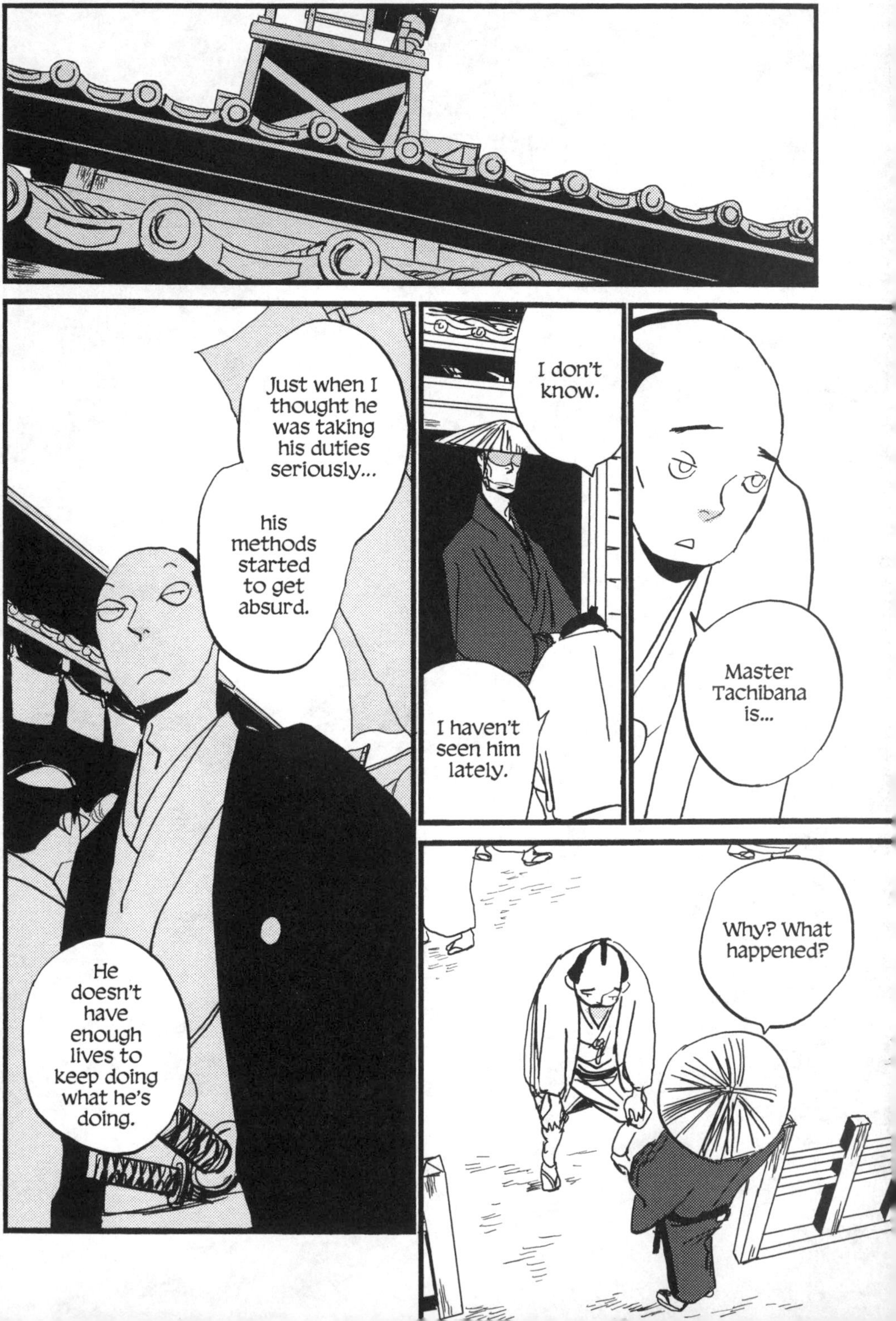
Master Tachibana is...
I don't know.
I haven't seen him lately.
Why? What happened?
Just when I thought he was taking his duties seriously...
his methods started to get absurd.
He doesn't have enough lives to keep doing what he's doing.

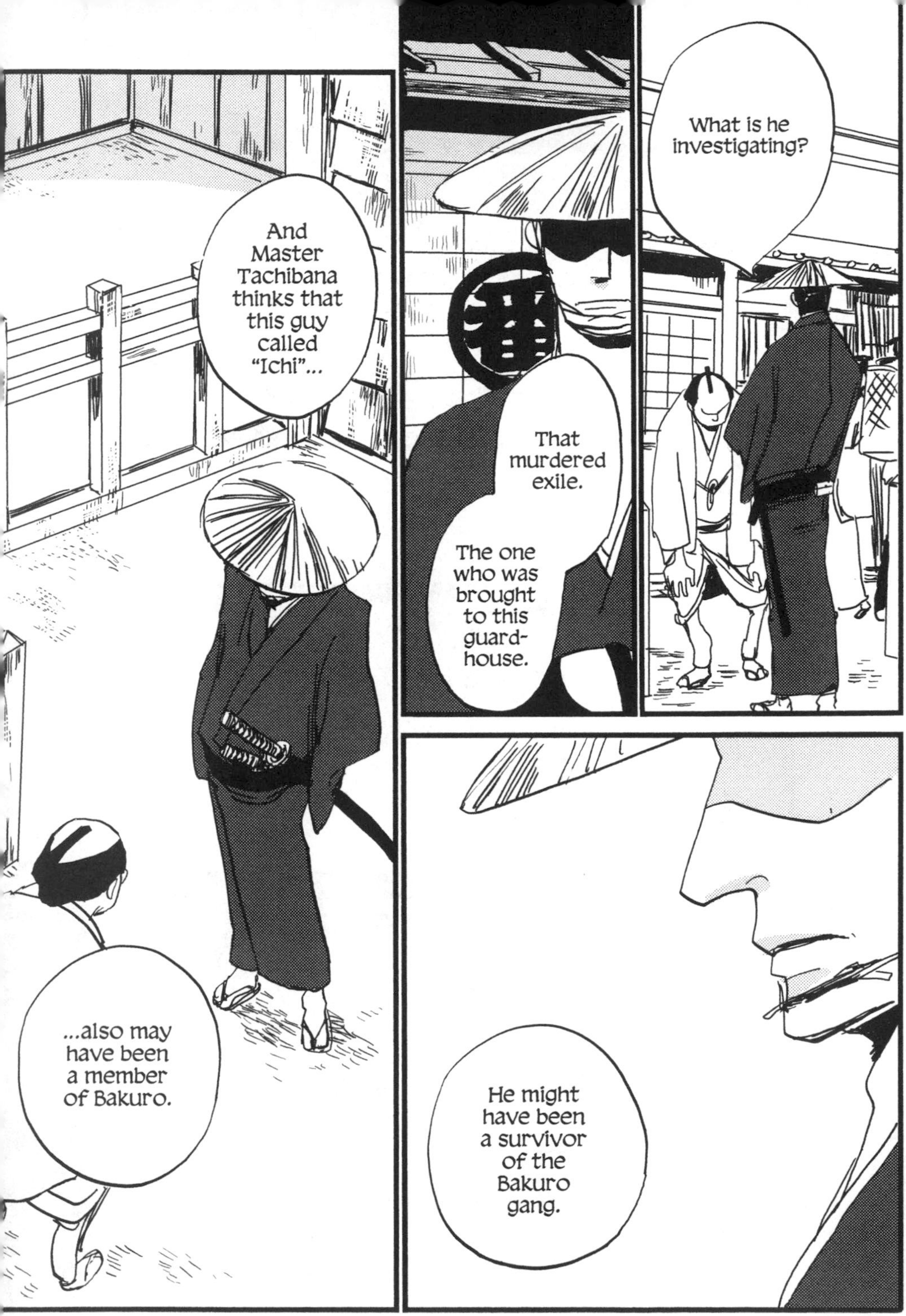
What is he investigating?
That murdered exile.
The one who was brought to this guardhouse.
He might have been a survivor of the Bakuro gang.
And Master Tachibana thinks that this guy called "Ichi"...
...also may have been a member of Bakuro.

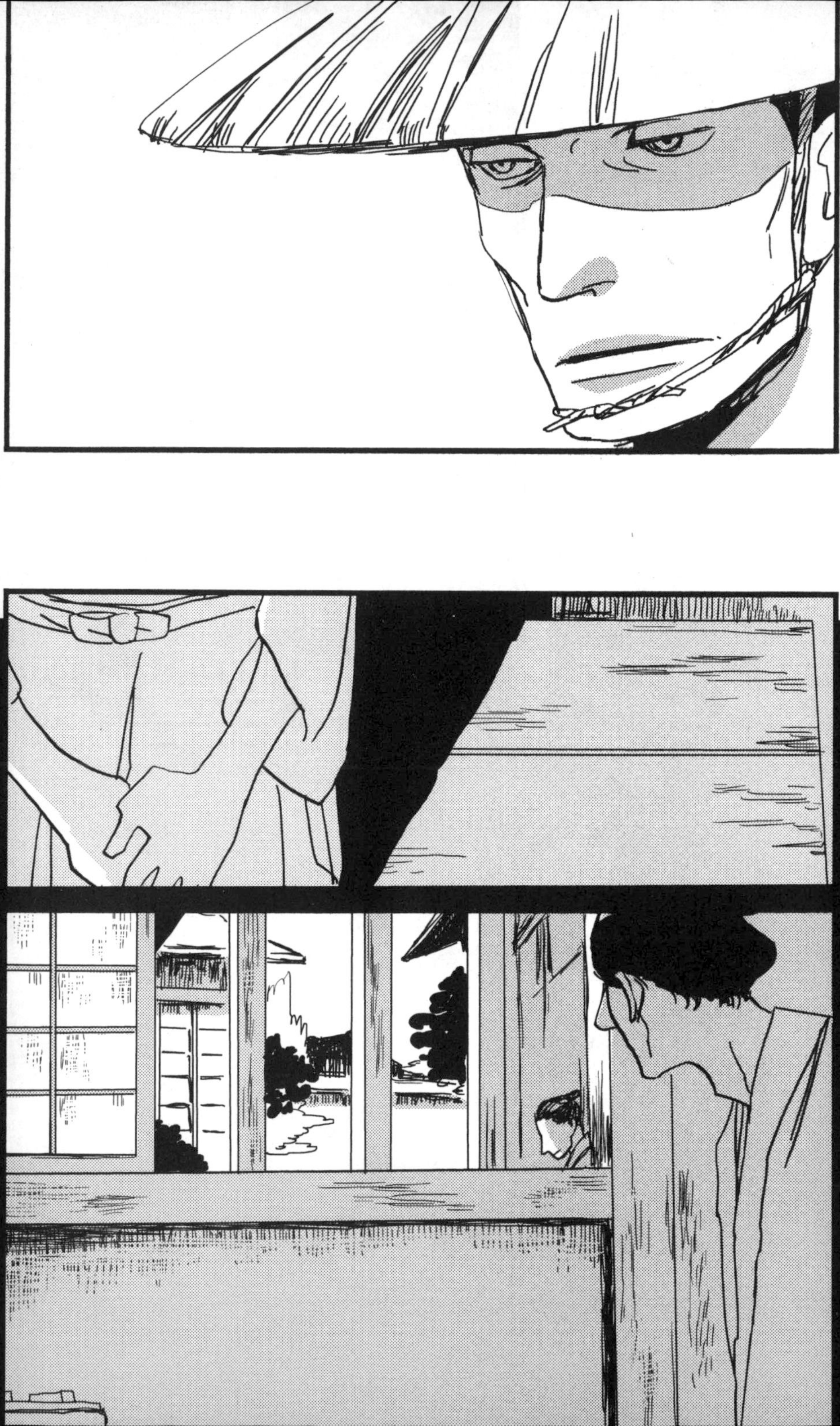

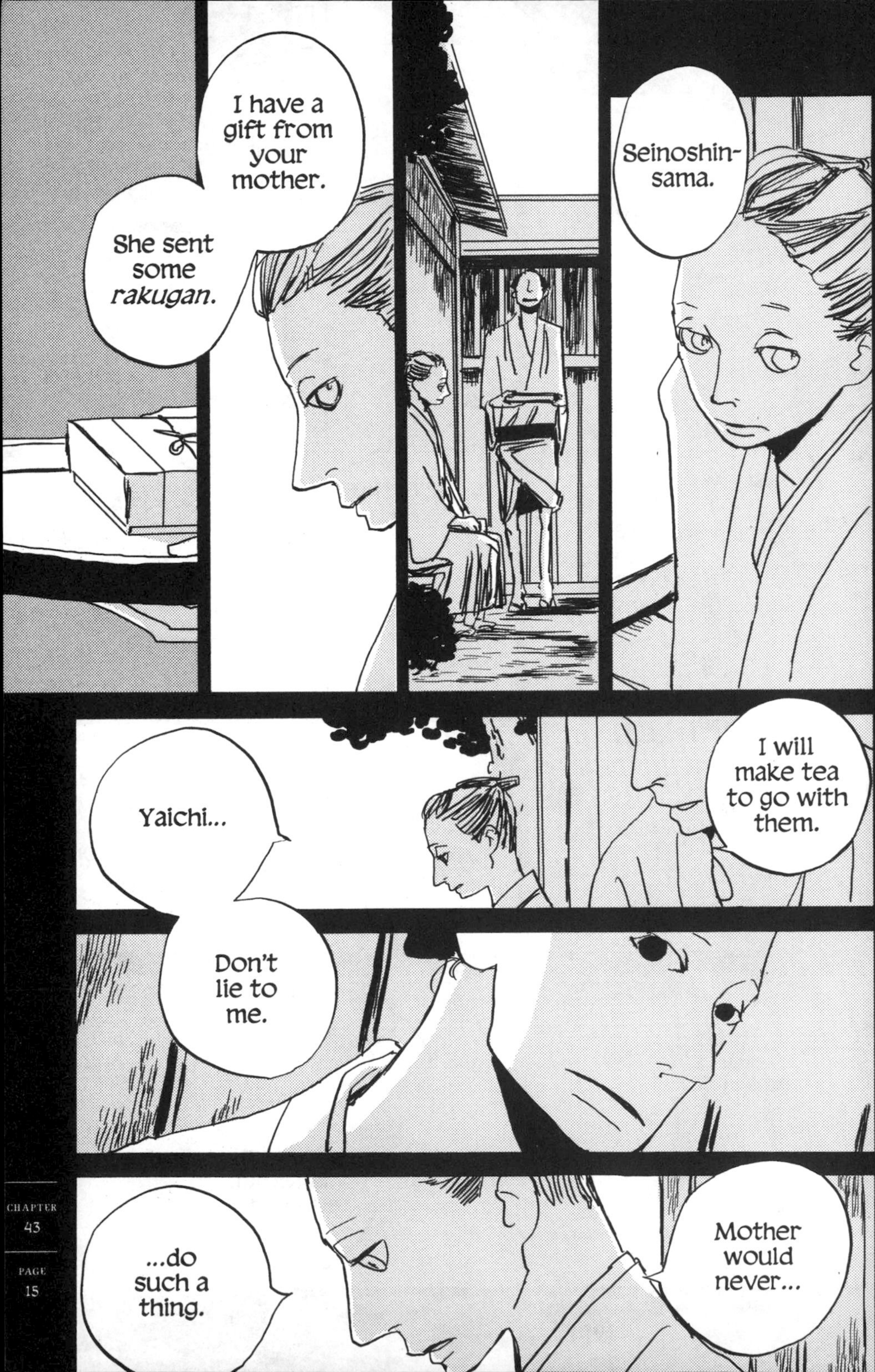
Seinoshin-sama.
I have a gift from your mother.
She sent some *rakugan*.
I will make tea to go with them.
Yaichi...
Don't lie to me.
Mother would never...
...do such a thing.

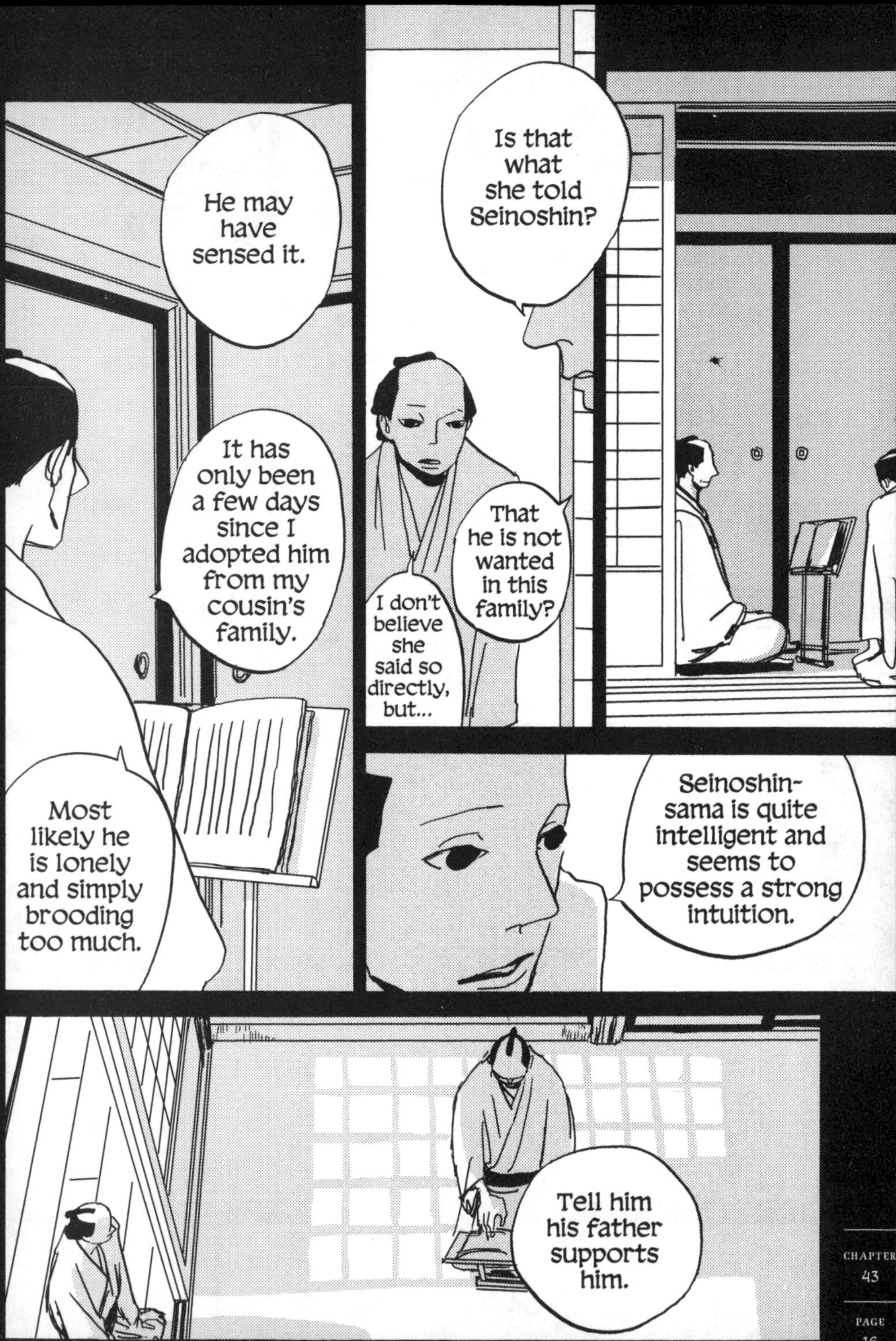
Is that what she told Seinoshin?
That he is not wanted in this family?
I don't believe she said so directly, but...
Seinoshin-sama is quite intelligent and seems to possess a strong intuition.
He may have sensed it.
It has only been a few days since I adopted him from my cousin's family.
Most likely he is lonely and simply brooding too much.
Tell him his father supports him.

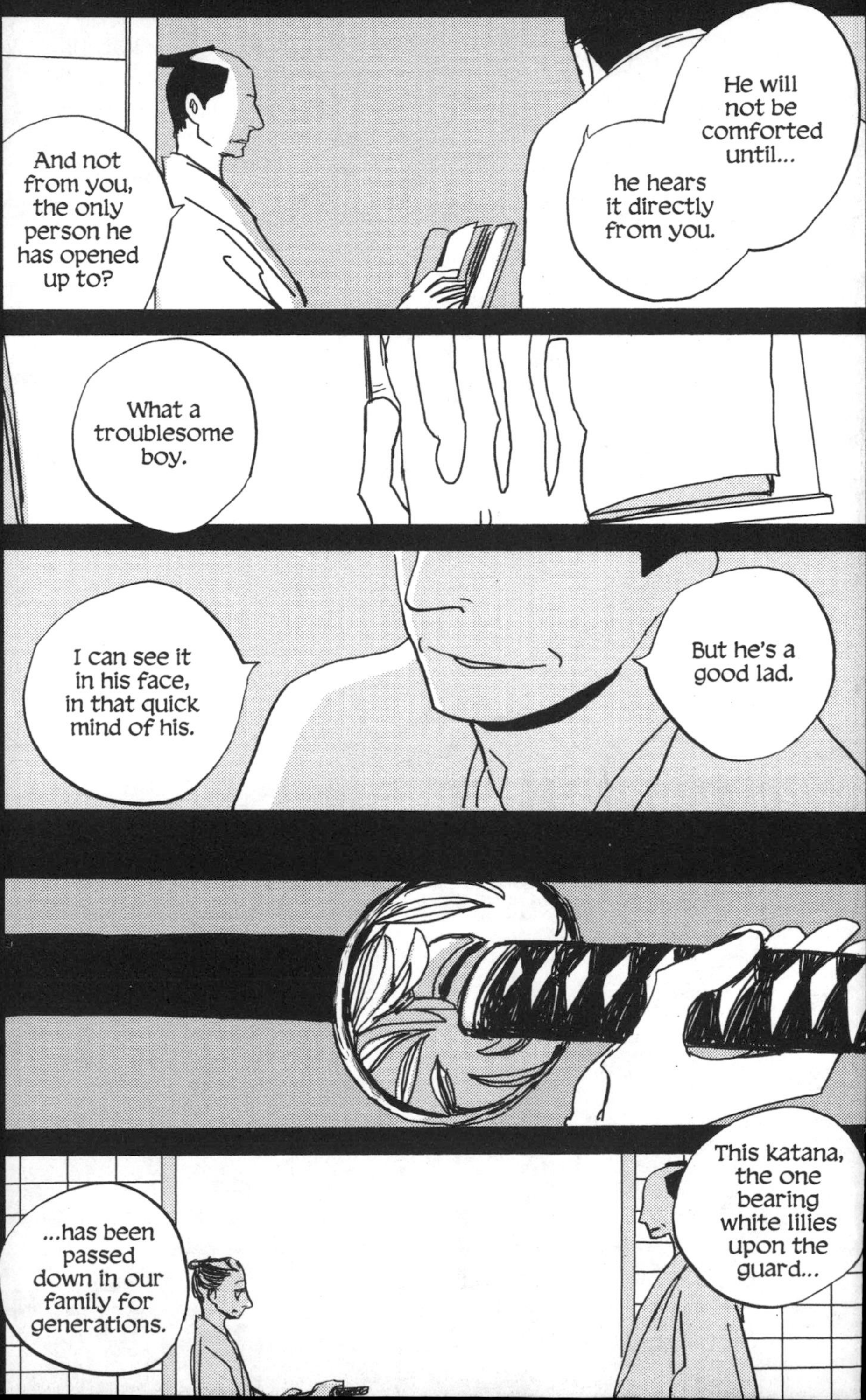
He will not be comforted until...
he hears it directly from you.
And not from you, the only person he has opened up to?
What a troublesome boy.
But he's a good lad.
I can see it in his face, in that quick mind of his.
This katana, the one bearing white lilies upon the guard...
...has been passed down in our family for generations.

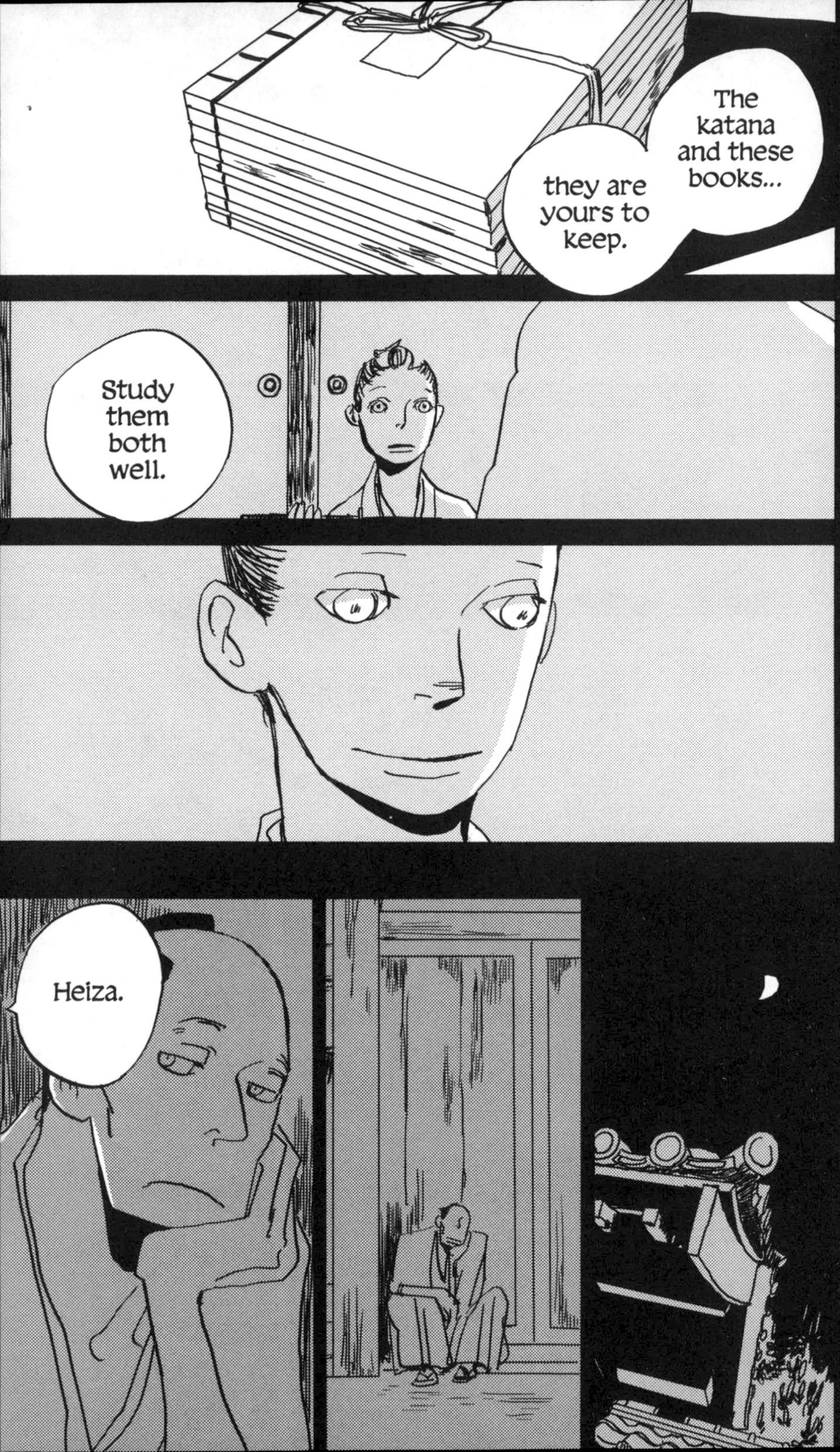
The katana and these books...
they are yours to keep.
Study them both well.
Heiza.

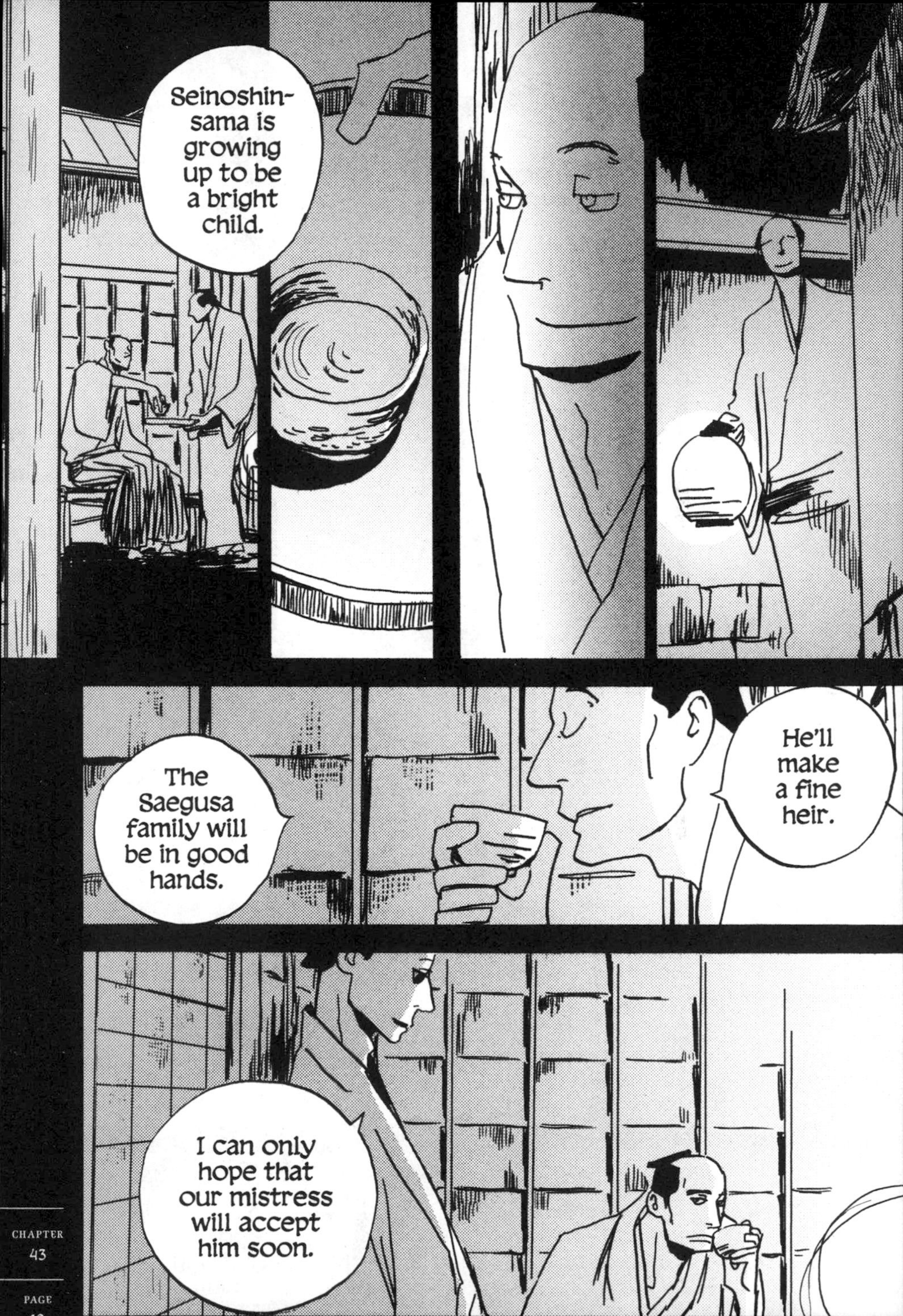
Seinoshin-sama is growing up to be a bright child.
He'll make a fine heir.
The Saegusa family will be in good hands.
I can only hope that our mistress will accept him soon.

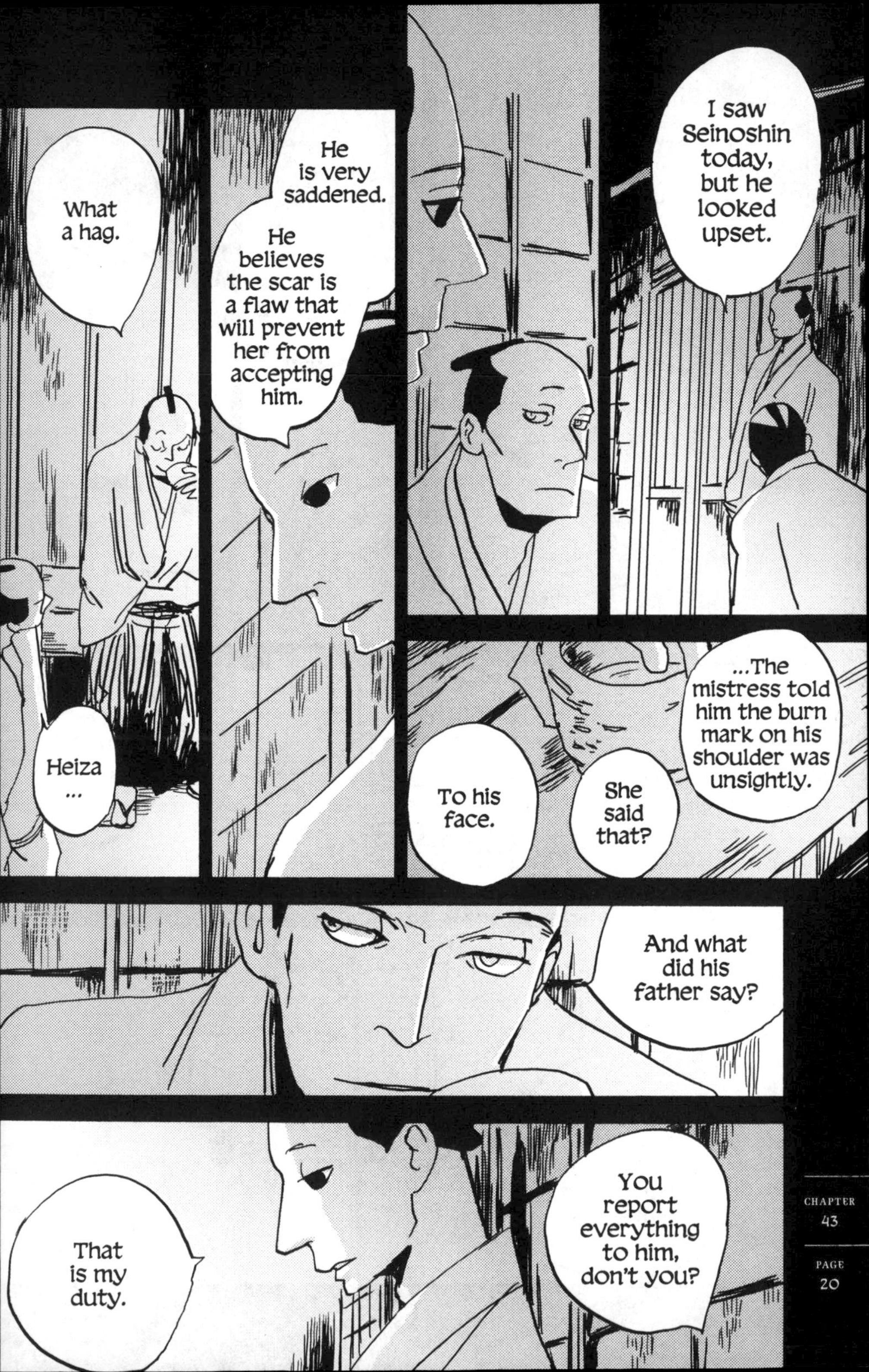
I saw Seinoshin today, but he looked upset.
...The mistress told him the burn mark on his shoulder was unsightly.
She said that?
To his face.
He is very saddened.
He believes the scar is a flaw that will prevent her from accepting him.
What a hag.
Heiza...
And what did his father say?
You report everything to him, don't you?
That is my duty.

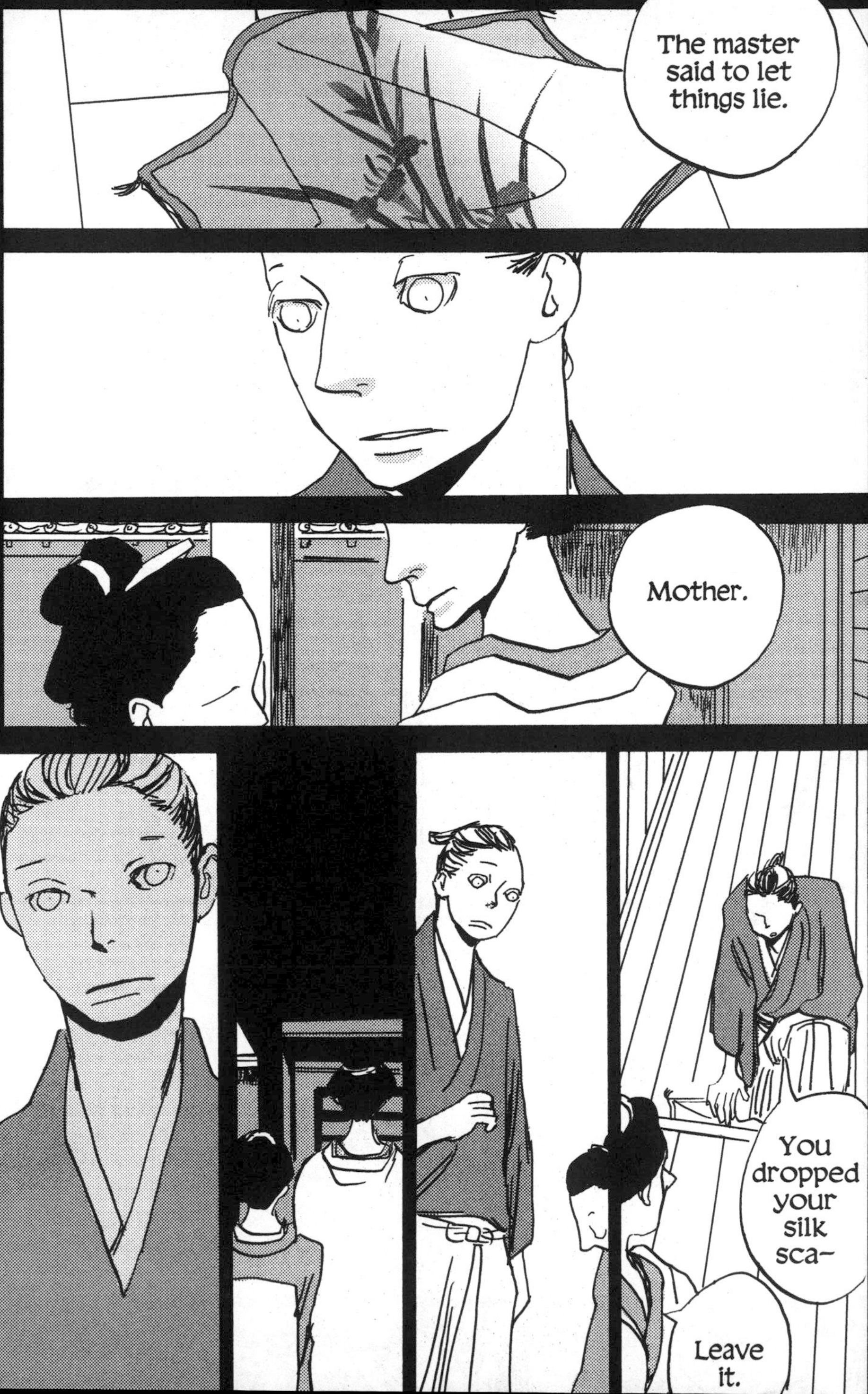
The master said to let things lie.
Mother.
You dropped your silk sca-
Leave it.

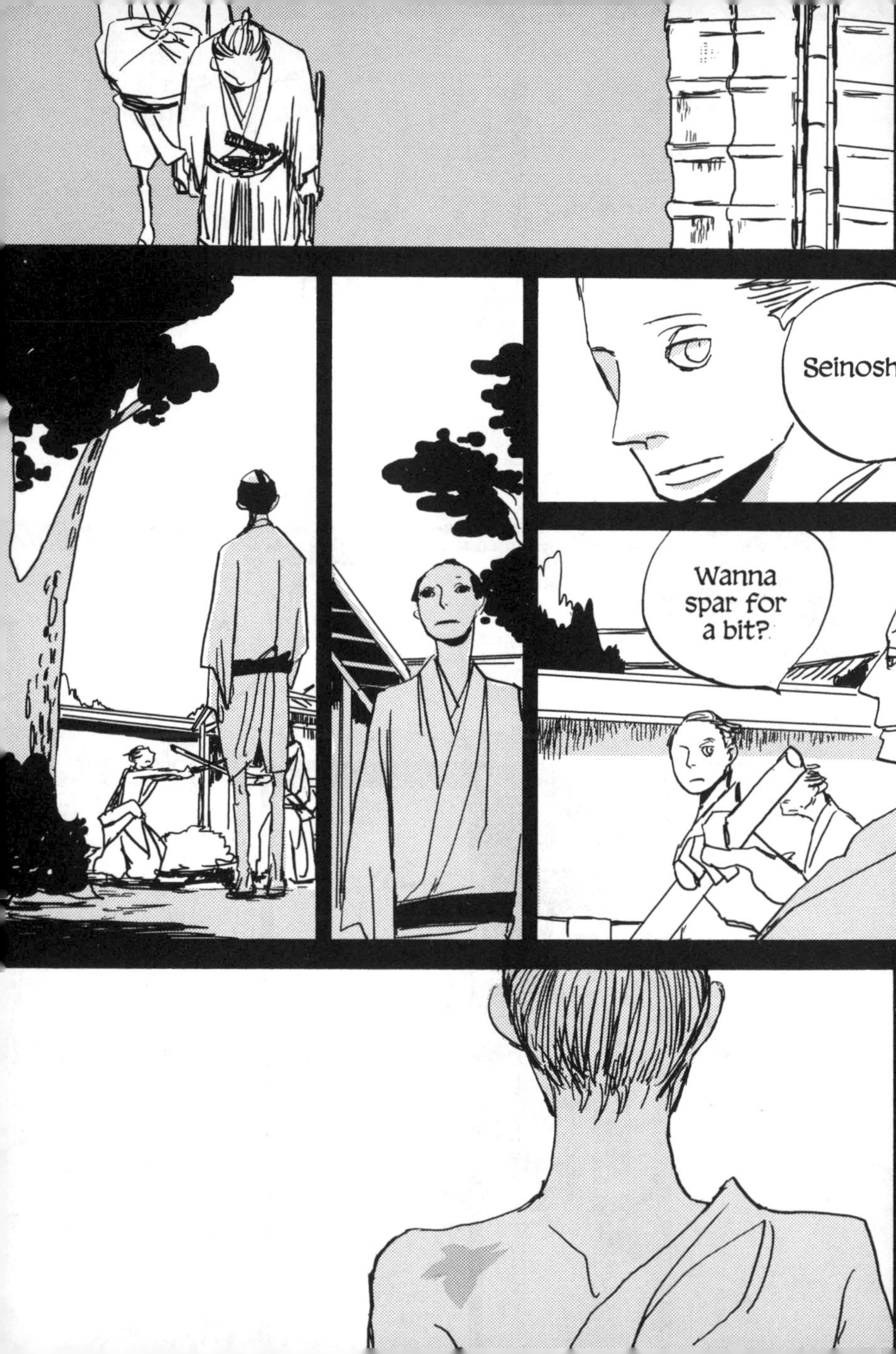
Seinoshin.
Wanna spar for a bit?

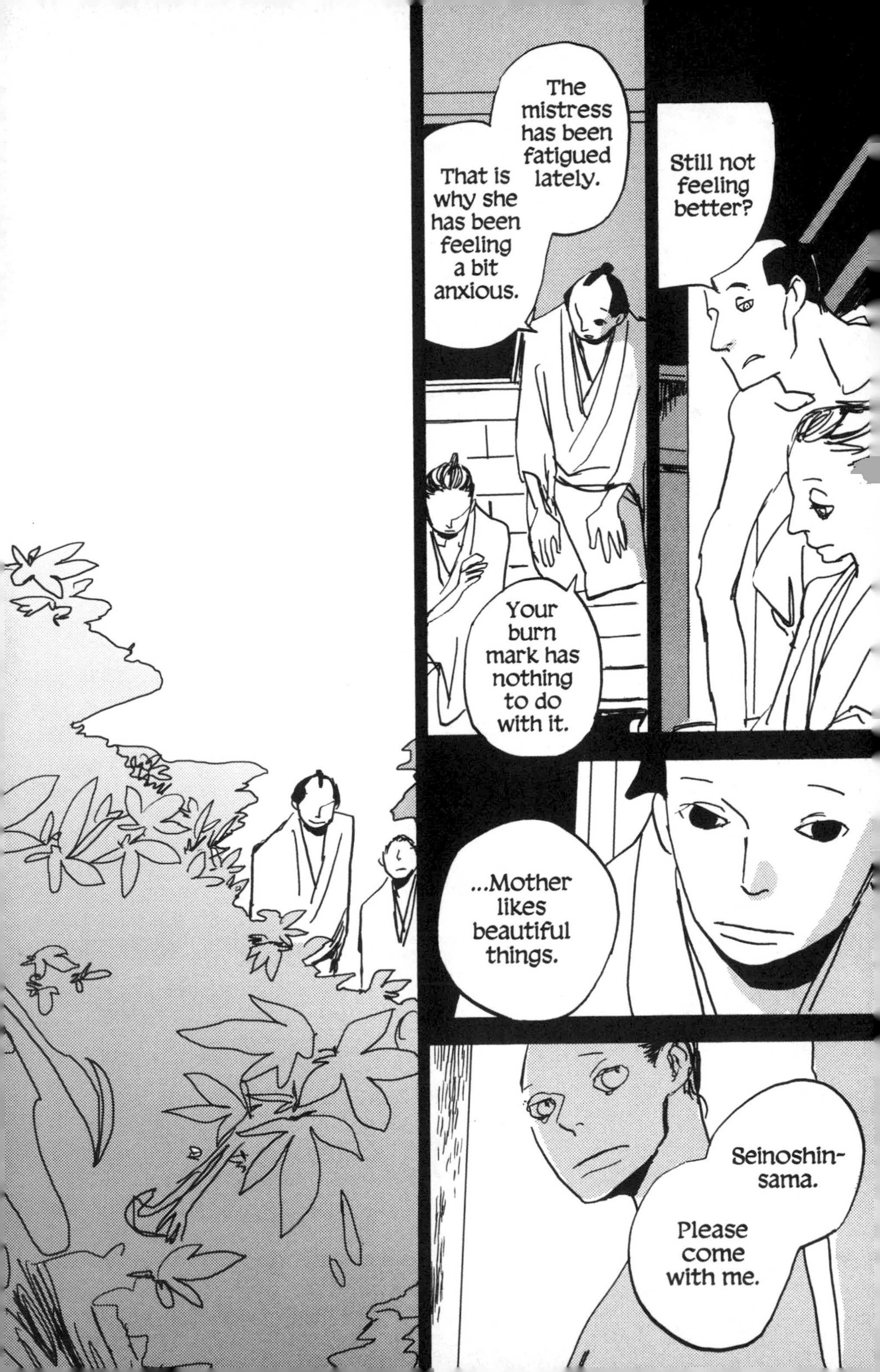
Still not feeling better?
The mistress has been fatigued lately.
That is why she has been feeling a bit anxious.
Your burn mark has nothing to do with it.
...Mother likes beautiful things.
Seinoshin-sama.
Please come with me.

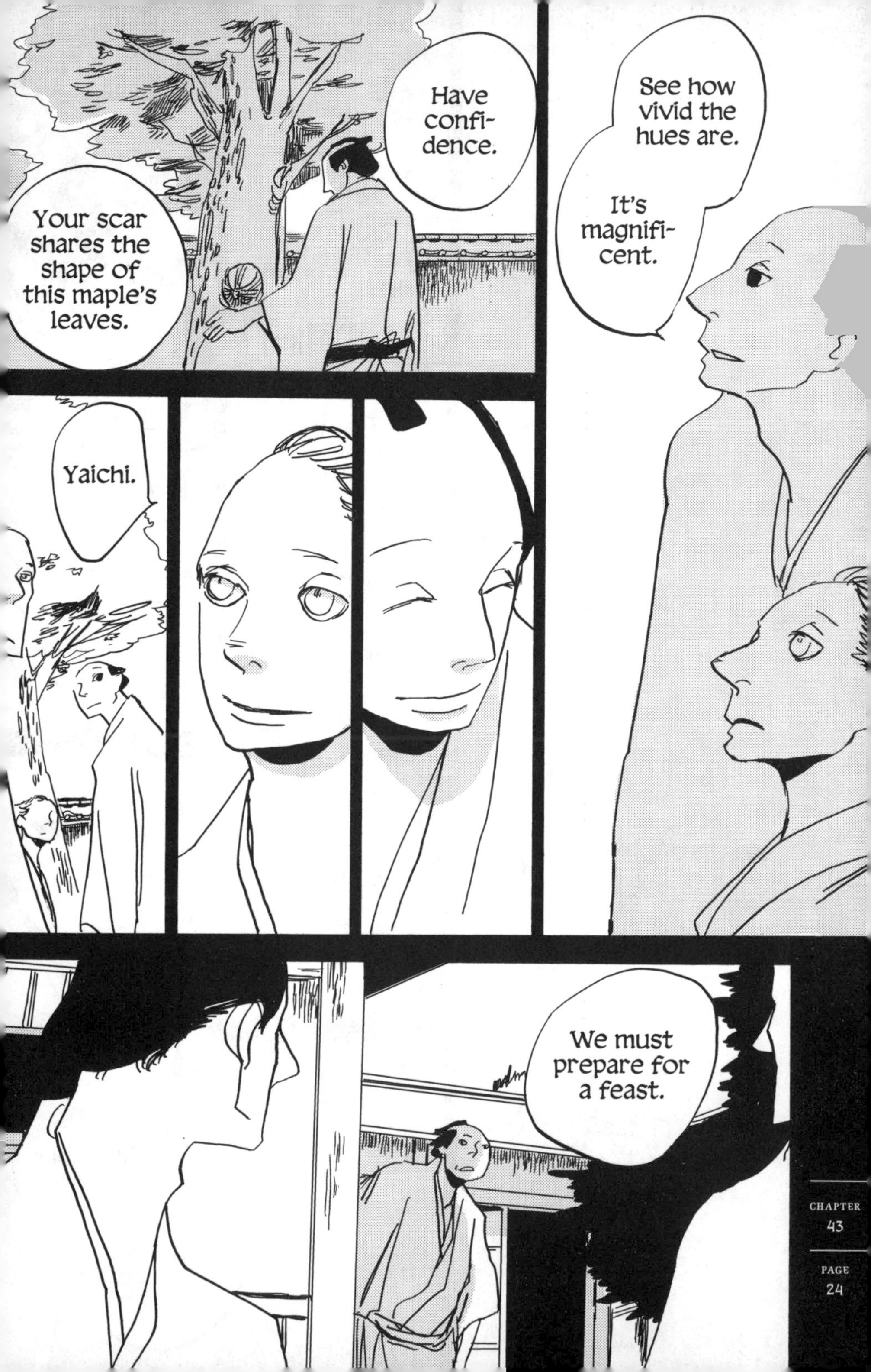
See how vivid the hues are.
It's magnificent.
Have confidence.
Your scar shares the shape of this maple's leaves.
Yaichi.
We must prepare for a feast.

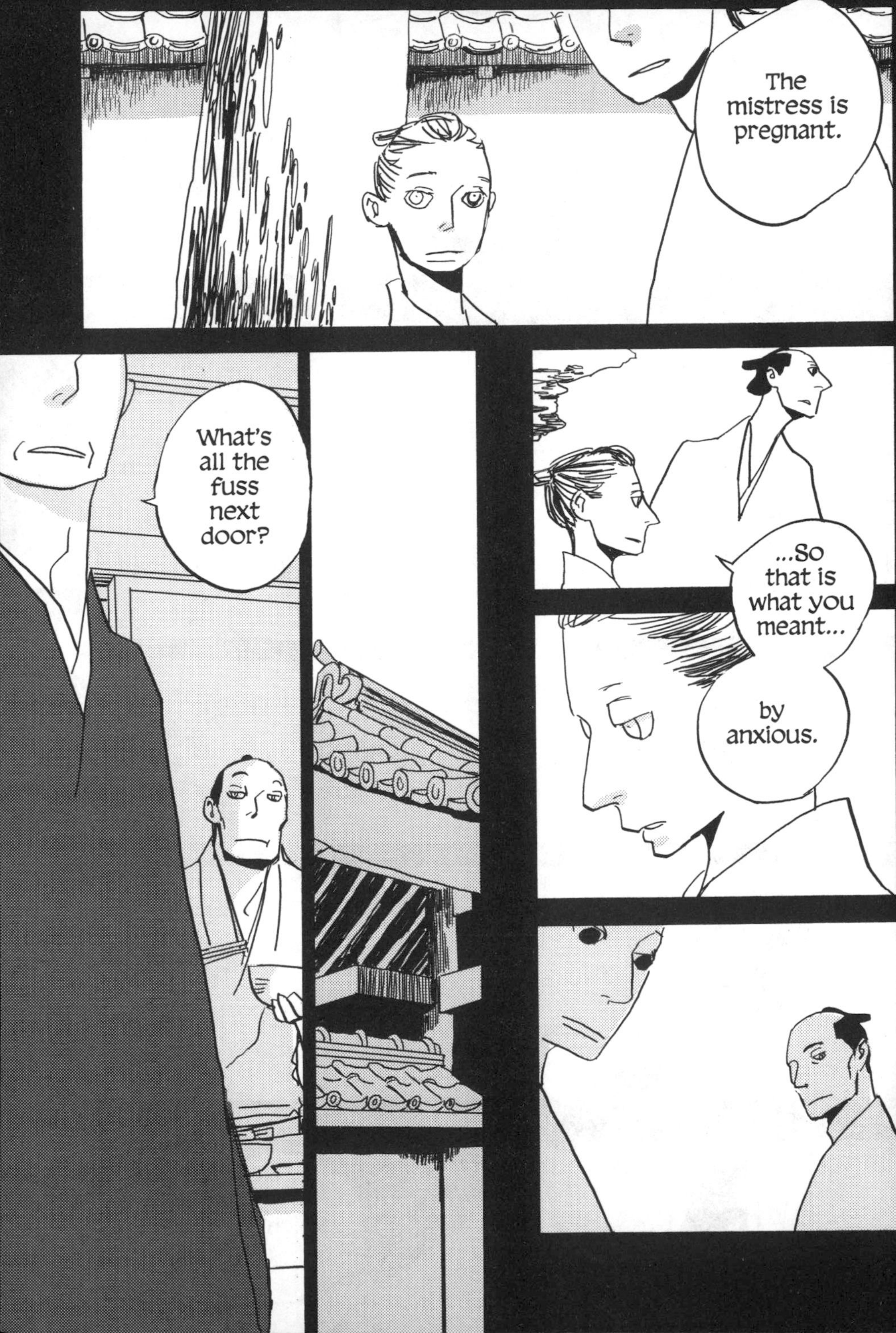
The mistress is pregnant.
...So that is what you meant...
by anxious.
What's all the fuss next door?

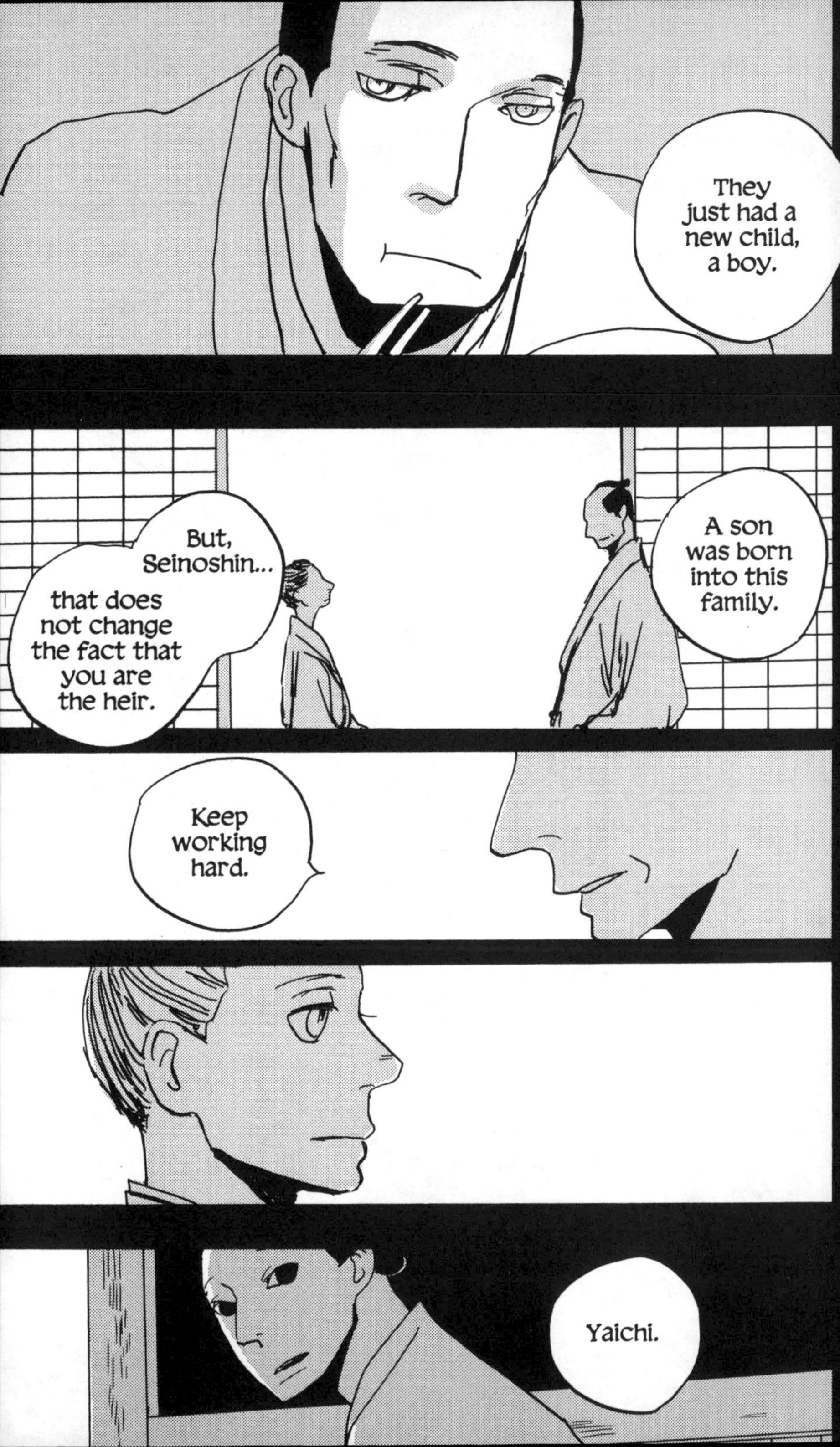
They just had a new child, a boy.
A son was born into this family.
But, Seinoshin...
that does not change the fact that you are the heir.
Keep working hard.
Yaichi.

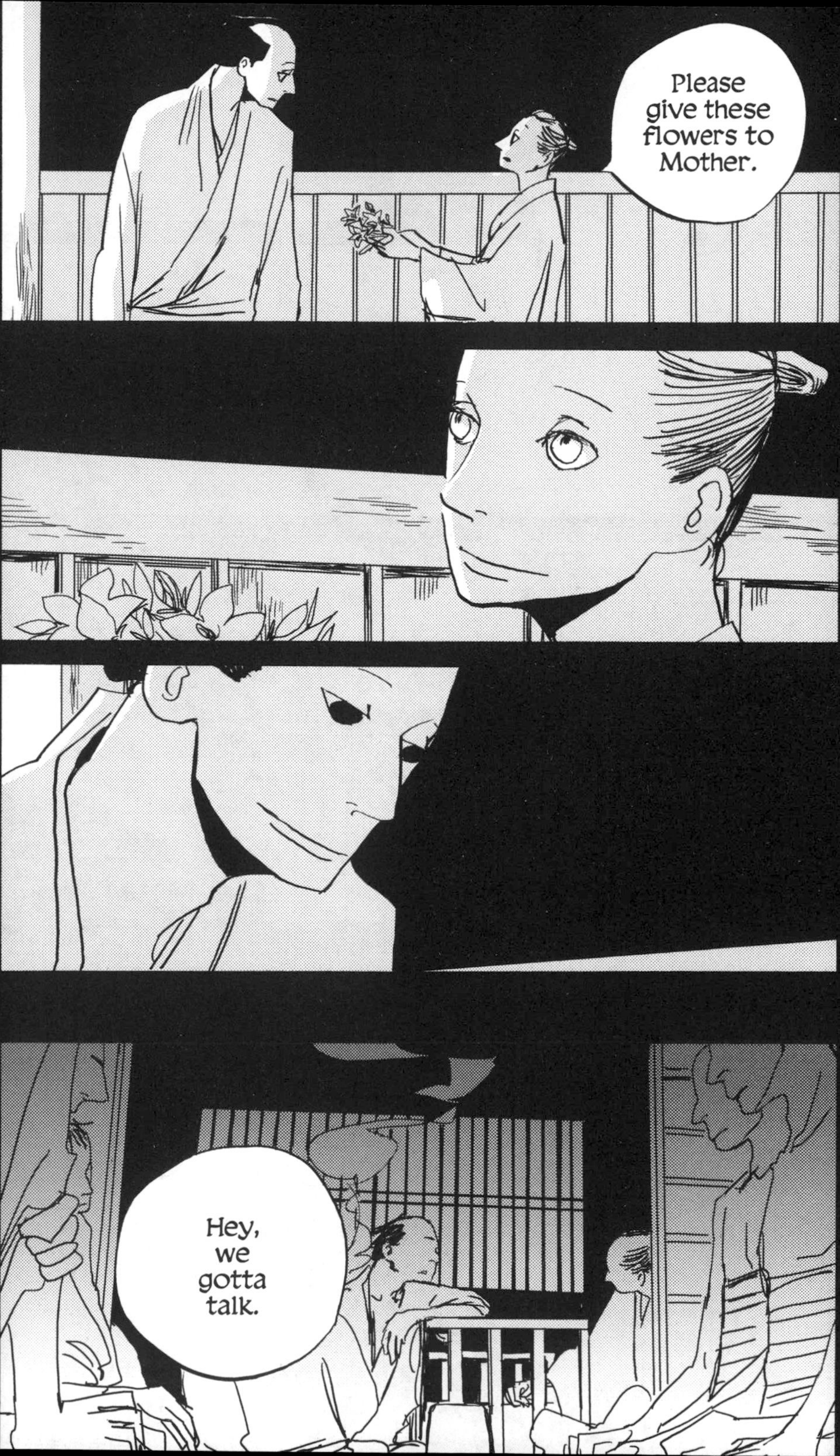
Please give these flowers to Mother.
Hey, we gotta talk.

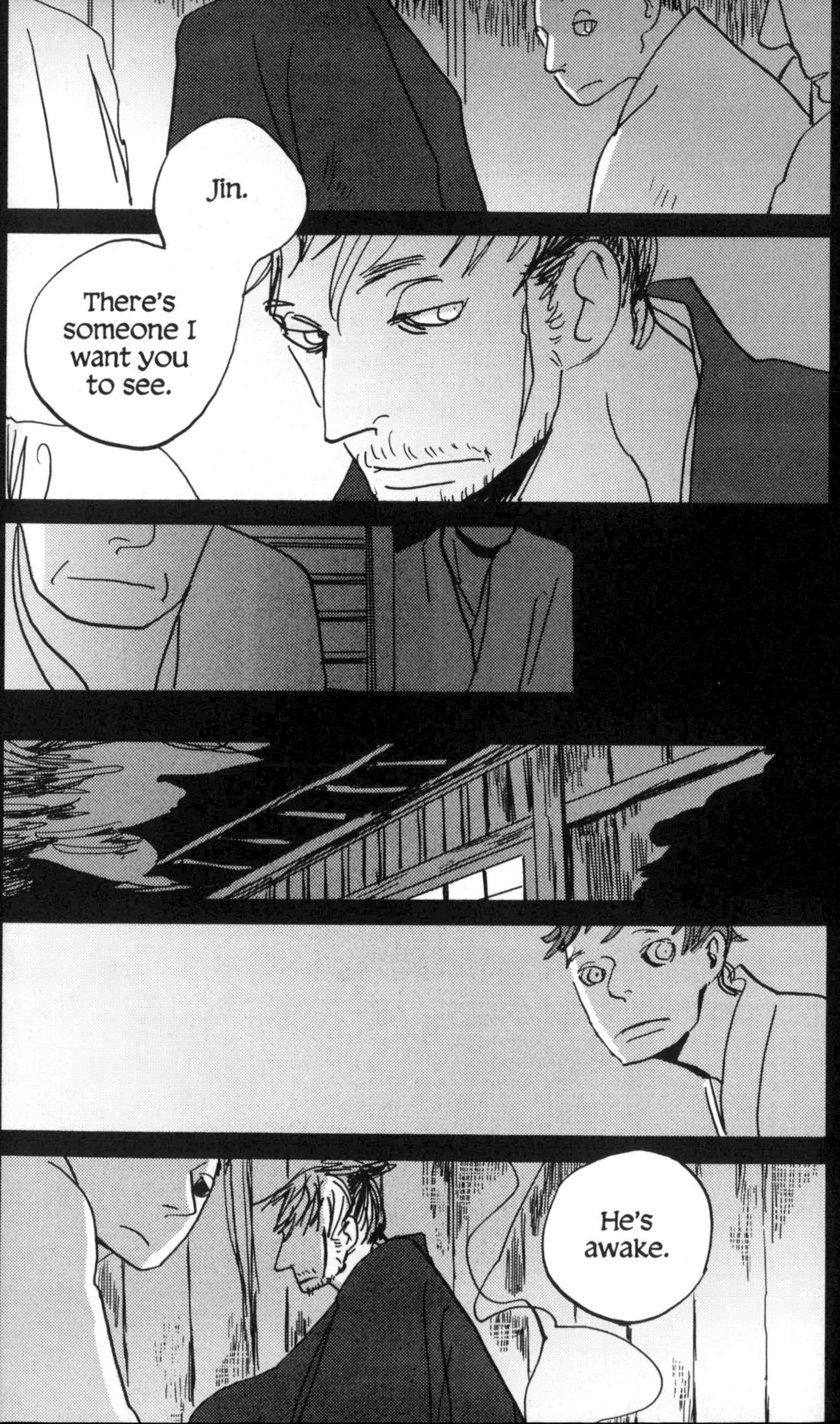
Jin.
There's someone I want you to see.
He's awake.

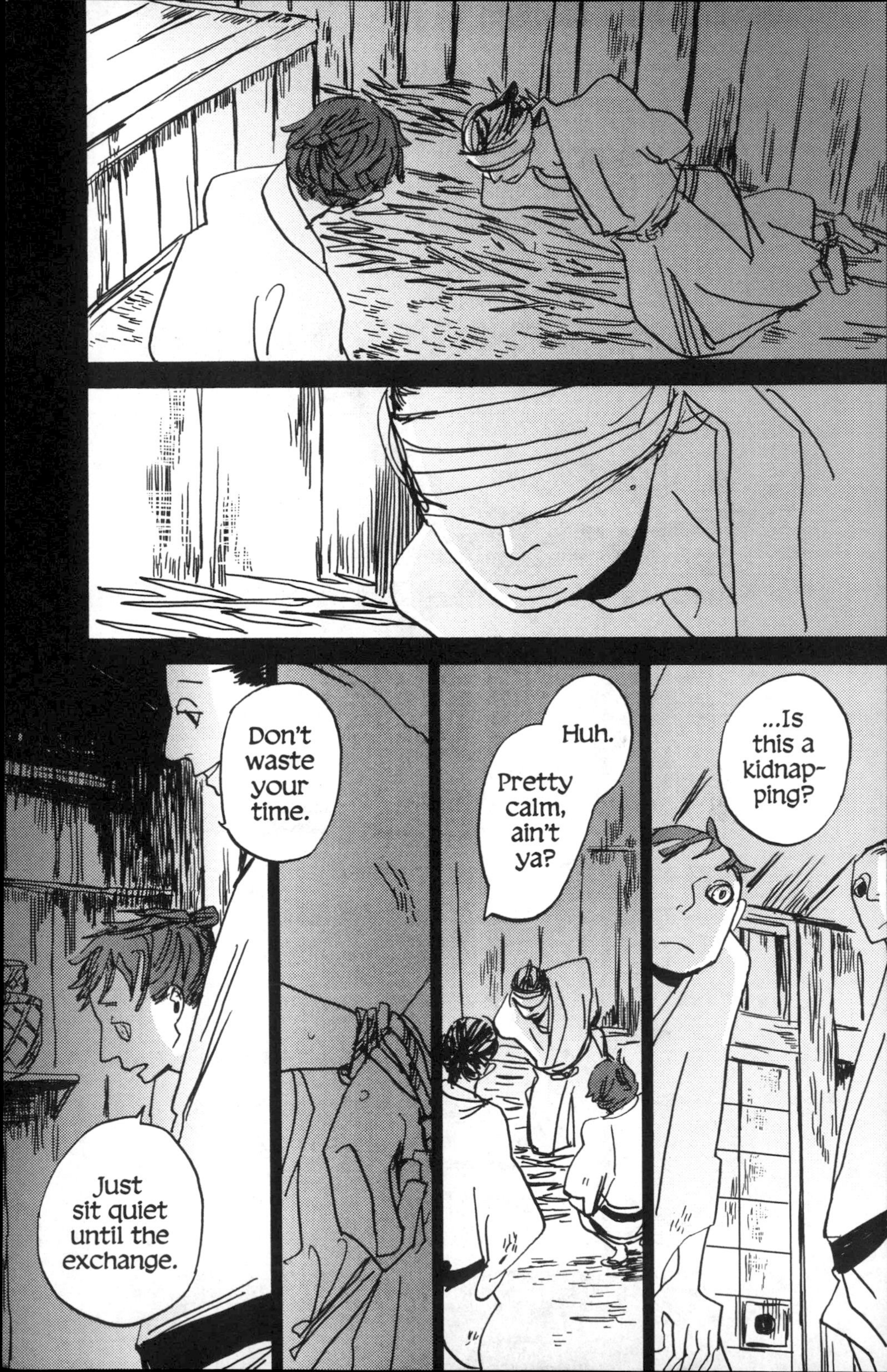
...Is this a kidnap-ping?
Huh.
Pretty calm, ain't ya?
Don't waste your time.
Just sit quiet until the exchange.

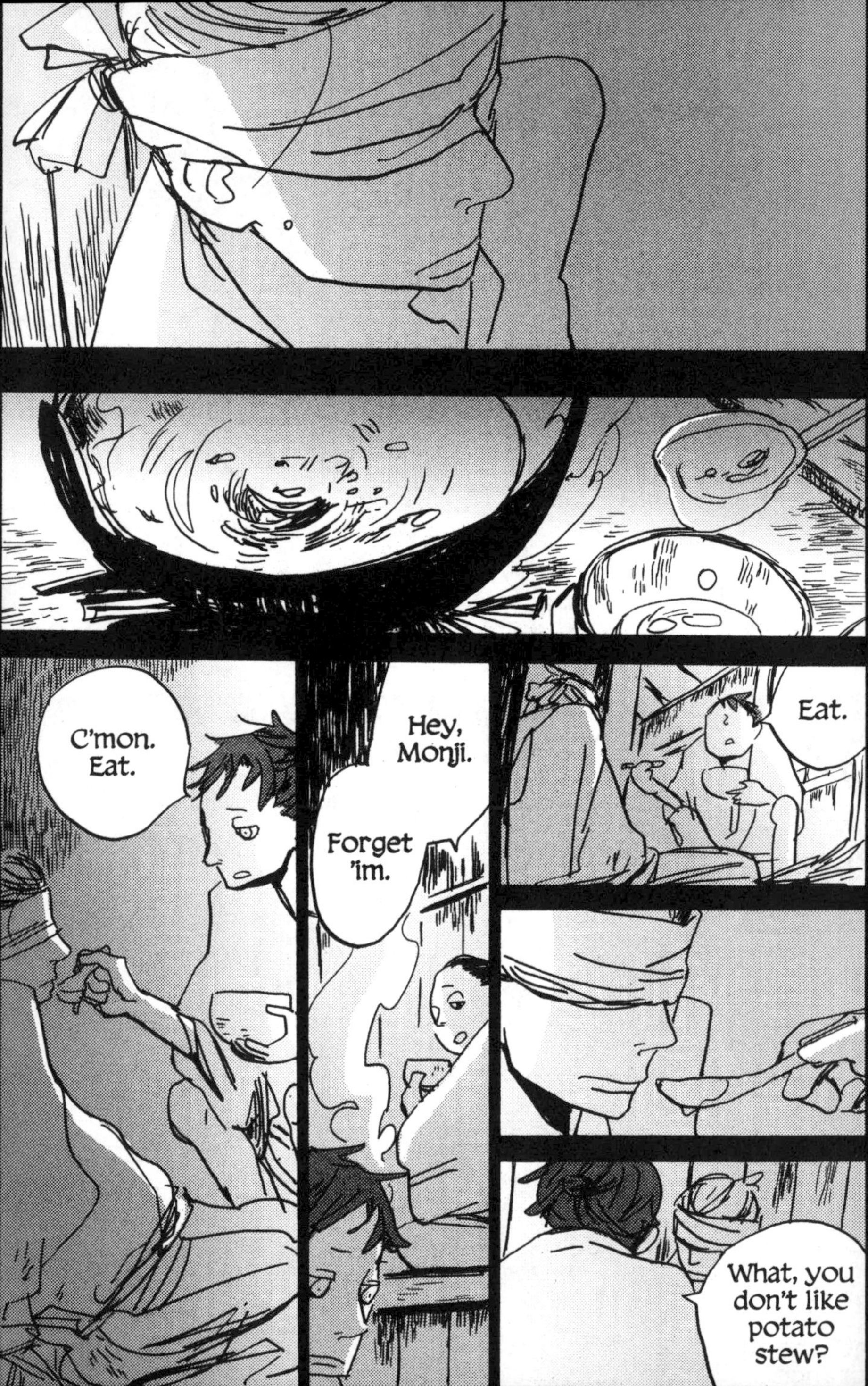
Eat.
What, you don't like potato stew?
Hey, Monji.
Forget 'im.
C'mon. Eat.

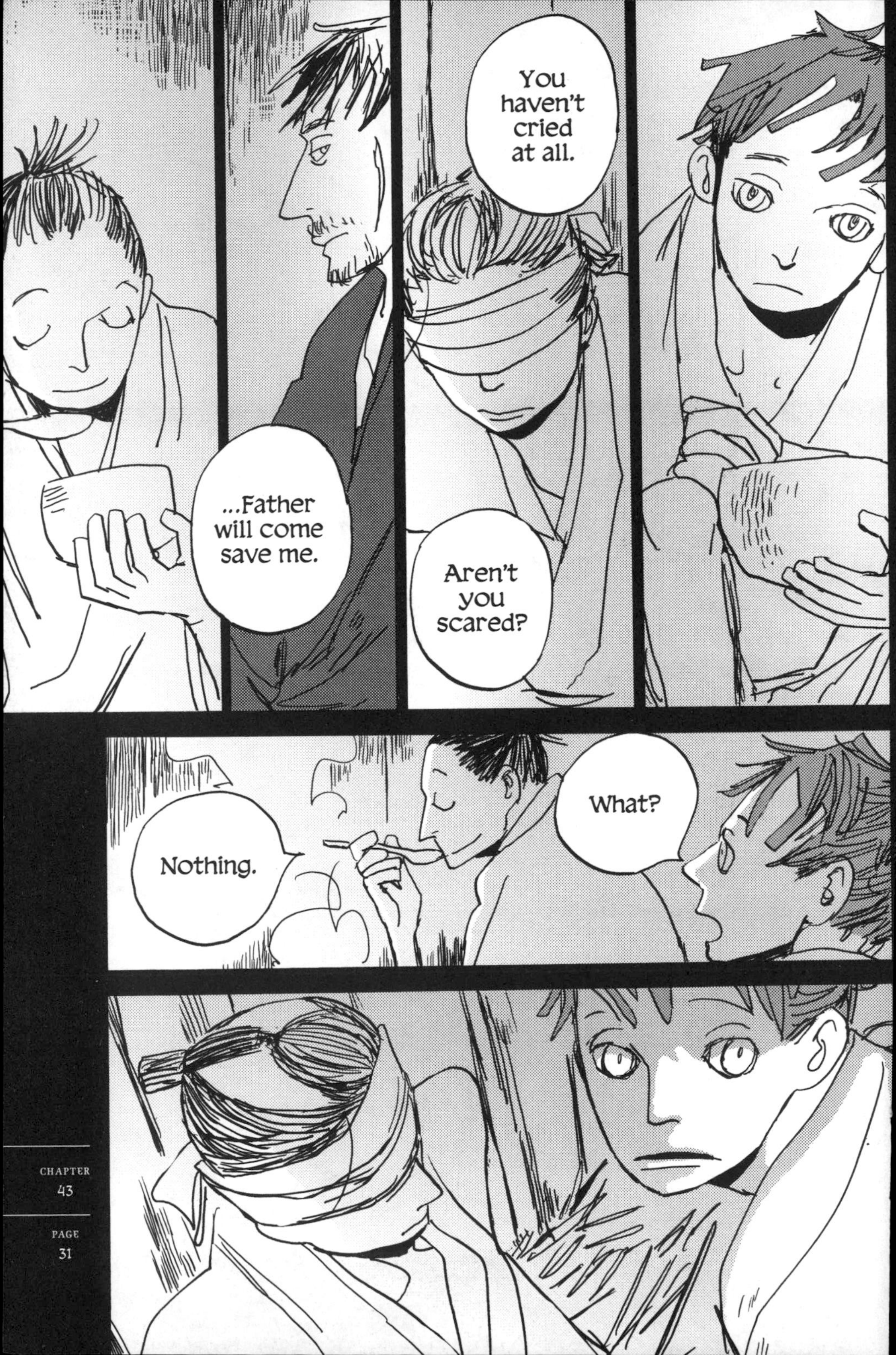
You haven't cried at all.
Aren't you scared?
...Father will come save me.
What?
Nothing.

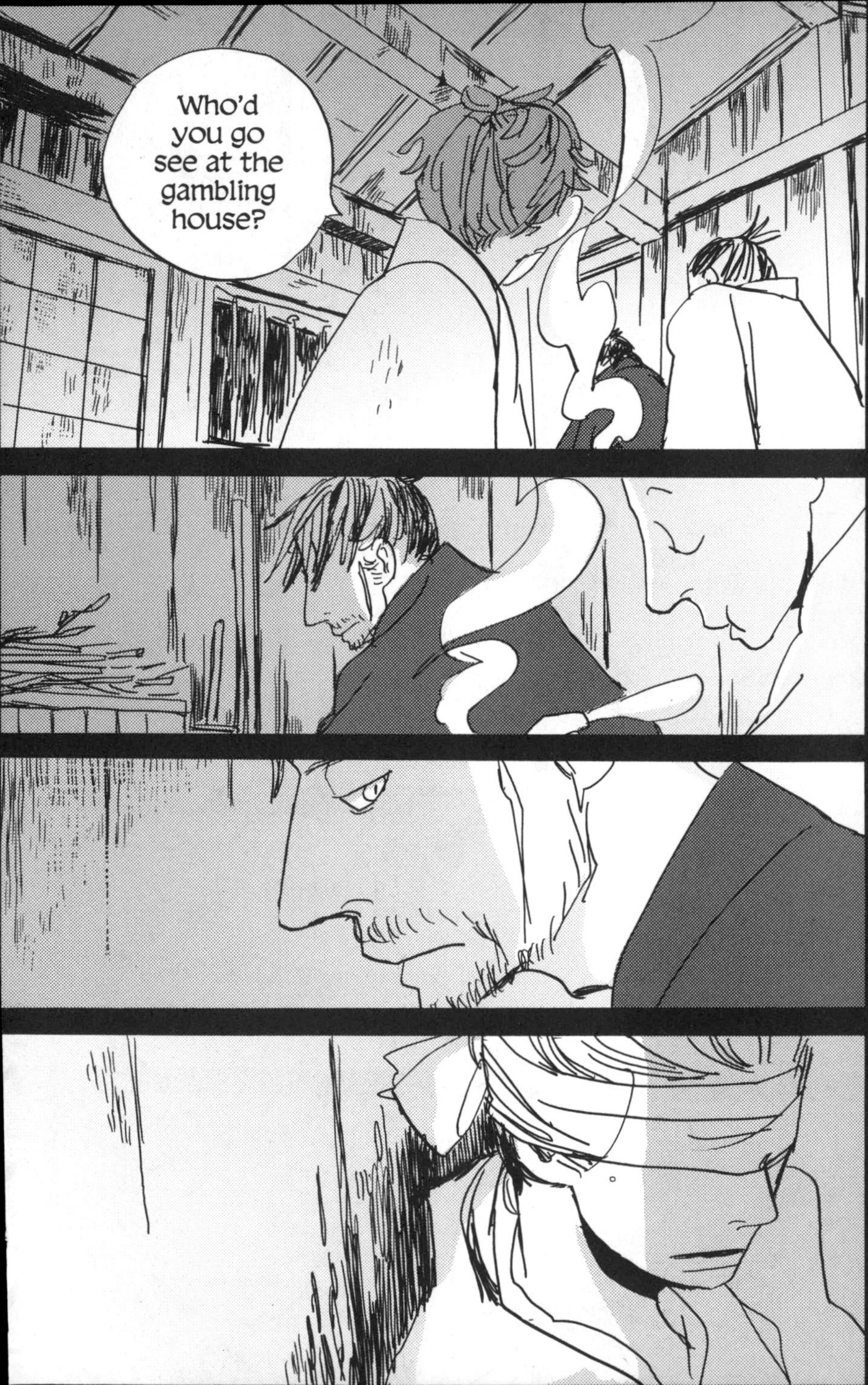
Who'd you go see at the gambling house?

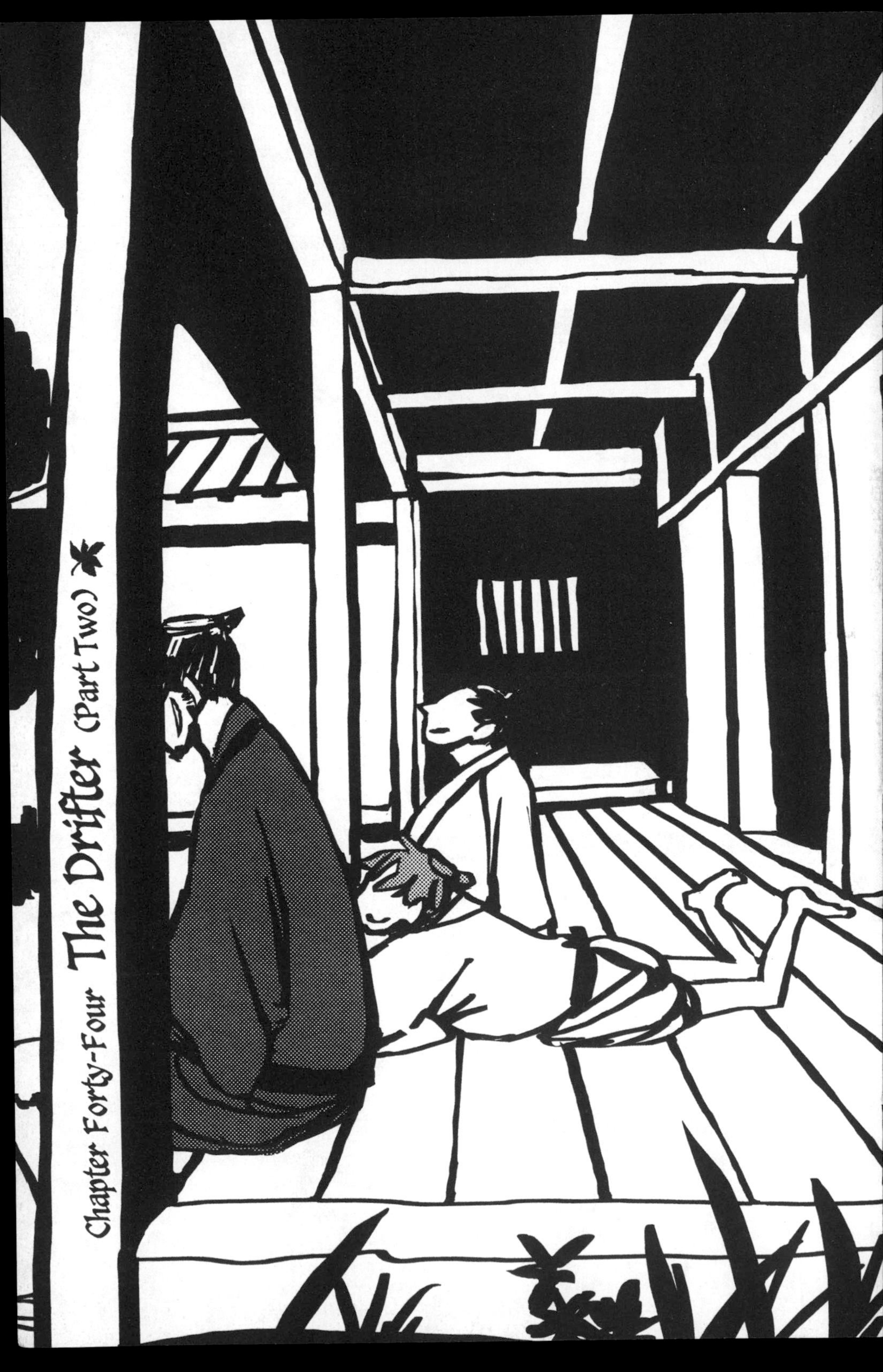
Chapter Forty-Four The Drifter (Part Two)

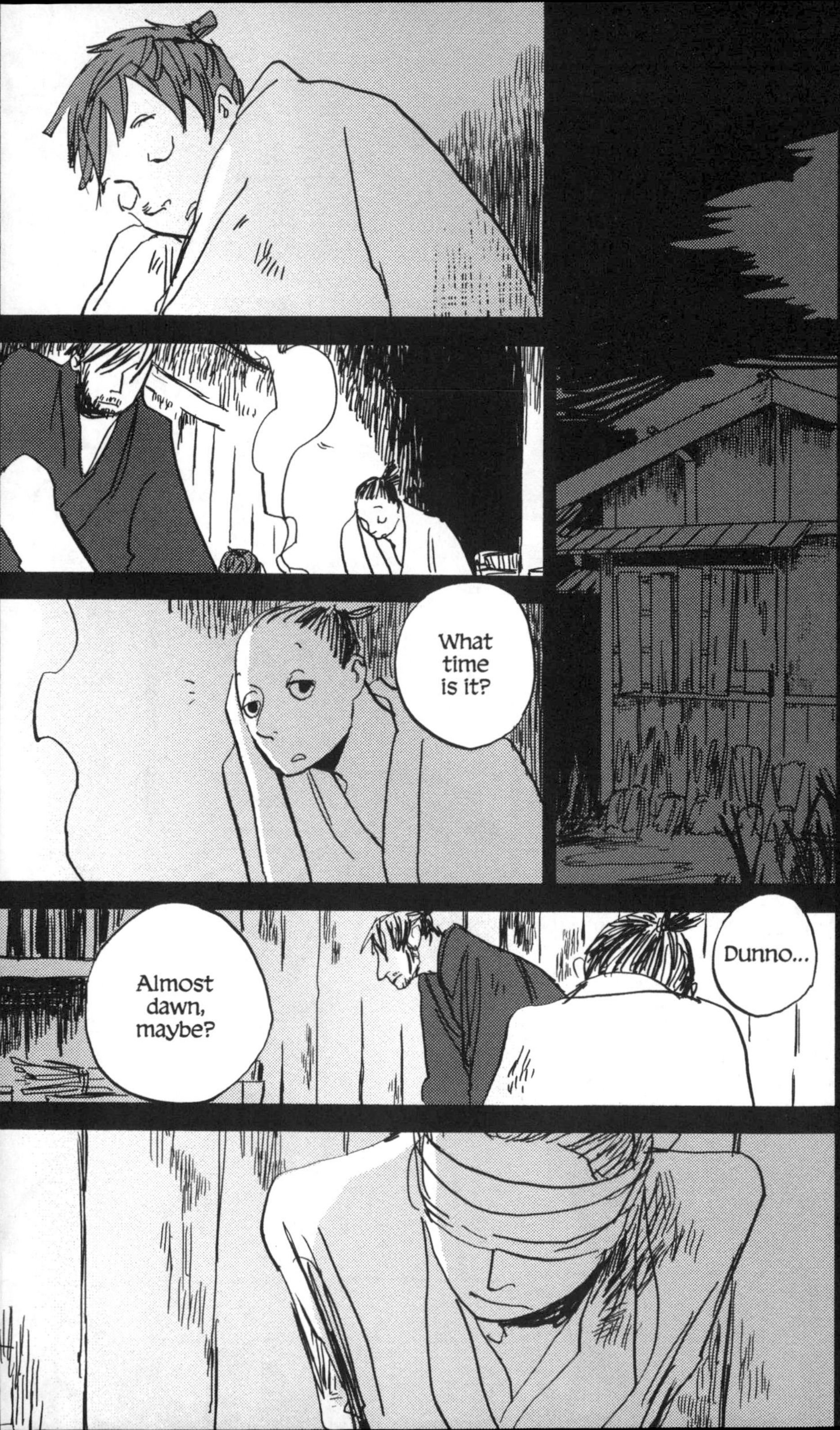
What time is it?
Dunno...
Almost dawn, maybe?

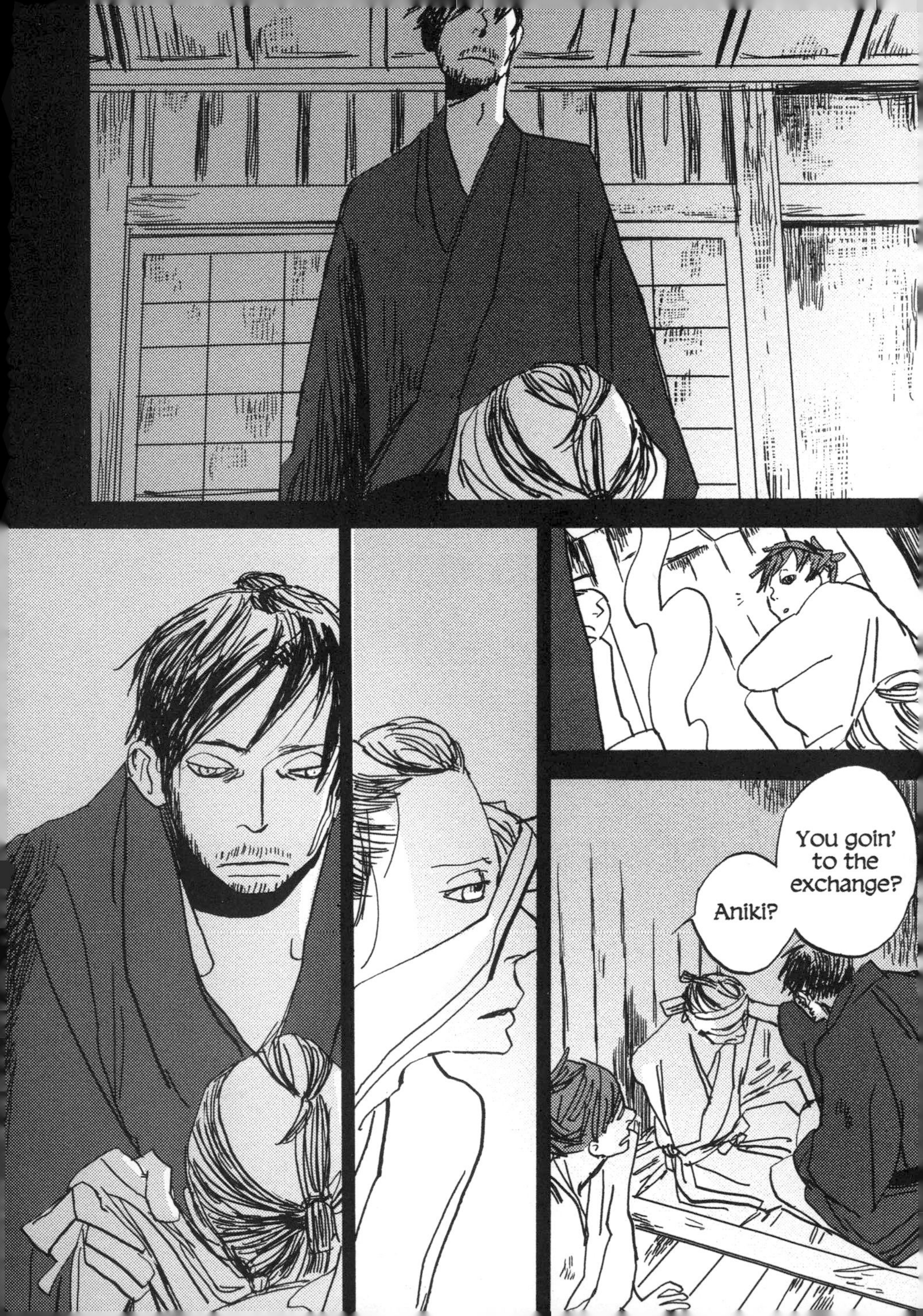
You goin' to the exchange?
Aniki?

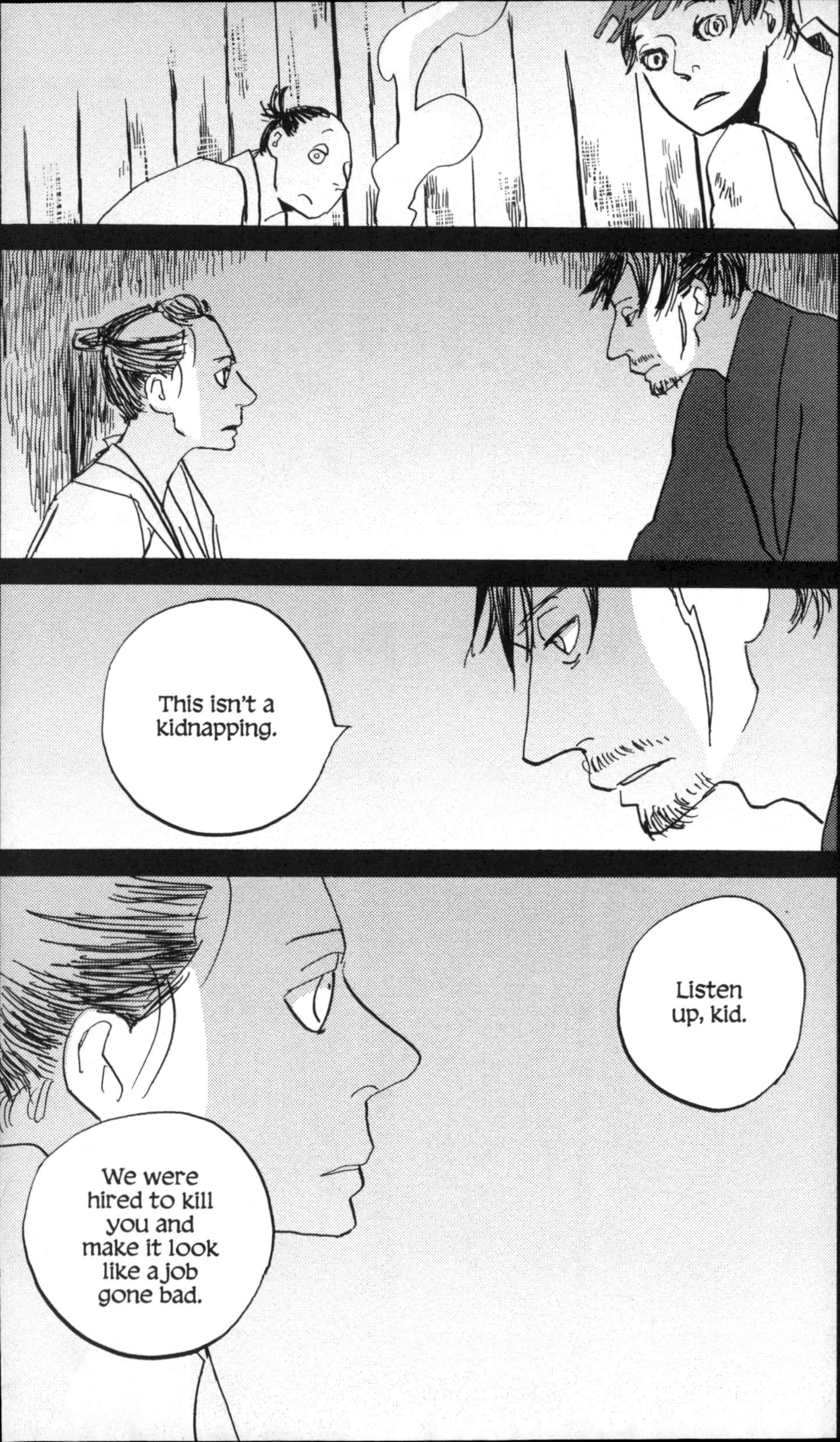
This isn't a kidnapping.
Listen up, kid.
We were hired to kill you and make it look like a job gone bad.

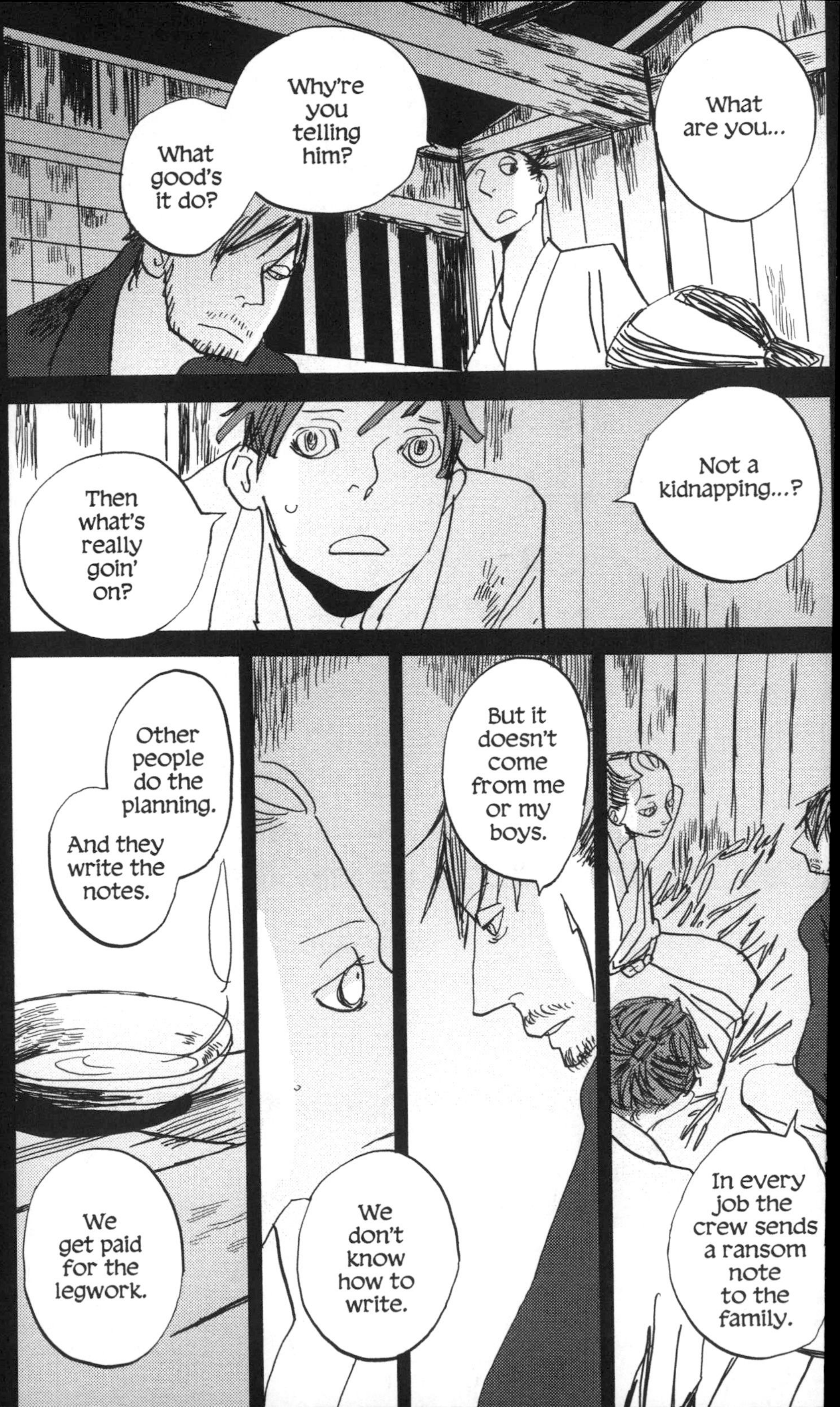
What are you...
Why're you telling him?
What good's it do?
Not a kidnapping...?
Then what's really goin' on?
In every job the crew sends a ransom note to the family.
But it doesn't come from me or my boys.
We don't know how to write.
Other people do the planning.
And they write the notes.
We get paid for the legwork.

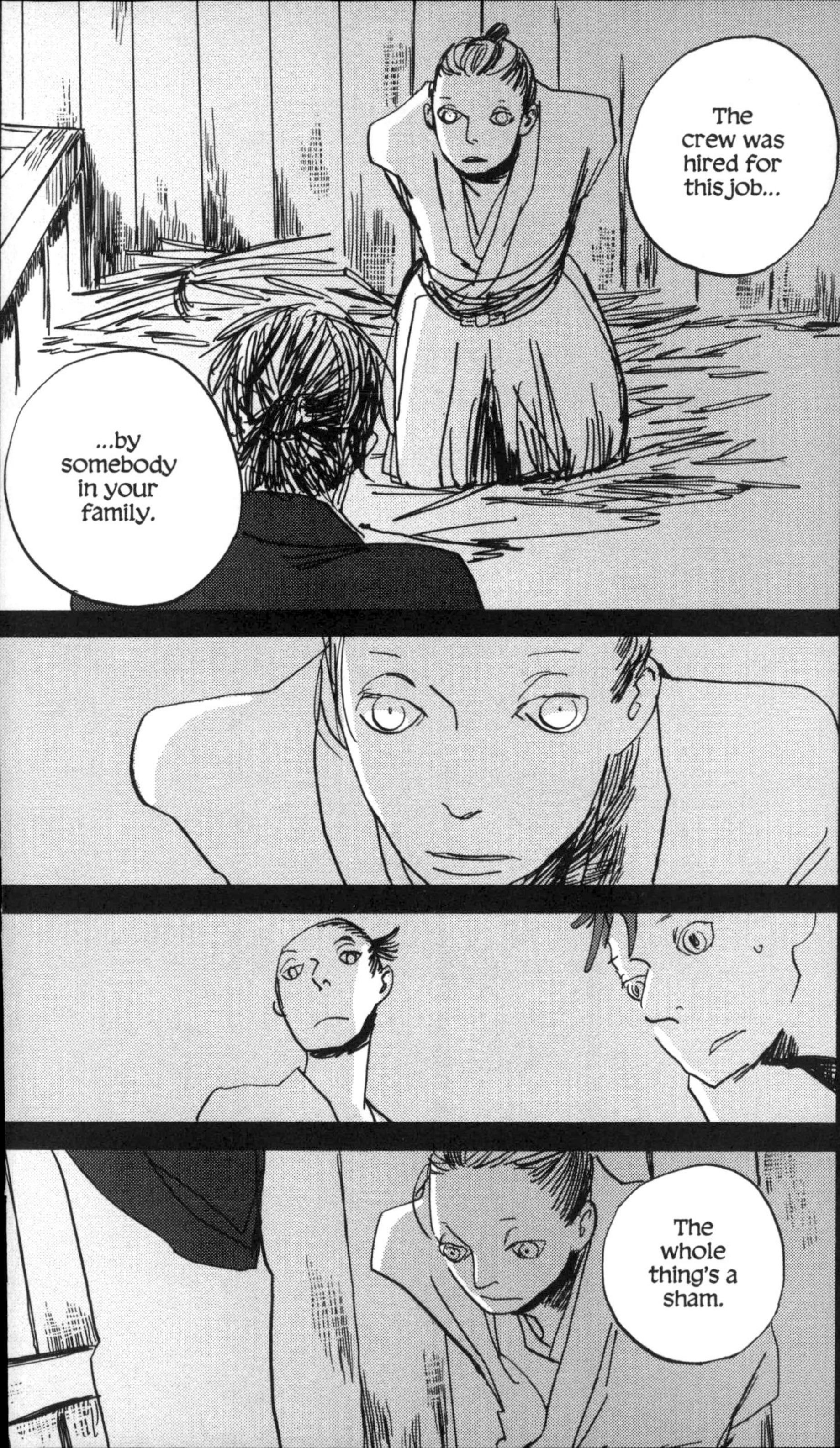
The crew was hired for this job...
...by somebody in your family.
The whole thing's a sham.

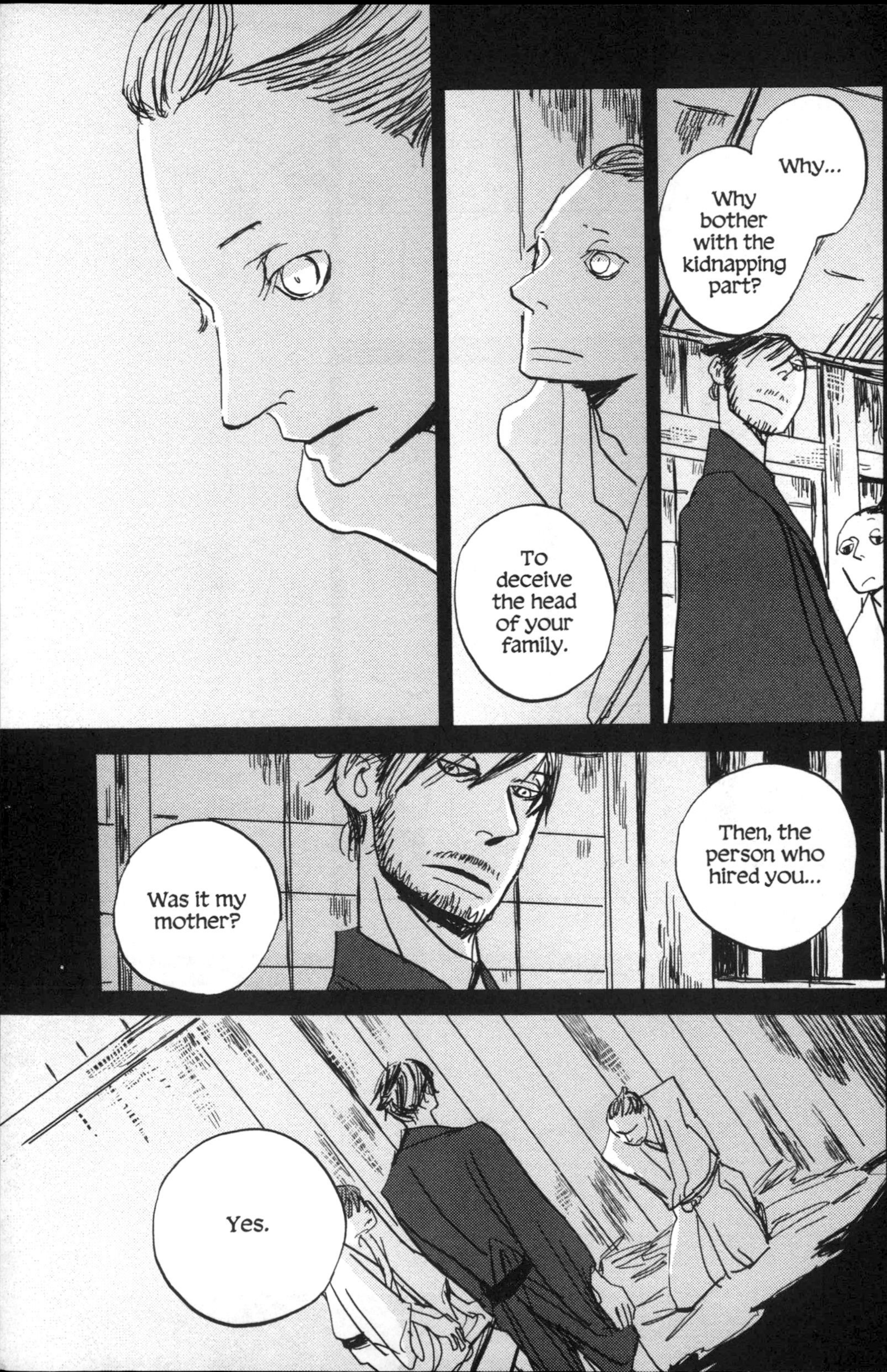
Why... Why bother with the kidnapping part?
To deceive the head of your family.
Then, the person who hired you...
Was it my mother?
Yes.

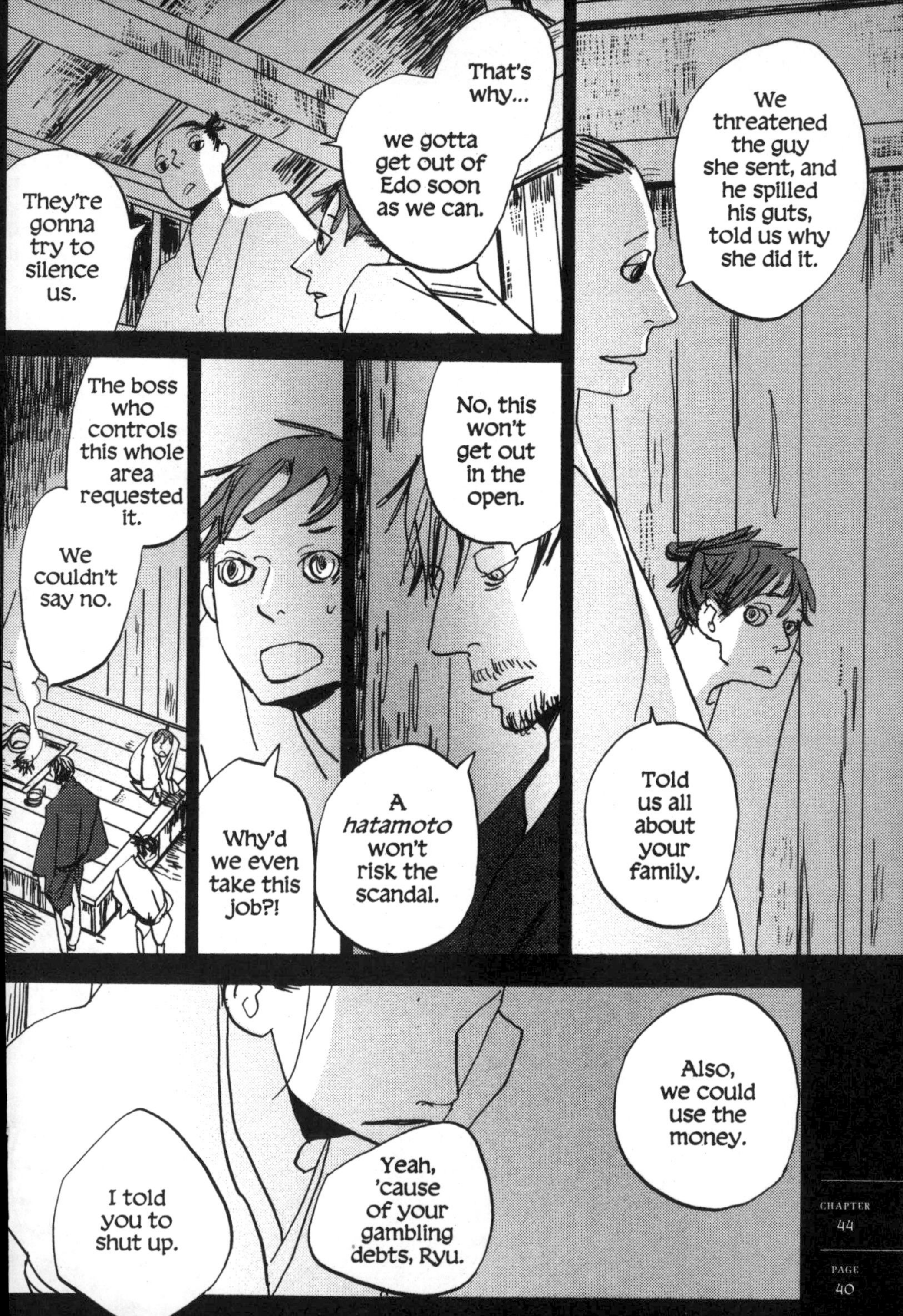
We threatened the guy she sent, and he spilled his guts, told us why she did it.
Told us all about your family.
That's why...
we gotta get out of Edo soon as we can.
They're gonna try to silence us.
No, this won't get out in the open.
A *hatamoto* won't risk the scandal.
Why'd we even take this job?!
The boss who controls this whole area requested it.
We couldn't say no.
Also, we could use the money.
Yeah, 'cause of your gambling debts, Ryu.
I told you to shut up.

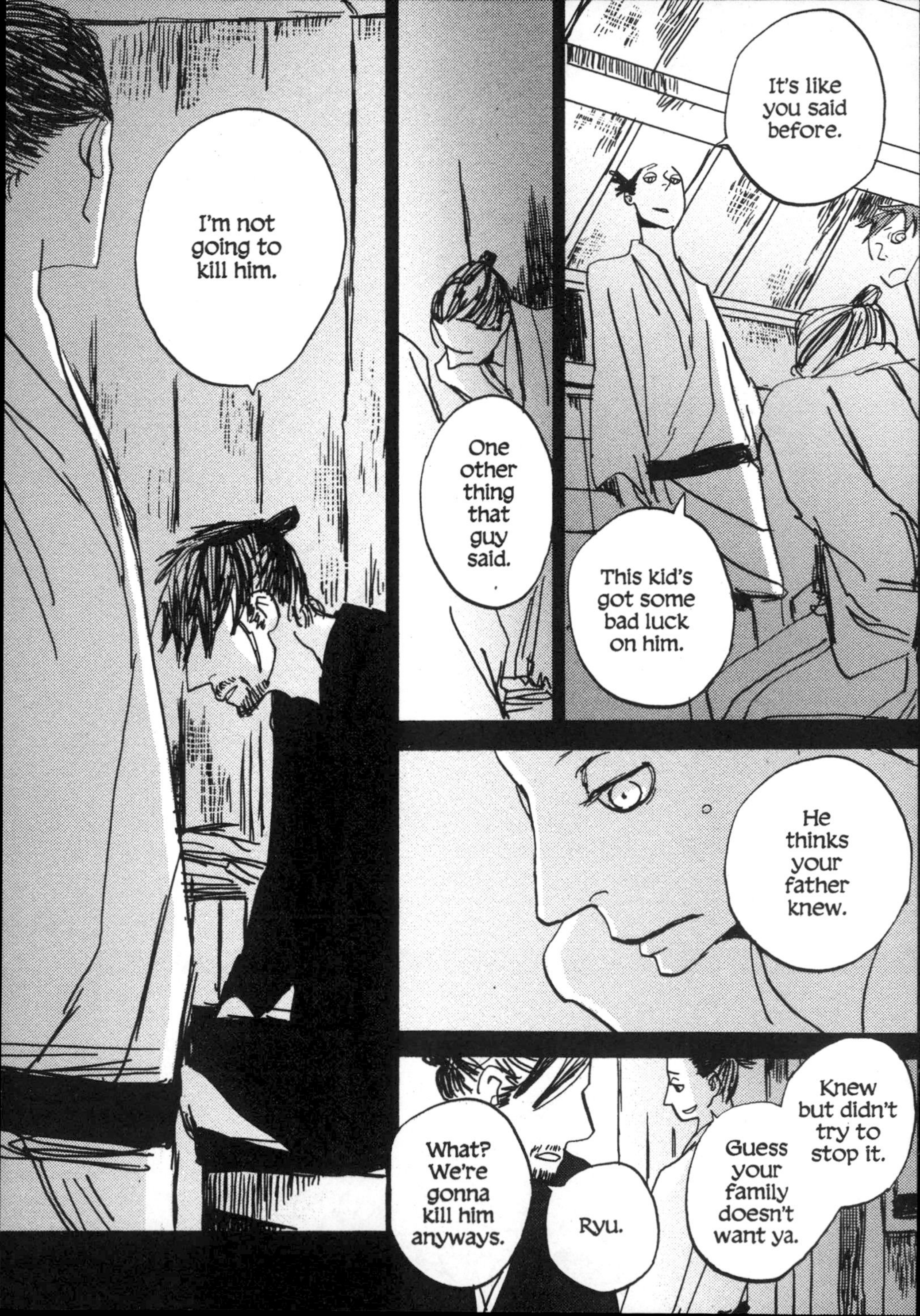
It's like you said before.
This kid's got some bad luck on him.
One other thing that guy said.
He thinks your father knew.
Knew but didn't try to stop it.
Guess your family doesn't want ya.
Ryu.
What? We're gonna kill him anyways.
I'm not going to kill him.

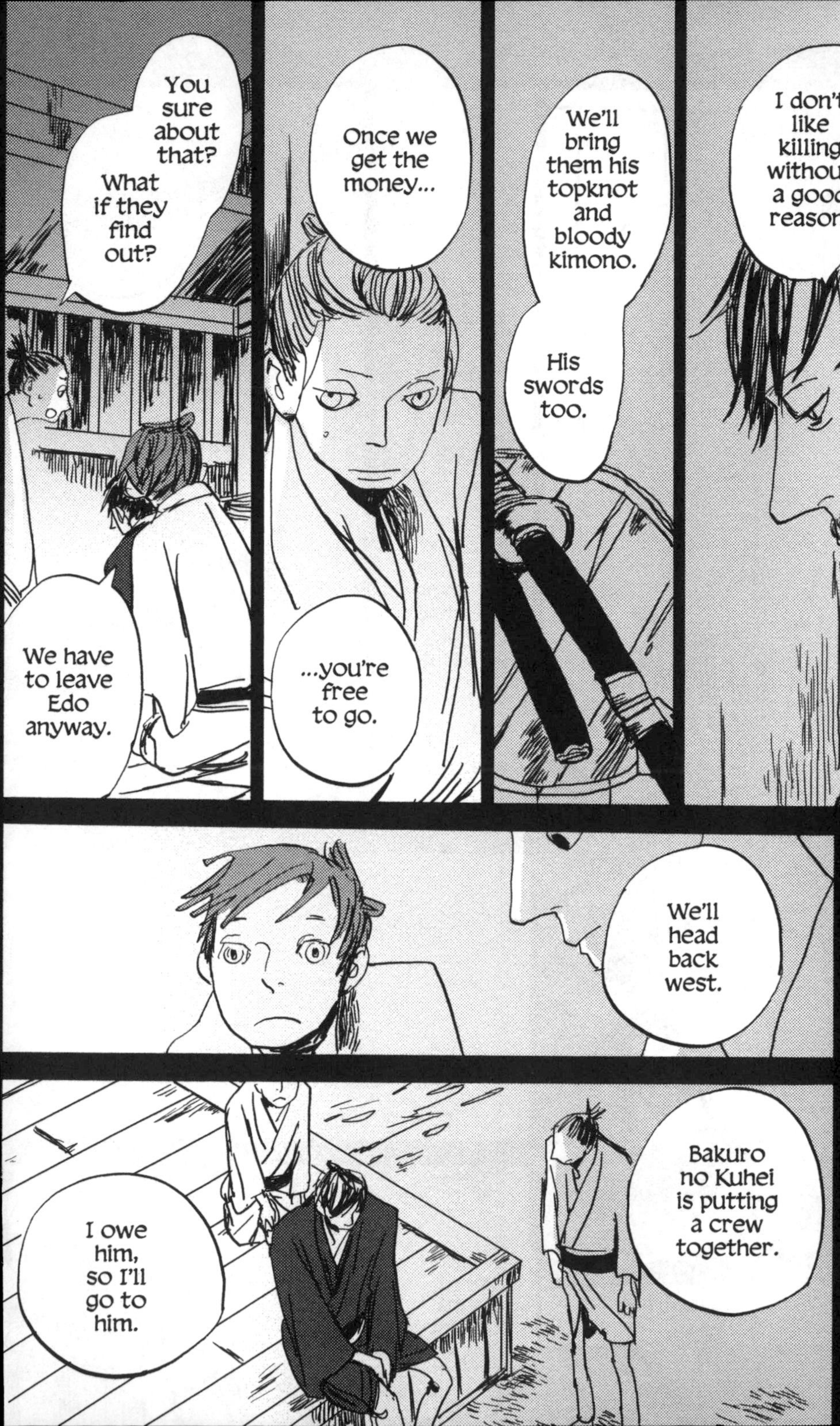

I don't like killing without a good reason.
We'll bring them his topknot and bloody kimono.
His swords too.
Once we get the money...
...you're free to go.
You sure about that? What if they find out?
We have to leave Edo anyway.
We'll head back west.
Bakuro no Kuhei is putting a crew together.
I owe him, so I'll go to him.

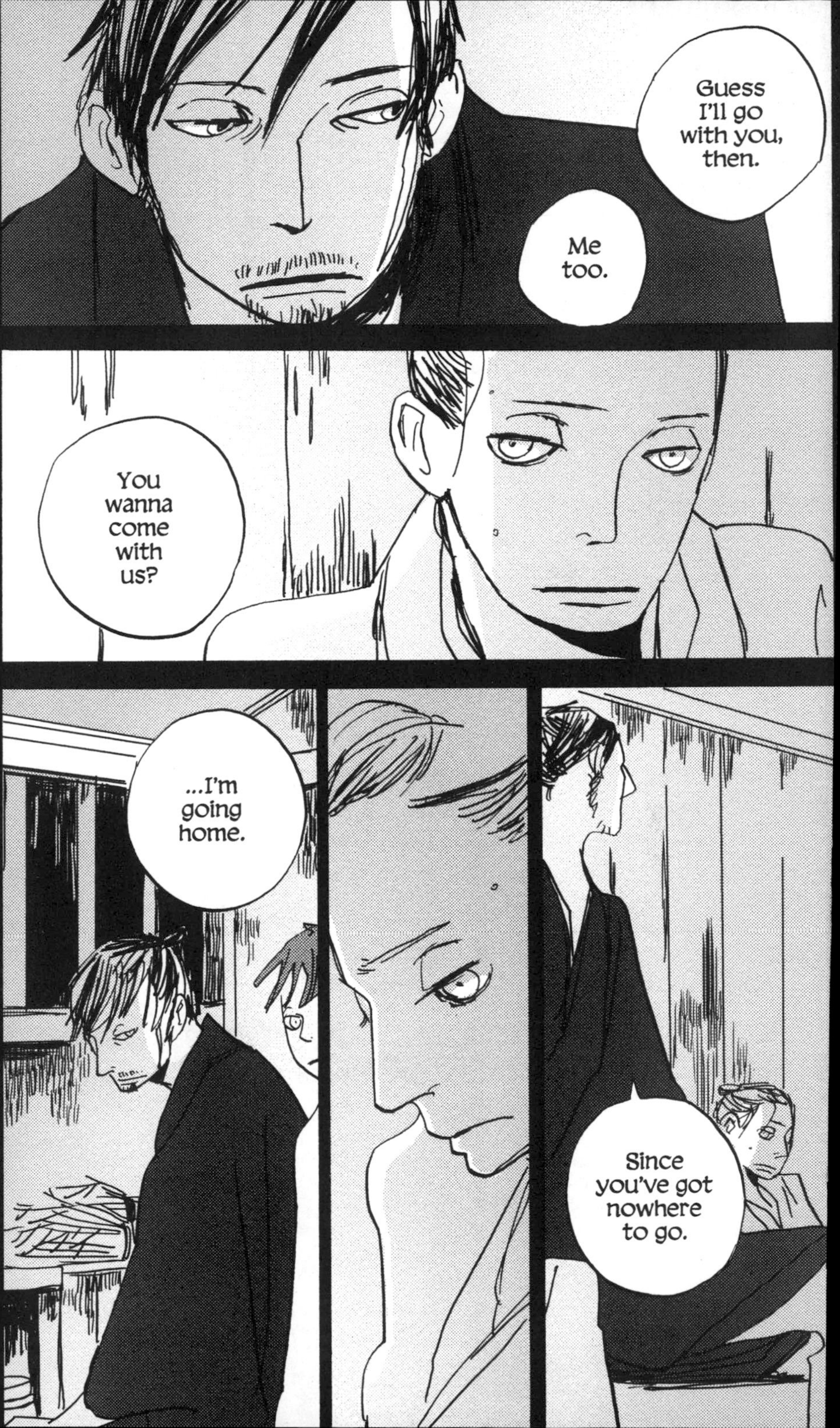
Guess I'll go with you, then.
Me too.
You wanna come with us?
Since you've got nowhere to go.
...I'm going home.

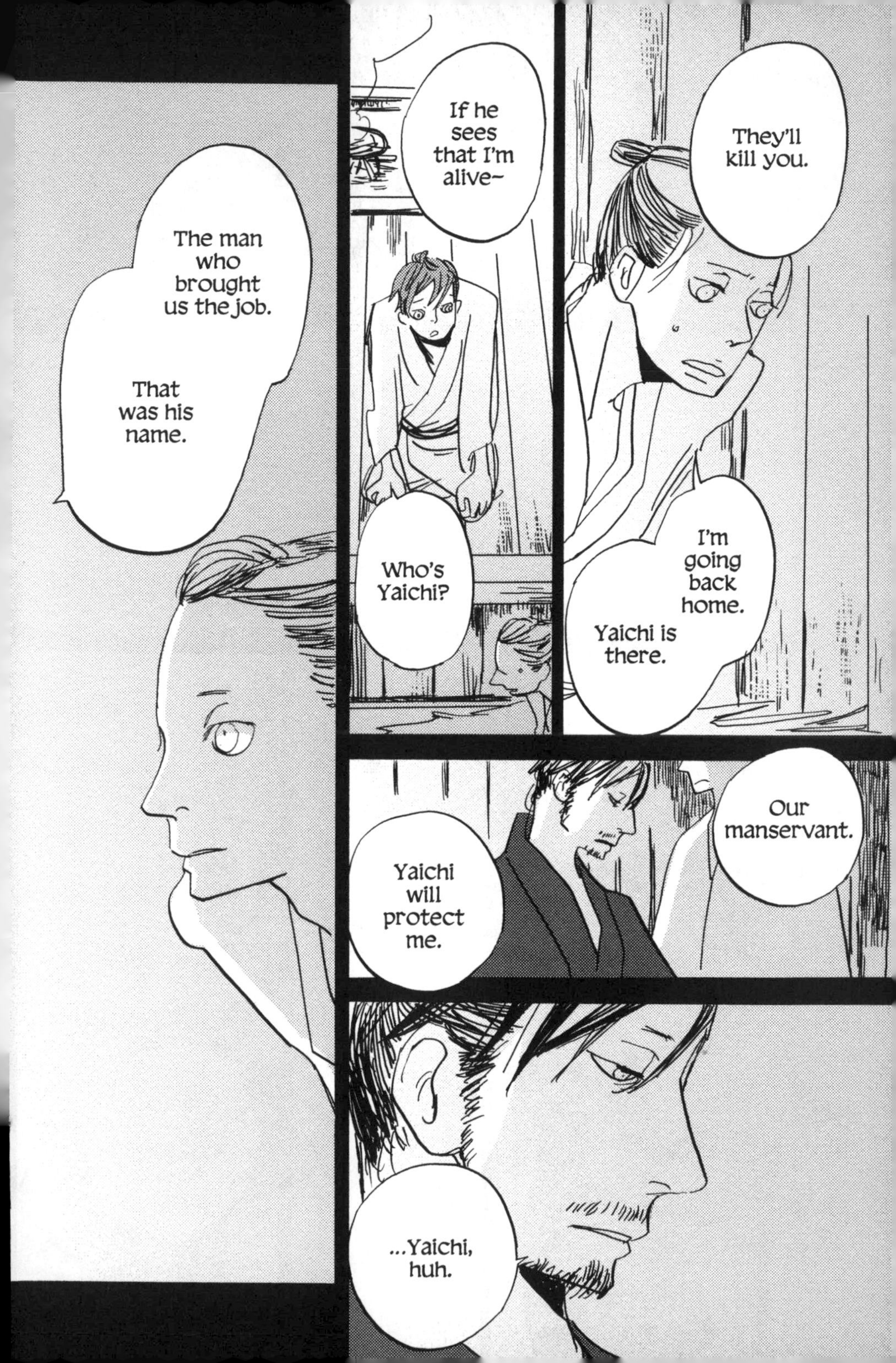
They'll kill you.
I'm going back home.
Yaichi is there.
If he sees that I'm alive~
Who's Yaichi?
Our manservant.
Yaichi will protect me.
...Yaichi, huh.
The man who brought us the job.
That was his name.

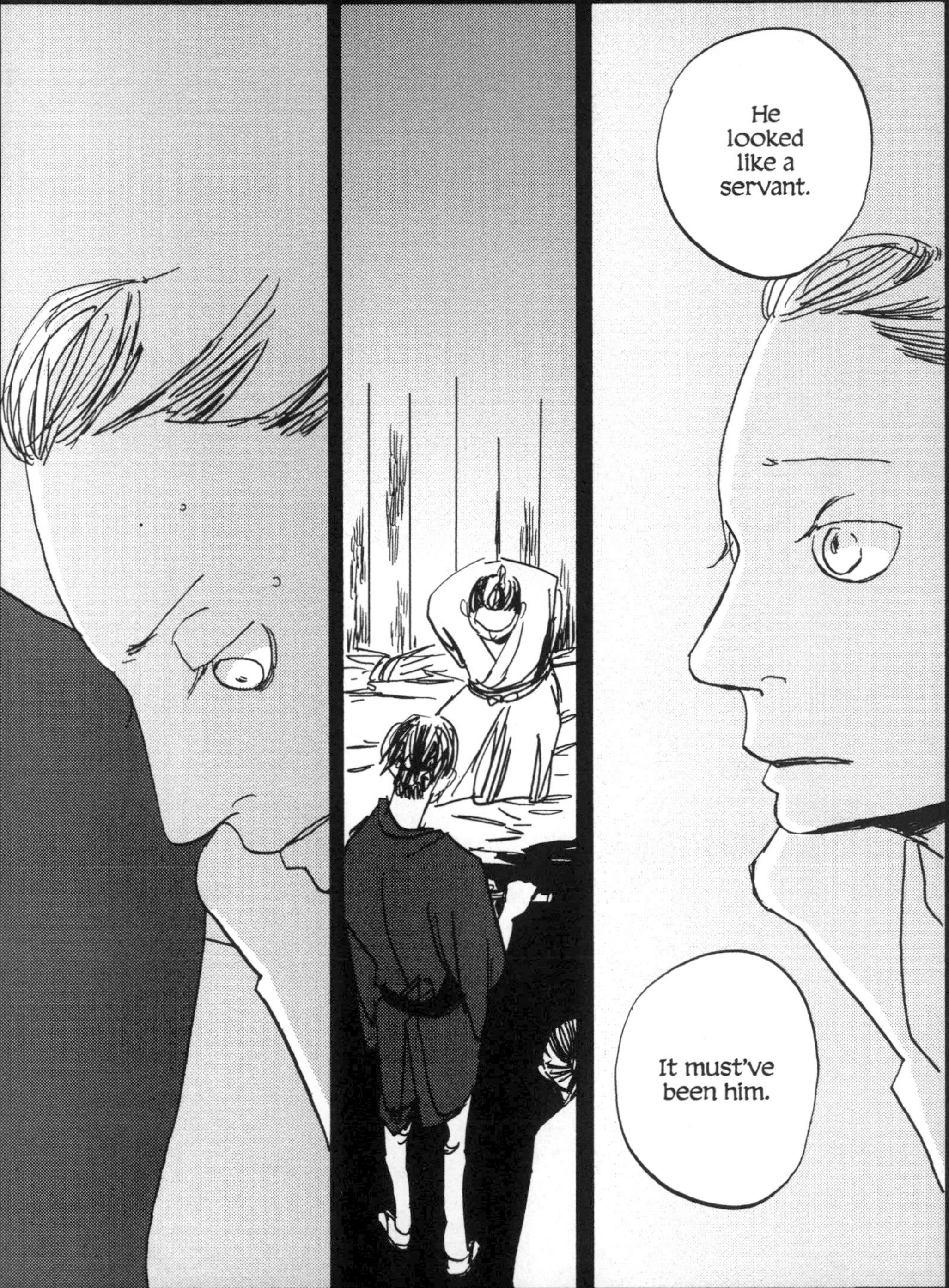
He looked like a servant.
It must've been him.

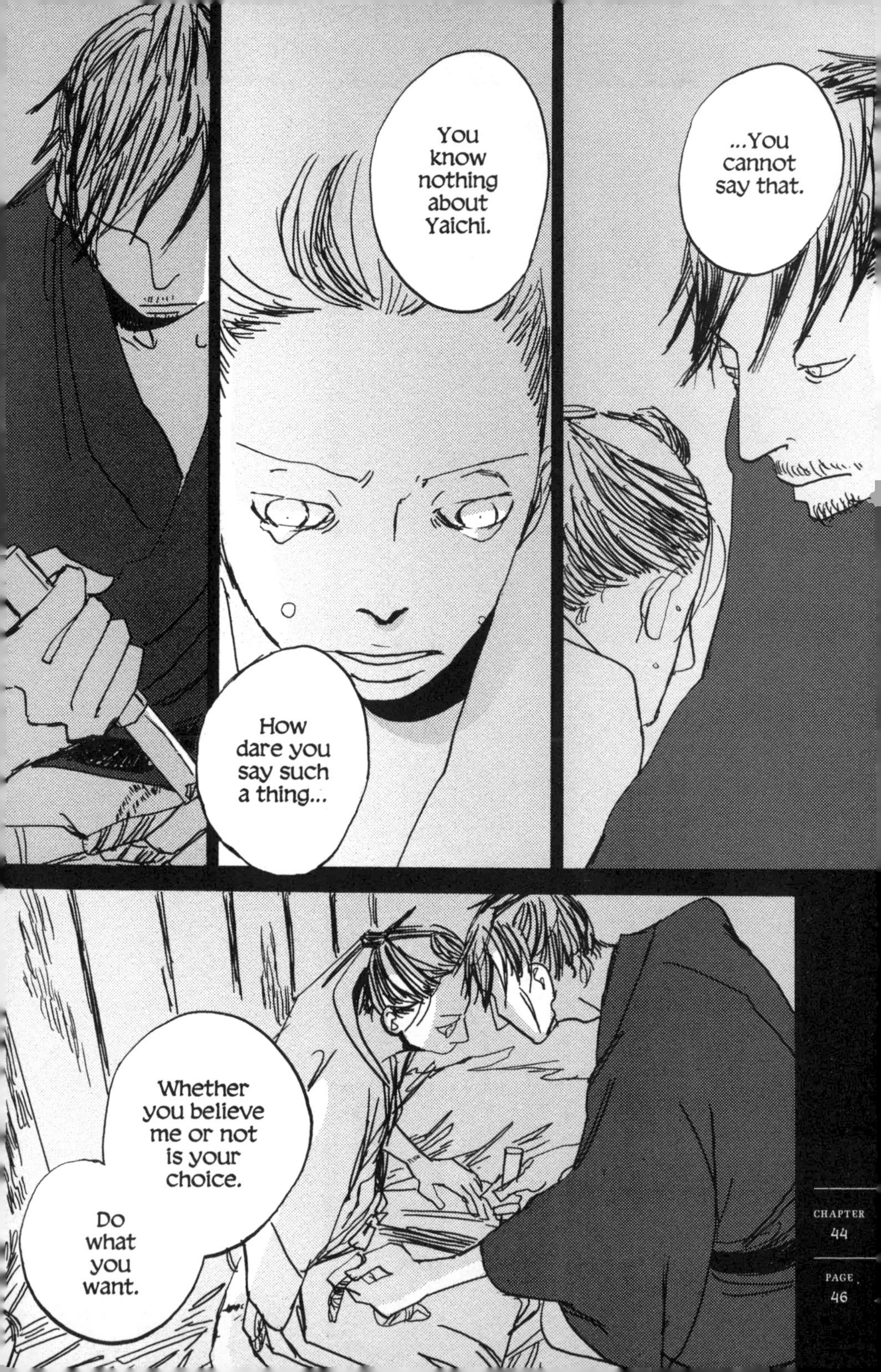
...You cannot say that.
You know nothing about Yaichi.
How dare you say such a thing...
Whether you believe me or not is your choice.
Do what you want.

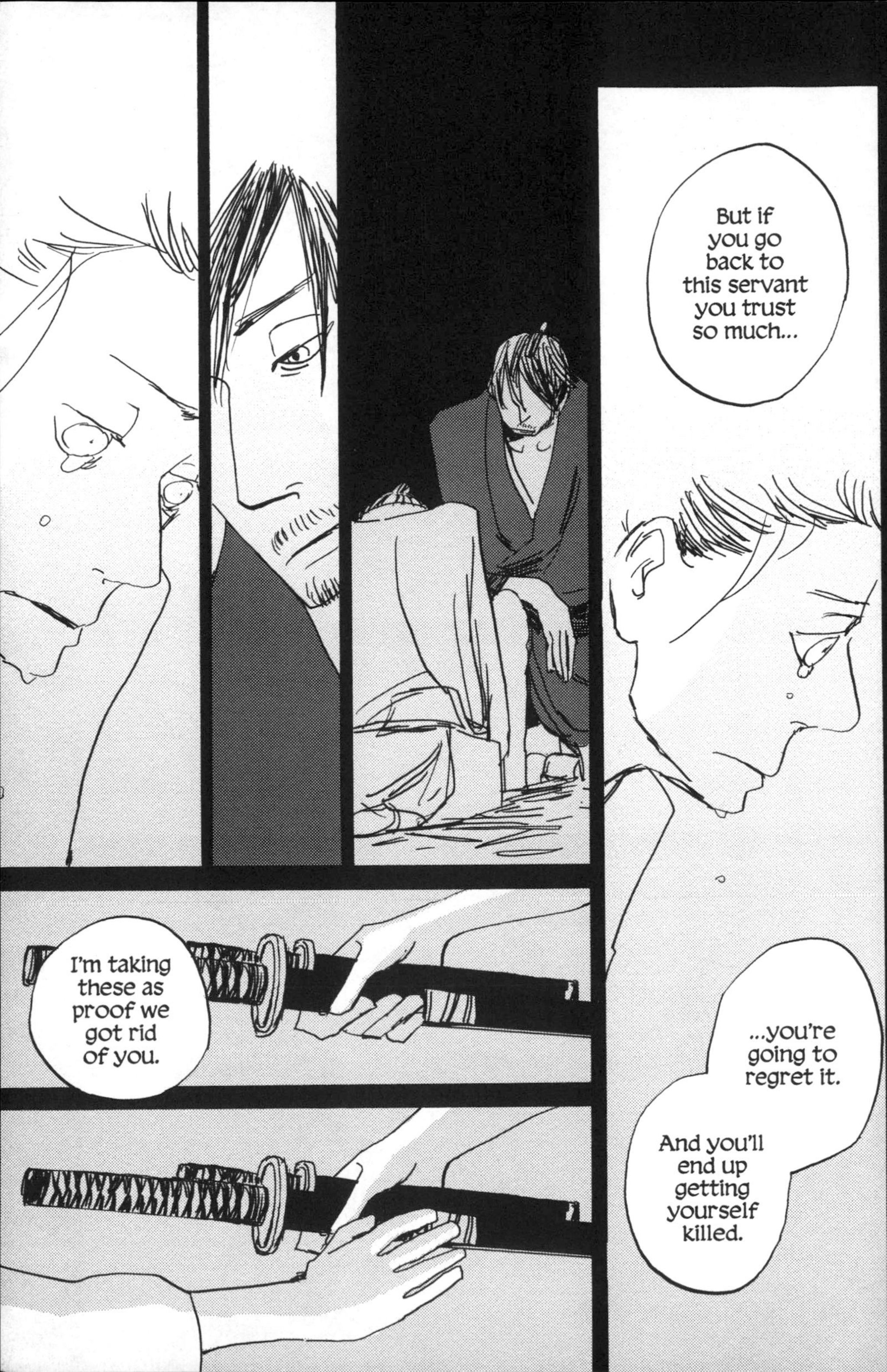
But if you go back to this servant you trust so much...
...you're going to regret it.
And you'll end up getting yourself killed.
I'm taking these as proof we got rid of you.

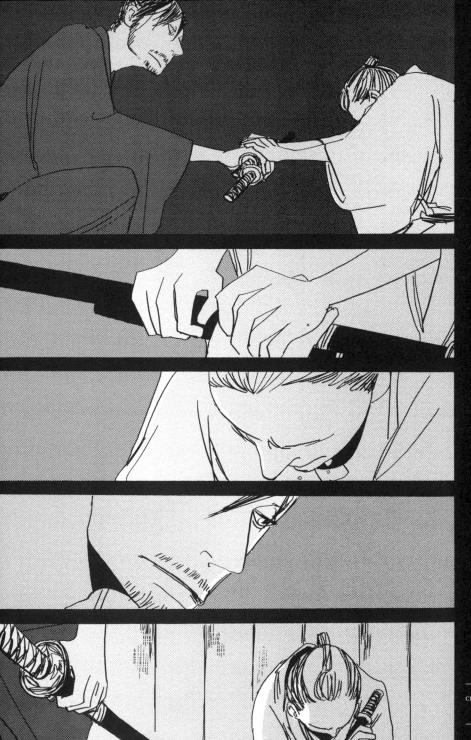

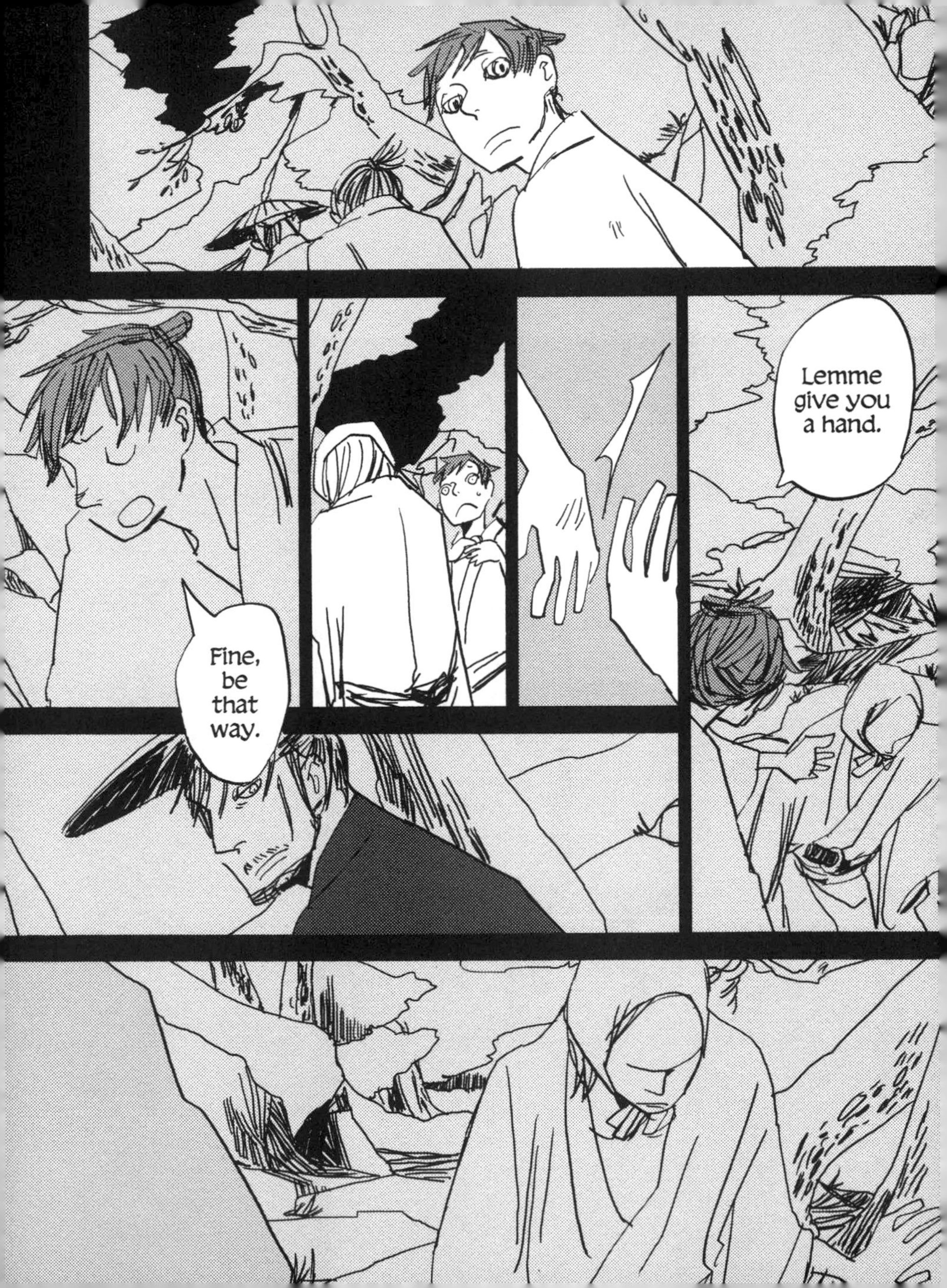
Lemme give you a hand.
Fine, be that way.

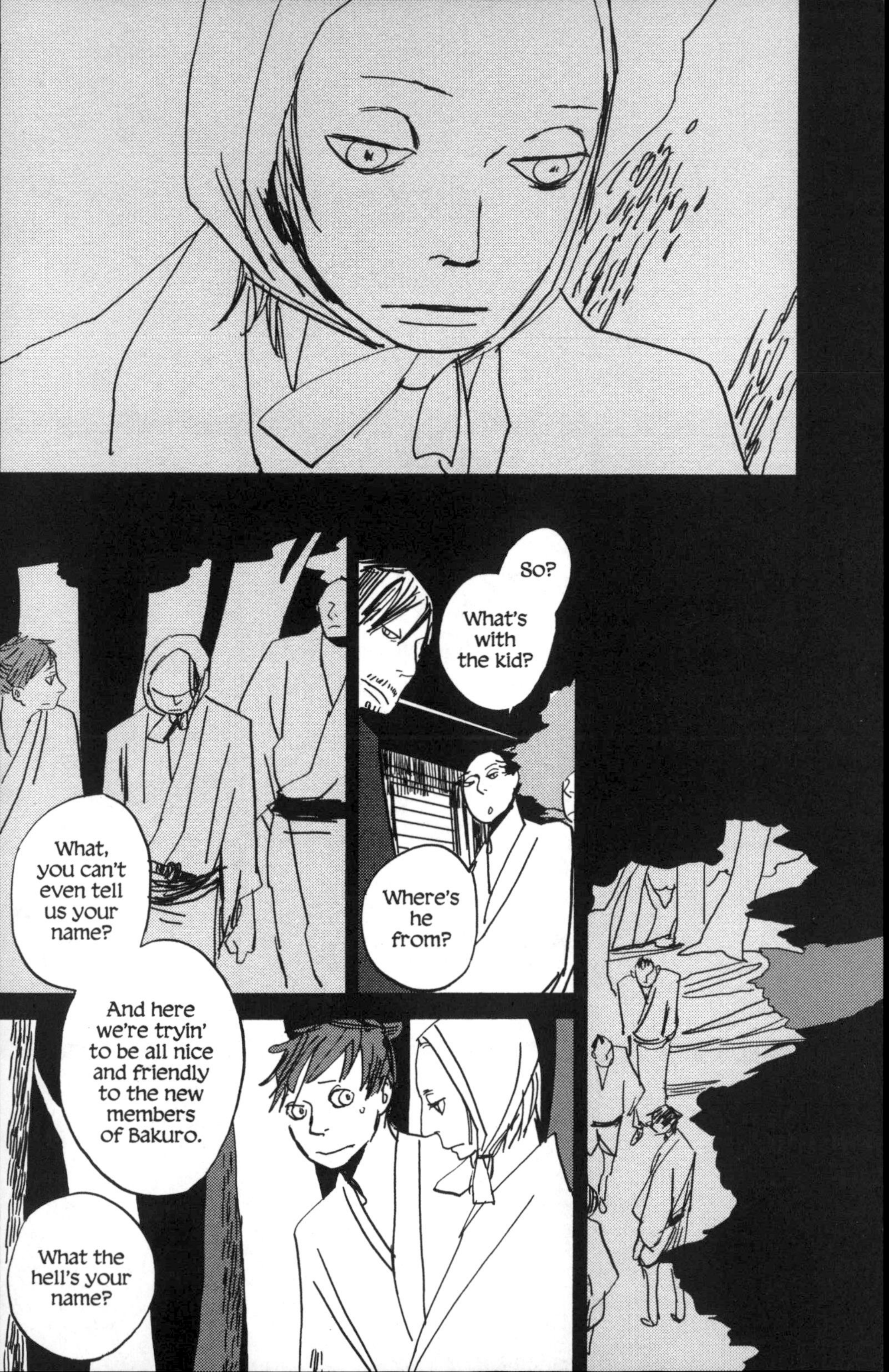
So?
What's with the kid?
Where's he from?
What, you can't even tell us your name?
And here we're tryin' to be all nice and friendly to the new members of Bakuro.
What the hell's your name?

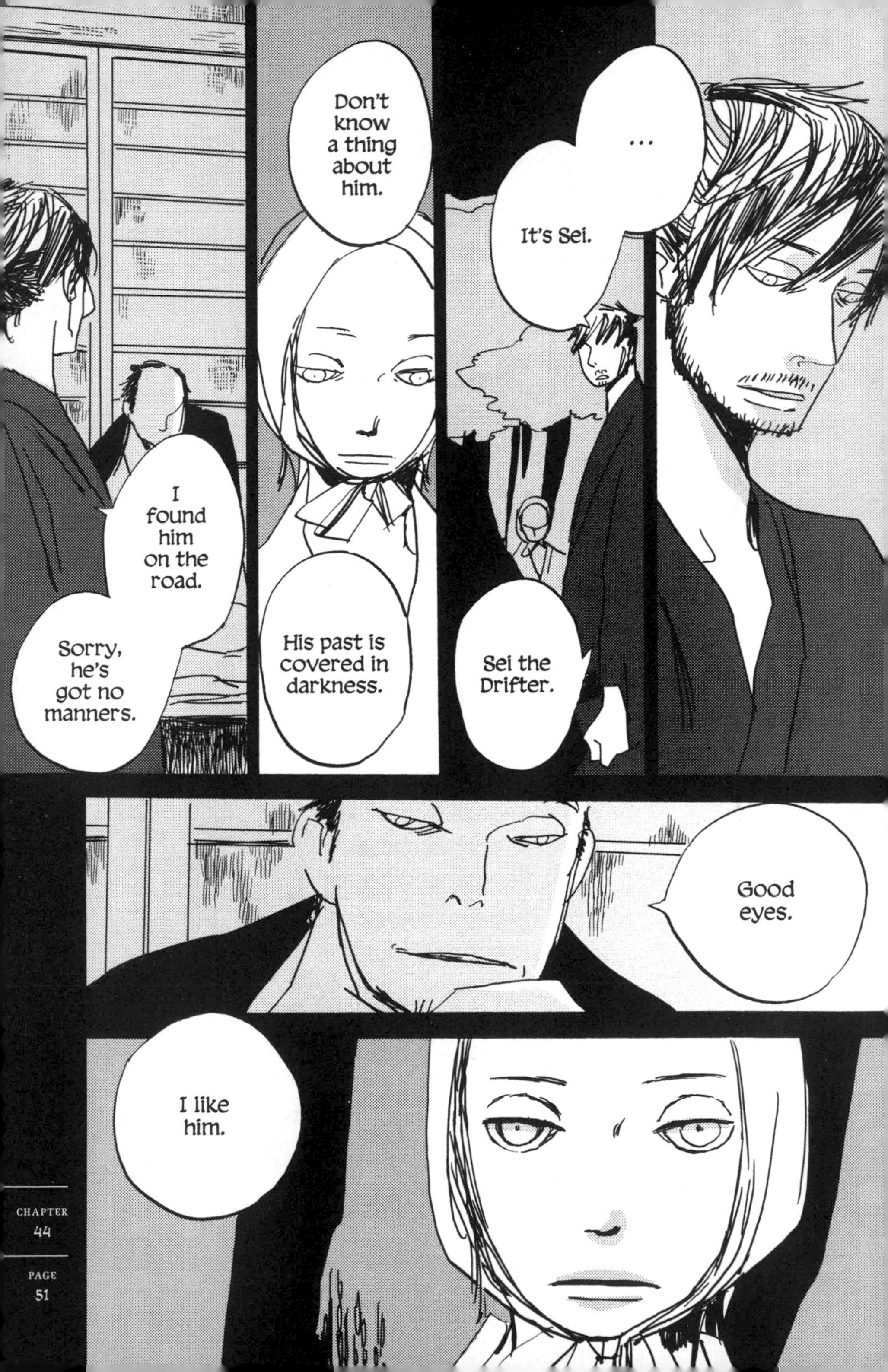
...
It's Sei.
Sei the Drifter.
Don't know a thing about him.
His past is covered in darkness.
I found him on the road.
Sorry, he's got no manners.
Good eyes.
I like him.

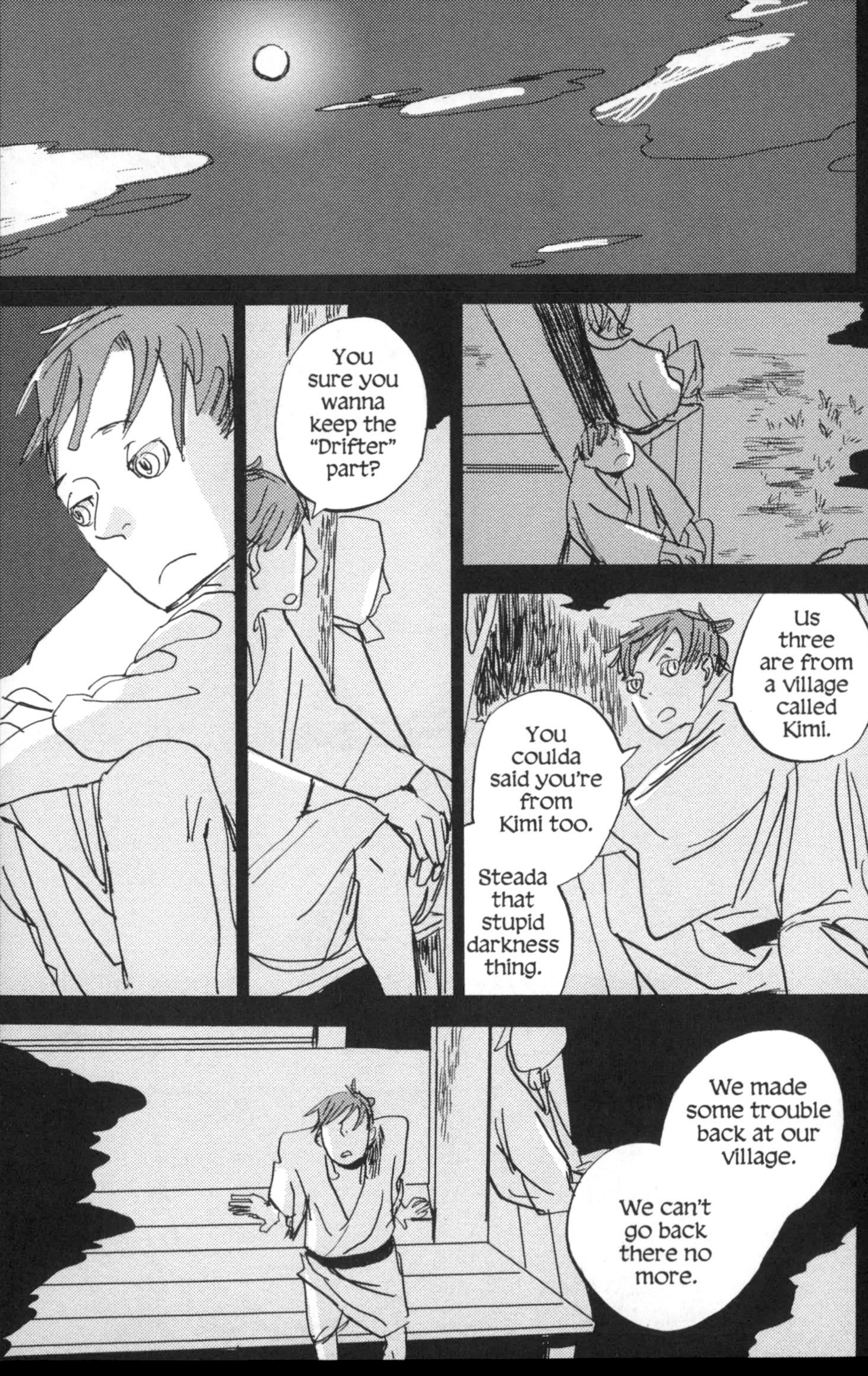
Us three are from a village called Kimi.
You coulda said you're from Kimi too.
Steada that stupid darkness thing.
You sure you wanna keep the "Drifter" part?
We made some trouble back at our village.
We can't go back there no more.

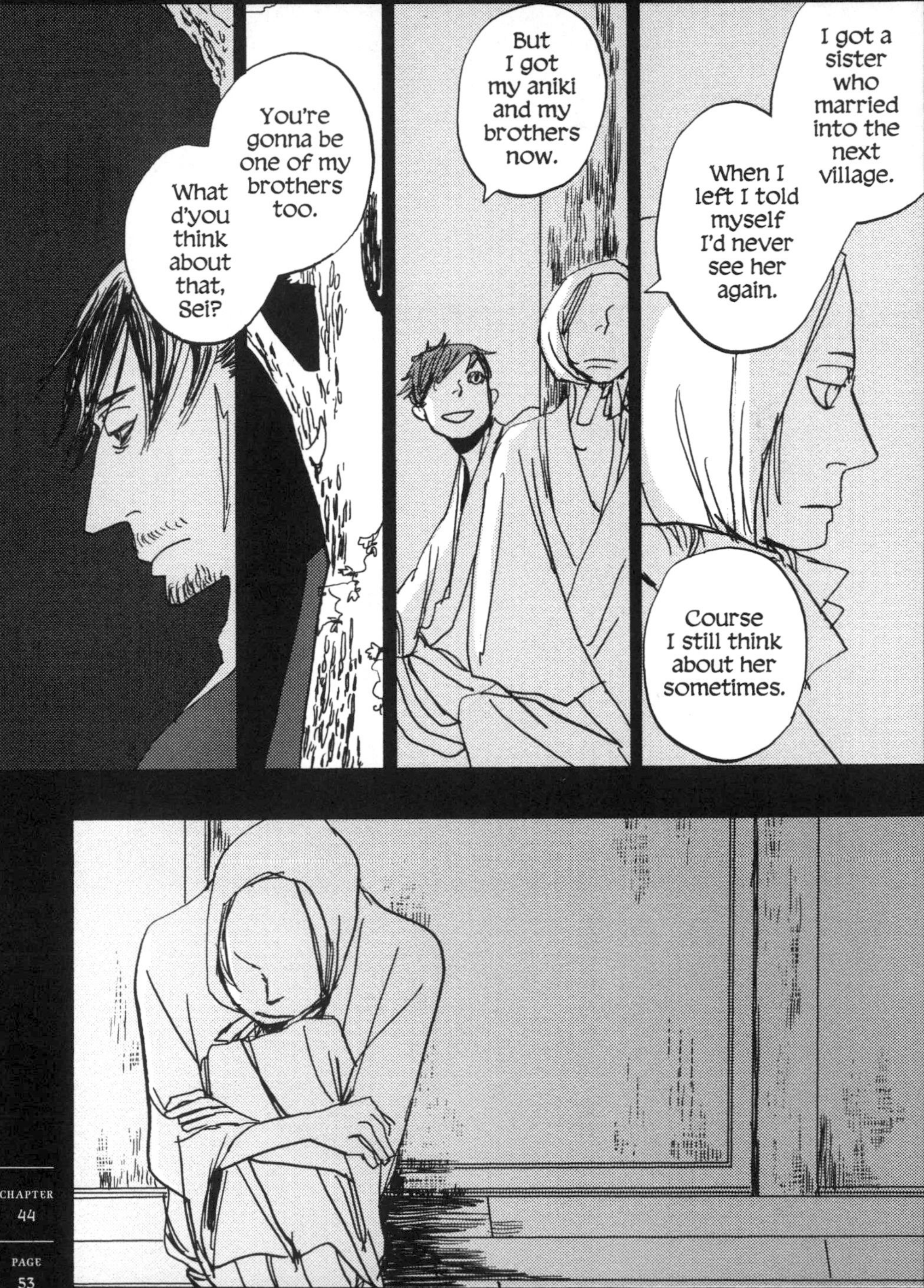
I got a sister who married into the next village.
When I left I told myself I'd never see her again.
Course I still think about her sometimes.
But I got my aniki and my brothers now.
You're gonna be one of my brothers too.
What d'you think about that, Sei?

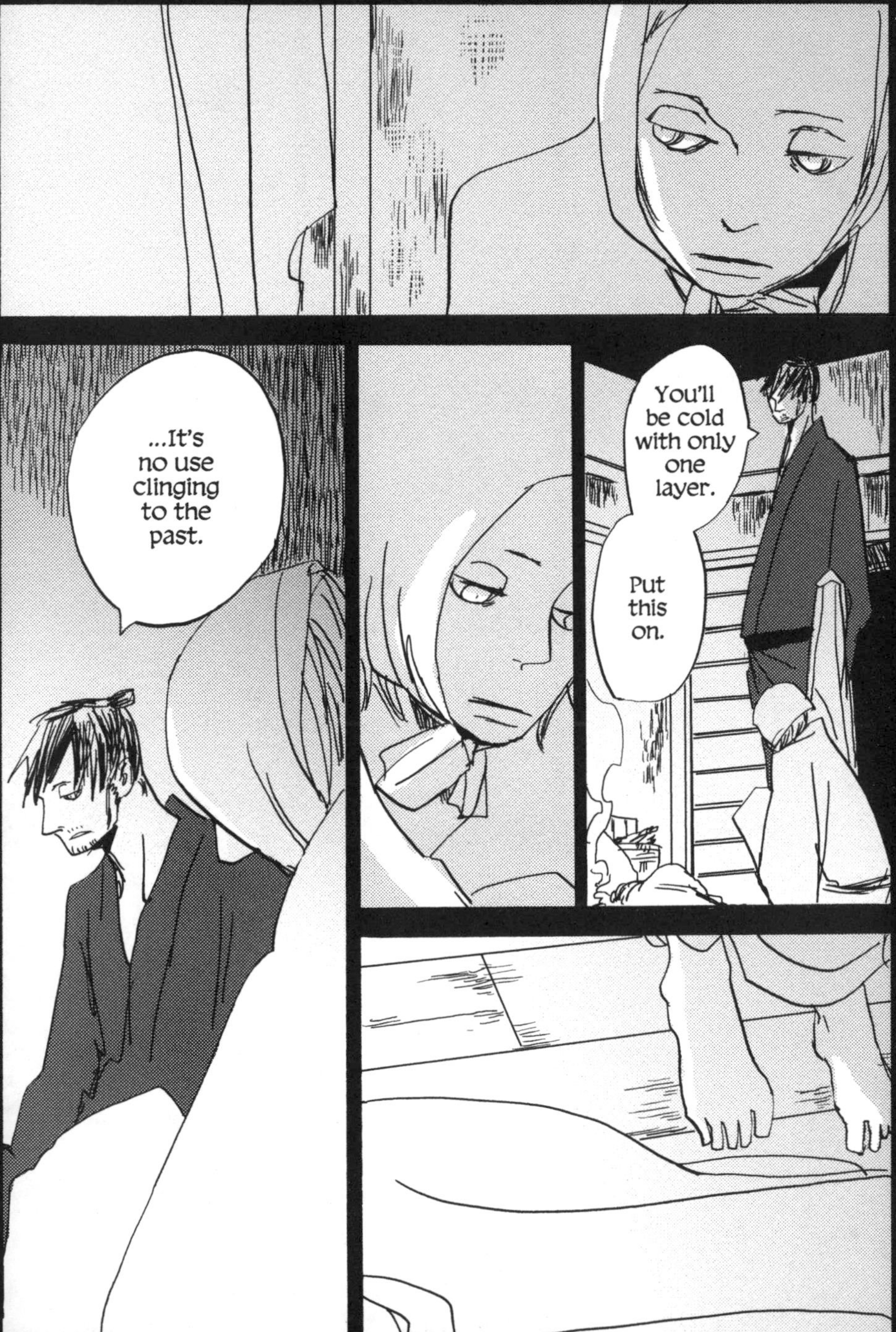

You'll be cold with only one layer.
Put this on.
...It's no use clinging to the past.

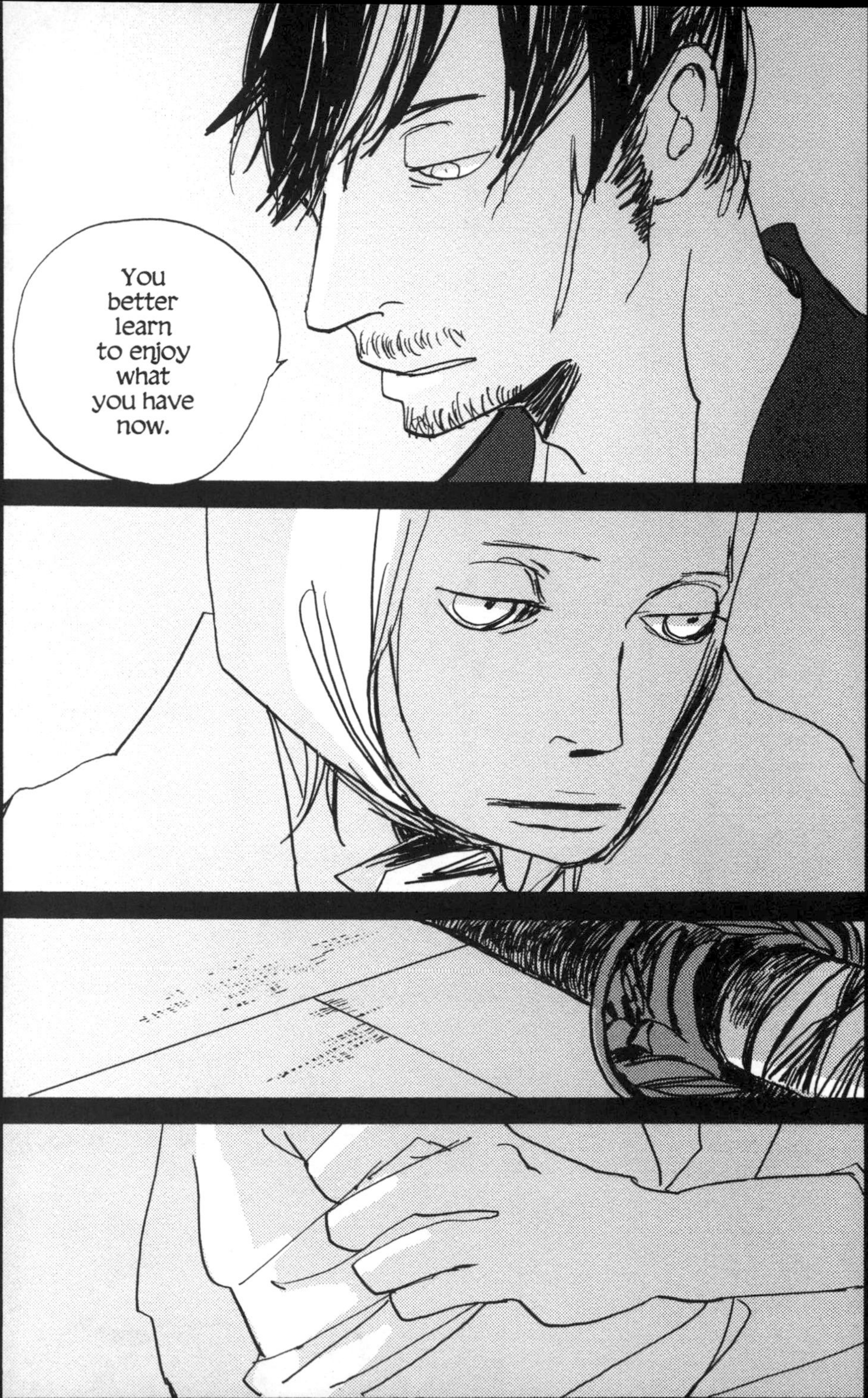

You better learn to enjoy what you have now.

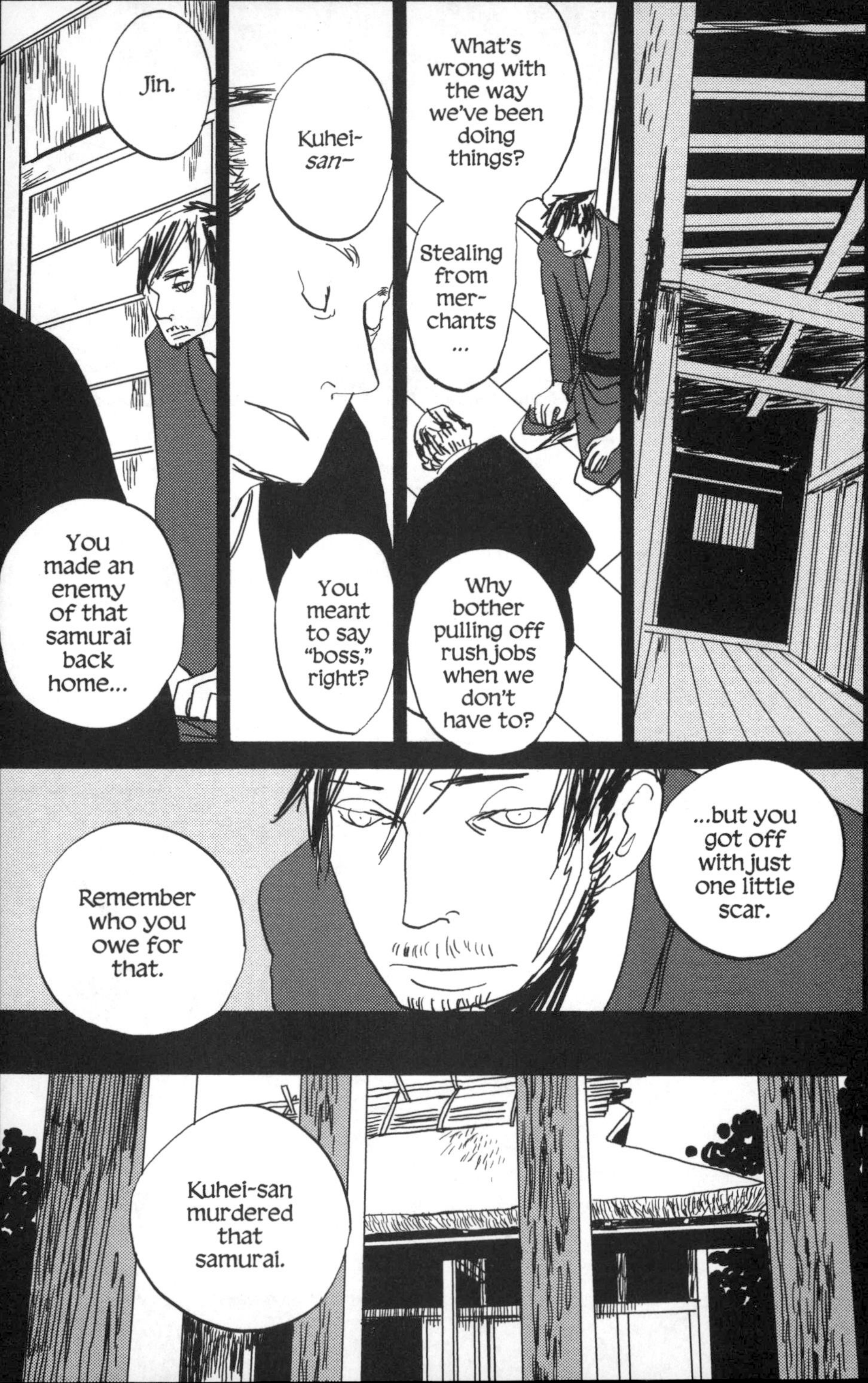
What's wrong with the way we've been doing things?
Stealing from mer-chants ...
Why bother pulling off rush jobs when we don't have to?
Kuhei-*san*—
You meant to say "boss," right?
Jin.
You made an enemy of that samurai back home...
...but you got off with just one little scar.
Remember who you owe for that.
Kuhei-san murdered that samurai.

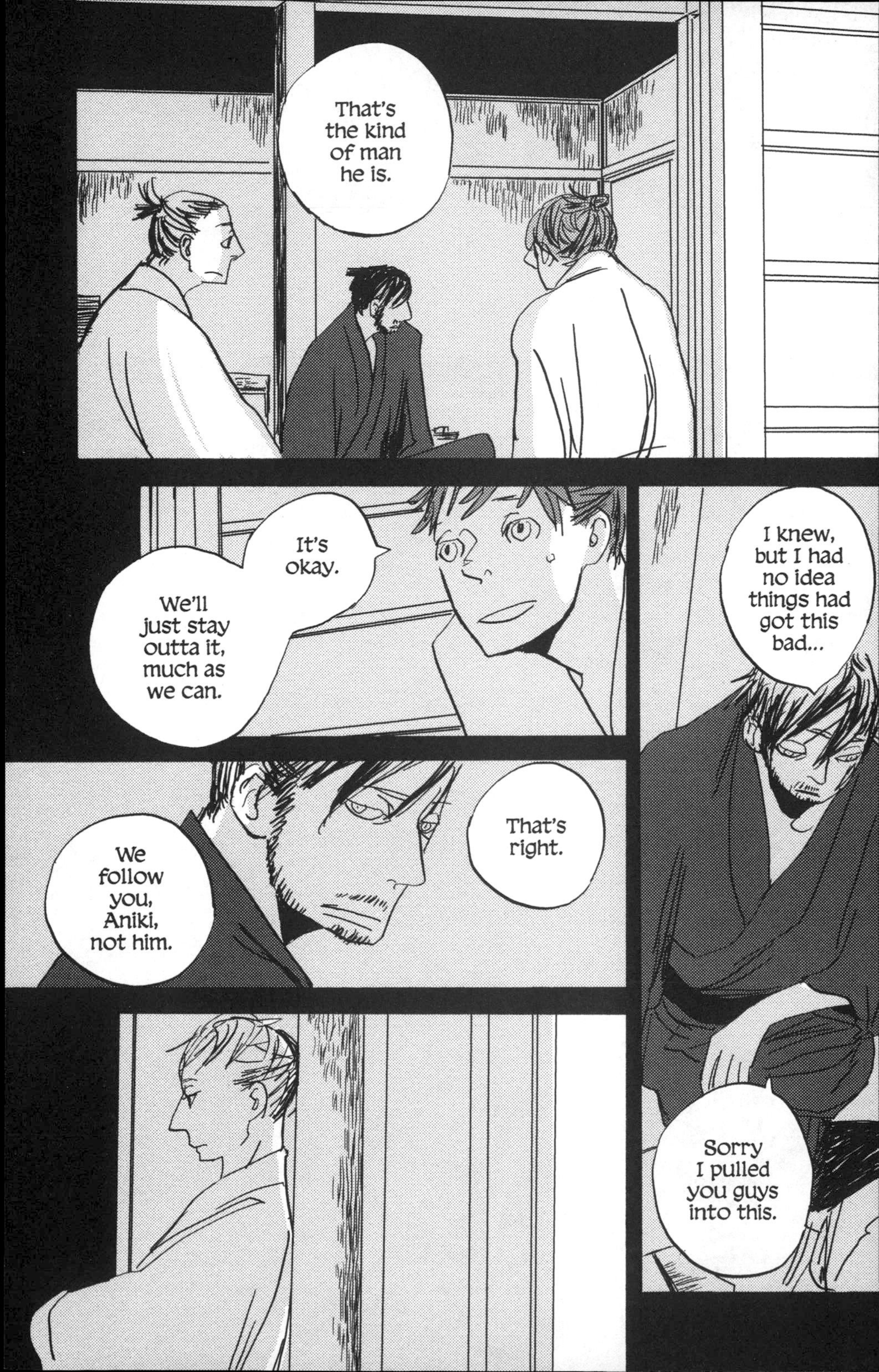
That's the kind of man he is.
I knew, but I had no idea things had got this bad...
Sorry I pulled you guys into this.
It's okay.
We'll just stay outta it, much as we can.
That's right.
We follow you, Aniki, not him.

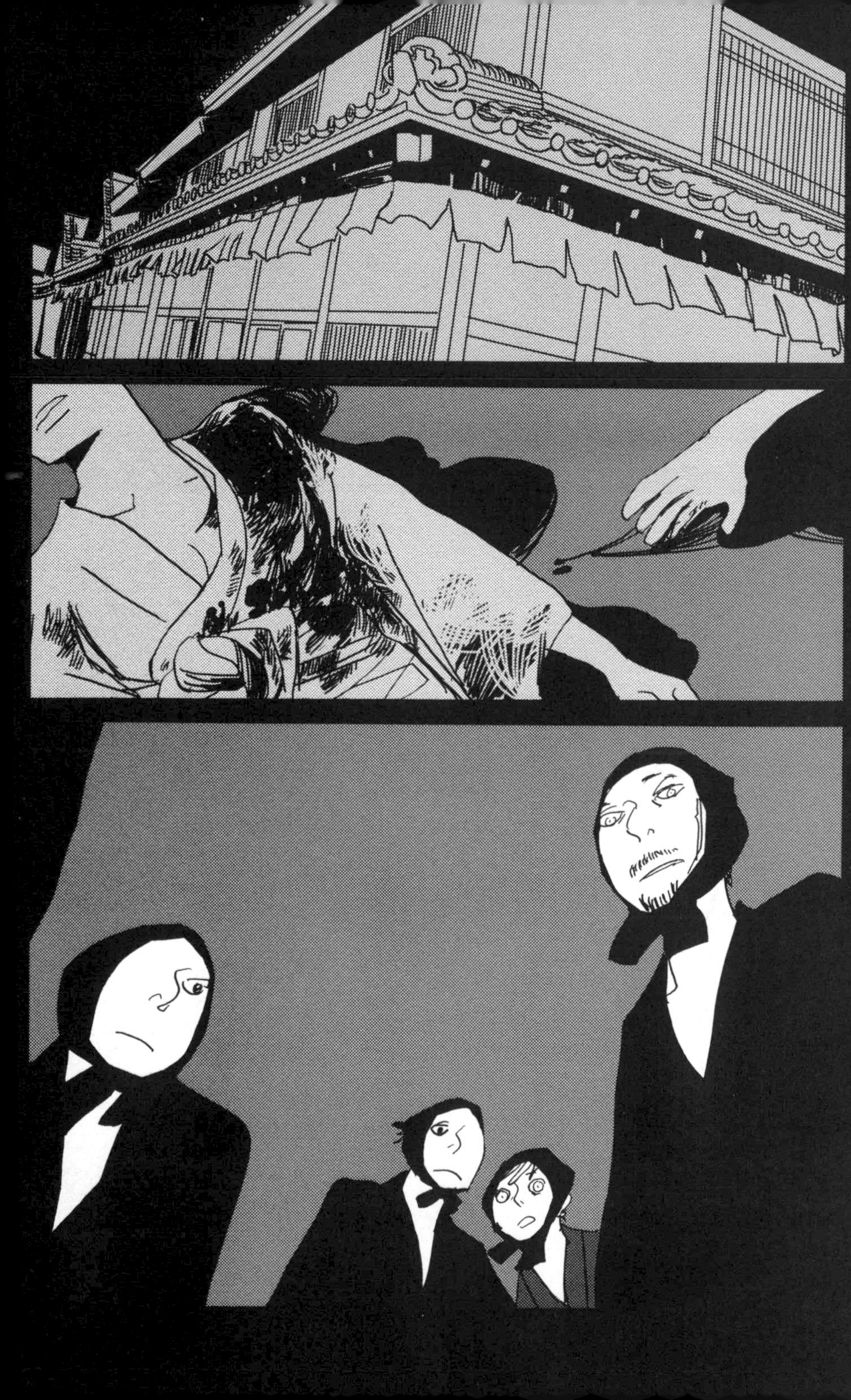

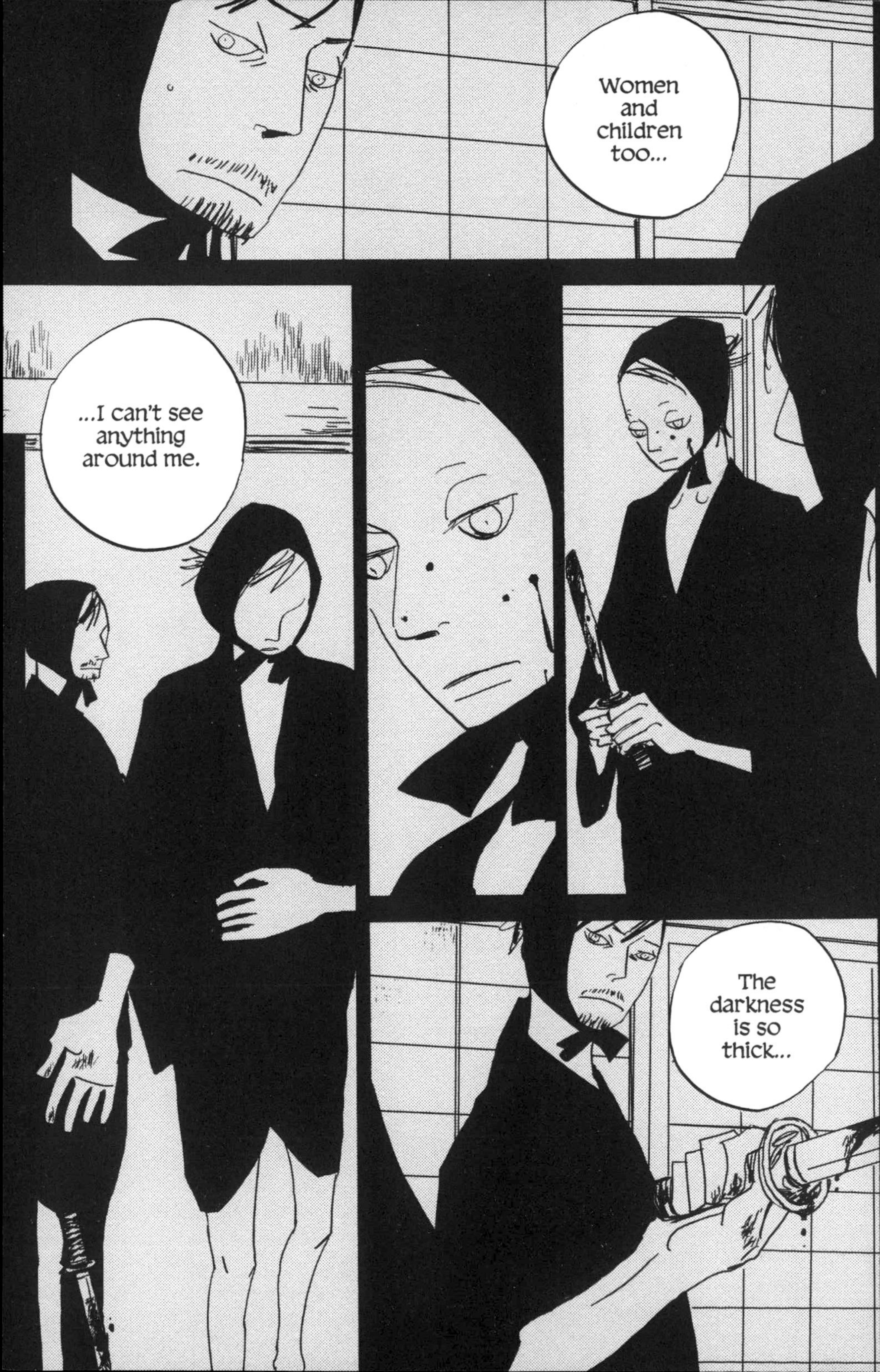
Women and children too...
...I can't see anything around me.
The darkness is so thick...

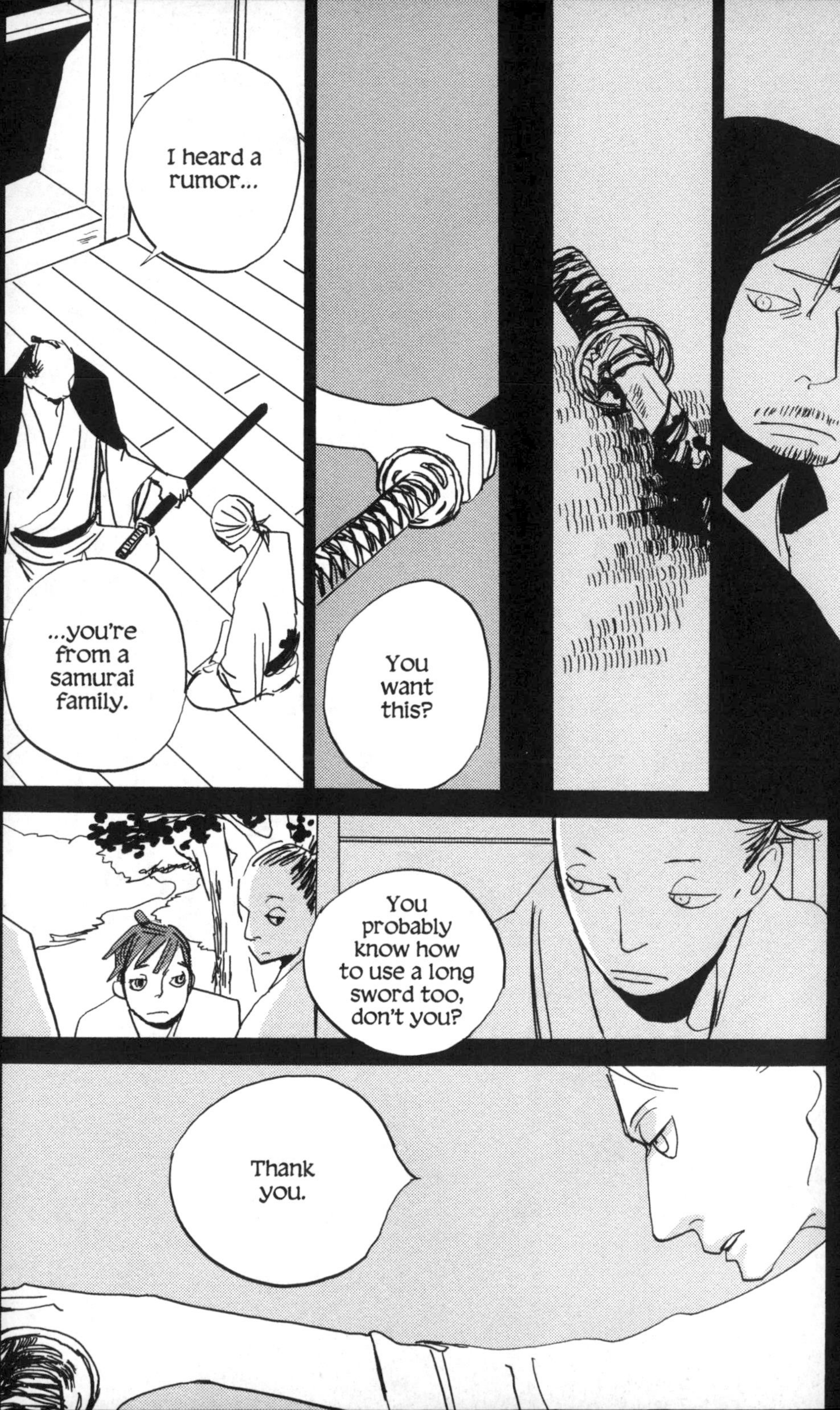
You want this?
I heard a rumor...
...you're from a samurai family.
You probably know how to use a long sword too, don't you?
Thank you.

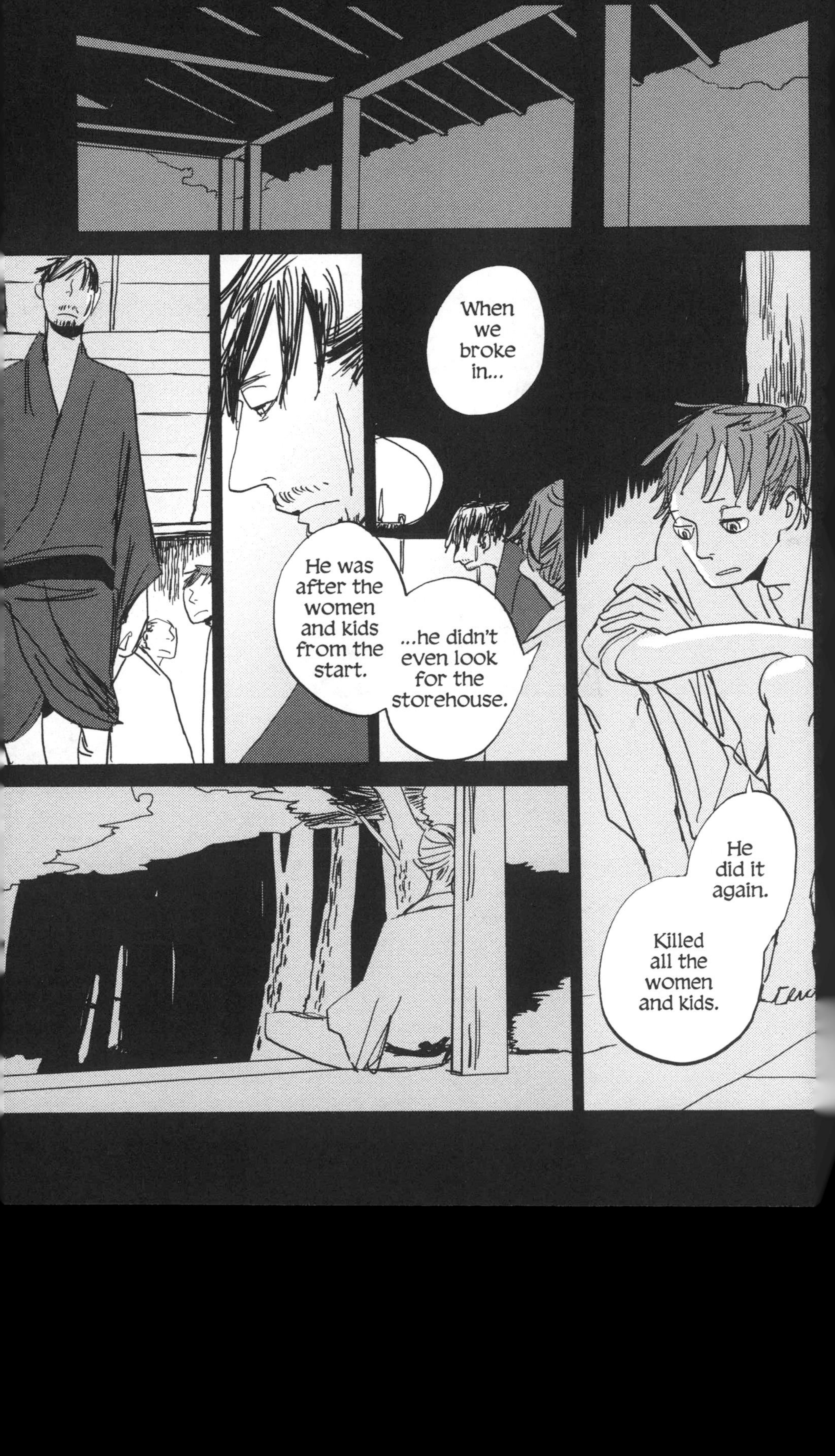
When we broke in...
...he didn't even look for the storehouse.
He was after the women and kids from the start.
He did it again.
Killed all the women and kids.

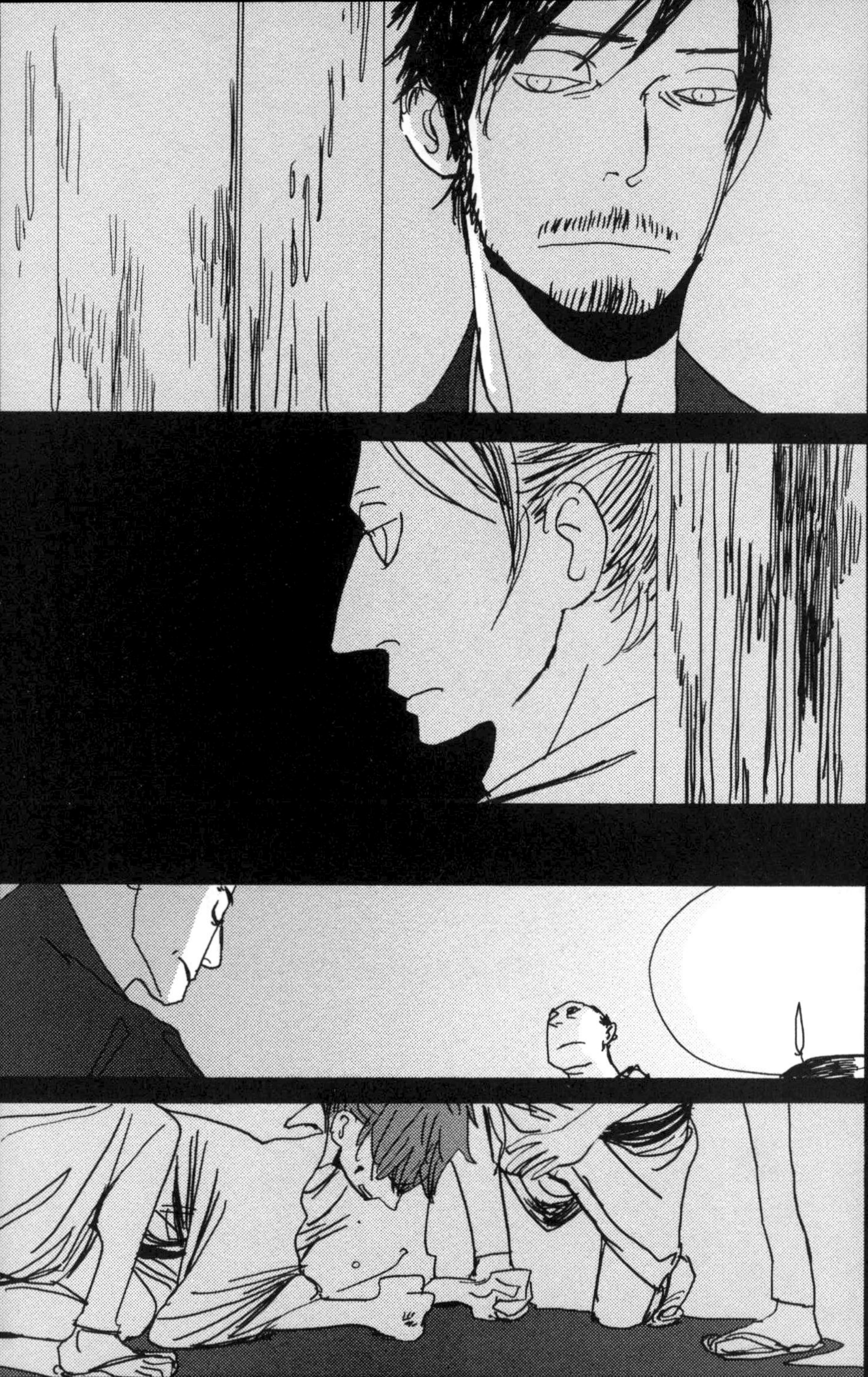

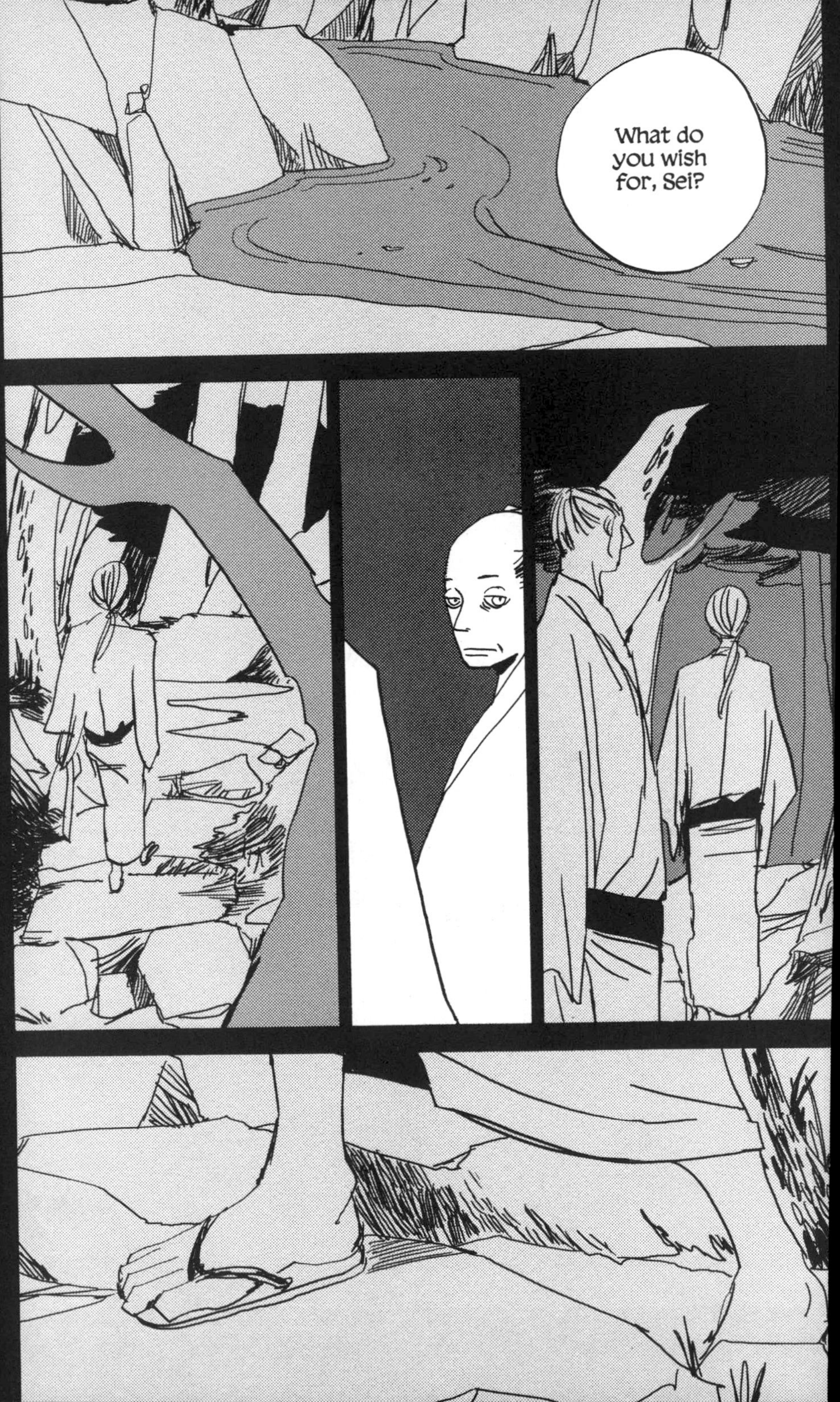
What do you wish for, Sei?

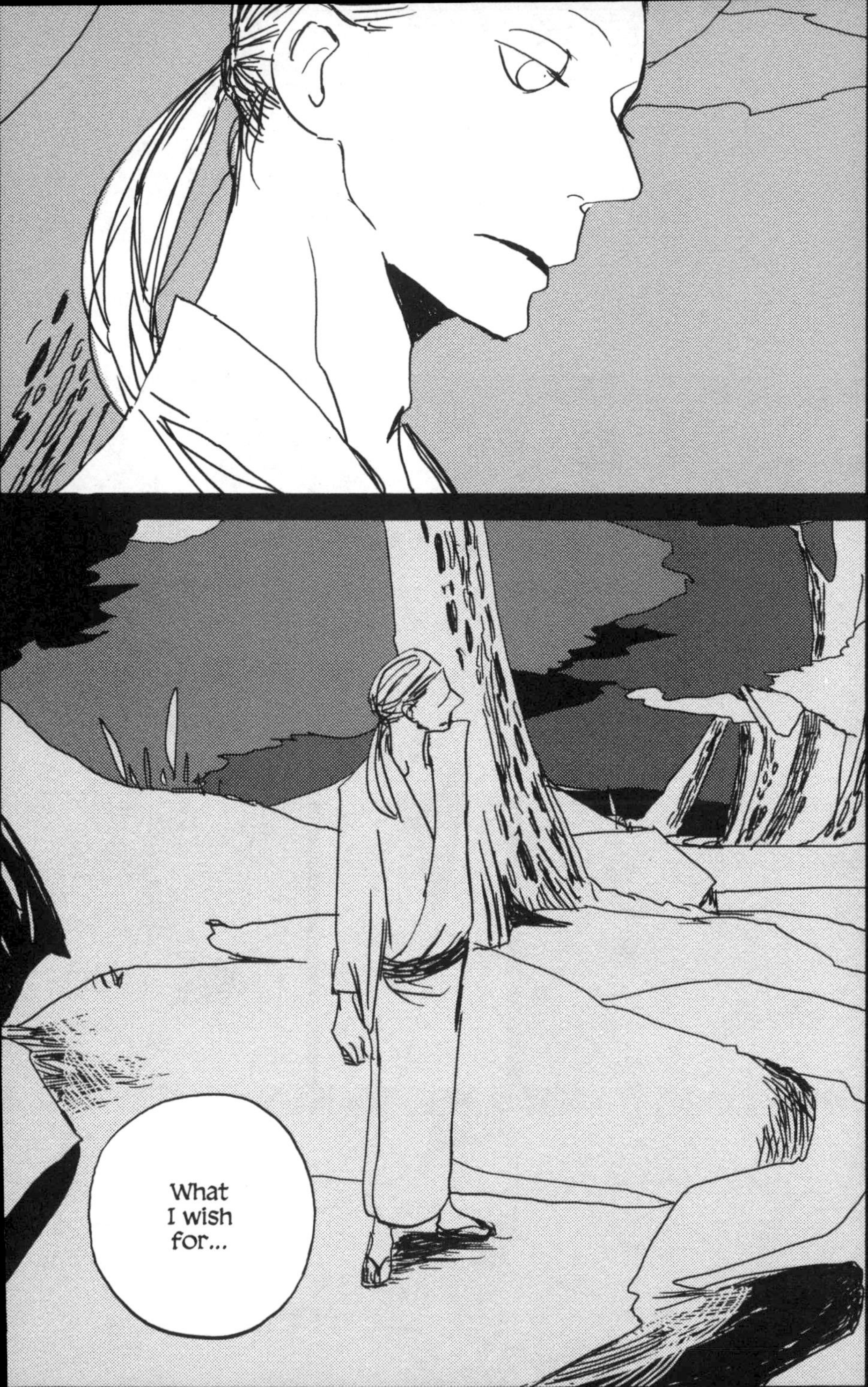
What I wish for...

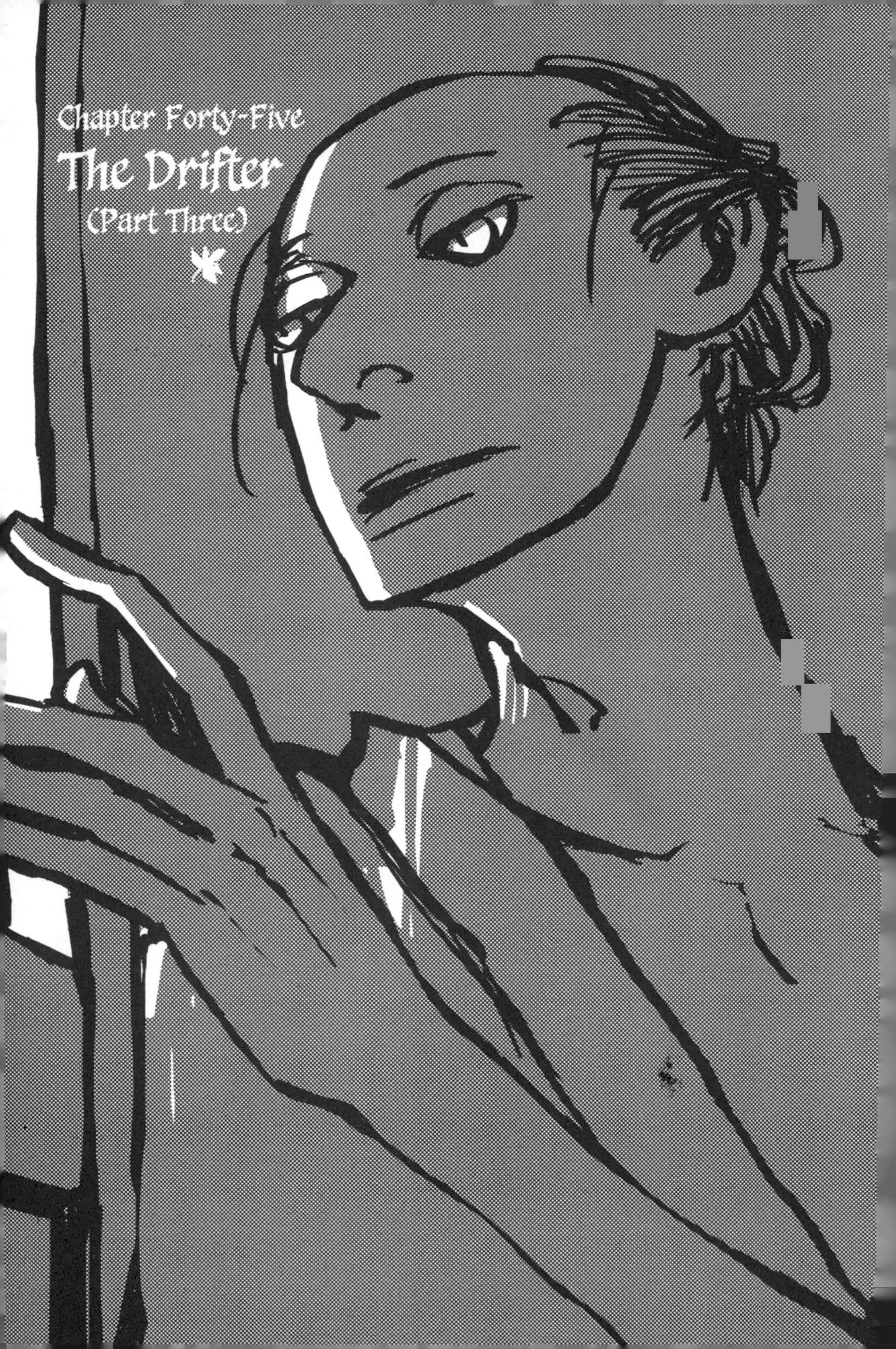
Chapter Forty-Five
The Drifter
(Part Three)

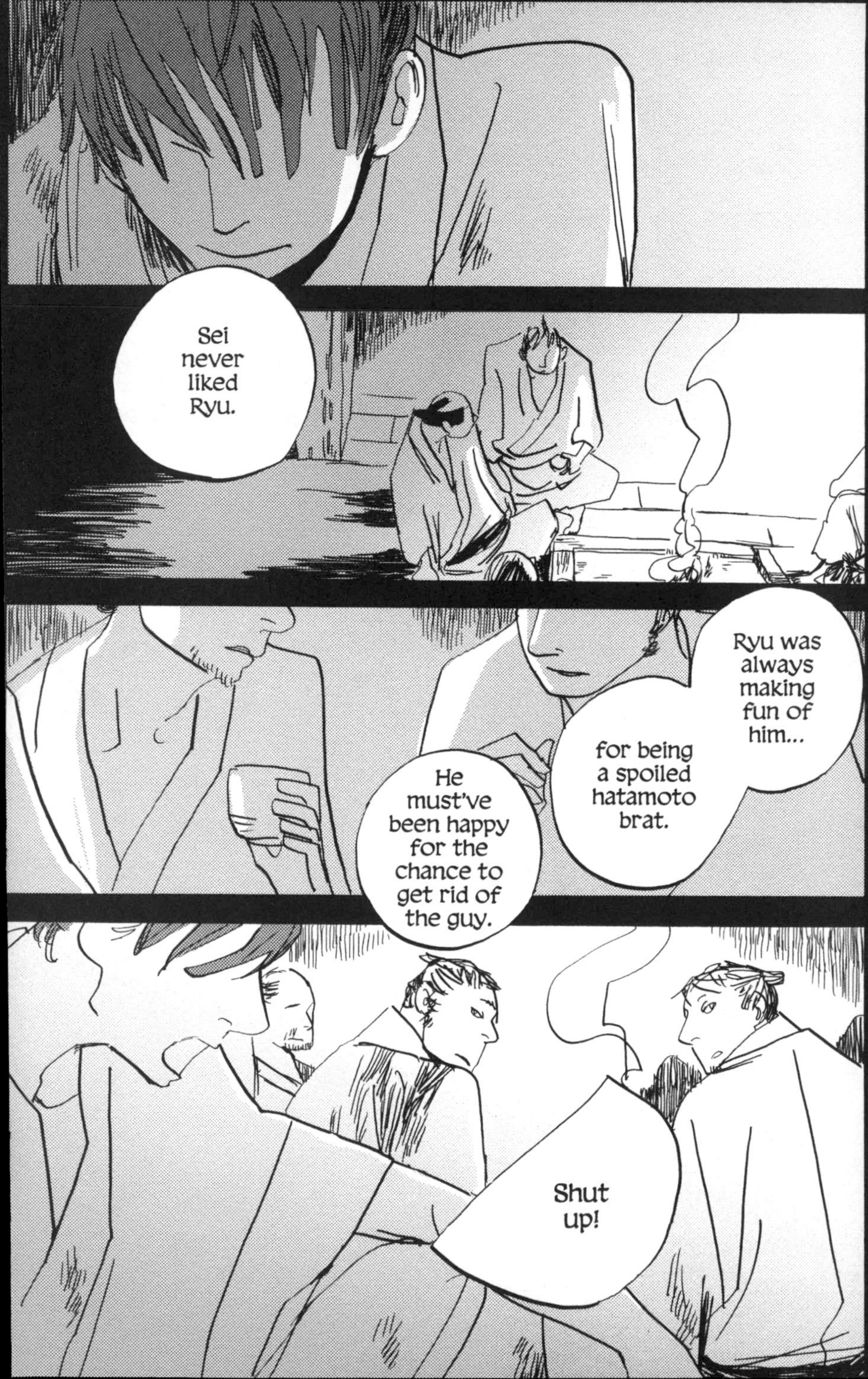
Sei never liked Ryu.
Ryu was always making fun of him...
for being a spoiled hatamoto brat.
He must've been happy for the chance to get rid of the guy.
Shut up!

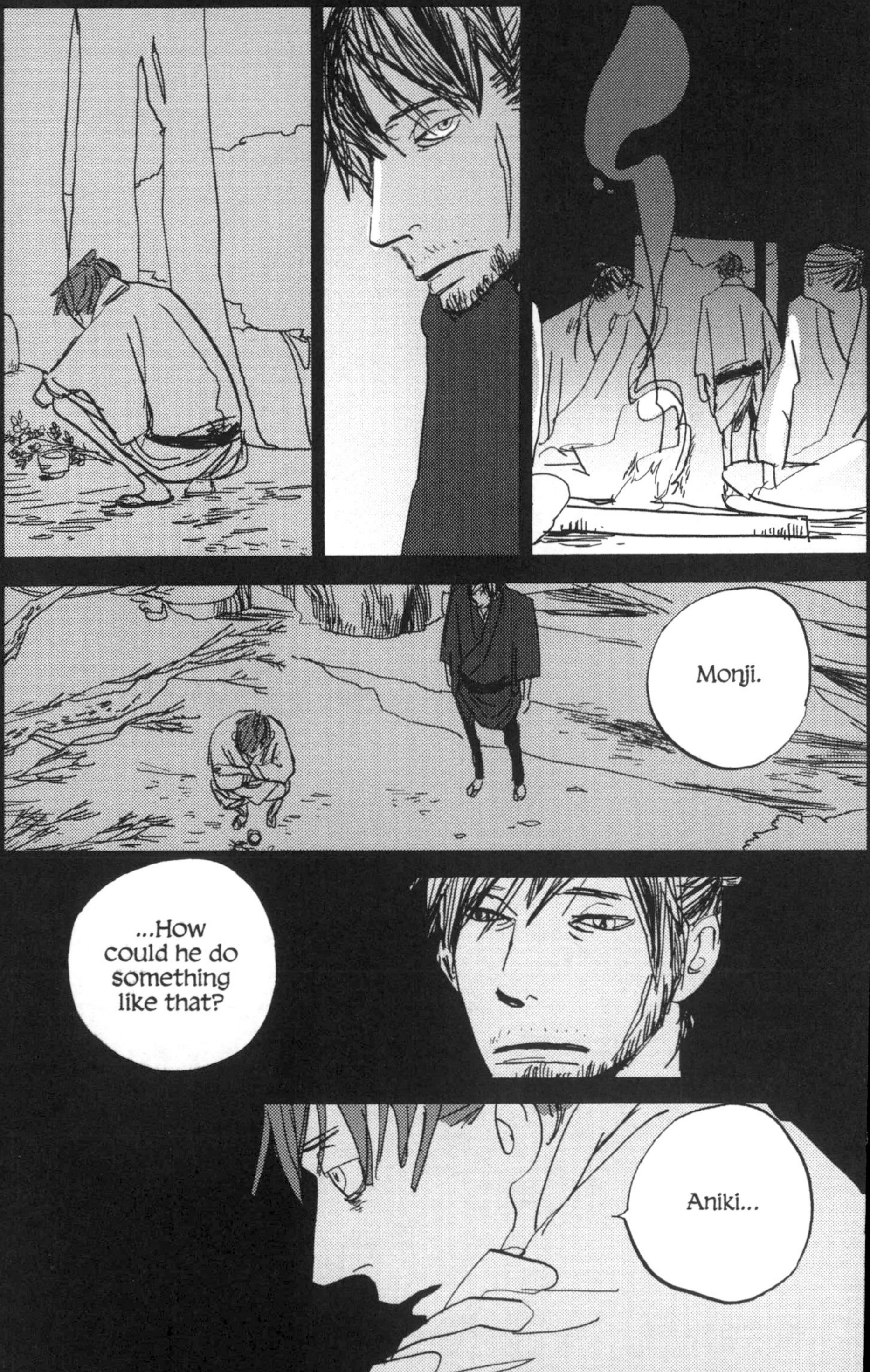
Monji.
...How could he do something like that?
Aniki...

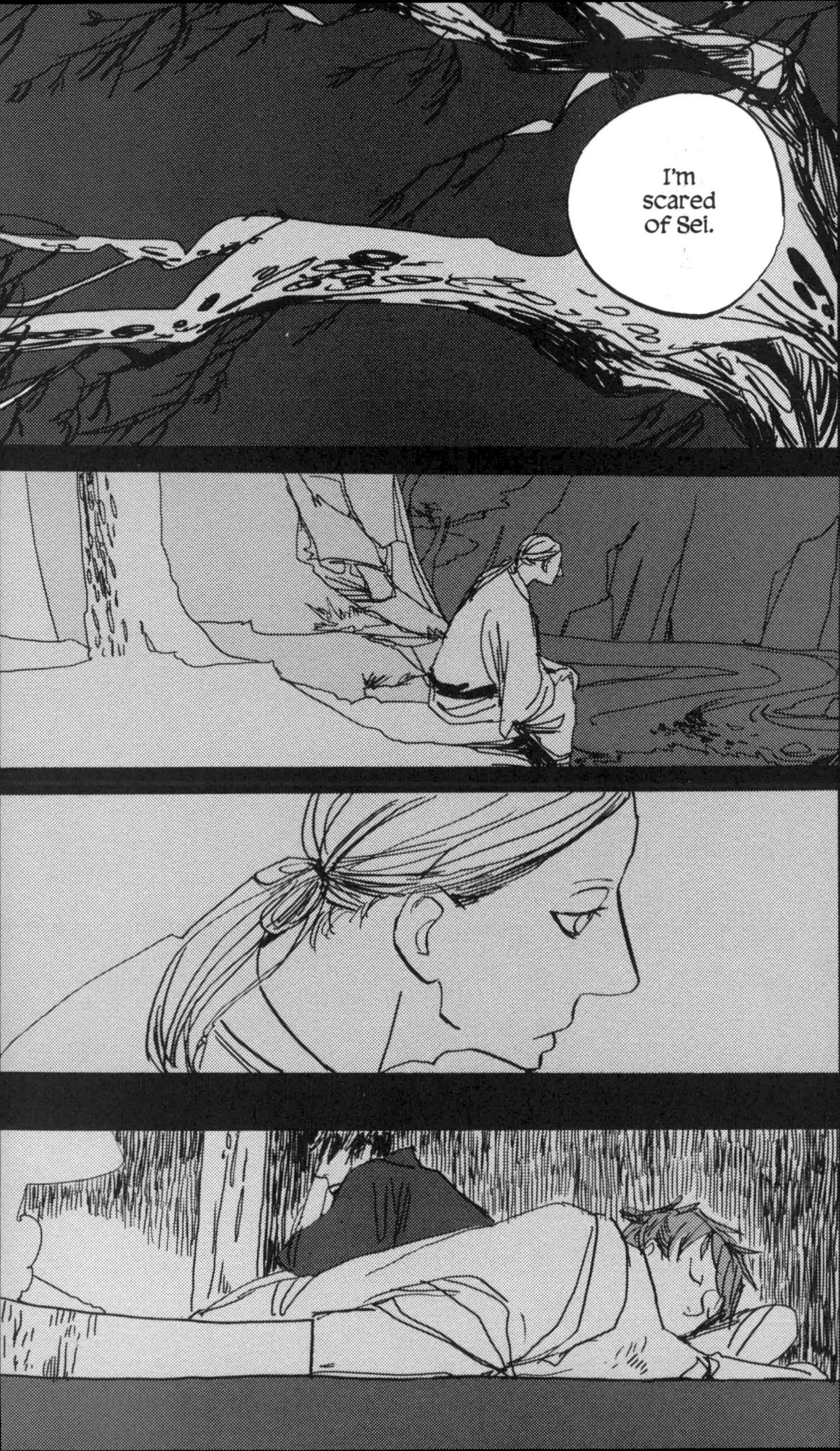
I'm scared of Sei.

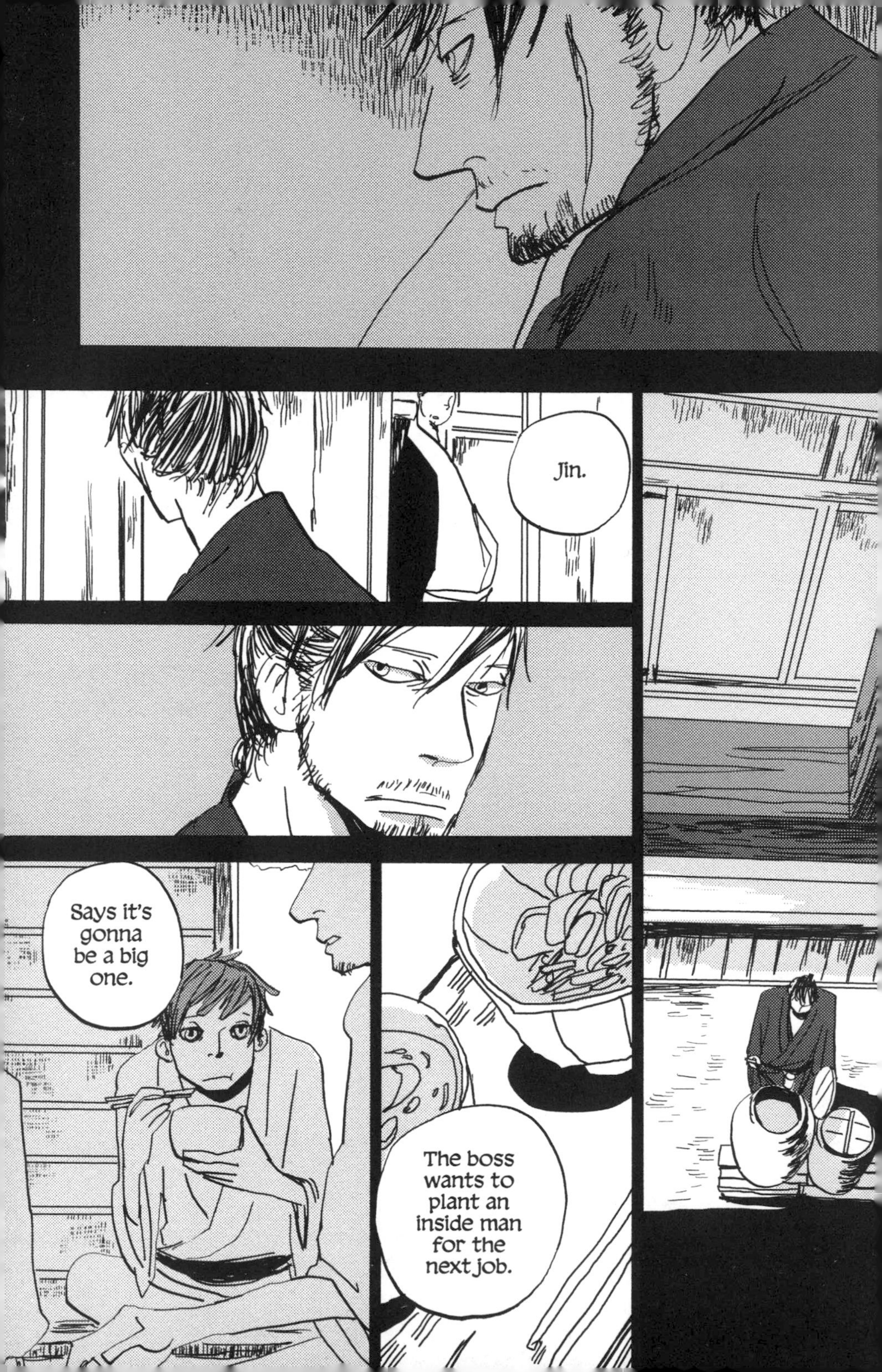
Jin.
The boss wants to plant an inside man for the next job.
Says it's gonna be a big one.

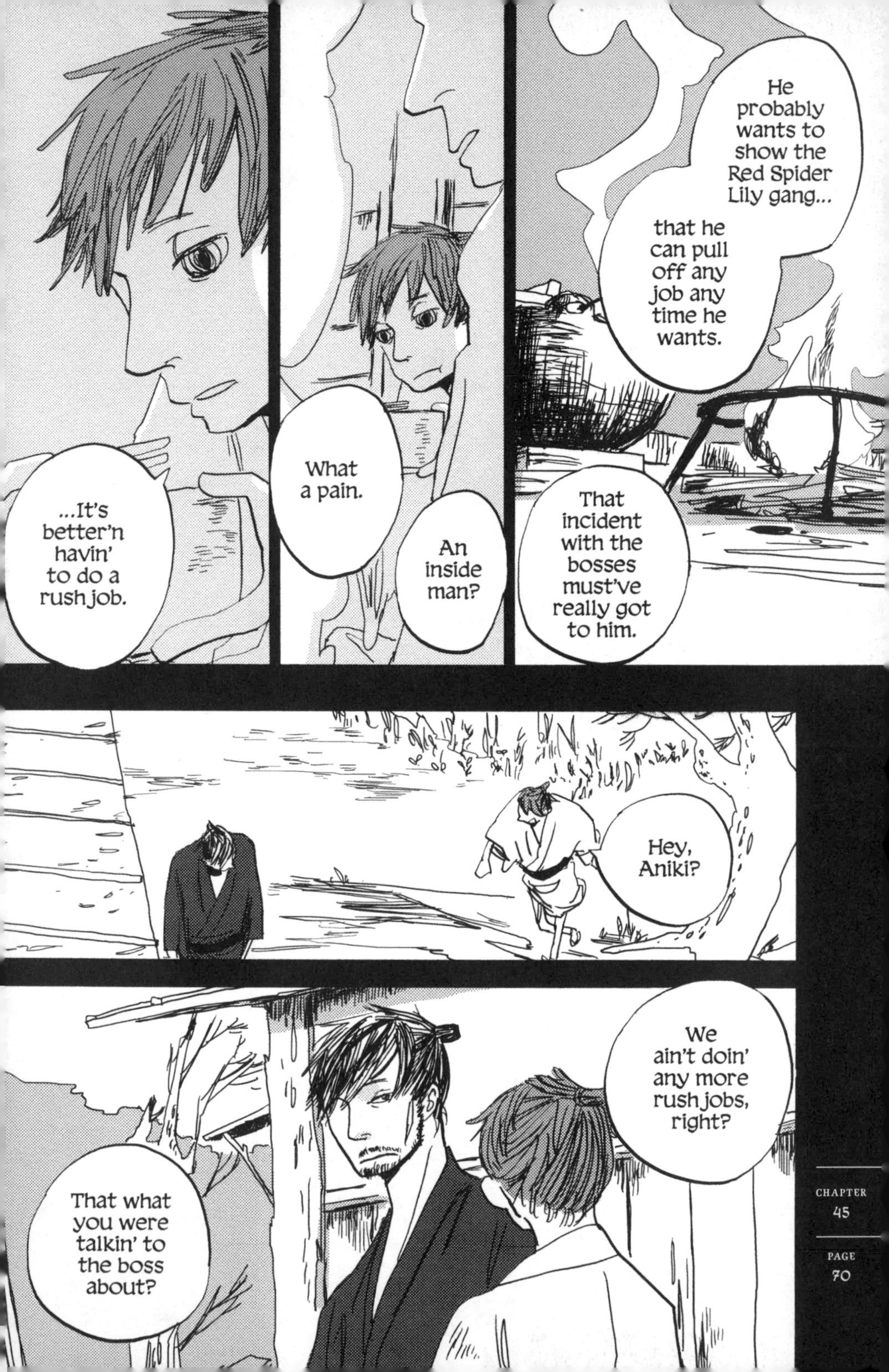
He probably wants to show the Red Spider Lily gang...
that he can pull off any job any time he wants.
That incident with the bosses must've really got to him.
What a pain.
An inside man?
...It's better'n havin' to do a rush job.
Hey, Aniki?
We ain't doin' any more rush jobs, right?
That what you were talkin' to the boss about?

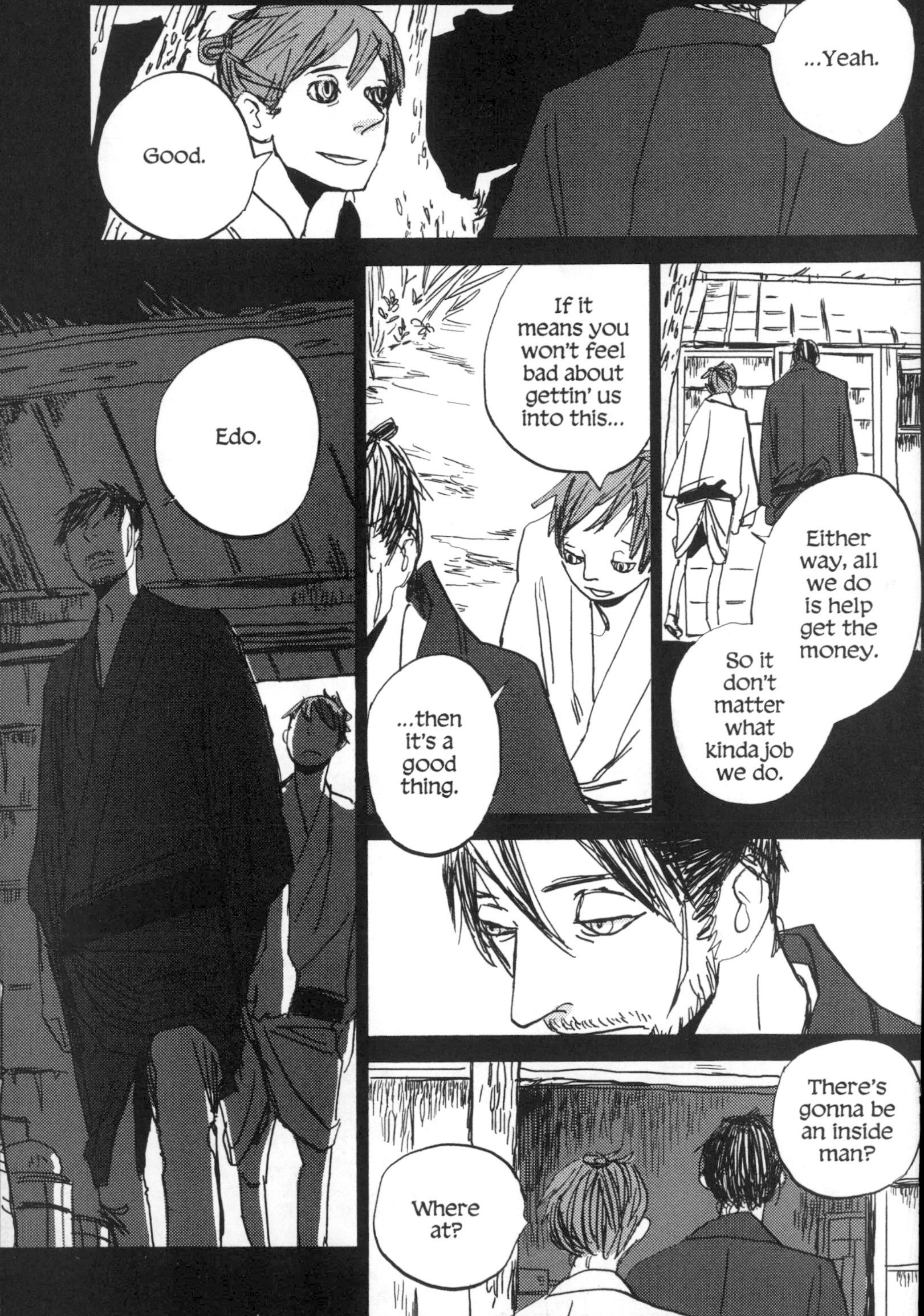
...Yeah.
Good.
Either way, all we do is help get the money.
So it don't matter what kinda job we do.
If it means you won't feel bad about gettin' us into this...
...then it's a good thing.
There's gonna be an inside man?
Where at?
Edo.

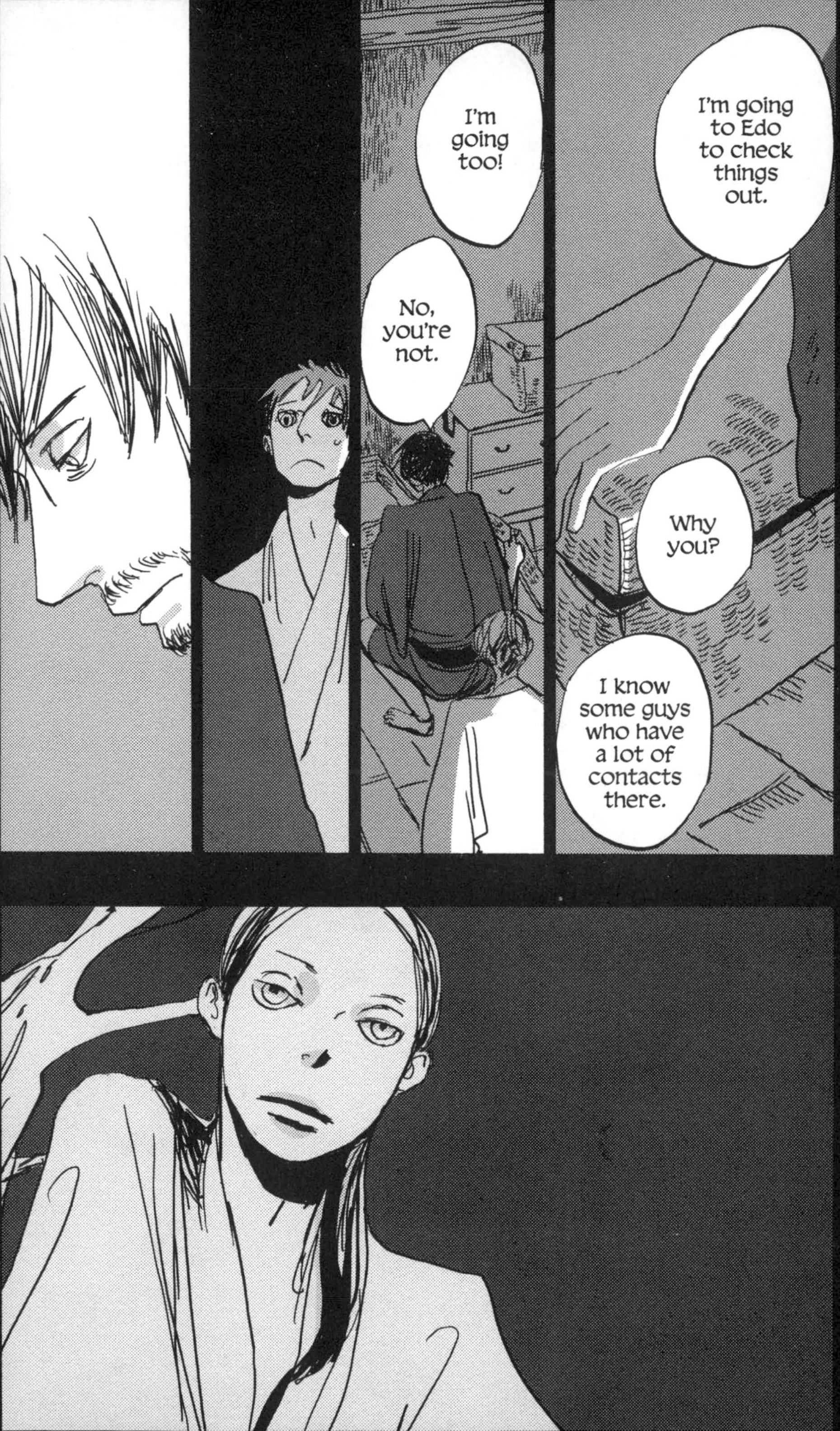
I'm going to Edo to check things out.
Why you?
I know some guys who have a lot of contacts there.
I'm going too!
No, you're not.

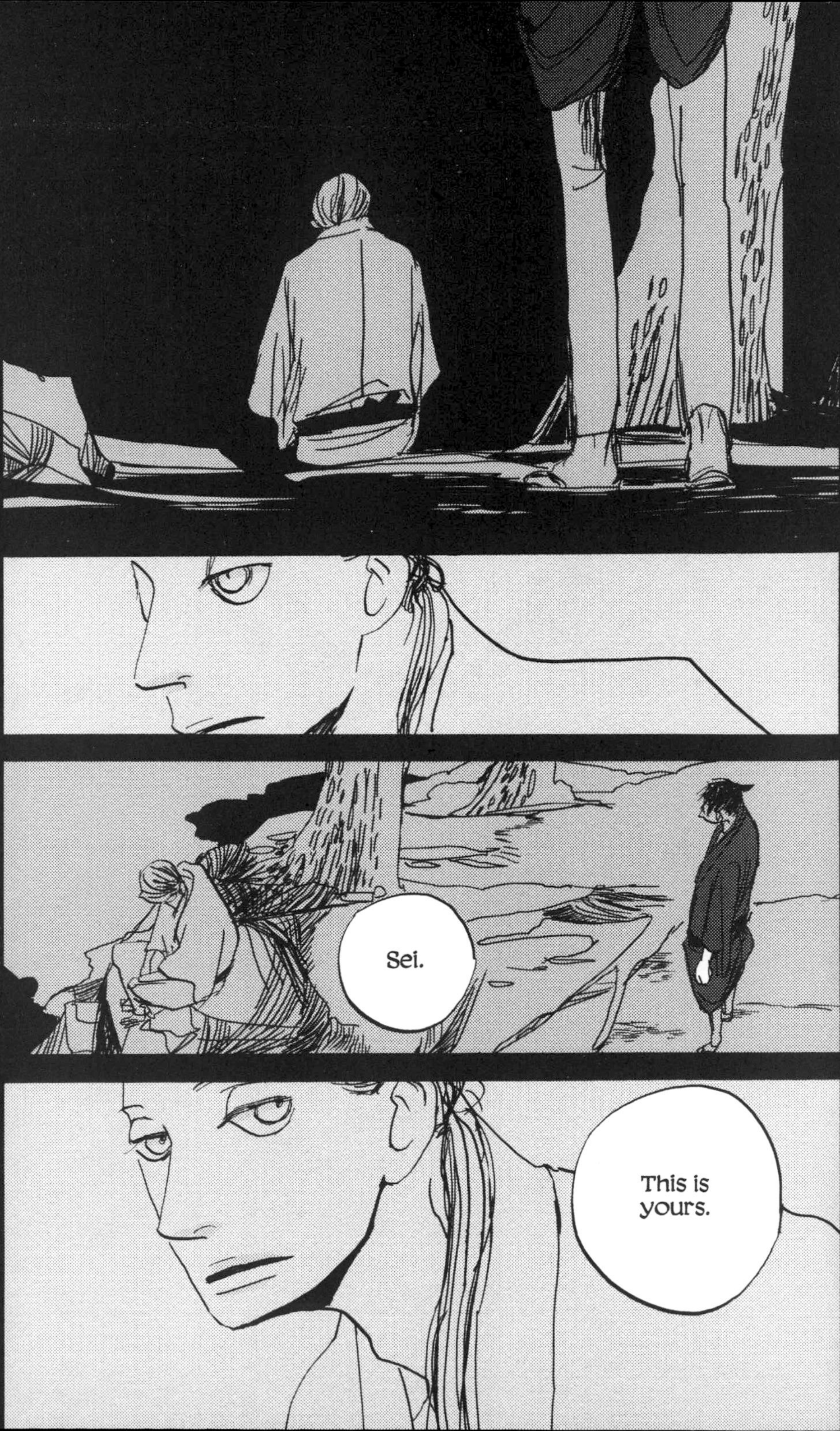
Sei.
This is yours.

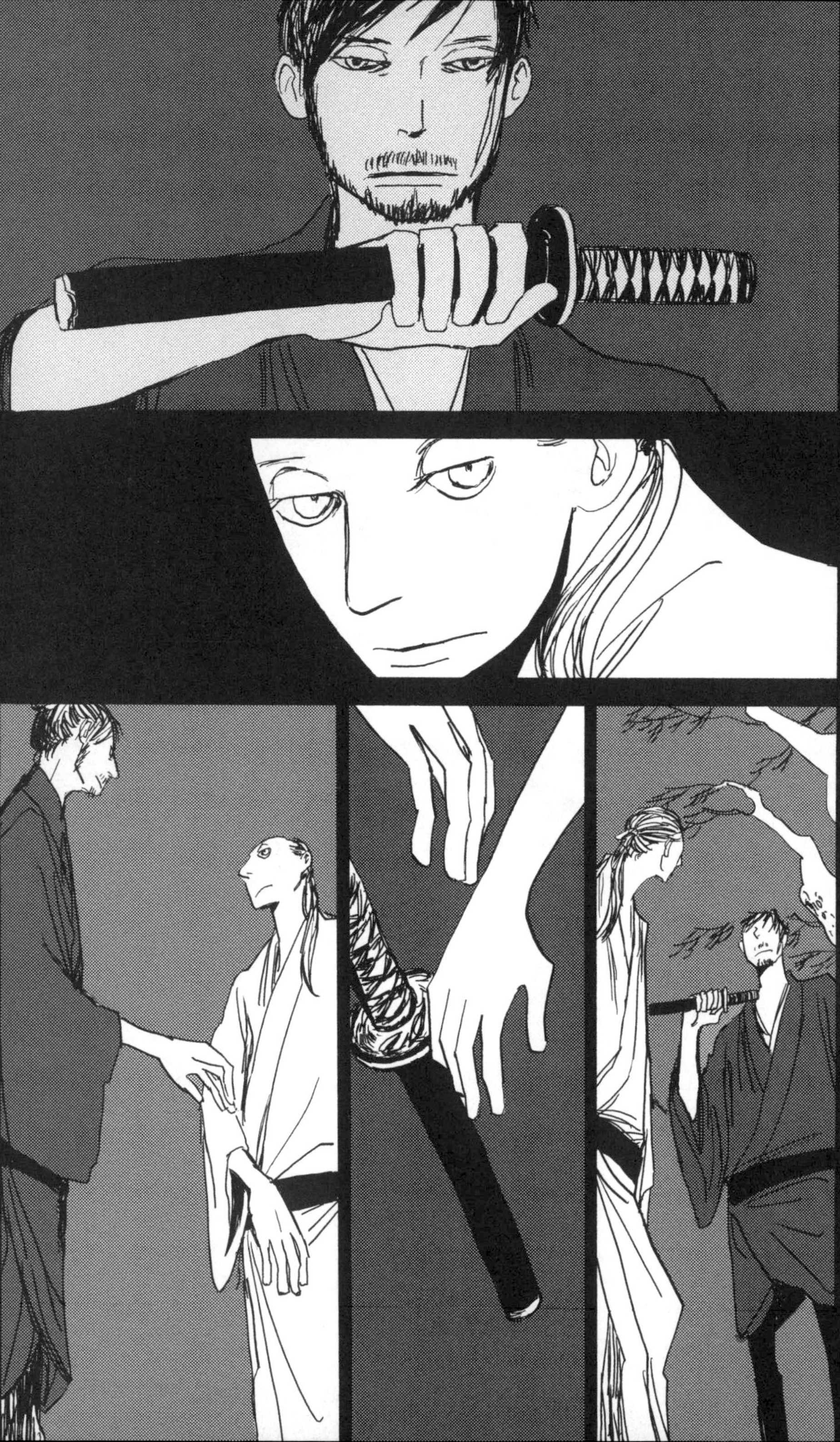

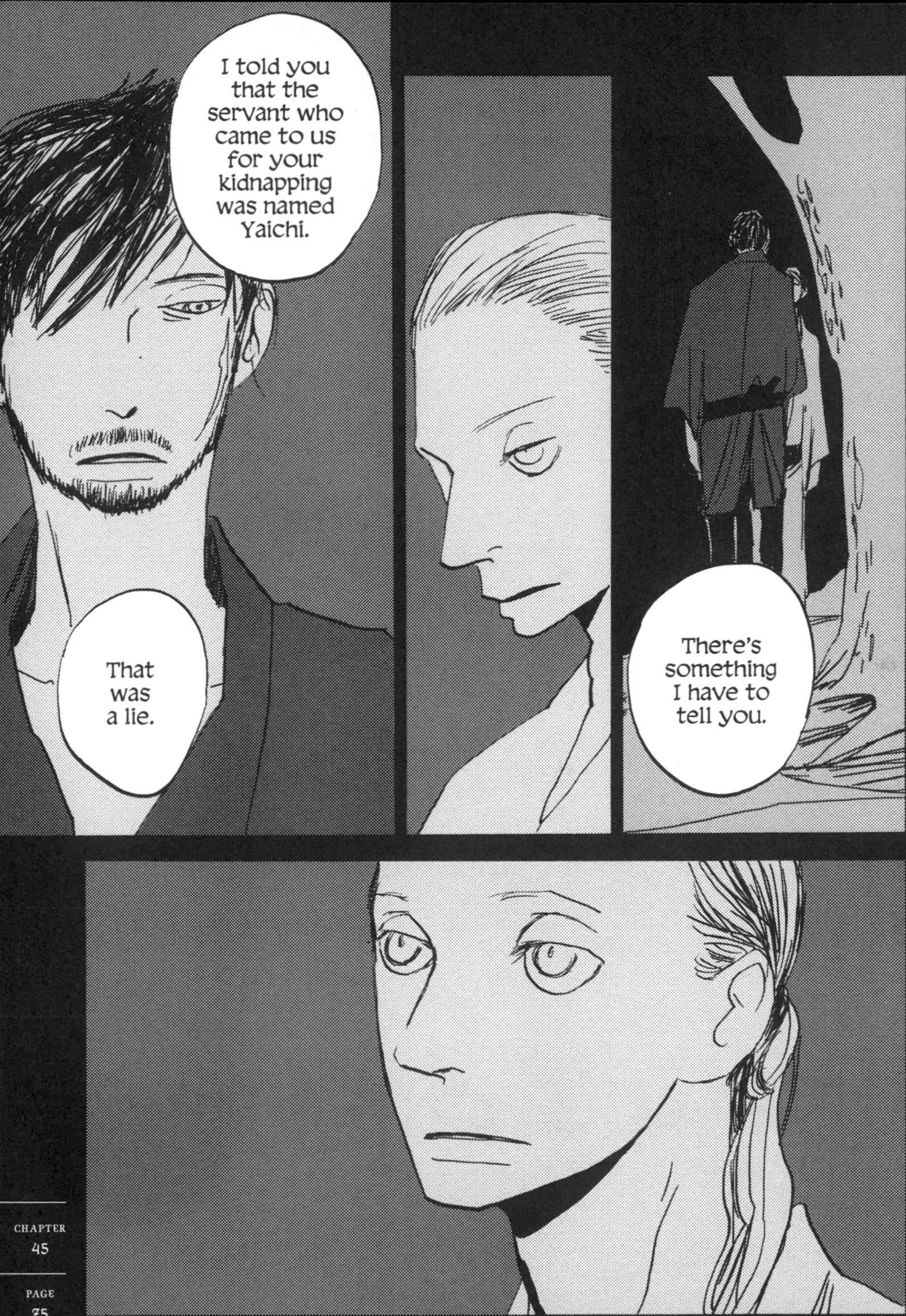
There's something I have to tell you.
I told you that the servant who came to us for your kidnapping was named Yaichi.
That was a lie.

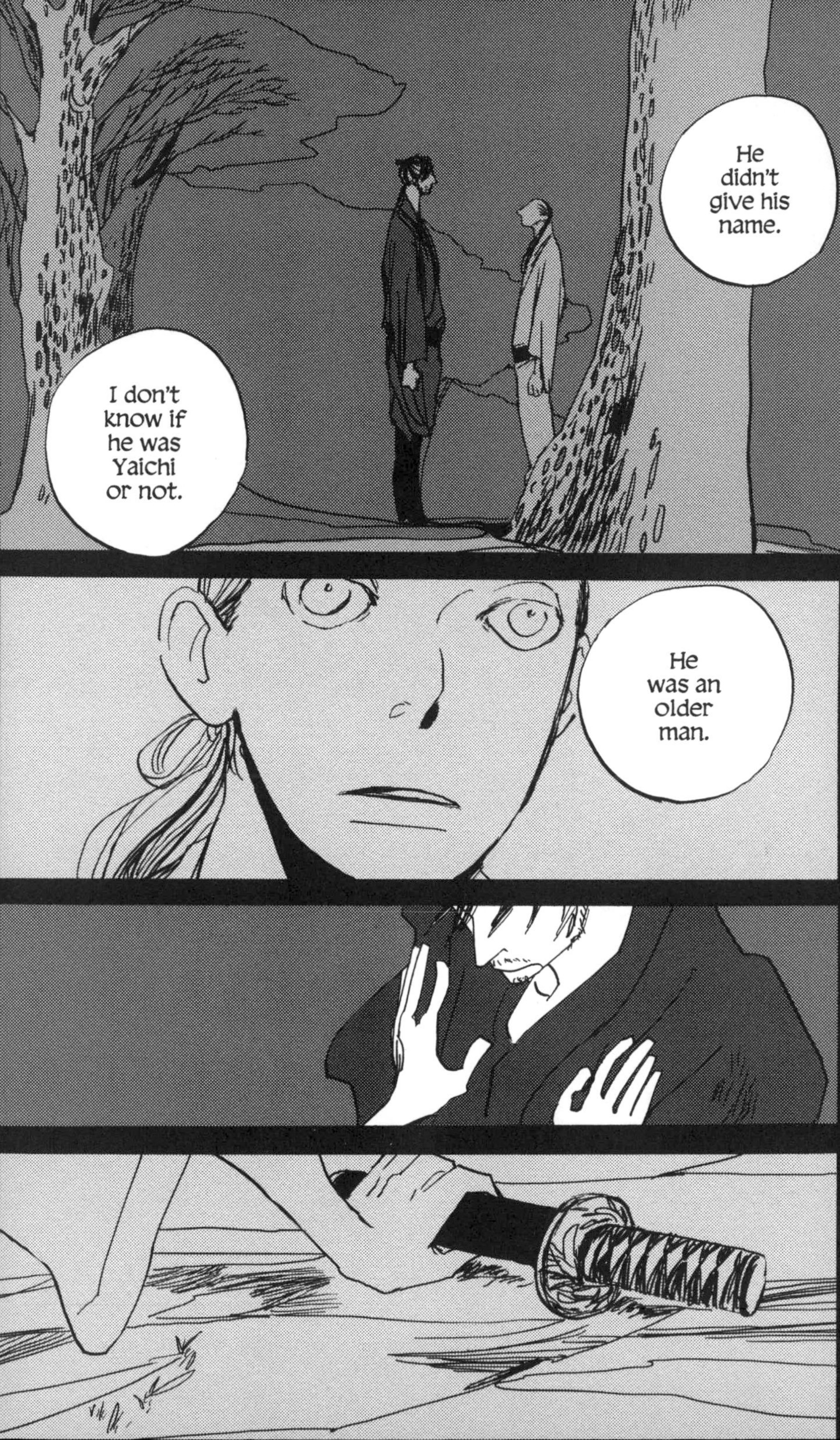
He didn't give his name.
I don't know if he was Yaichi or not.
He was an older man.

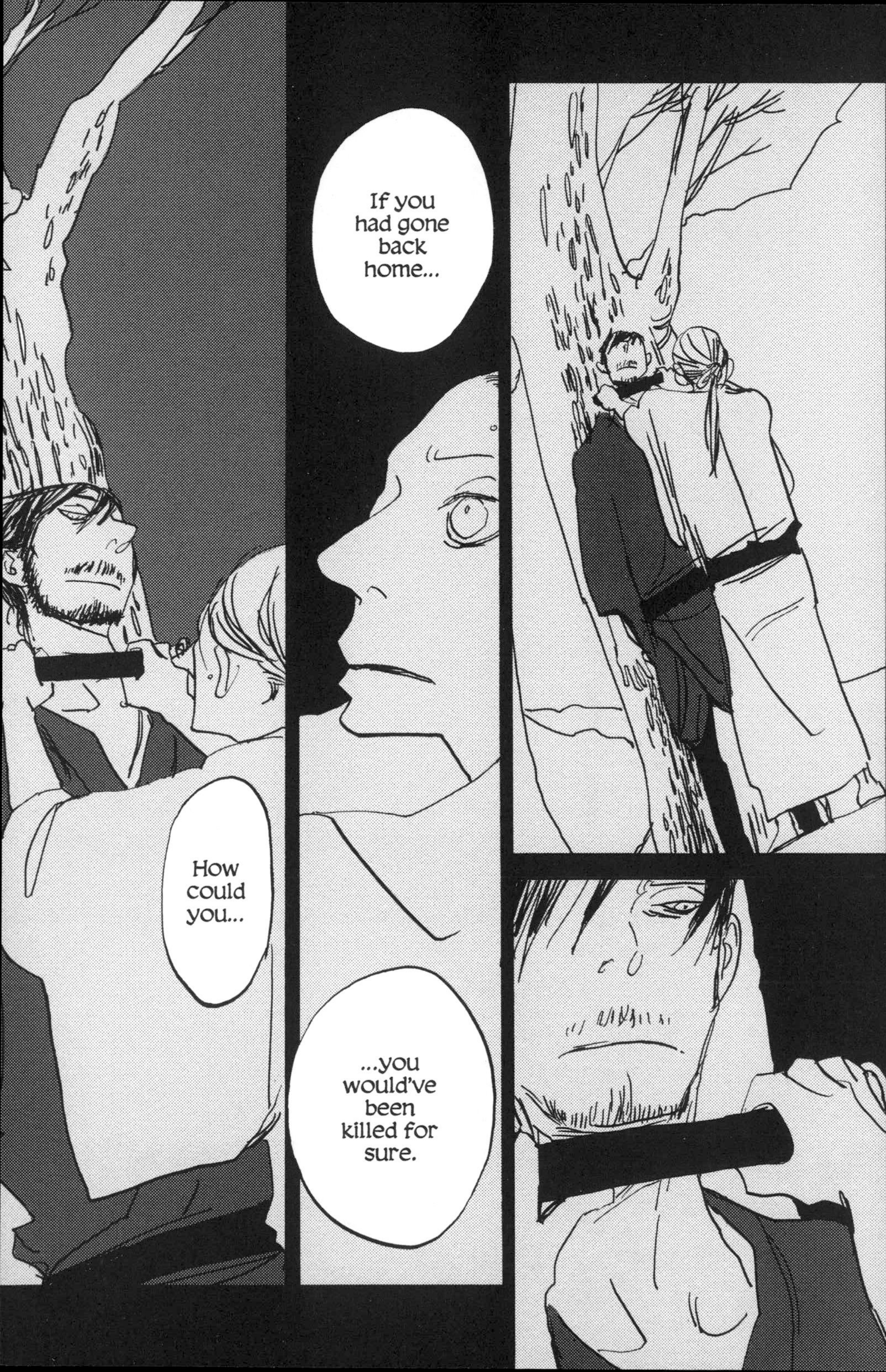
If you had gone back home...
...you would've been killed for sure.
How could you...

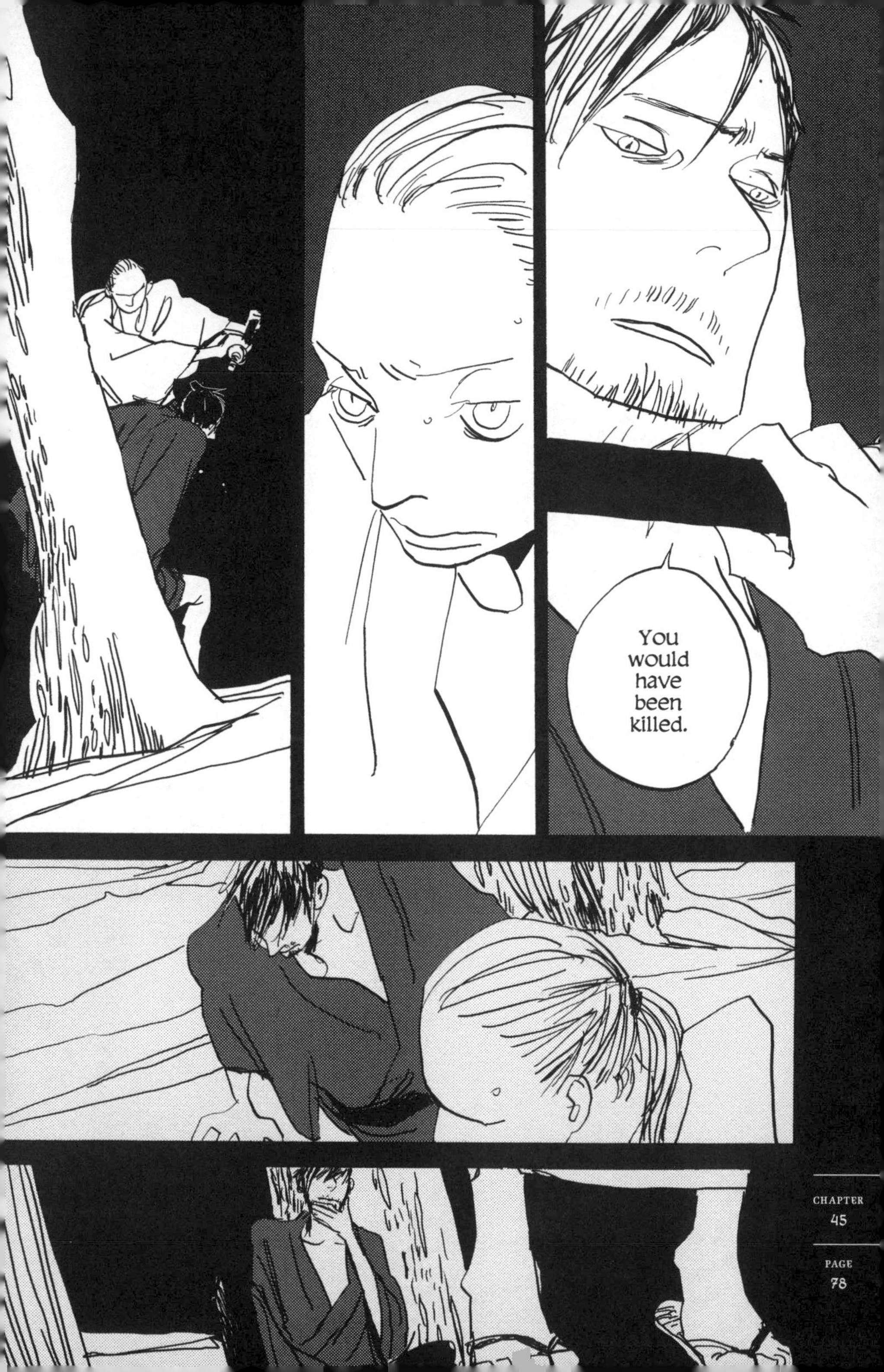
You would have been killed.

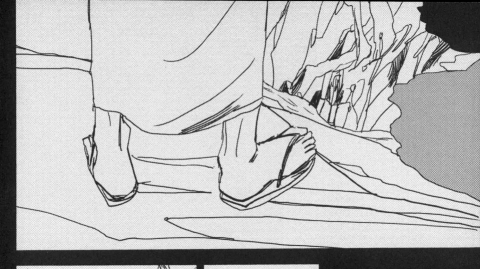

You'll stand out looking like that.

You should wear your hair...

in a *sakayaki*.

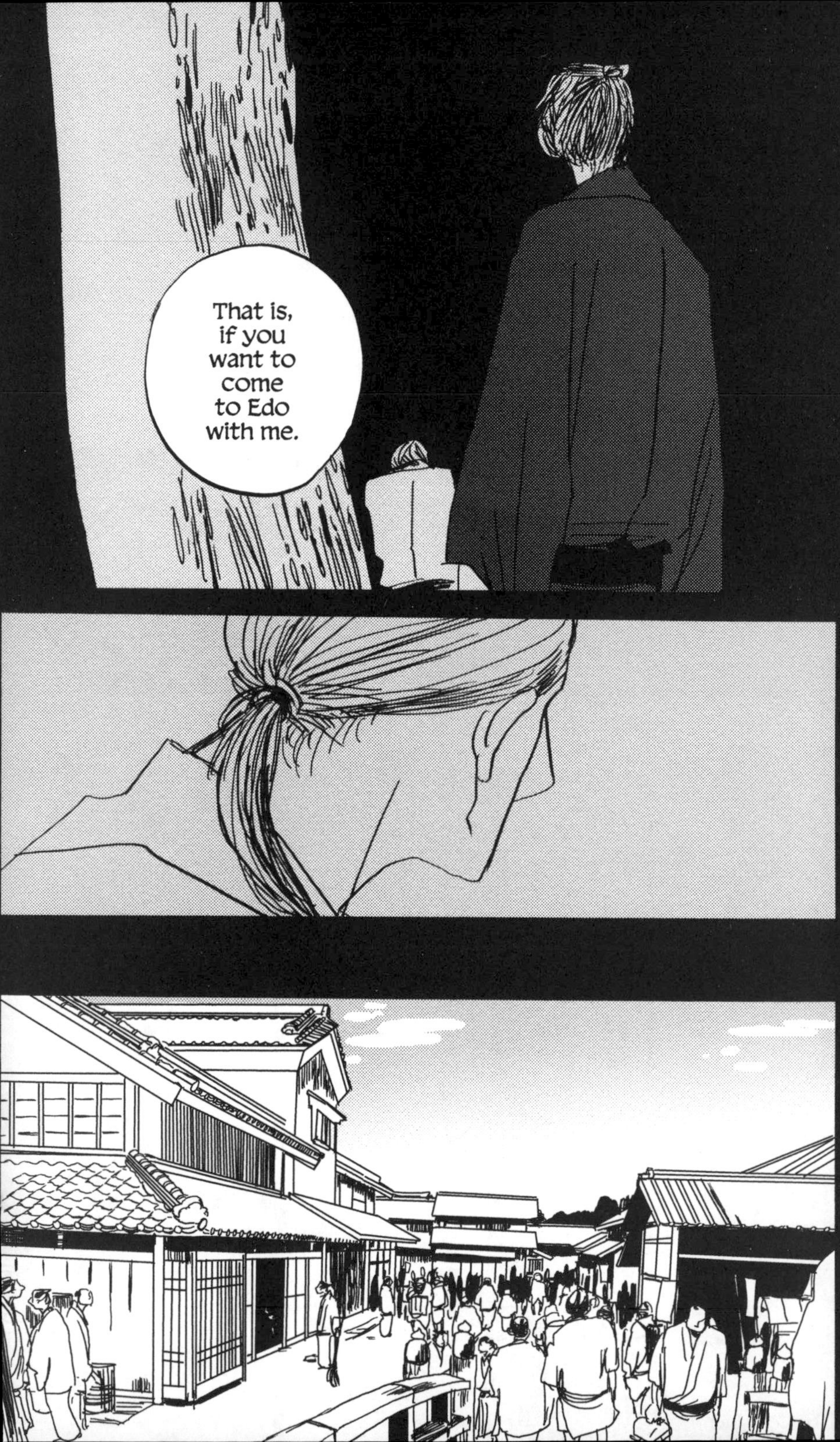
That is, if you want to come to Edo with me.

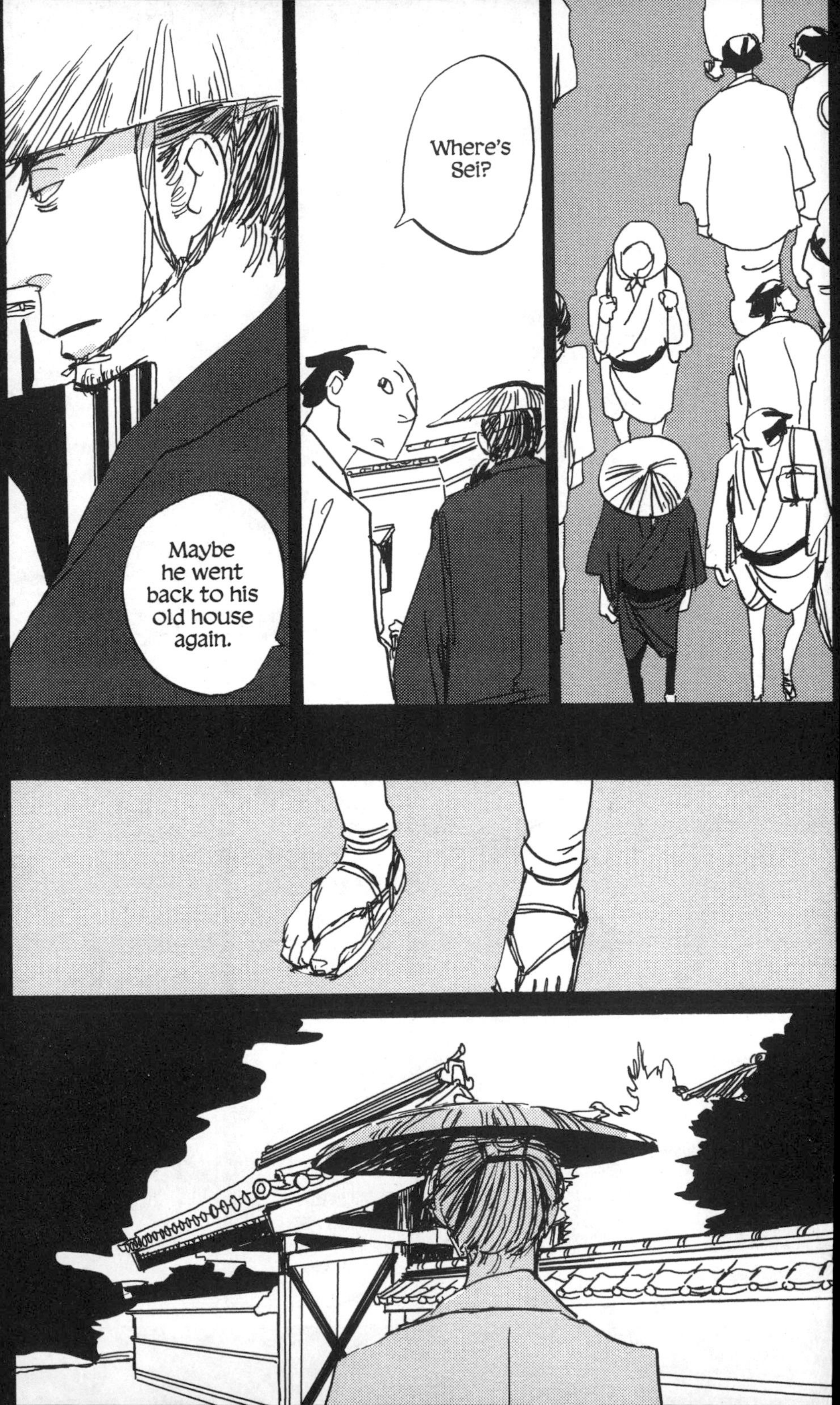
Where's Sei?
Maybe he went back to his old house again.

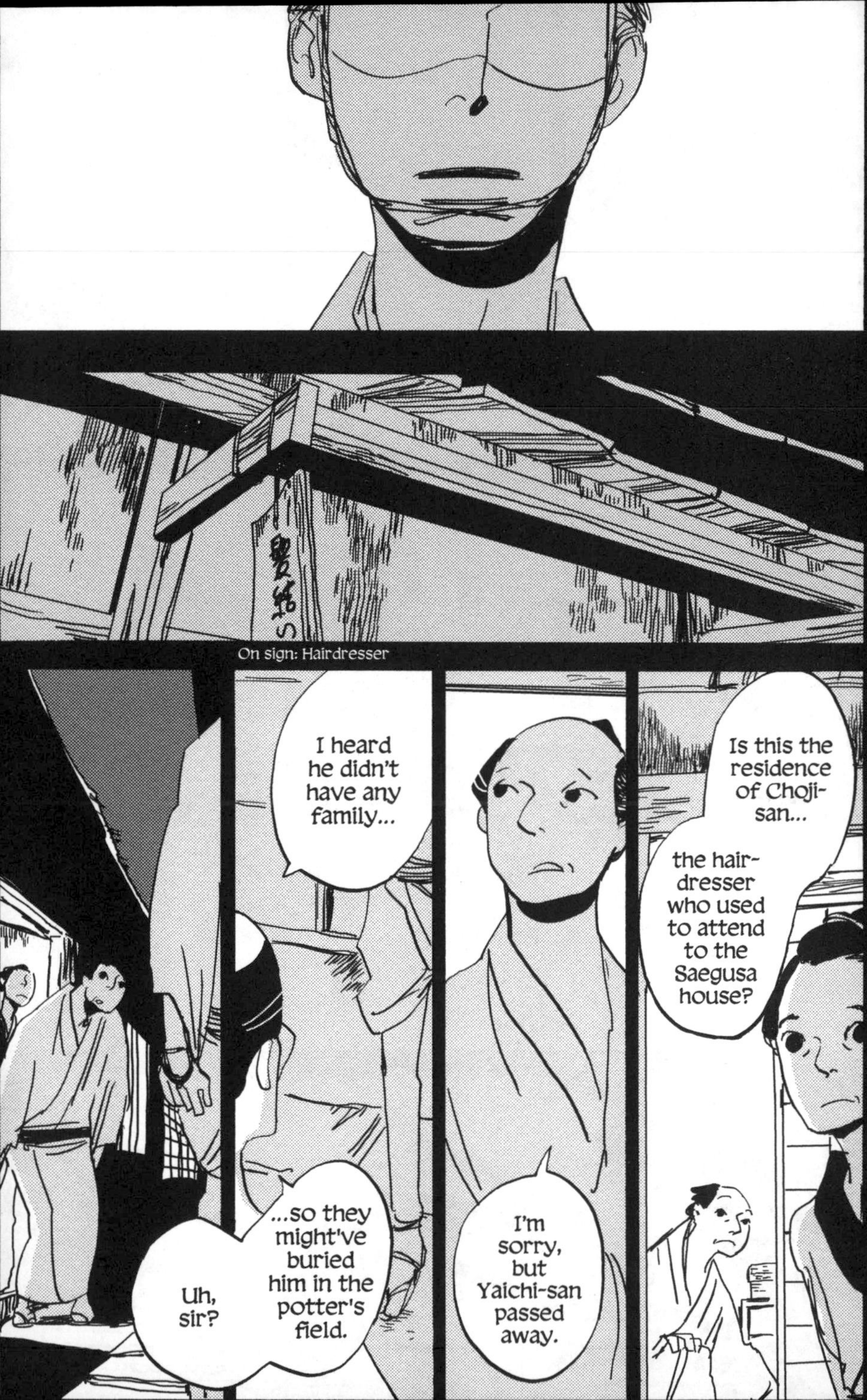
Is this the residence of Choji-san...
the hair-dresser who used to attend to the Saegusa house?
I'm sorry, but Yaichi-san passed away.
I heard he didn't have any family...
...so they might've buried him in the potter's field.
Uh, sir?
On sign: Hairdresser

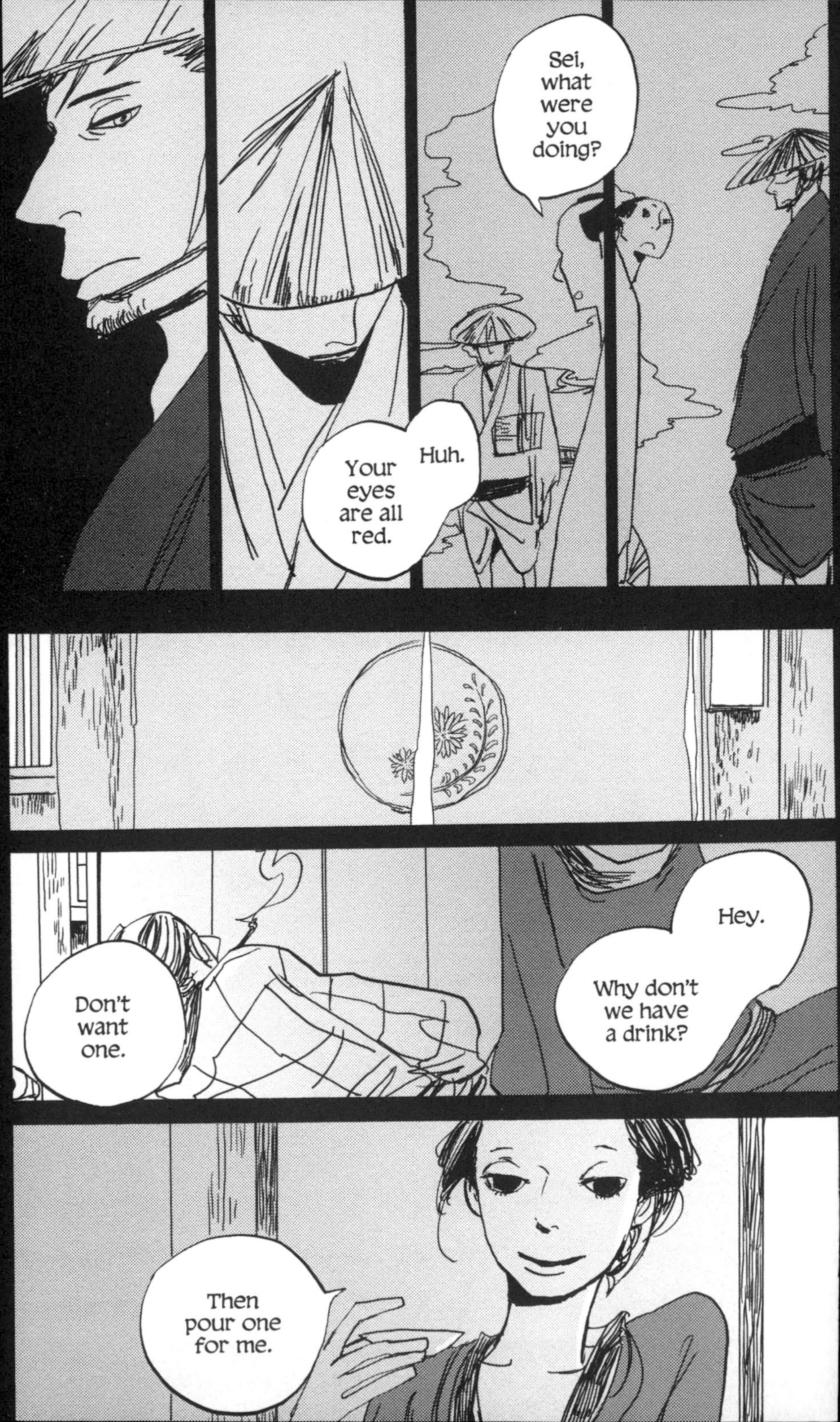
Sei, what were you doing?
Huh.
Your eyes are all red.
Hey.
Why don't we have a drink?
Don't want one.
Then pour one for me.

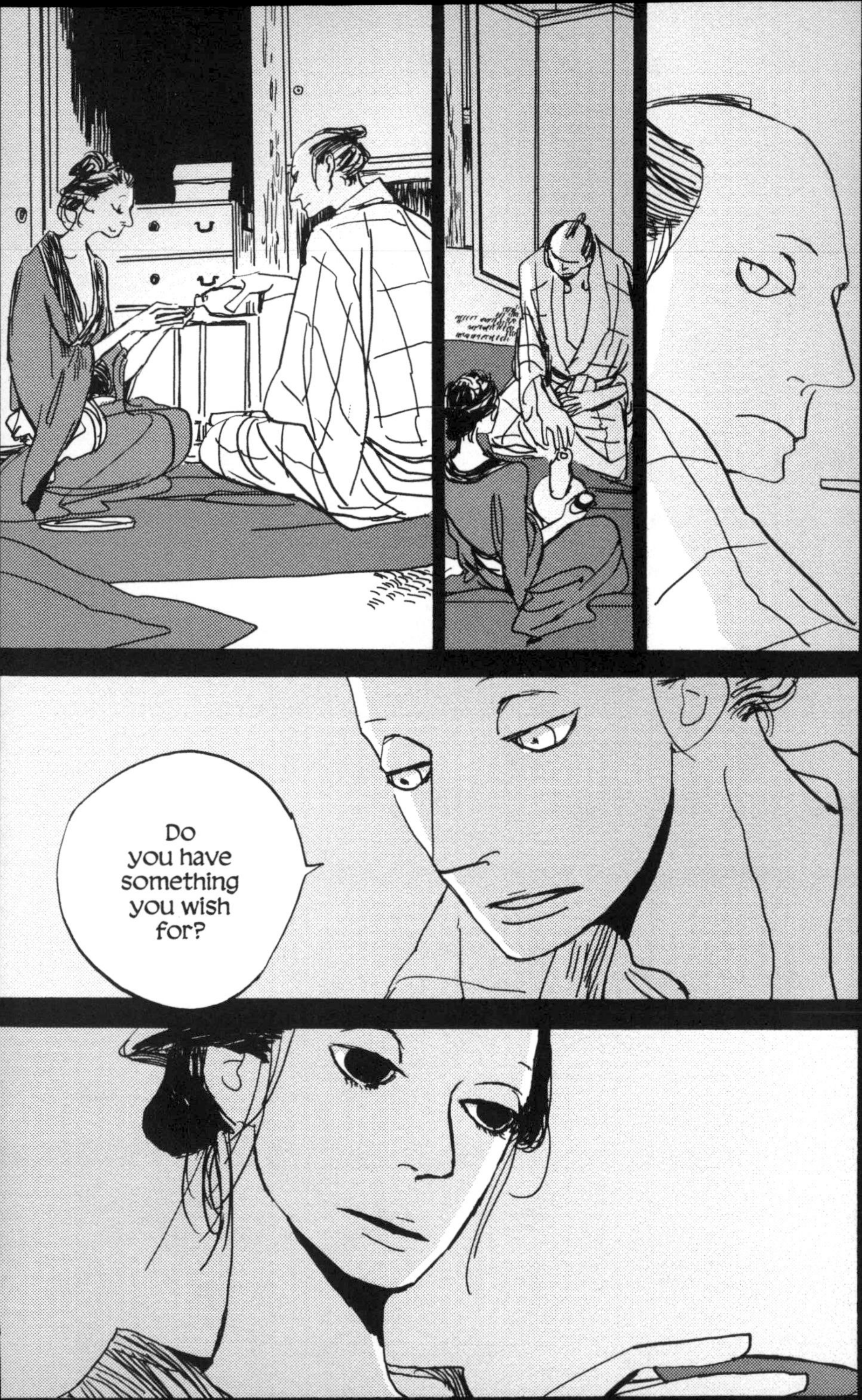
Do you have something you wish for?

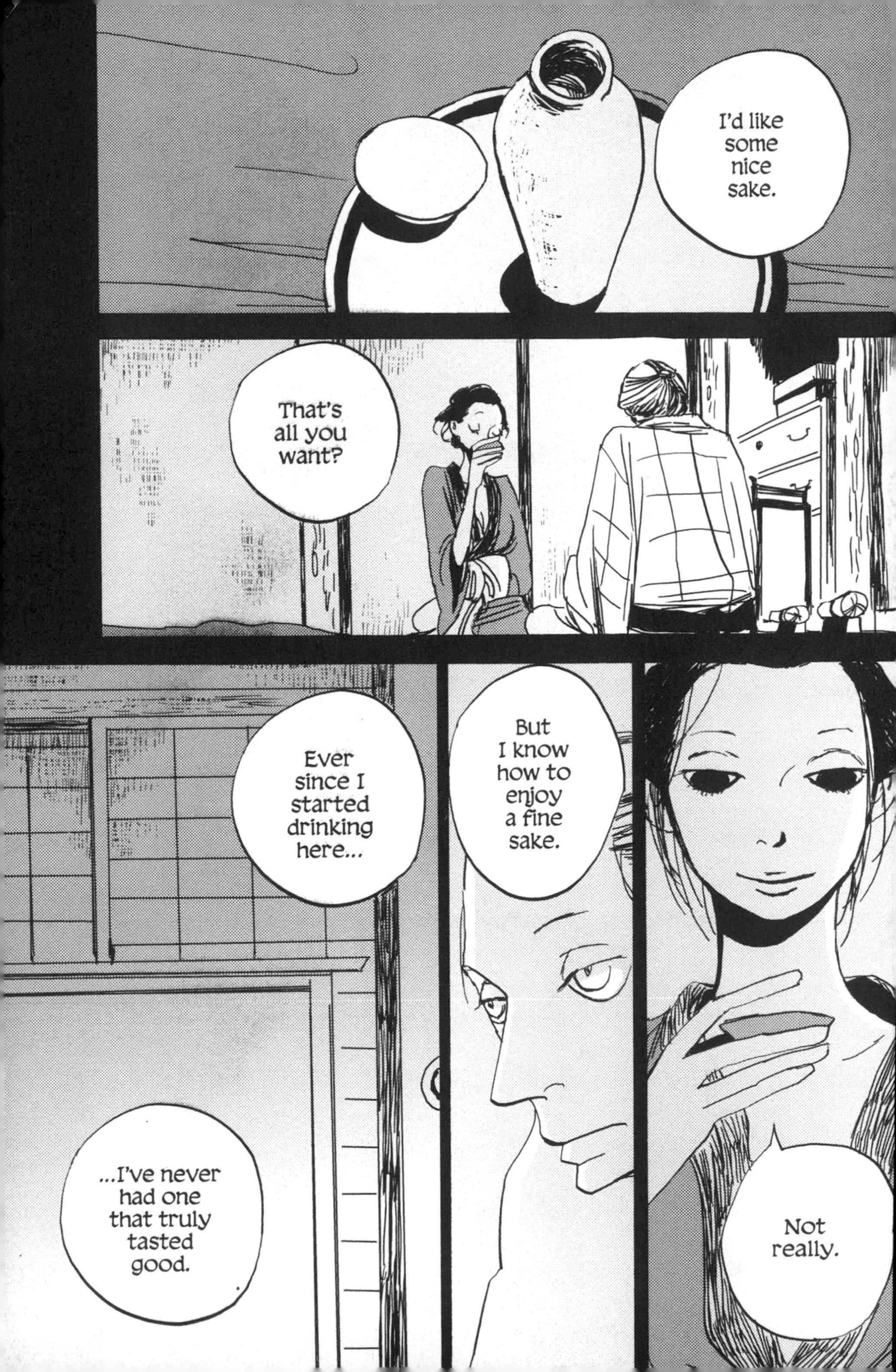
I'd like some nice sake.
That's all you want?
Not really.
But I know how to enjoy a fine sake.
Ever since I started drinking here...
...I've never had one that truly tasted good.

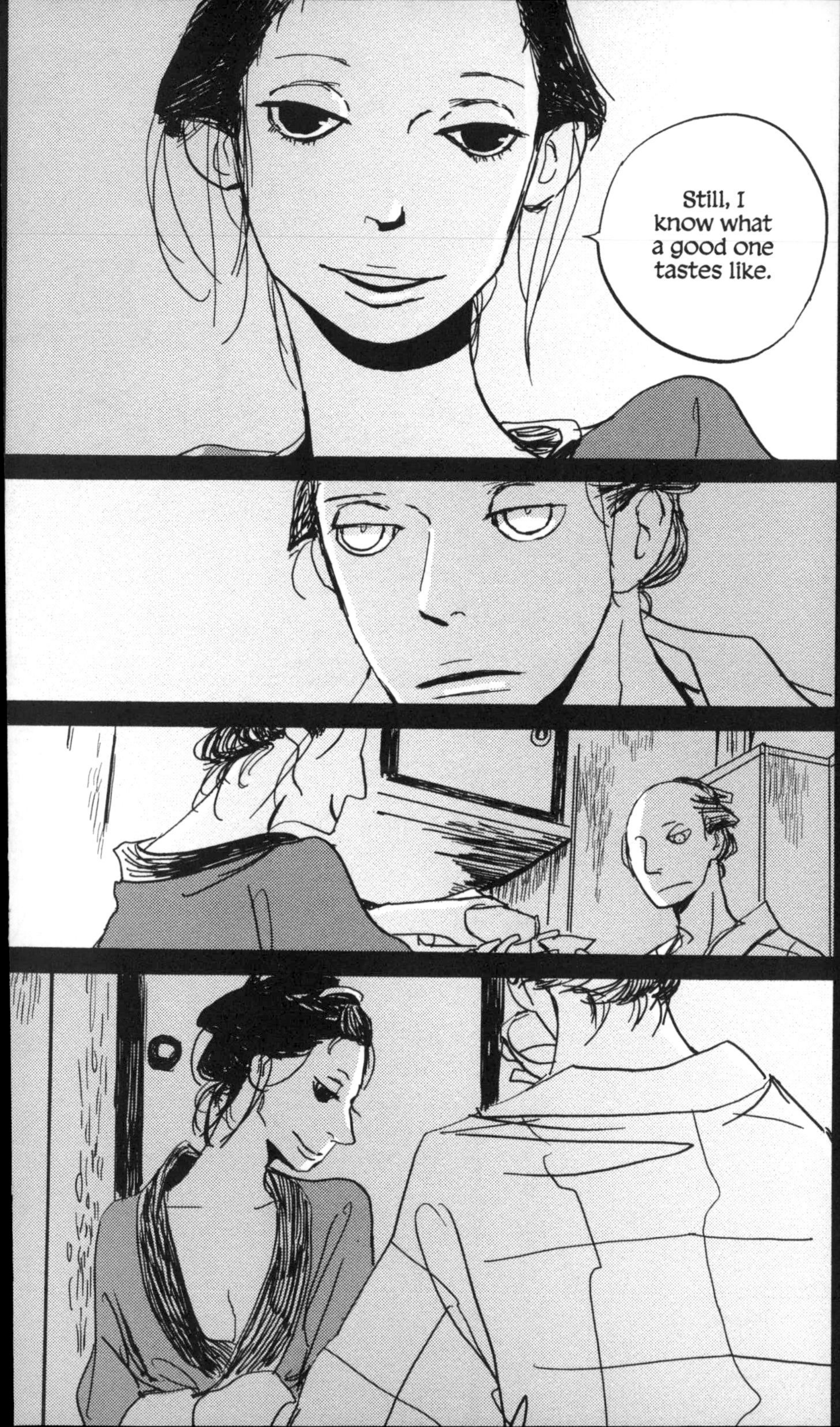
Still, I know what a good one tastes like.

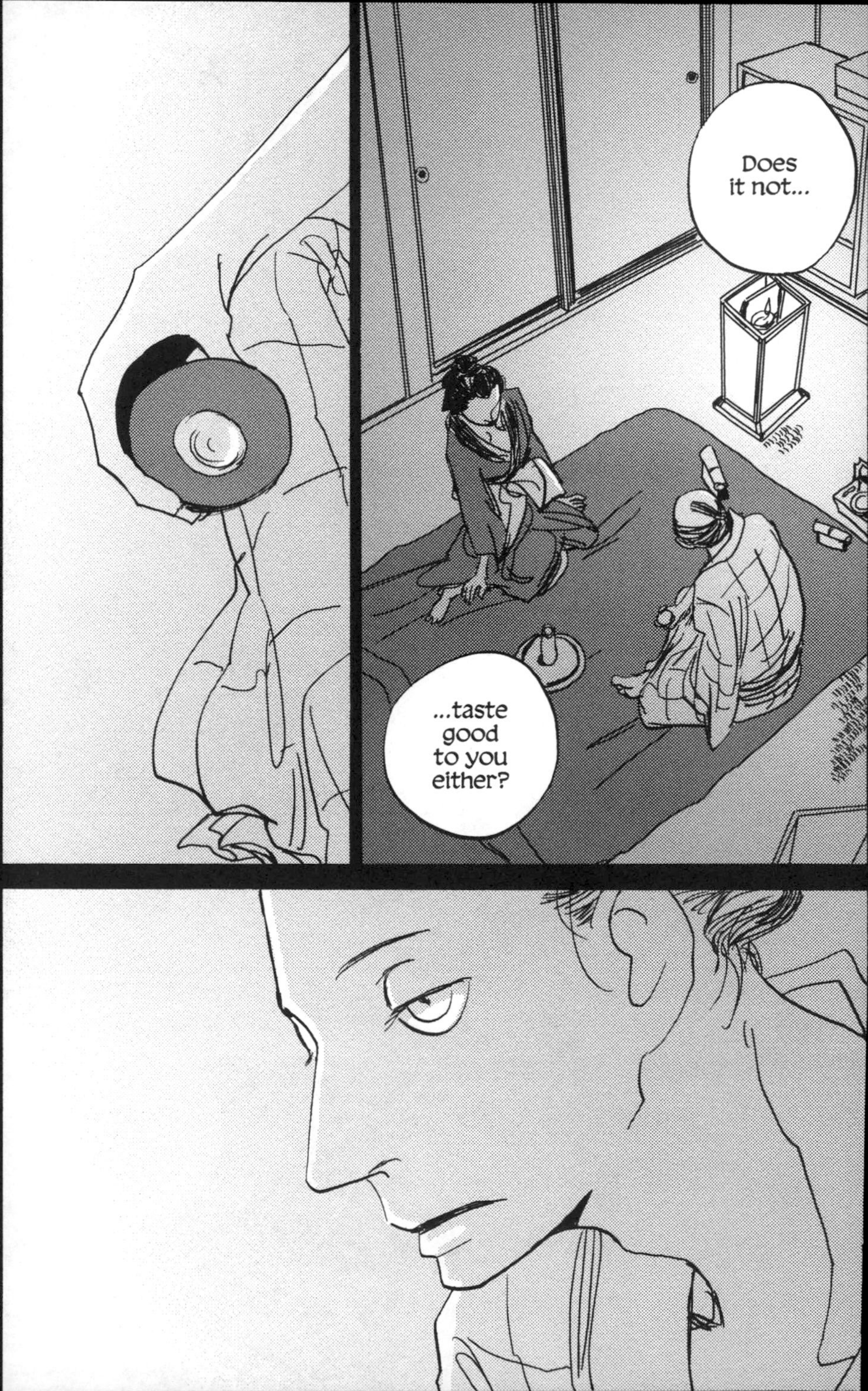
Does it not...
...taste good to you either?

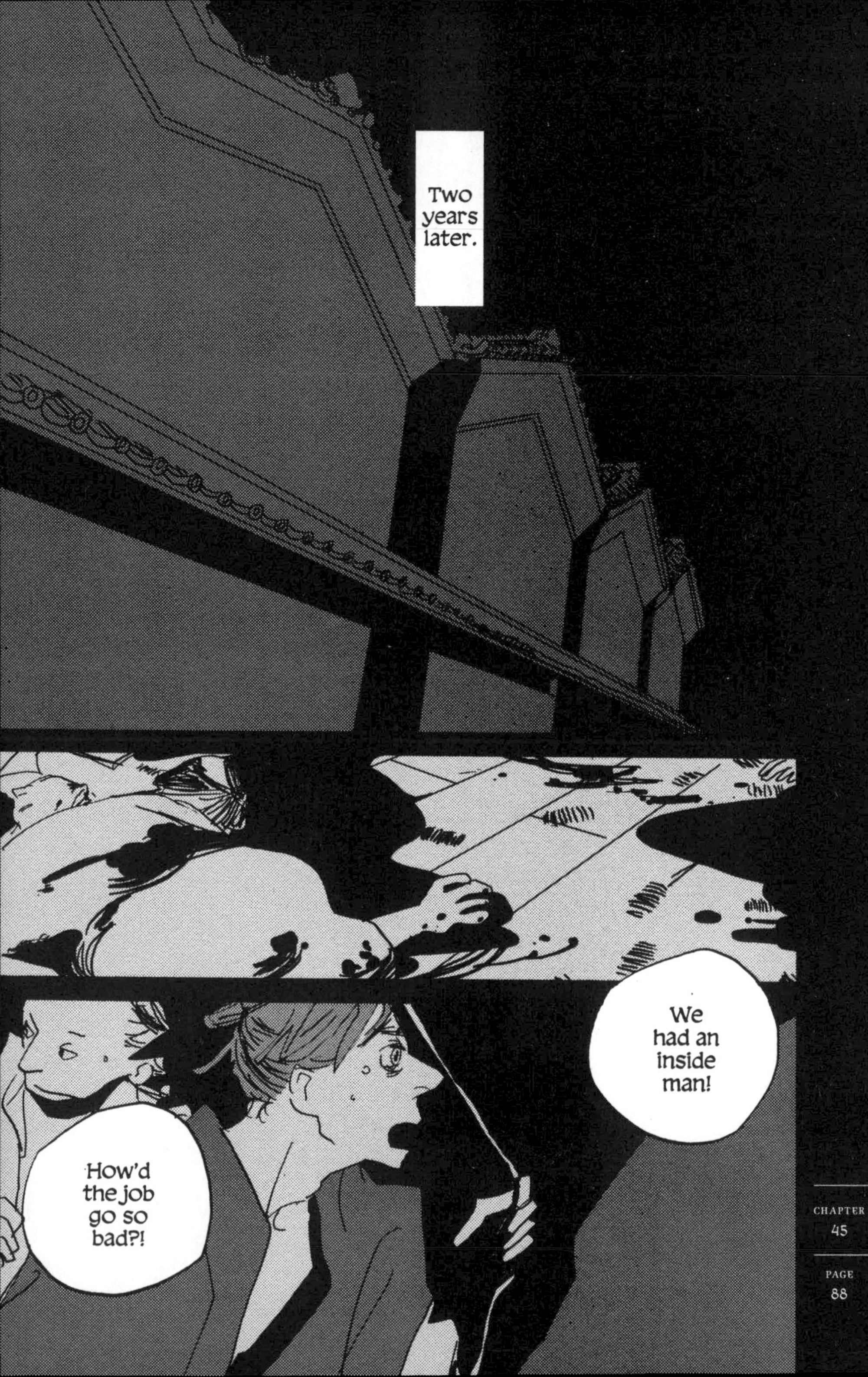
Two years later.
We had an inside man!
How'd the job go so bad?!

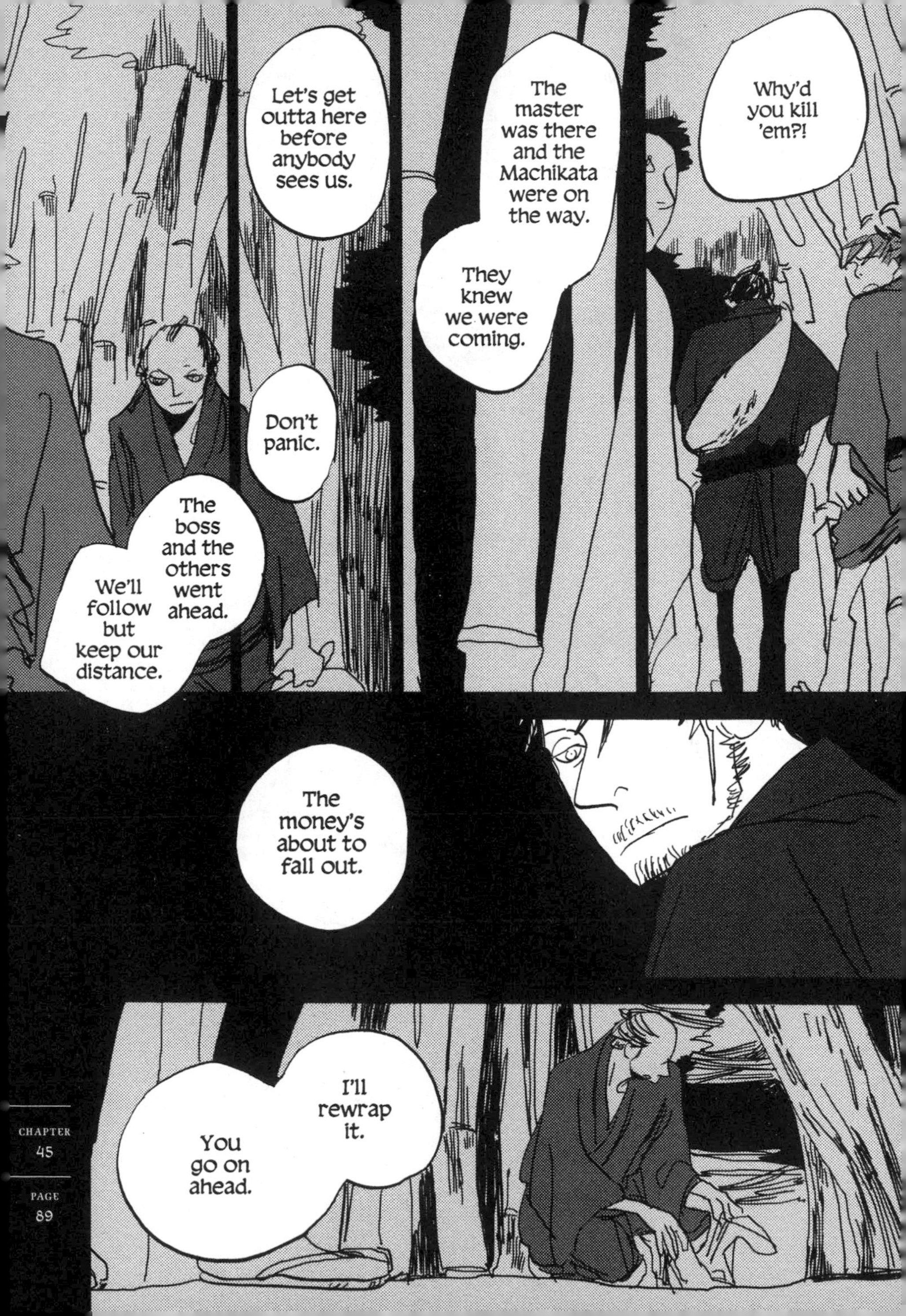
Why'd you kill 'em?!
The master was there and the Machikata were on the way.
They knew we were coming.
Let's get outta here before anybody sees us.
Don't panic.
The boss and the others went ahead.
We'll follow but keep our distance.
The money's about to fall out.
I'll rewrap it.
You go on ahead.

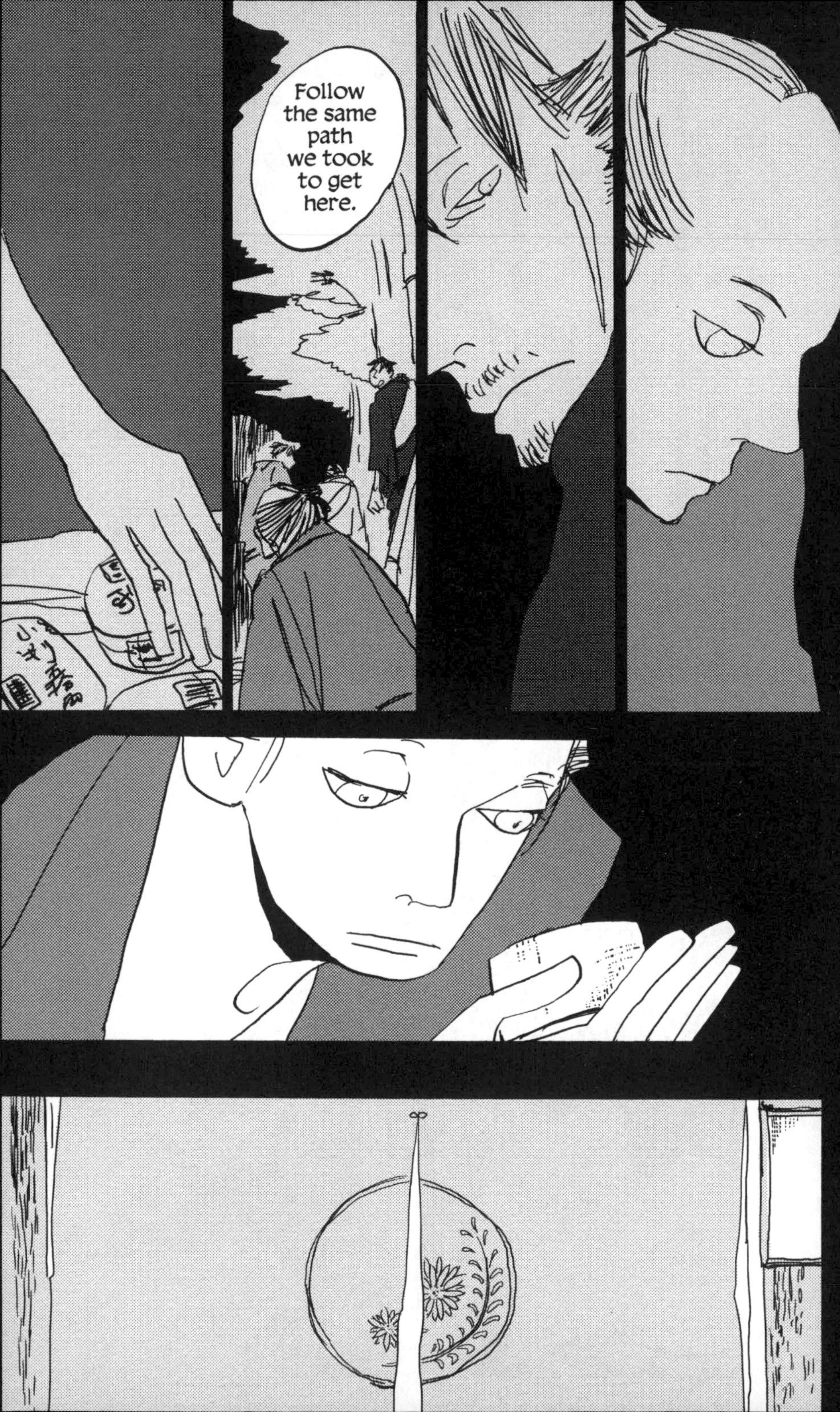
Follow the same path we took to get here.

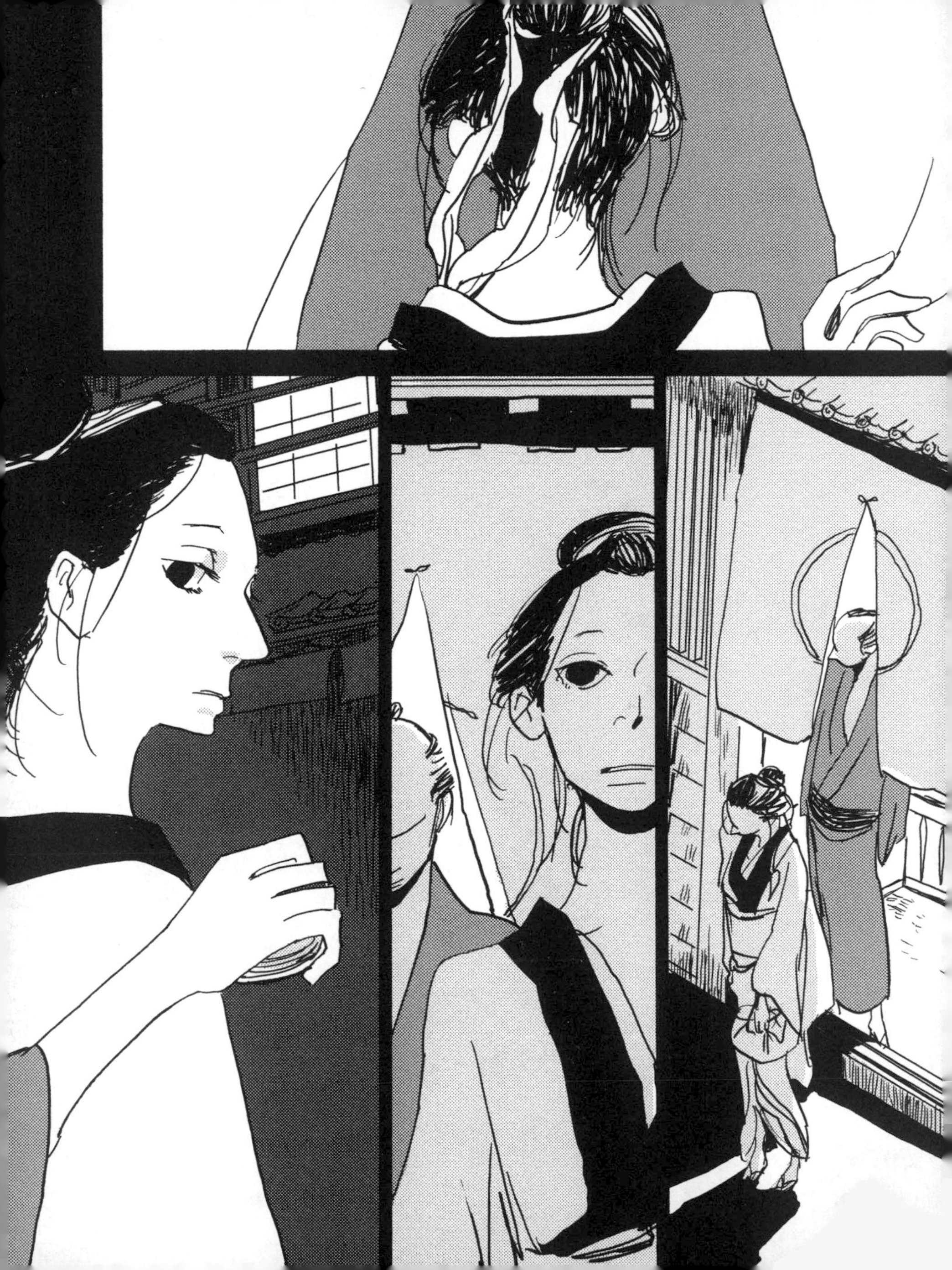

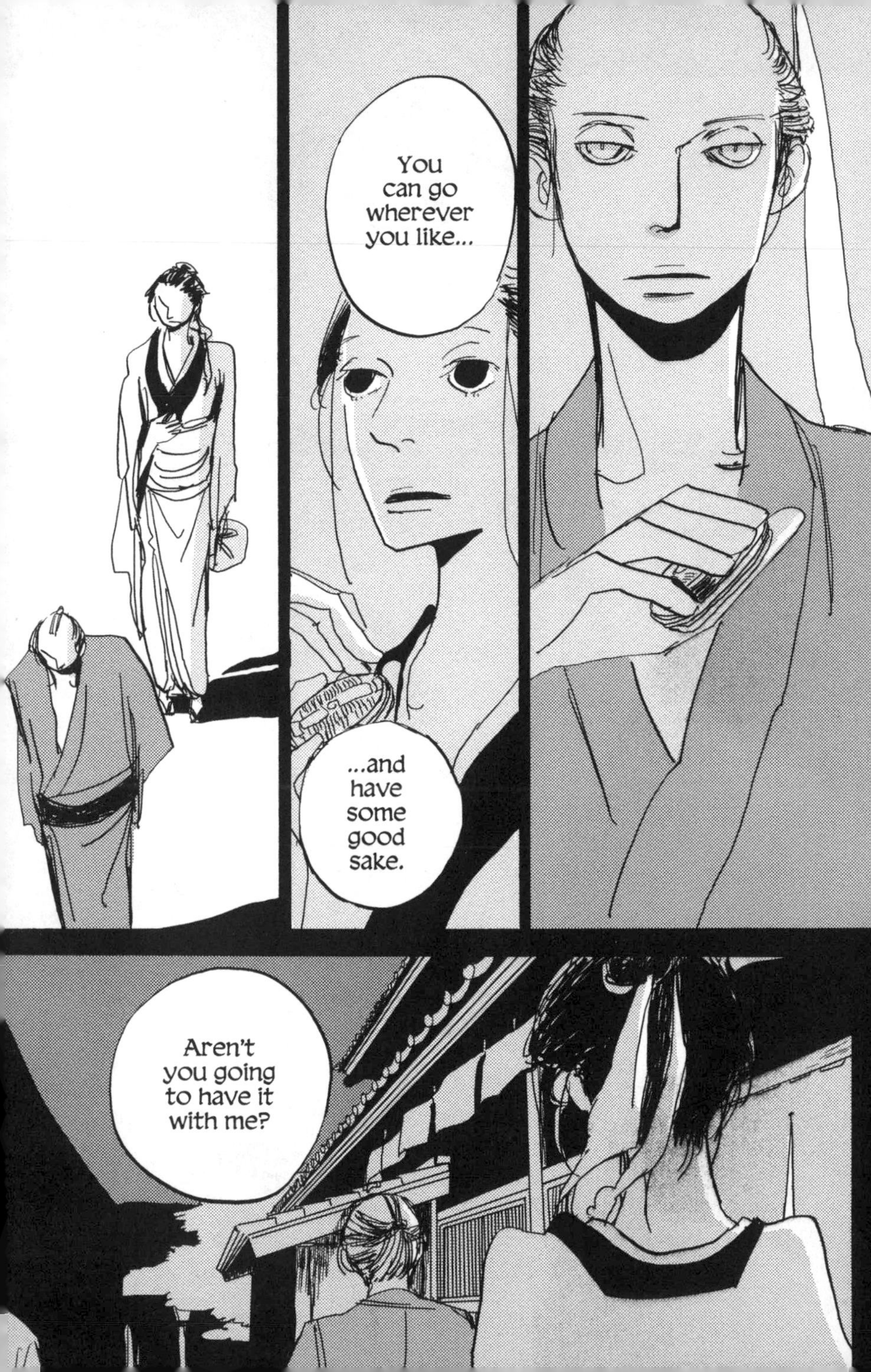
You can go wherever you like...
...and have some good sake.
Aren't you going to have it with me?

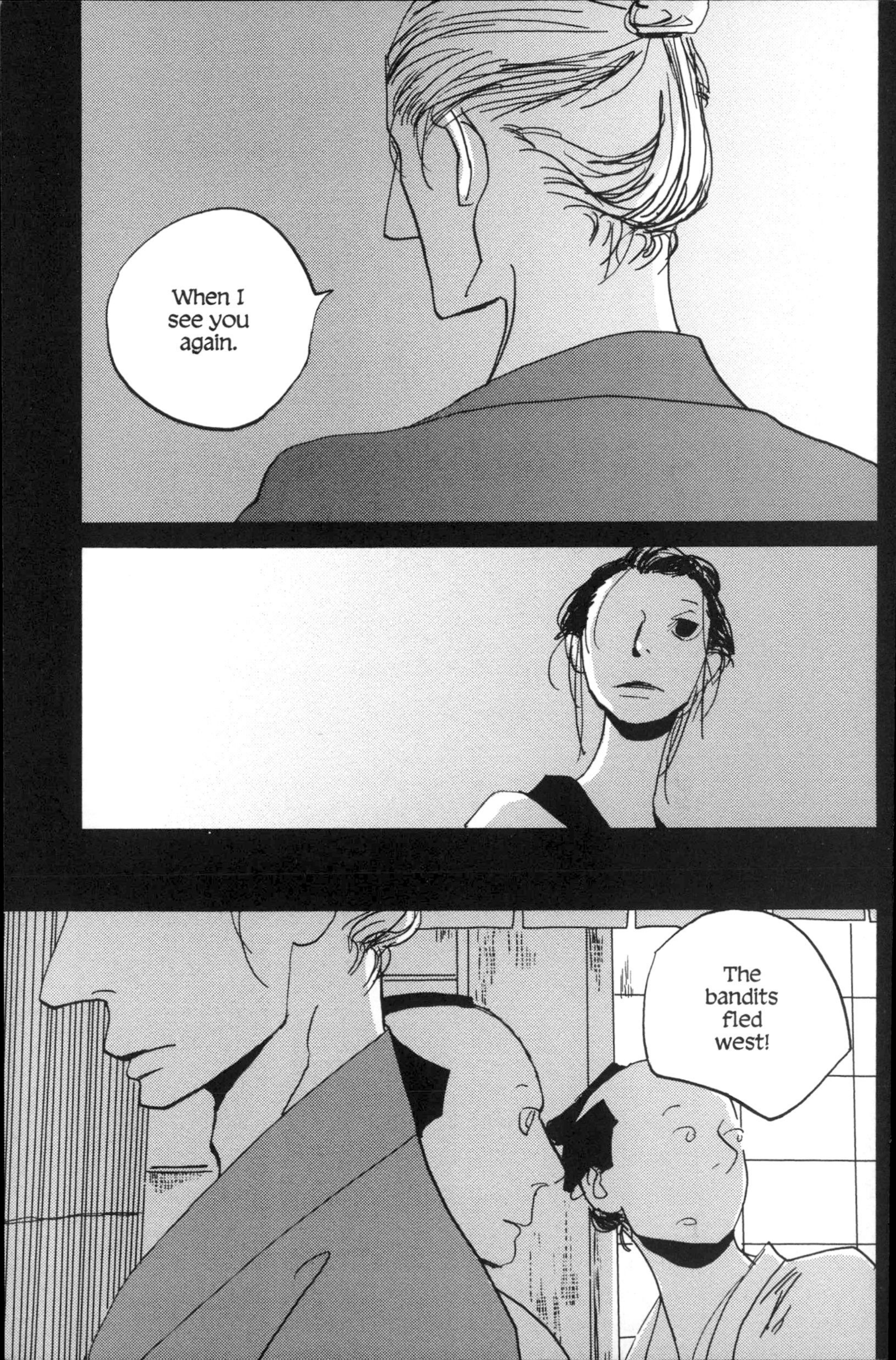
When I see you again.
The bandits fled west!

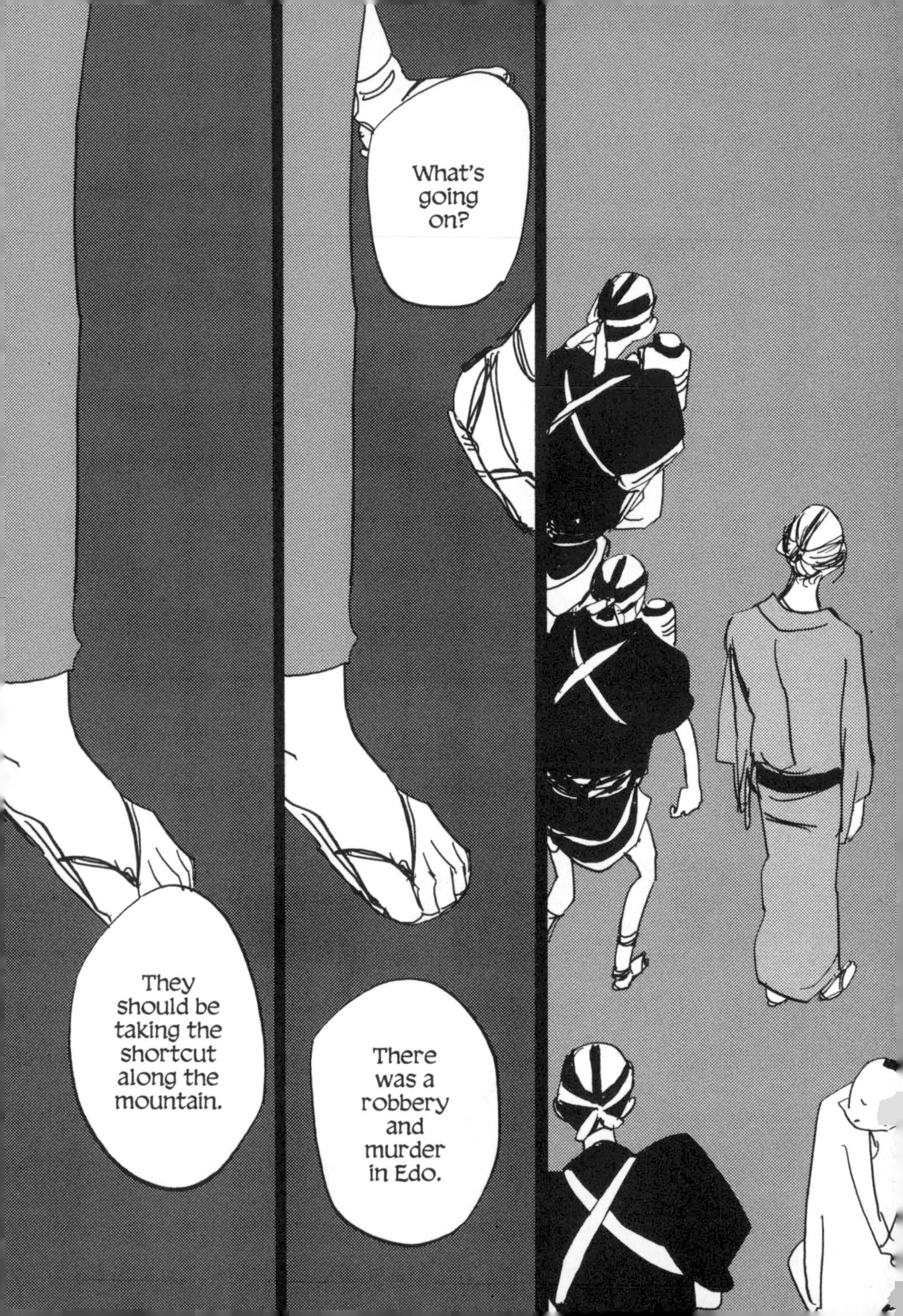
What's going on?
There was a robbery and murder in Edo.
They should be taking the shortcut along the mountain.

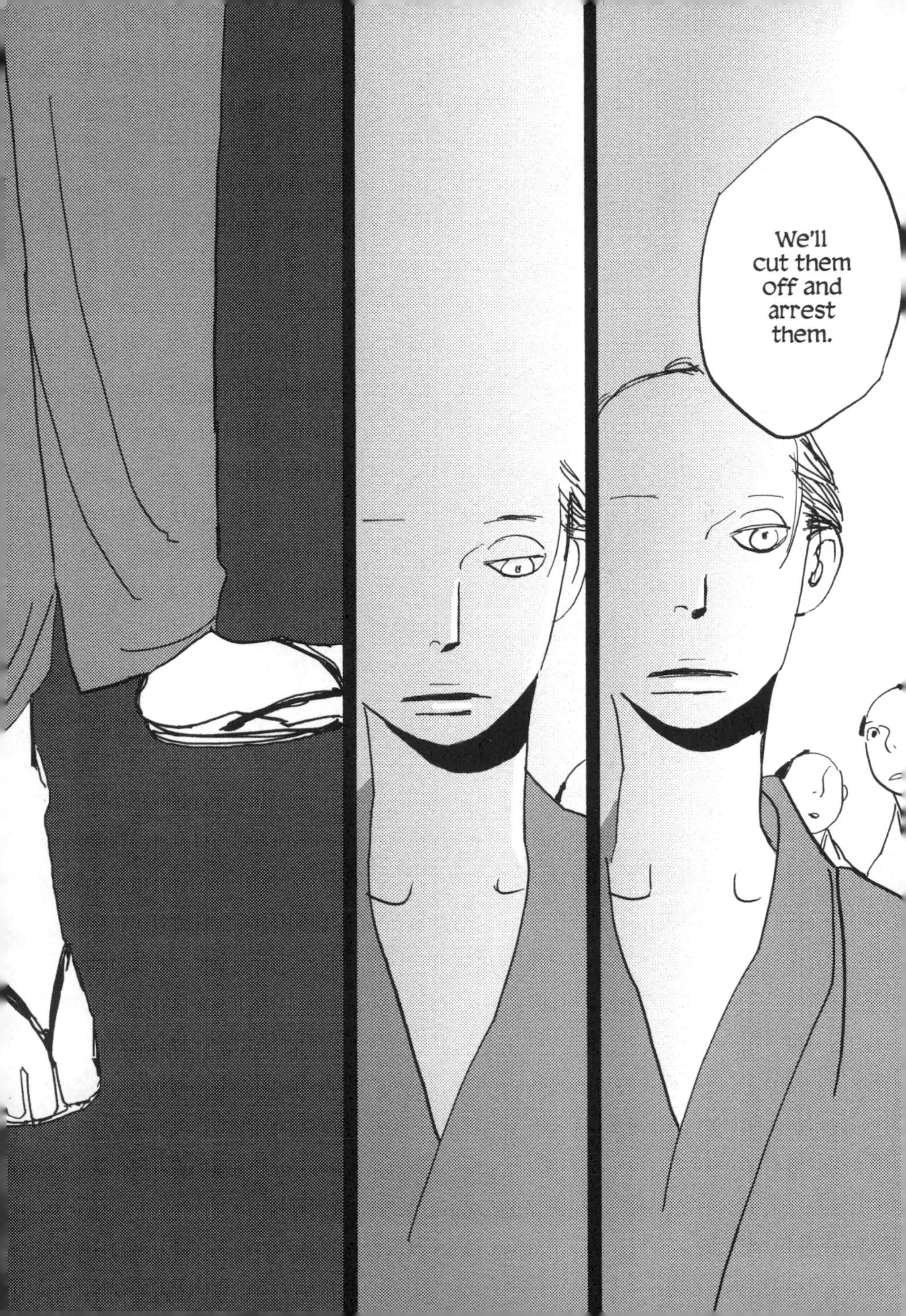
We'll cut them off and arrest them.

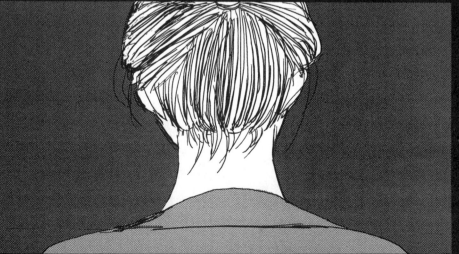

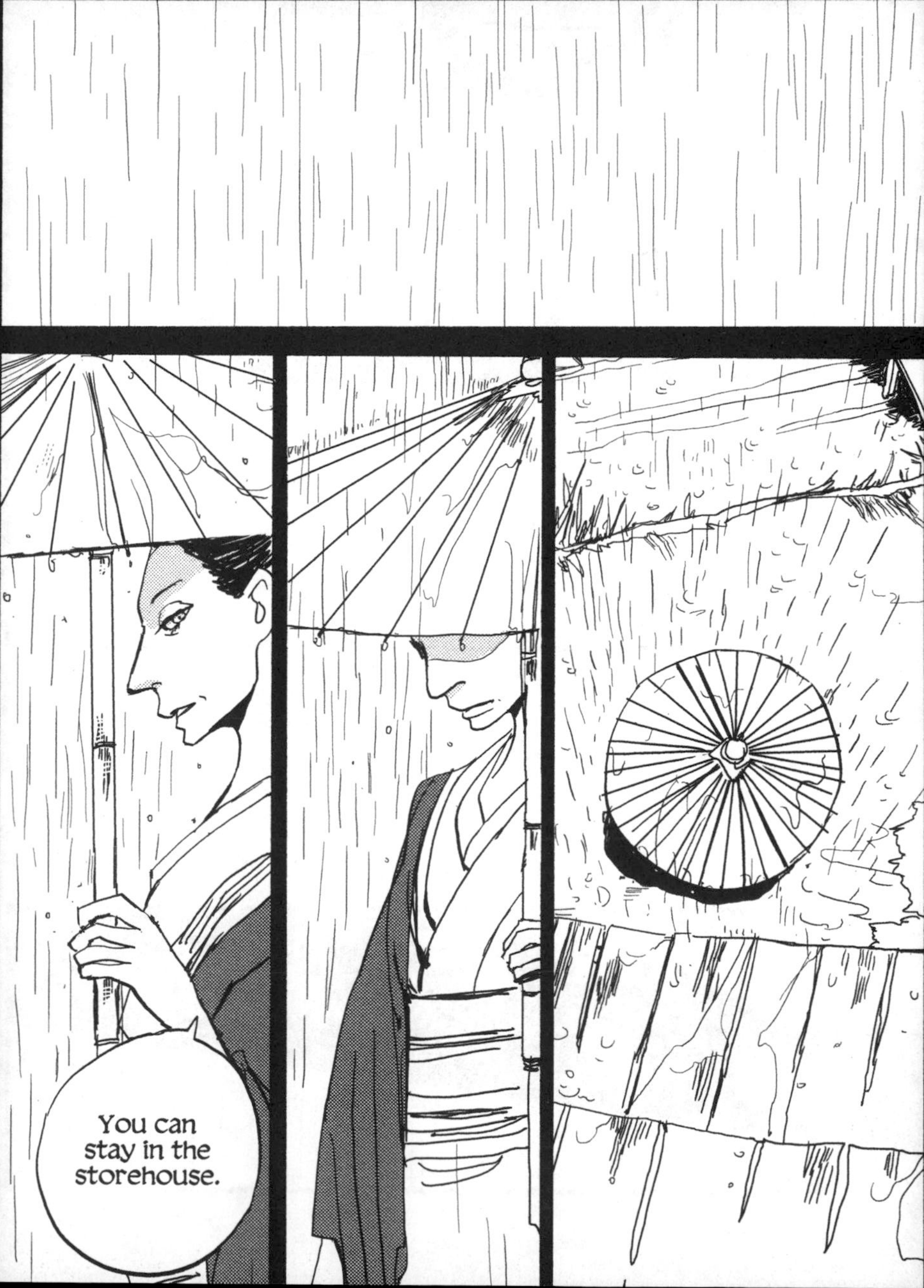
You can stay in the storehouse.

If that's what you want.

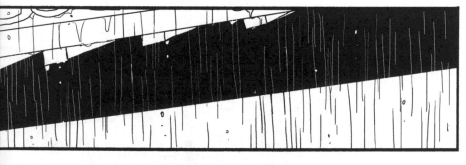

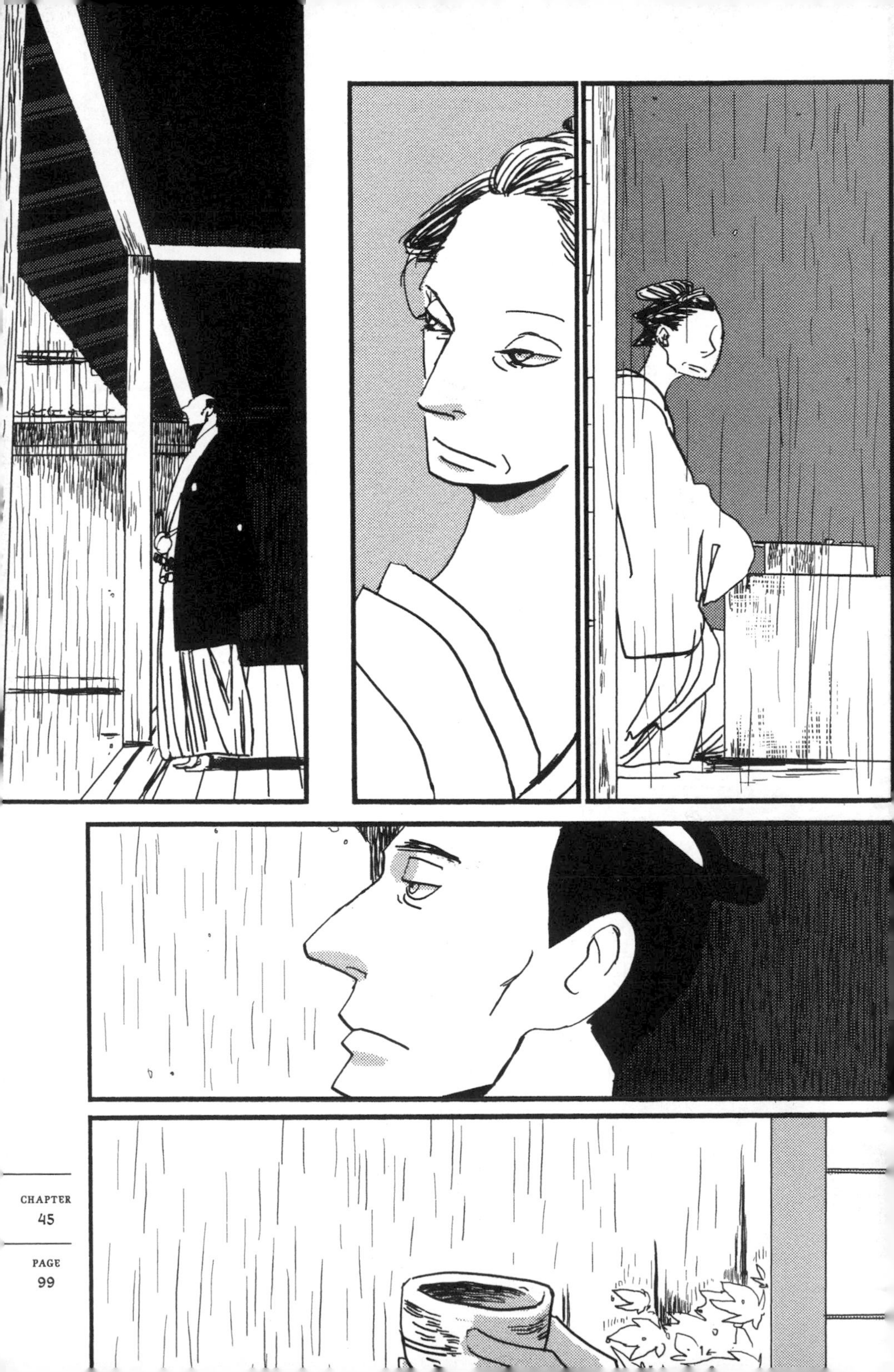

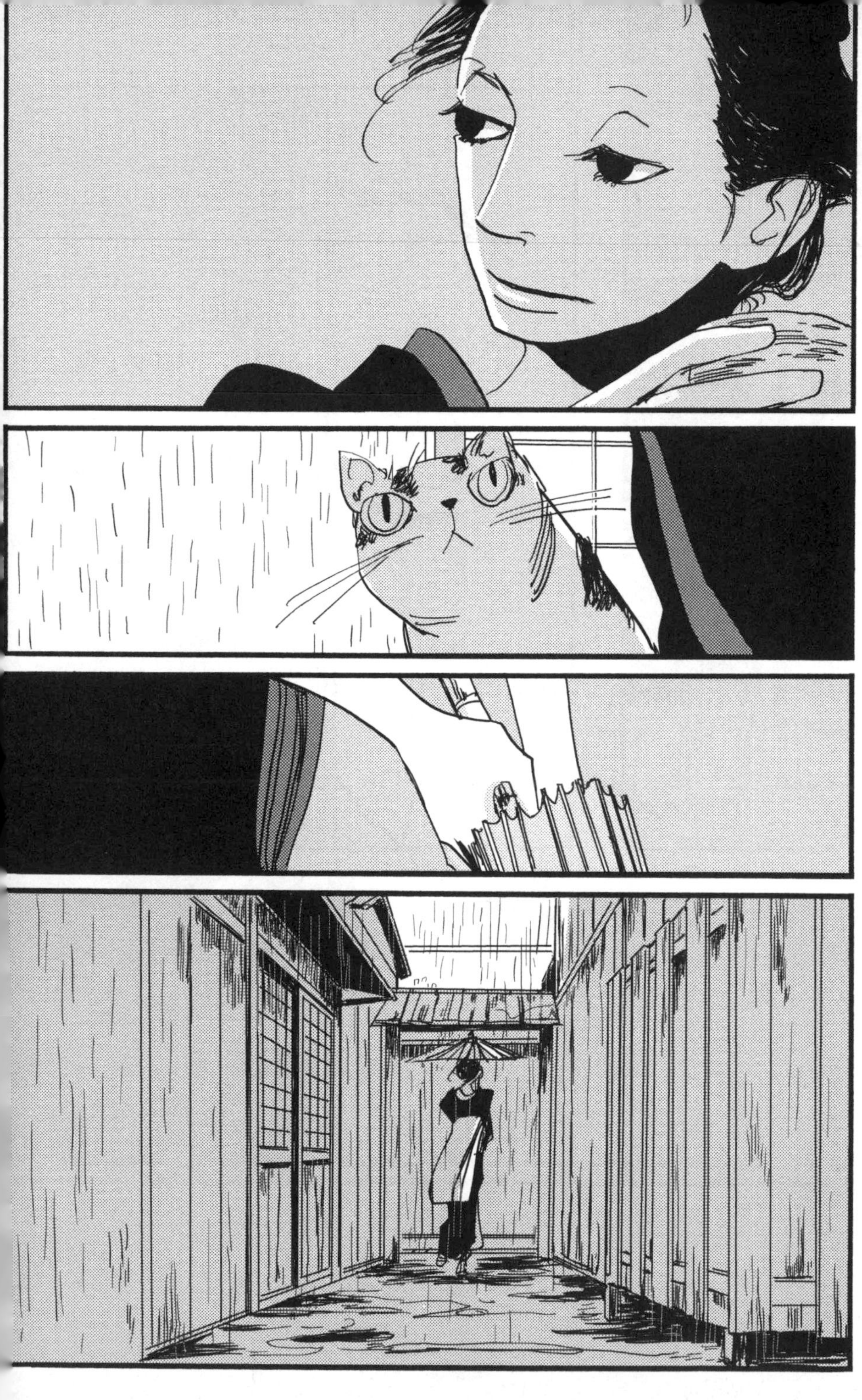

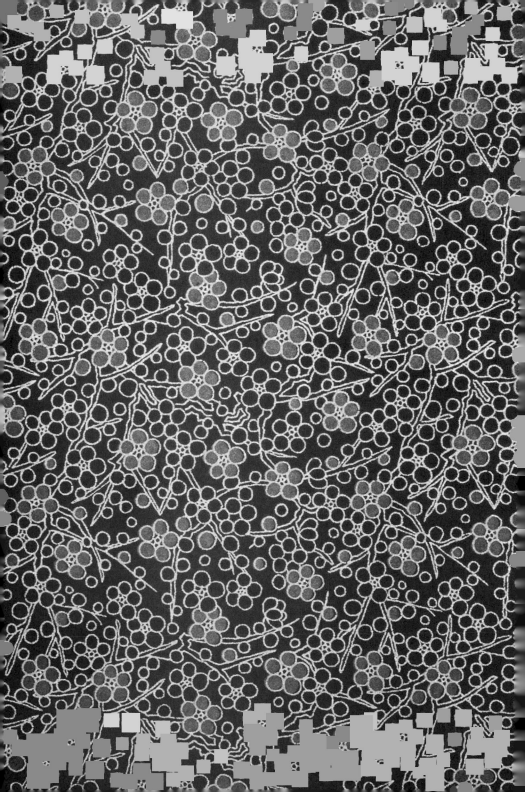

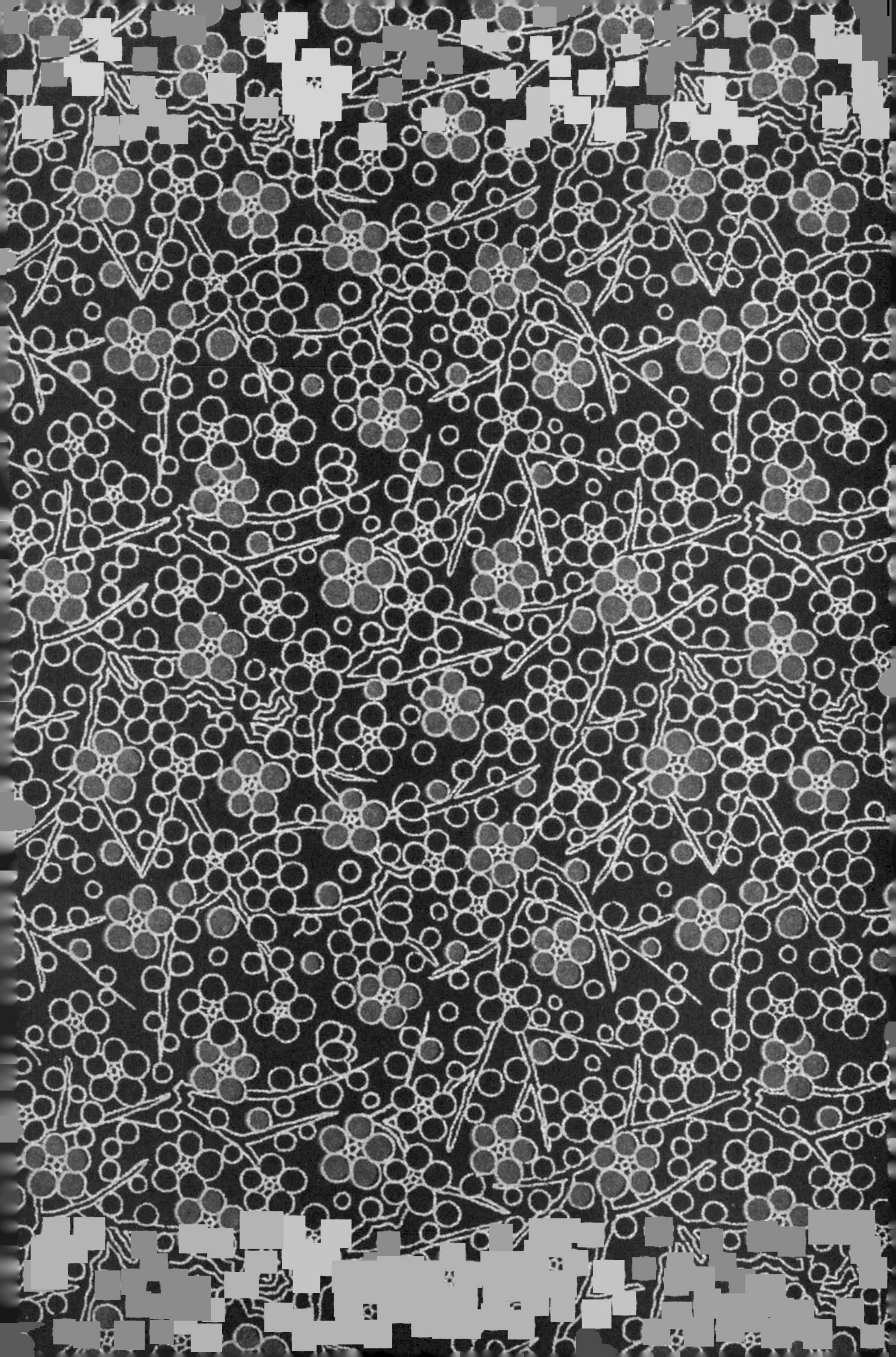

Chapter Forty-Six
A Long Rain
(Part One)

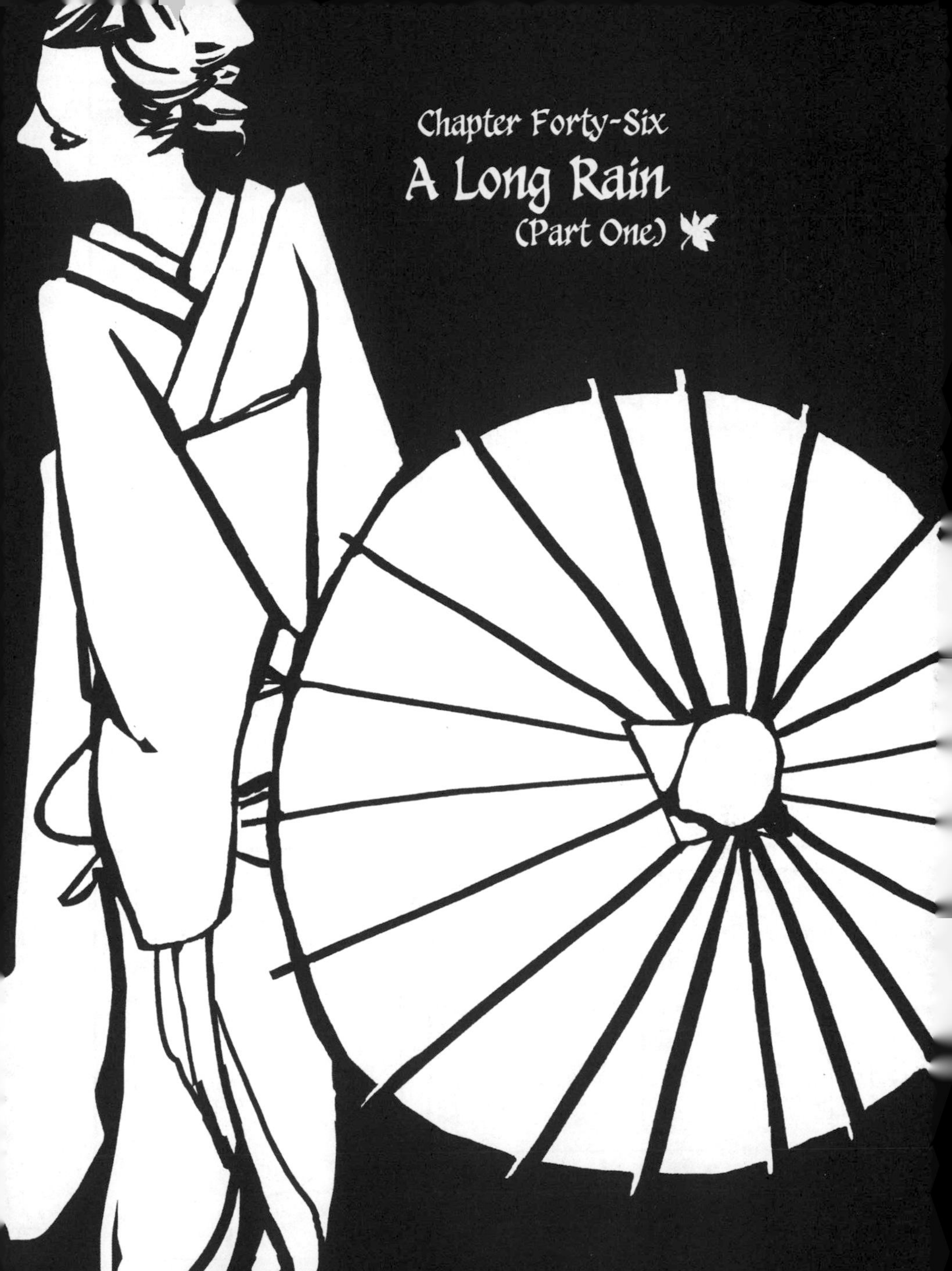

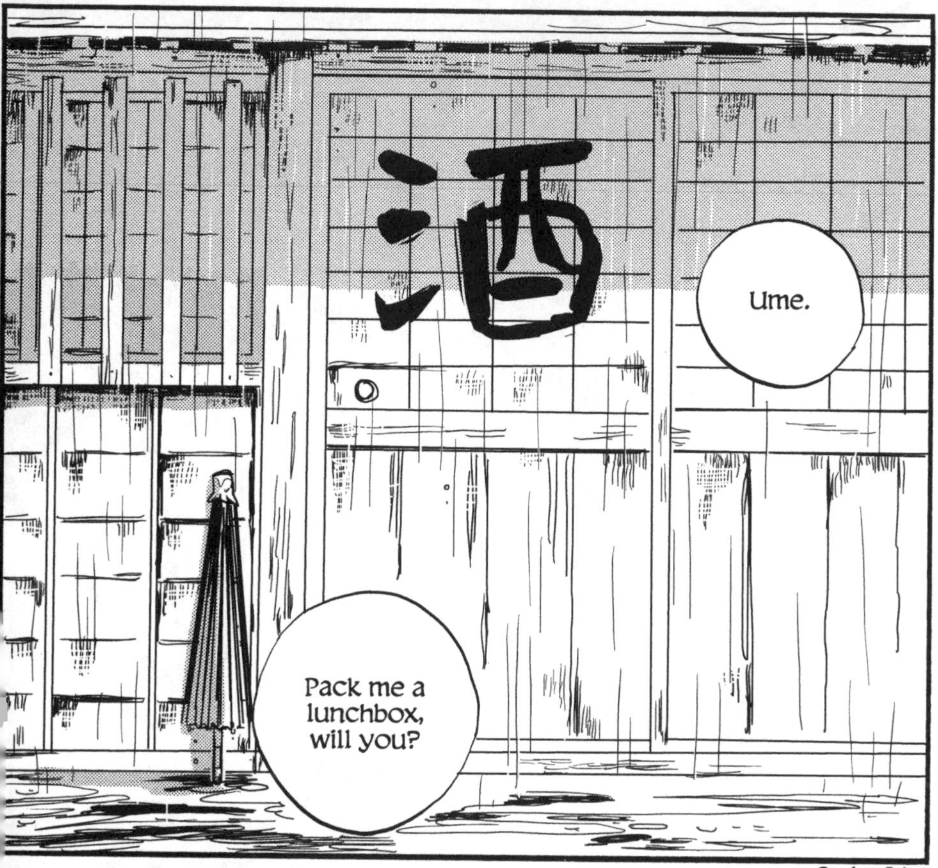
酒
Ume.
Pack me a lunchbox, will you?
On sign: Sake

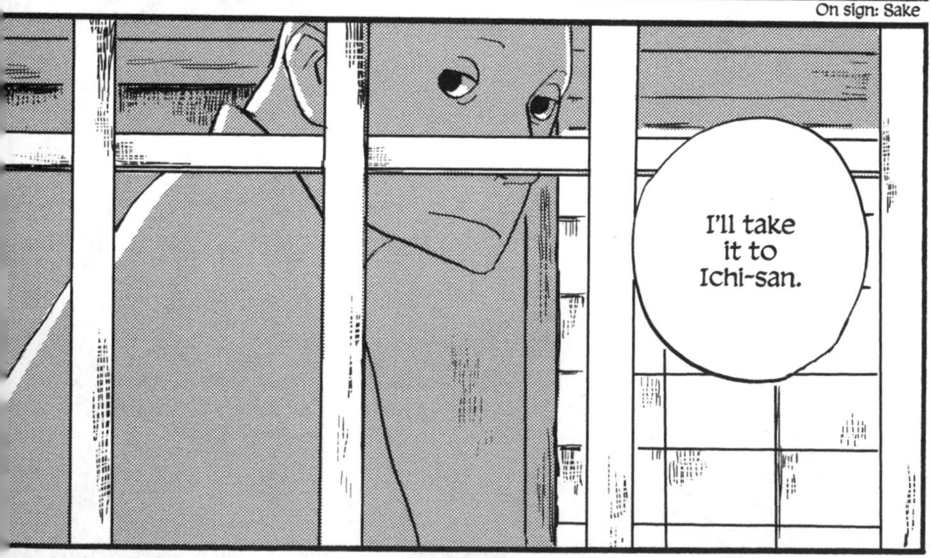
I'll take it to Ichi-san.

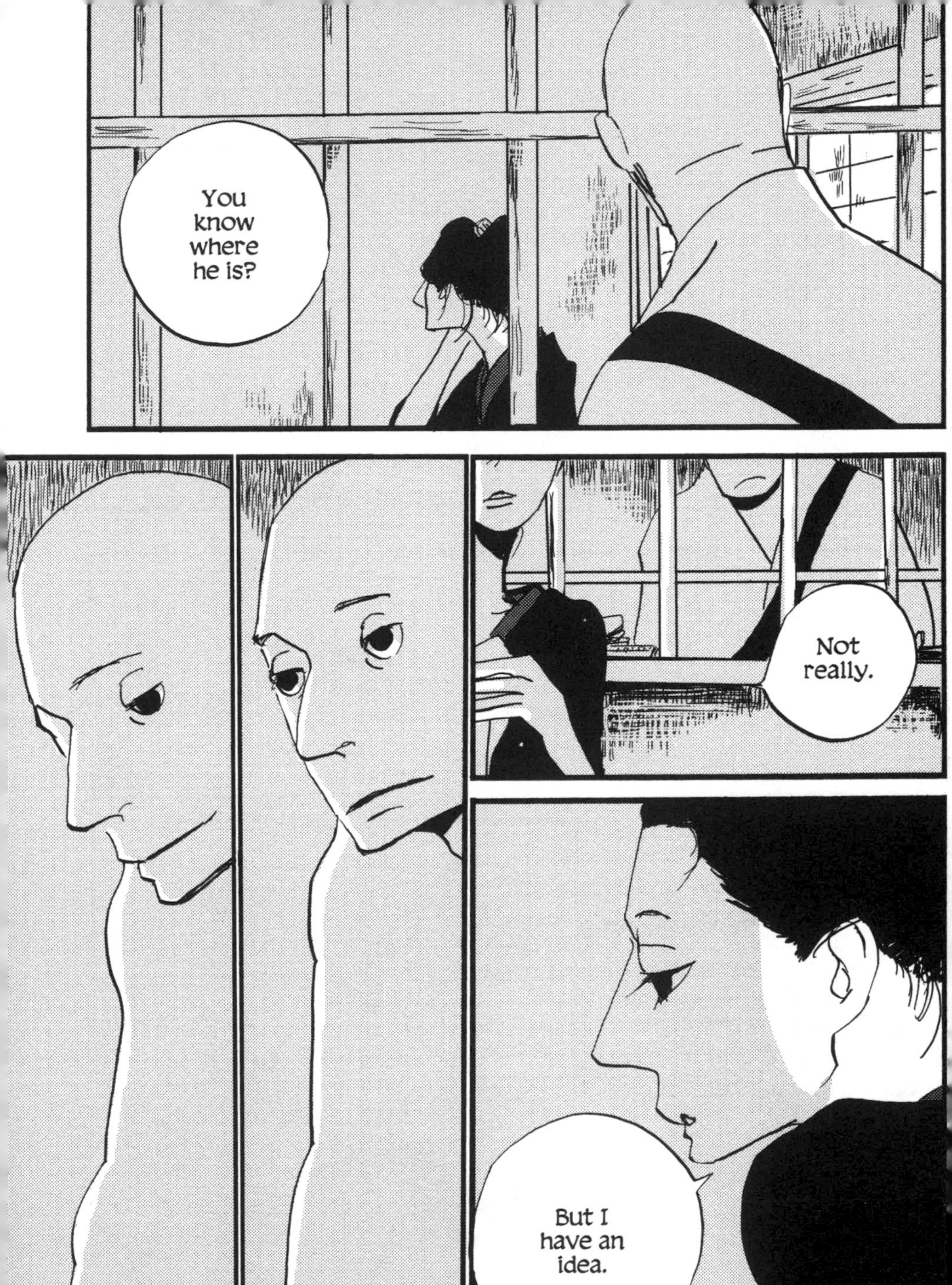
You know where he is?
Not really.
But I have an idea.

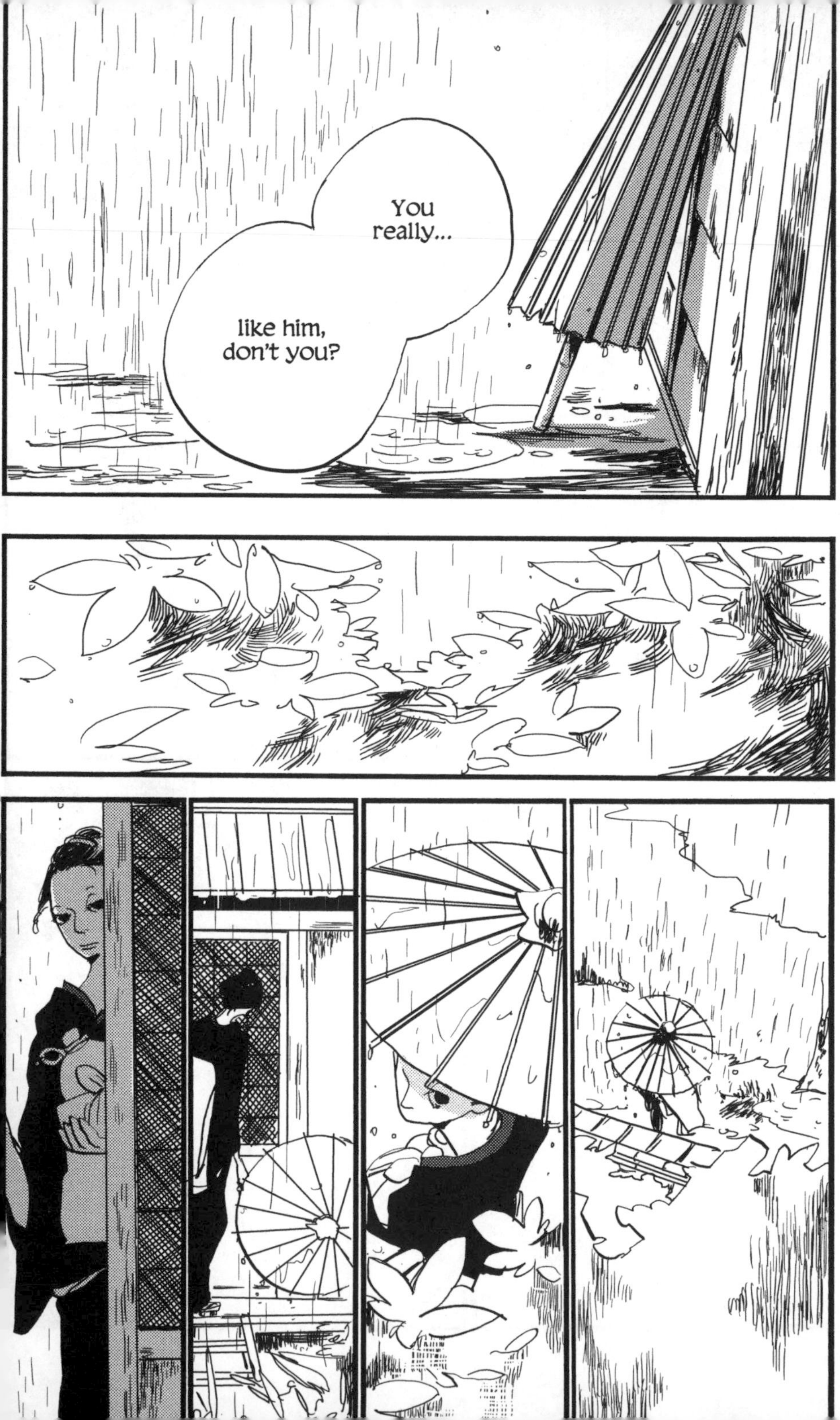
You really...
like him, don't you?

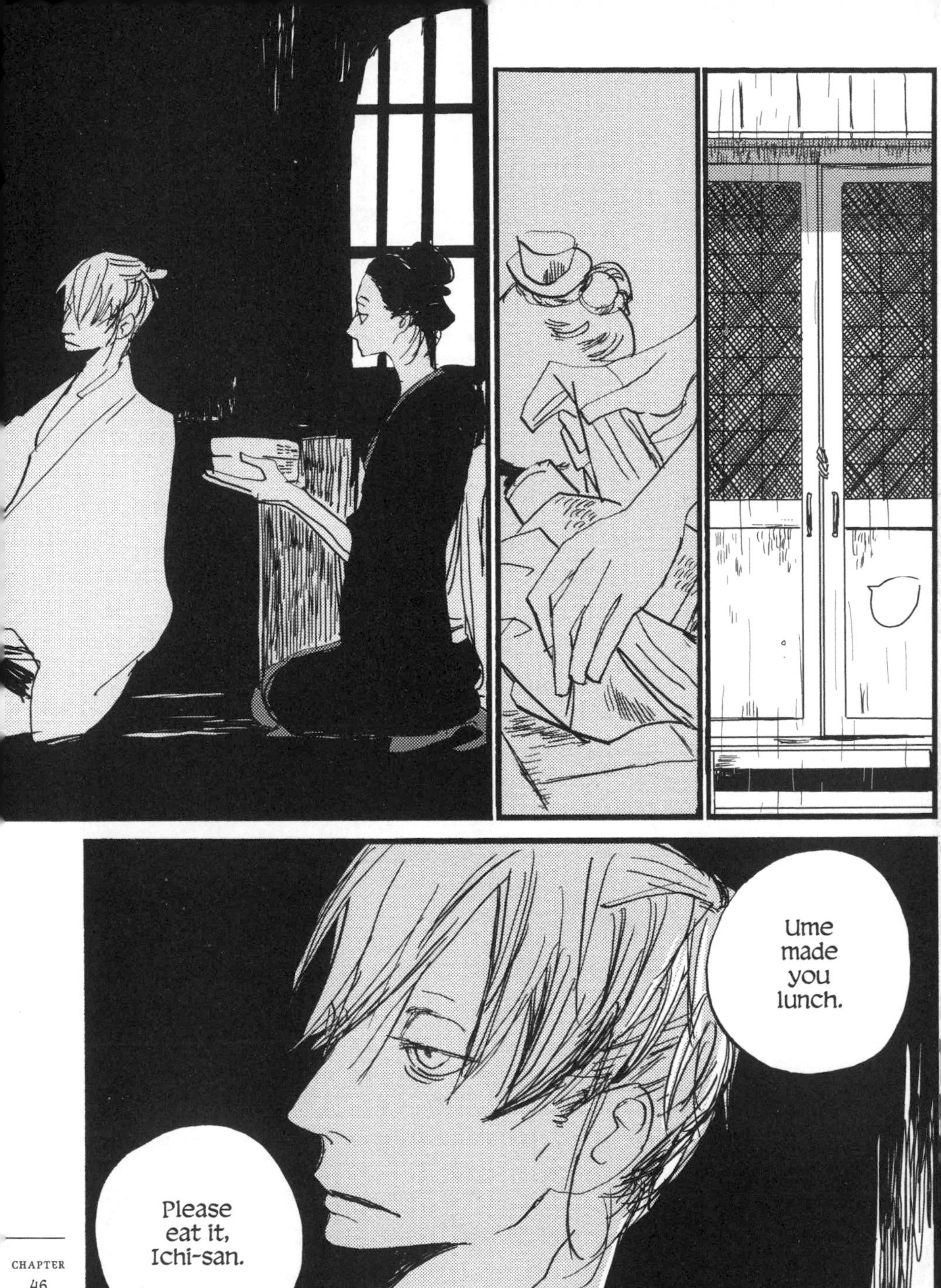
Ume made you lunch.
Please eat it, Ichi-san.

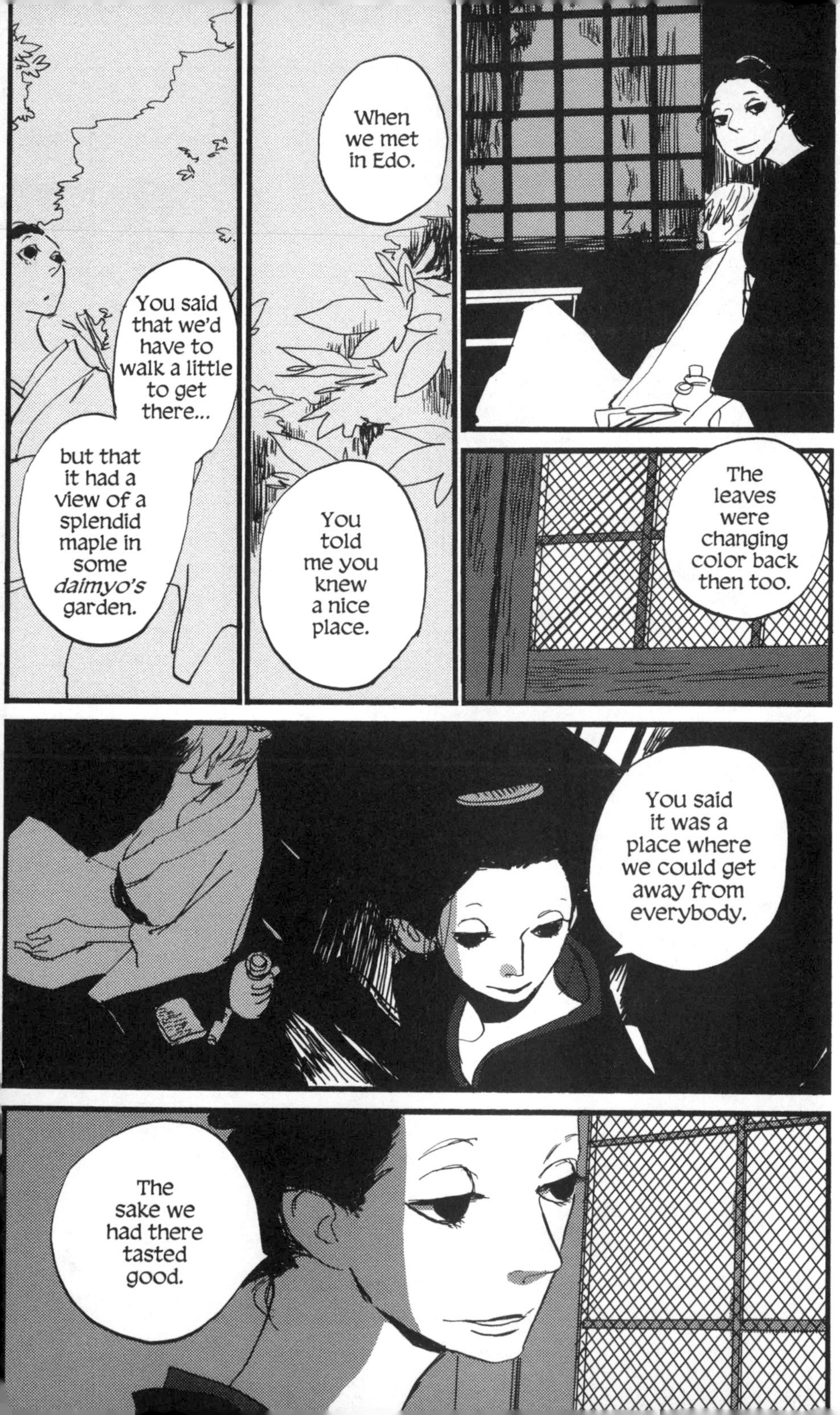

The leaves were changing color back then too.
When we met in Edo.
You told me you knew a nice place.
You said that we'd have to walk a little to get there...
but that it had a view of a splendid maple in some *daimyo's* garden.
You said it was a place where we could get away from everybody.
The sake we had there tasted good.

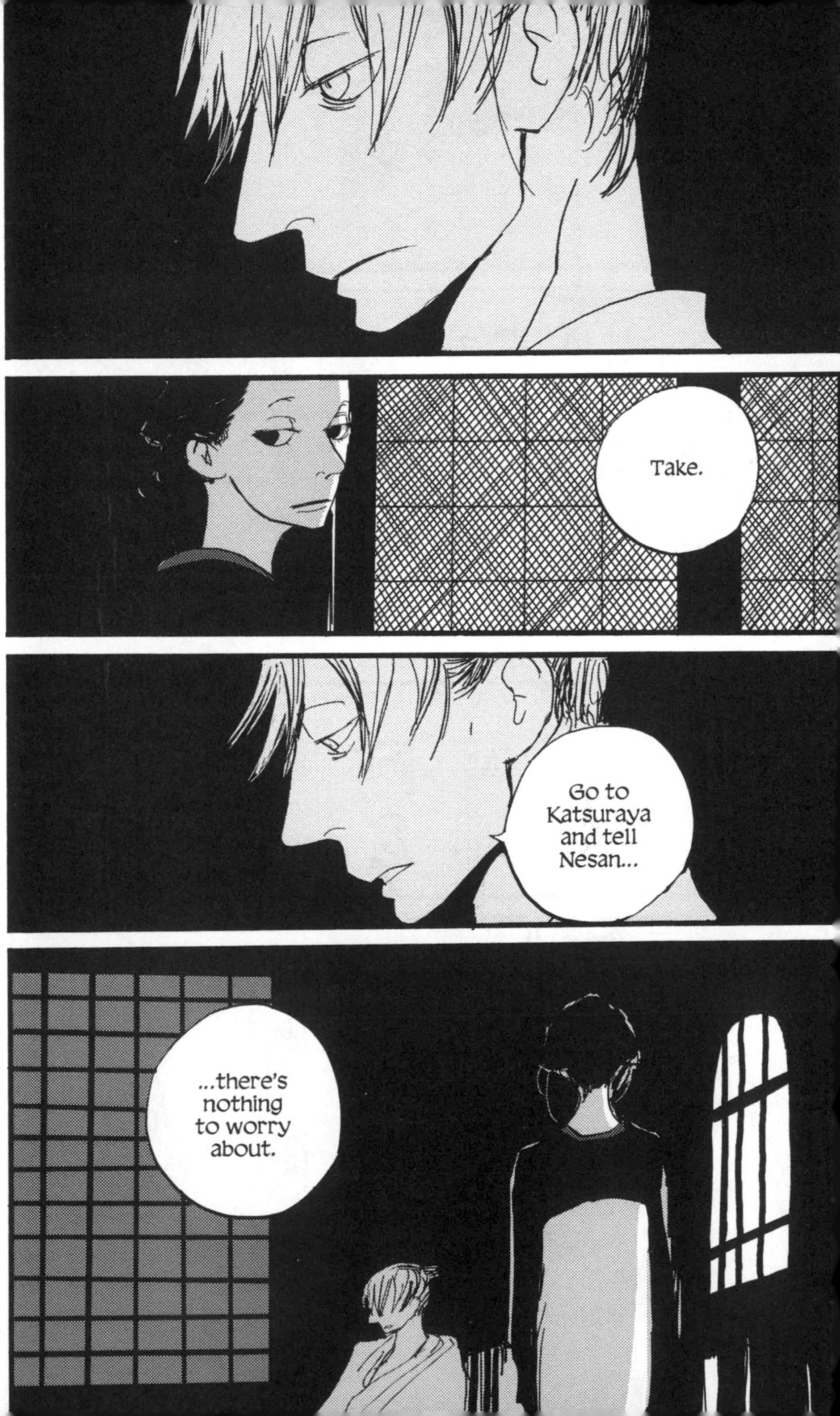
Take.
Go to Katsuraya and tell Nesan...
...there's nothing to worry about.

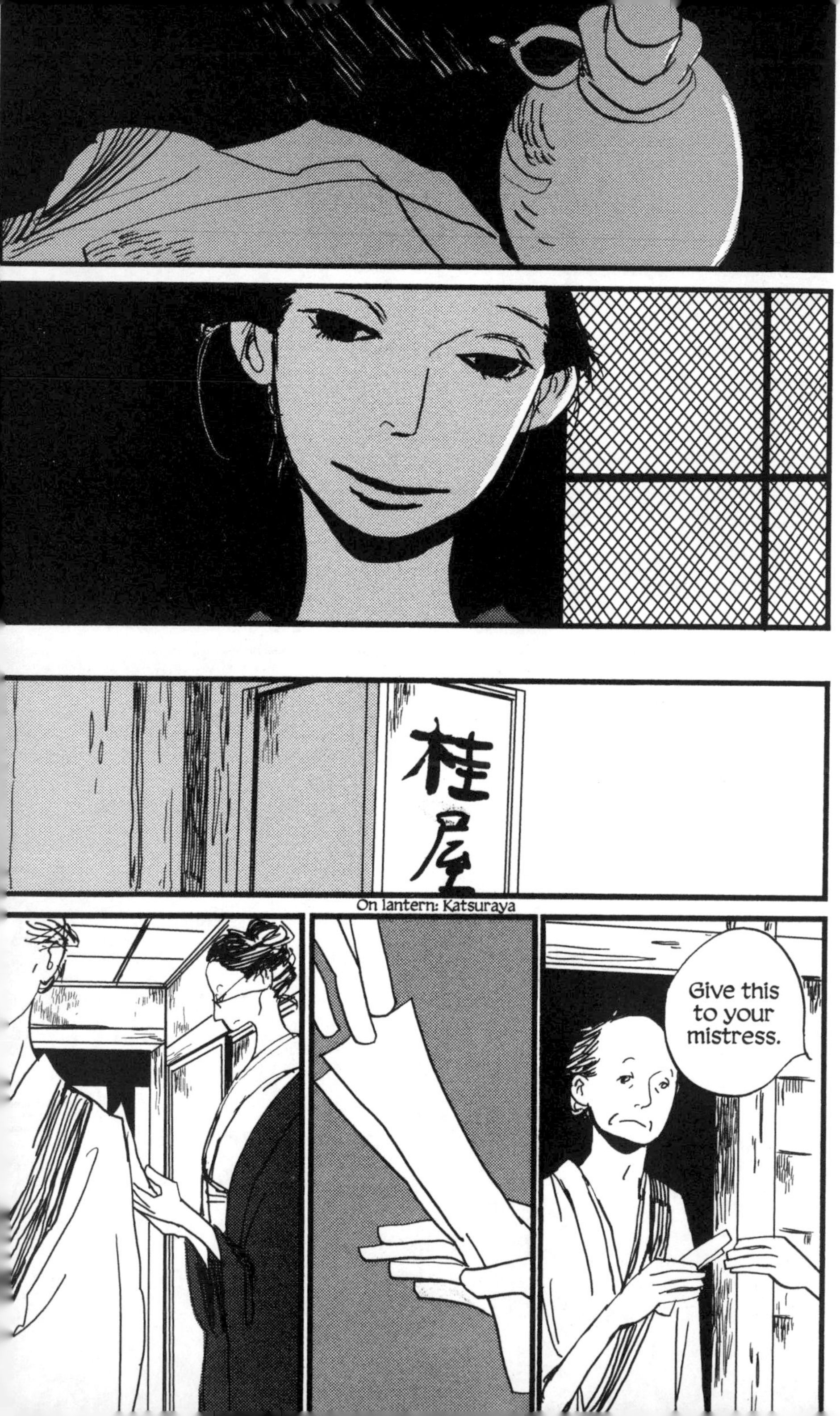
桂屋
On lantern: Katsuraya
Give this to your mistress.

Wait.

Is all this nonsense because that ronin showed up?

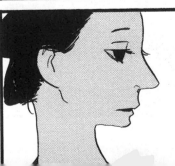

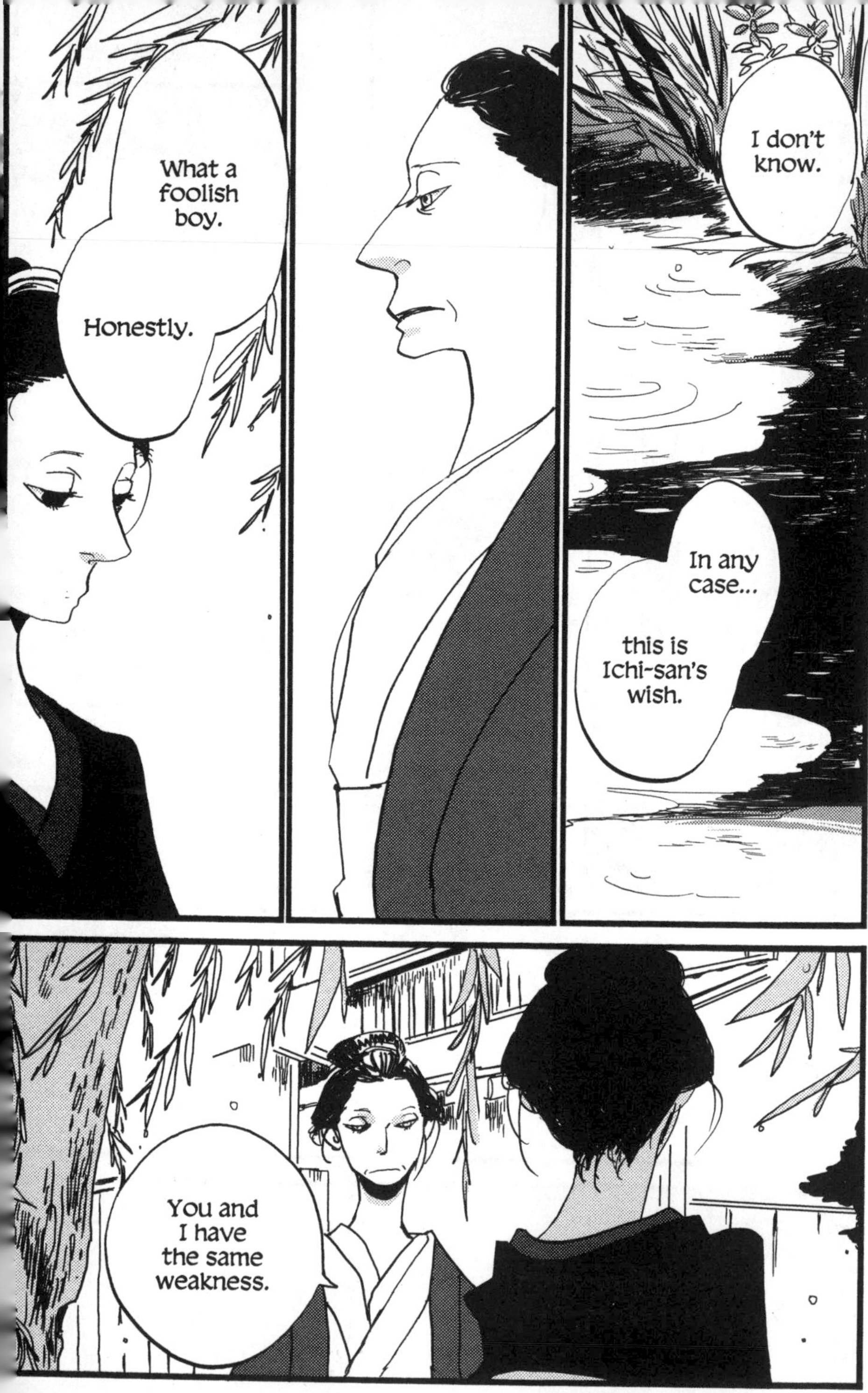
I don't know.
In any case...
this is Ichi-san's wish.
What a foolish boy.
Honestly.
You and I have the same weakness.

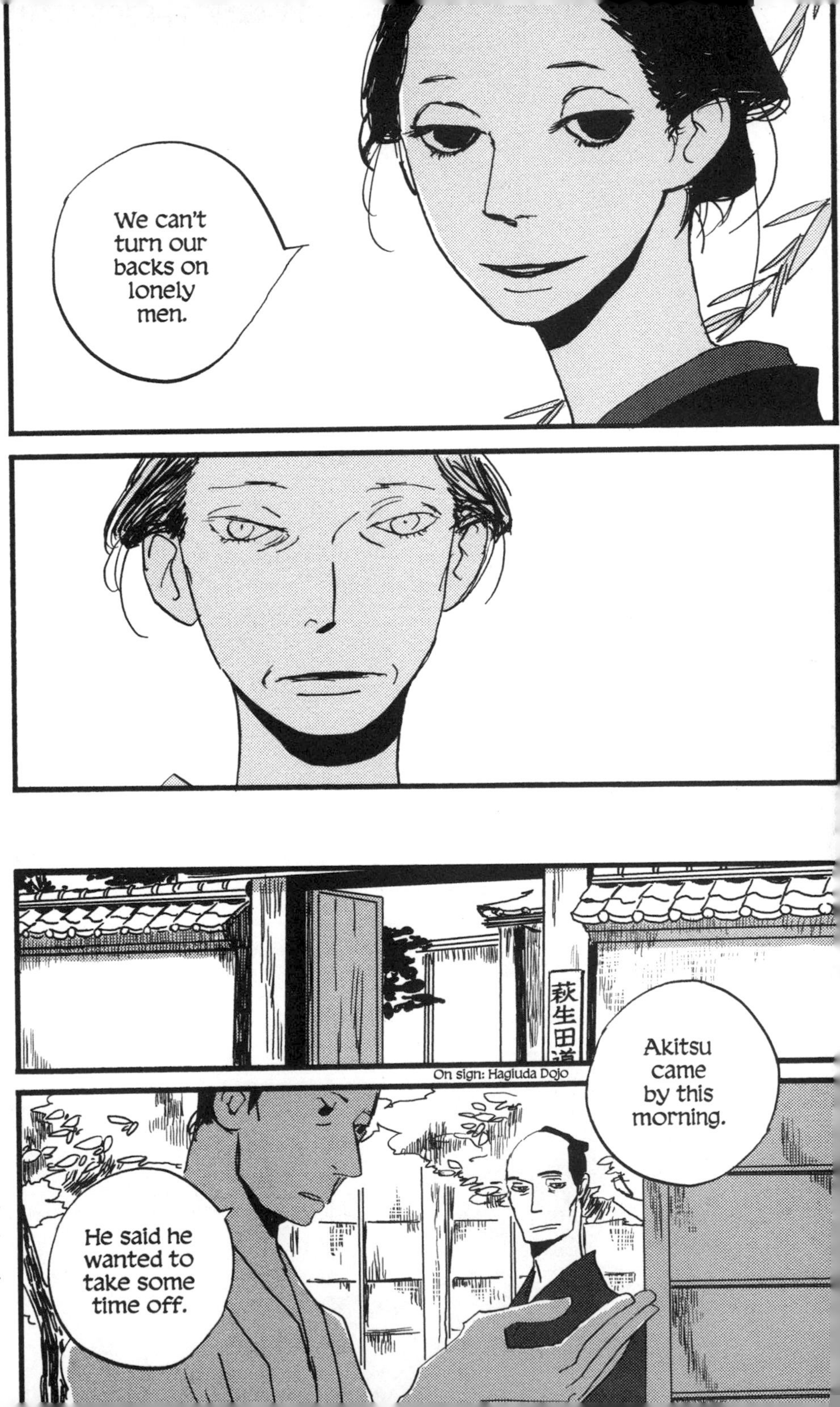
We can't turn our backs on lonely men.
萩生田道
On sign: Hagiuda Dojo
Akitsu came by this morning.
He said he wanted to take some time off.

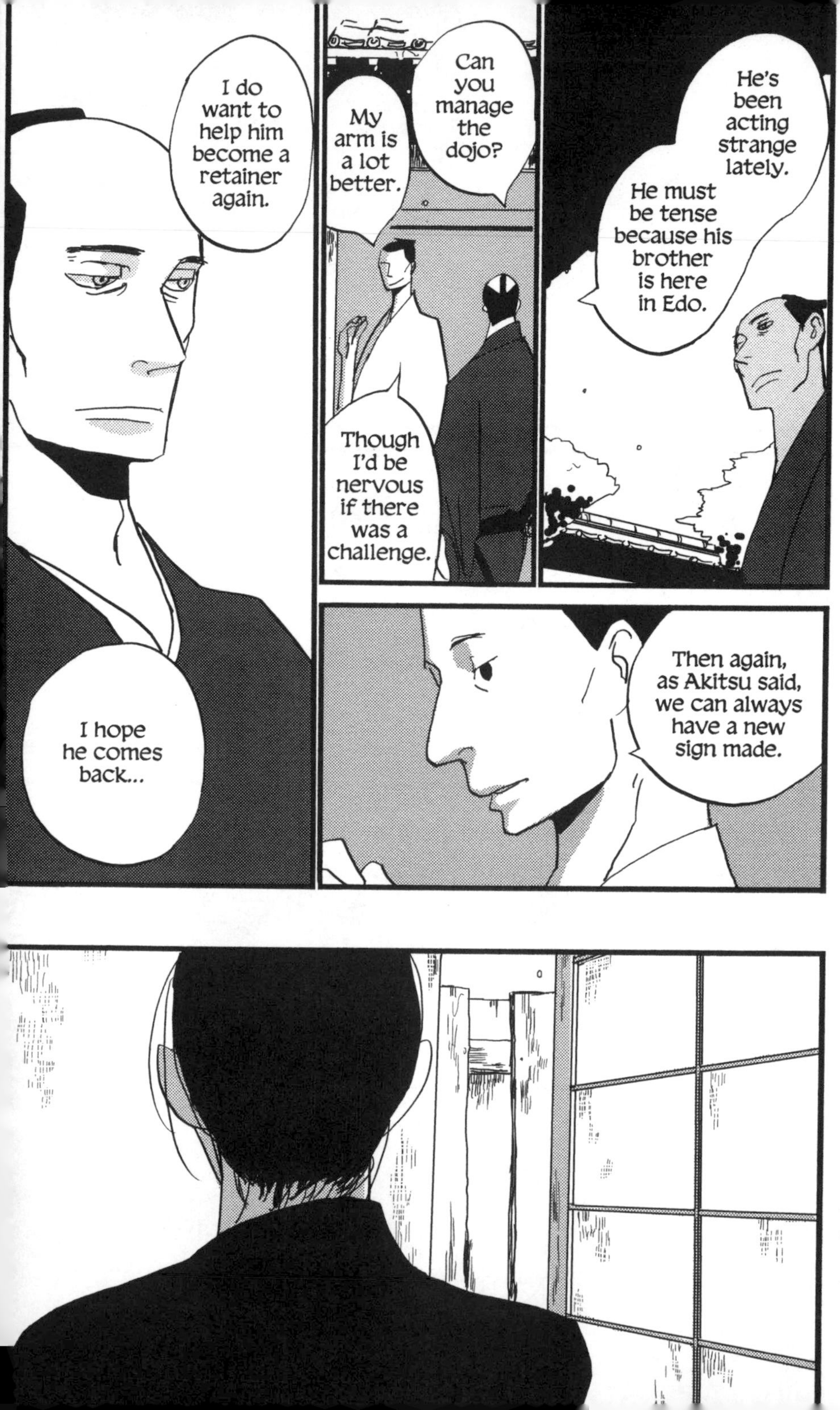
He's been acting strange lately.
He must be tense because his brother is here in Edo.
Can you manage the dojo?
My arm is a lot better.
Though I'd be nervous if there was a challenge.
Then again, as Akitsu said, we can always have a new sign made.
I do want to help him become a retainer again.
I hope he comes back...

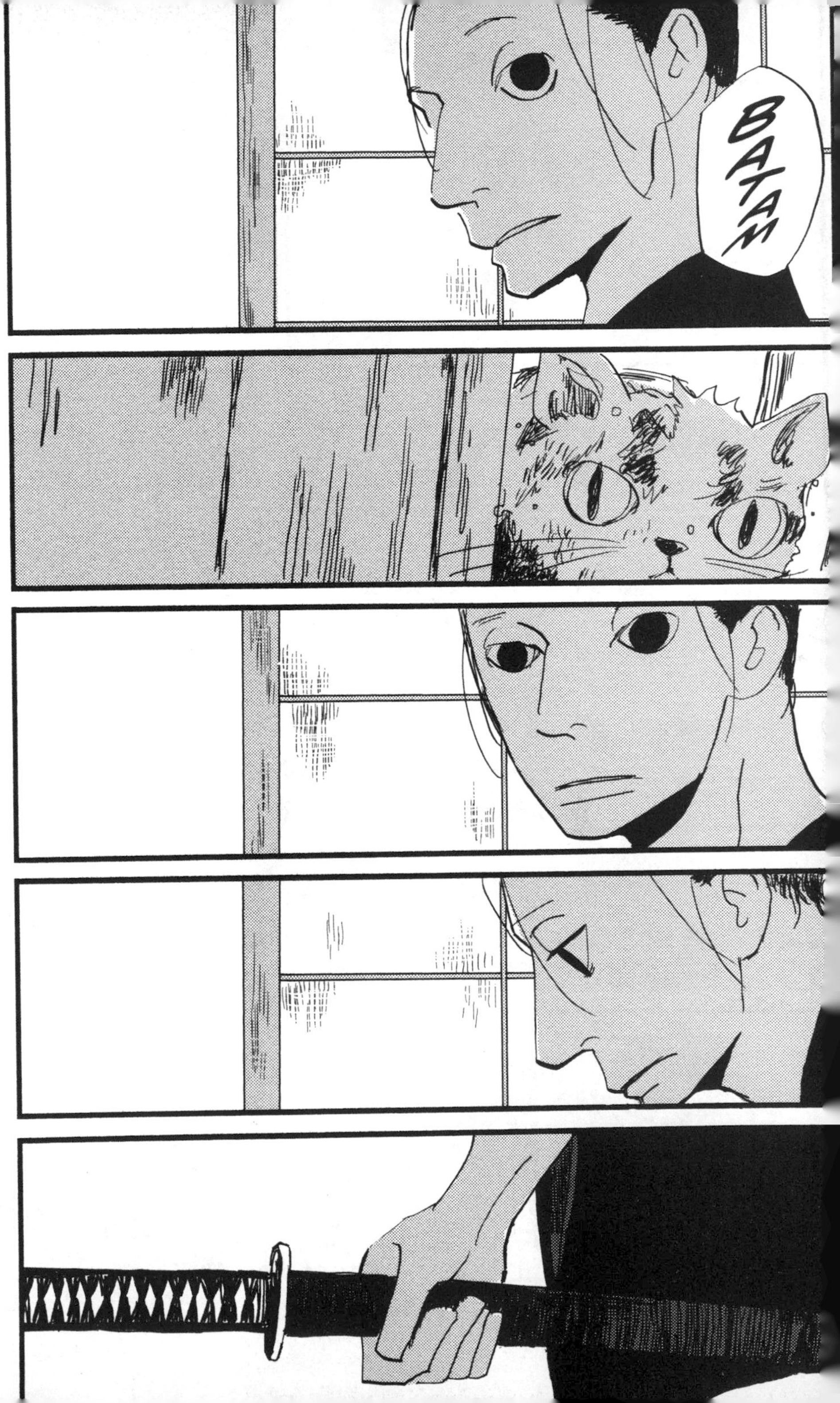
BATAM

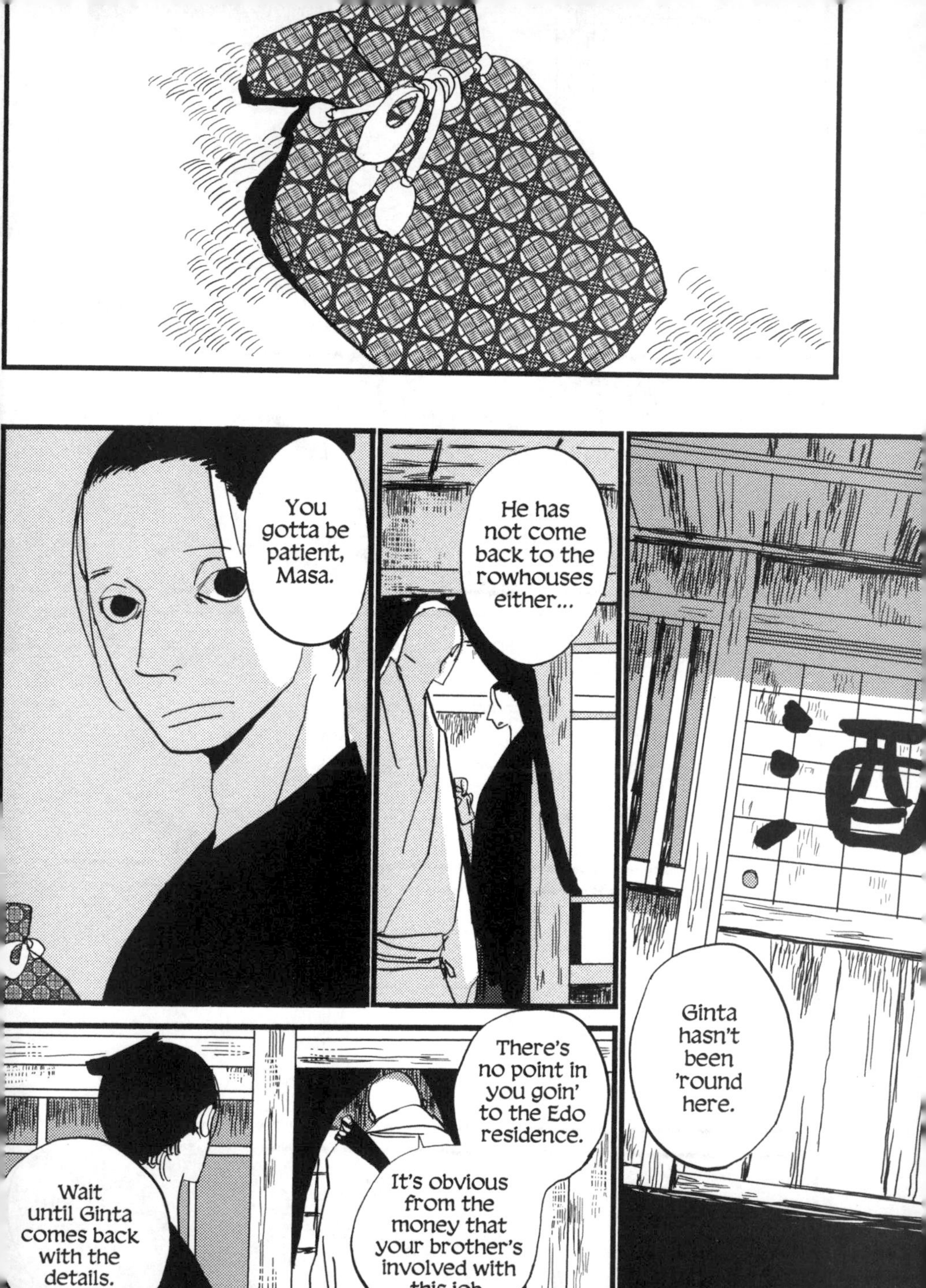
酒
Ginta hasn't been 'round here.
He has not come back to the rowhouses either...
You gotta be patient, Masa.
There's no point in you goin' to the Edo residence.
It's obvious from the money that your brother's involved with this job.
Wait until Ginta comes back with the details.

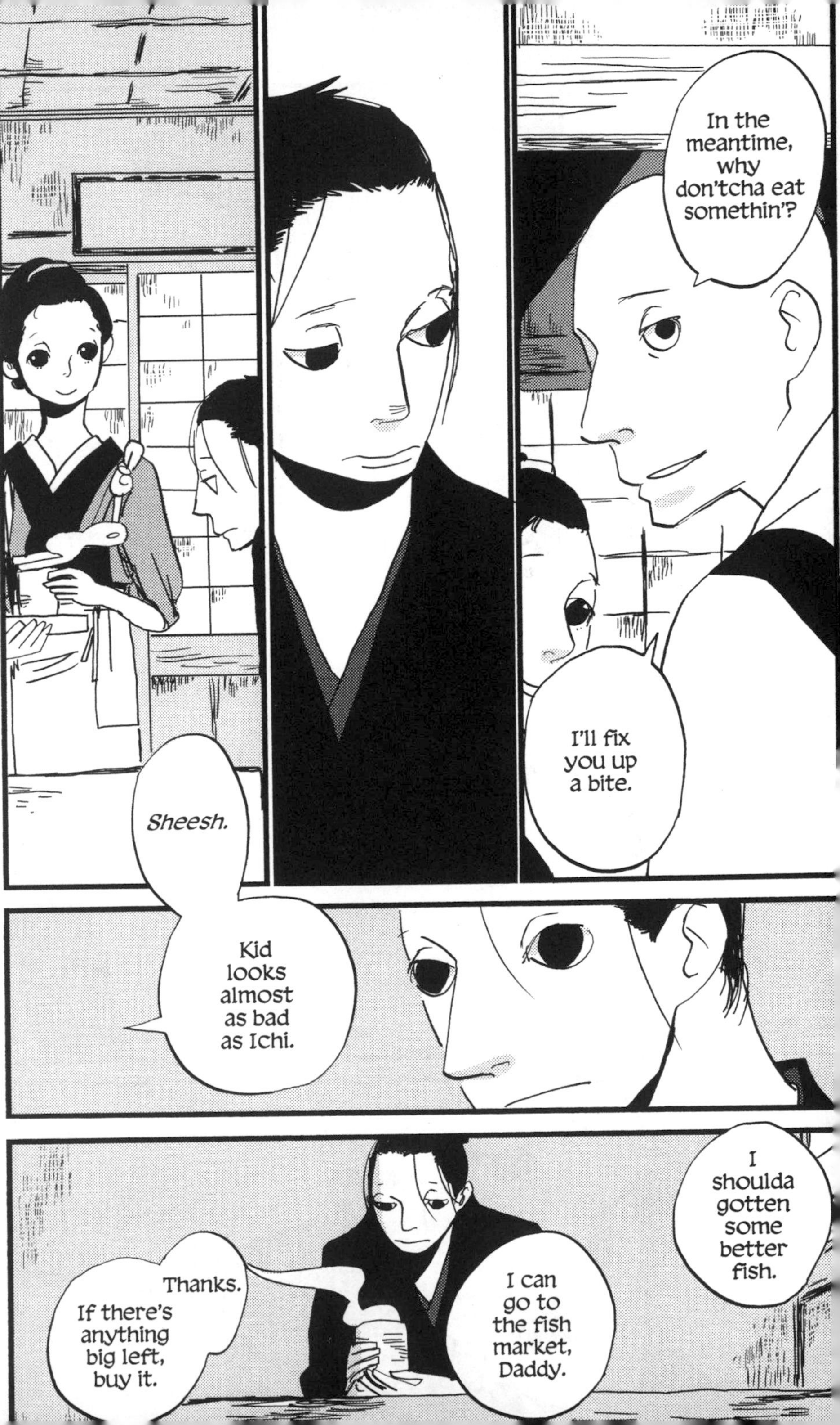
In the meantime, why don'tcha eat somethin'?
I'll fix you up a bite.
Sheesh.
Kid looks almost as bad as Ichi.
I shoulda gotten some better fish.
I can go to the fish market, Daddy.
Thanks. If there's anything big left, buy it.

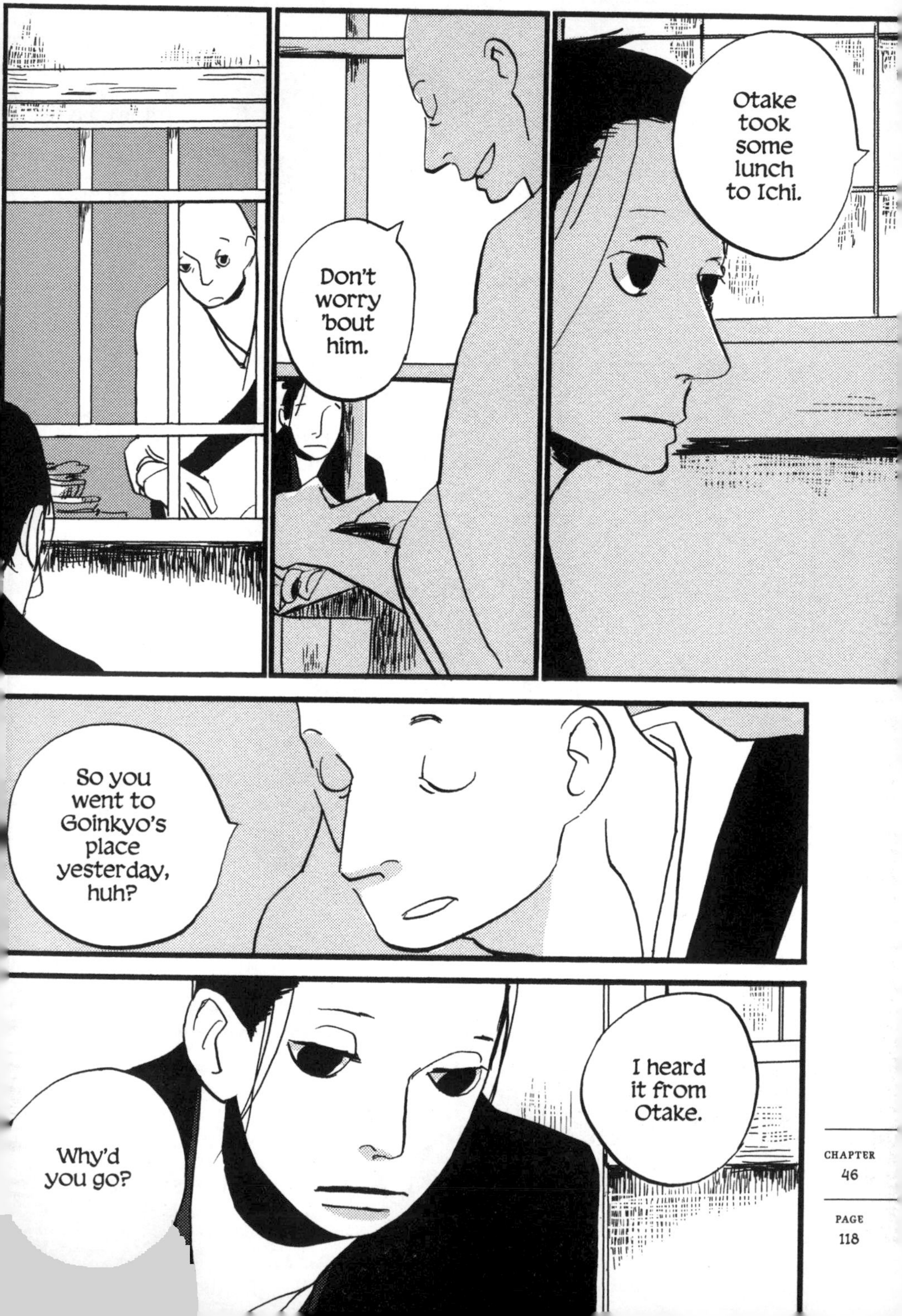
Otake took some lunch to Ichi.
Don't worry 'bout him.
So you went to Goinkyo's place yesterday, huh?
I heard it from Otake.
Why'd you go?

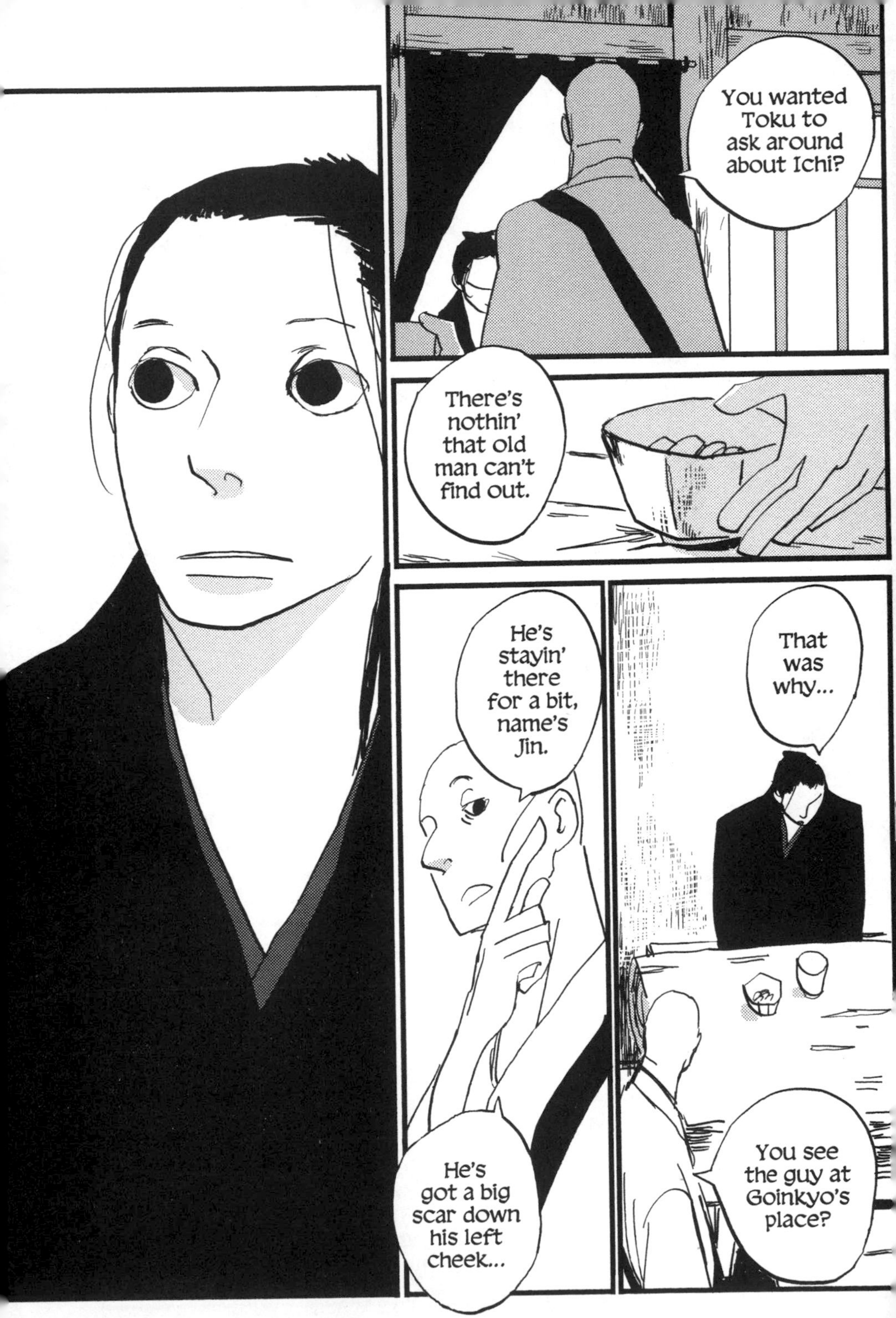
You wanted Toku to ask around about Ichi?
There's nothin' that old man can't find out.
That was why...
You see the guy at Goinkyo's place?
He's stayin' there for a bit, name's Jin.
He's got a big scar down his left cheek...

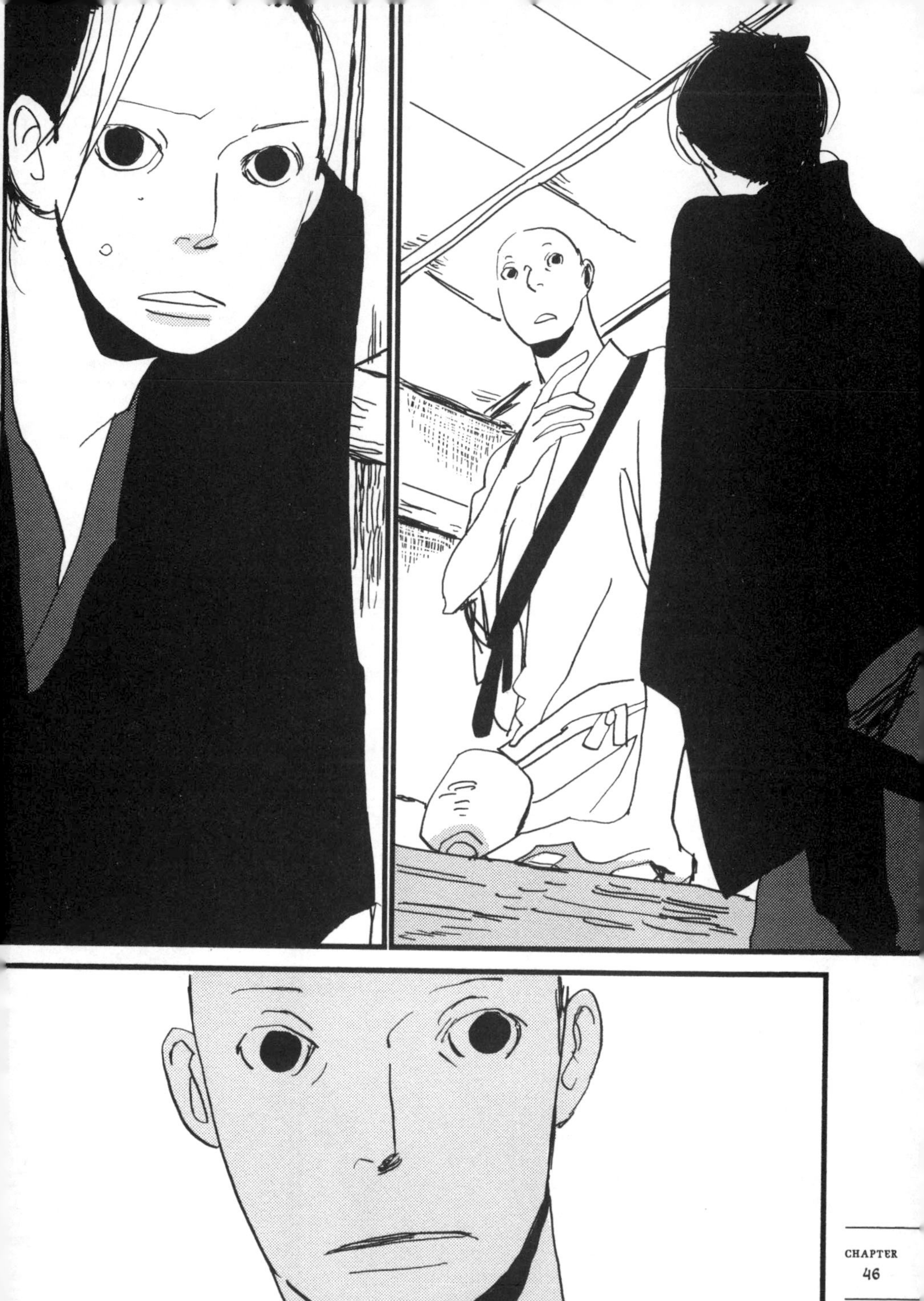

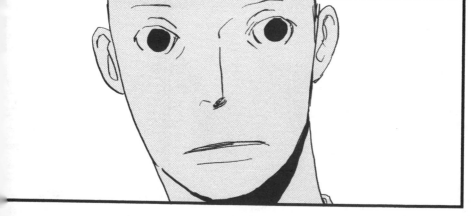

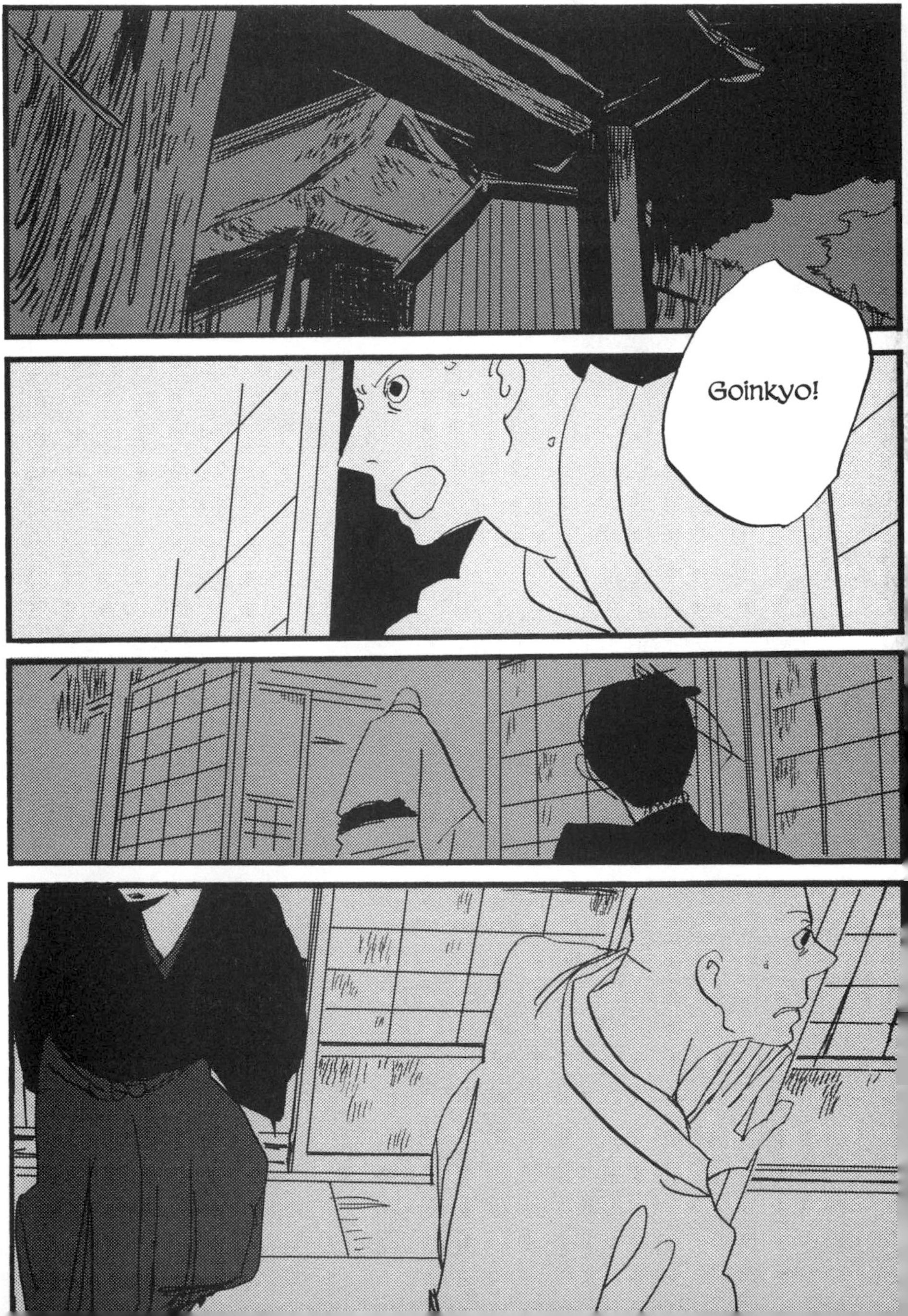
Goinkyo!

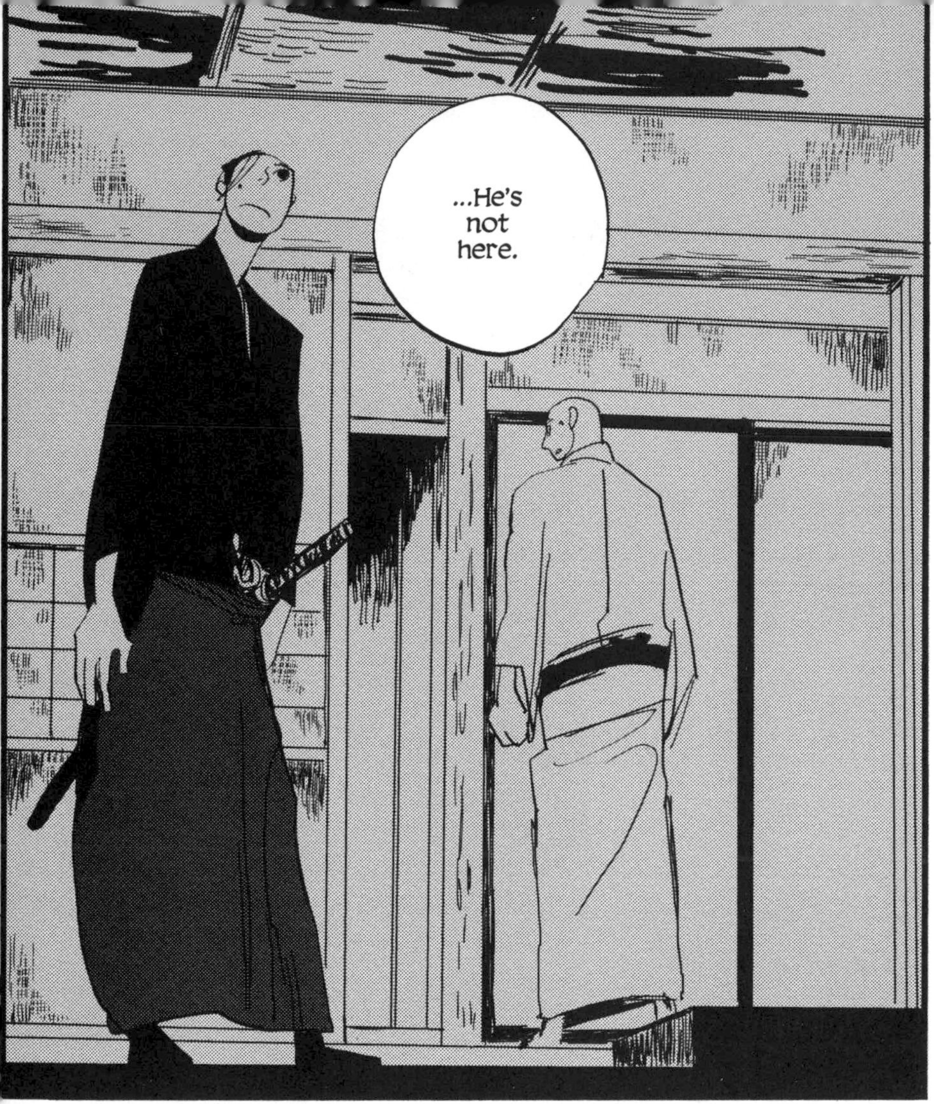
...He's not here.

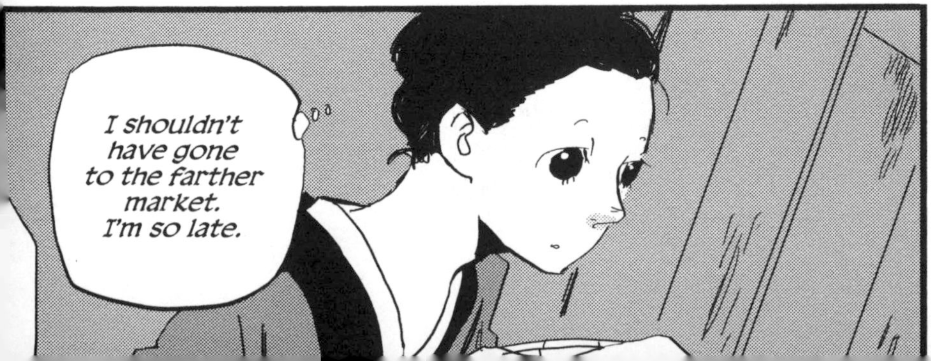
I shouldn't have gone to the farther market. I'm so late.

I wonder if Masa-san is still there.

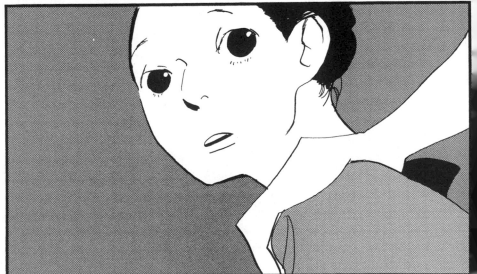

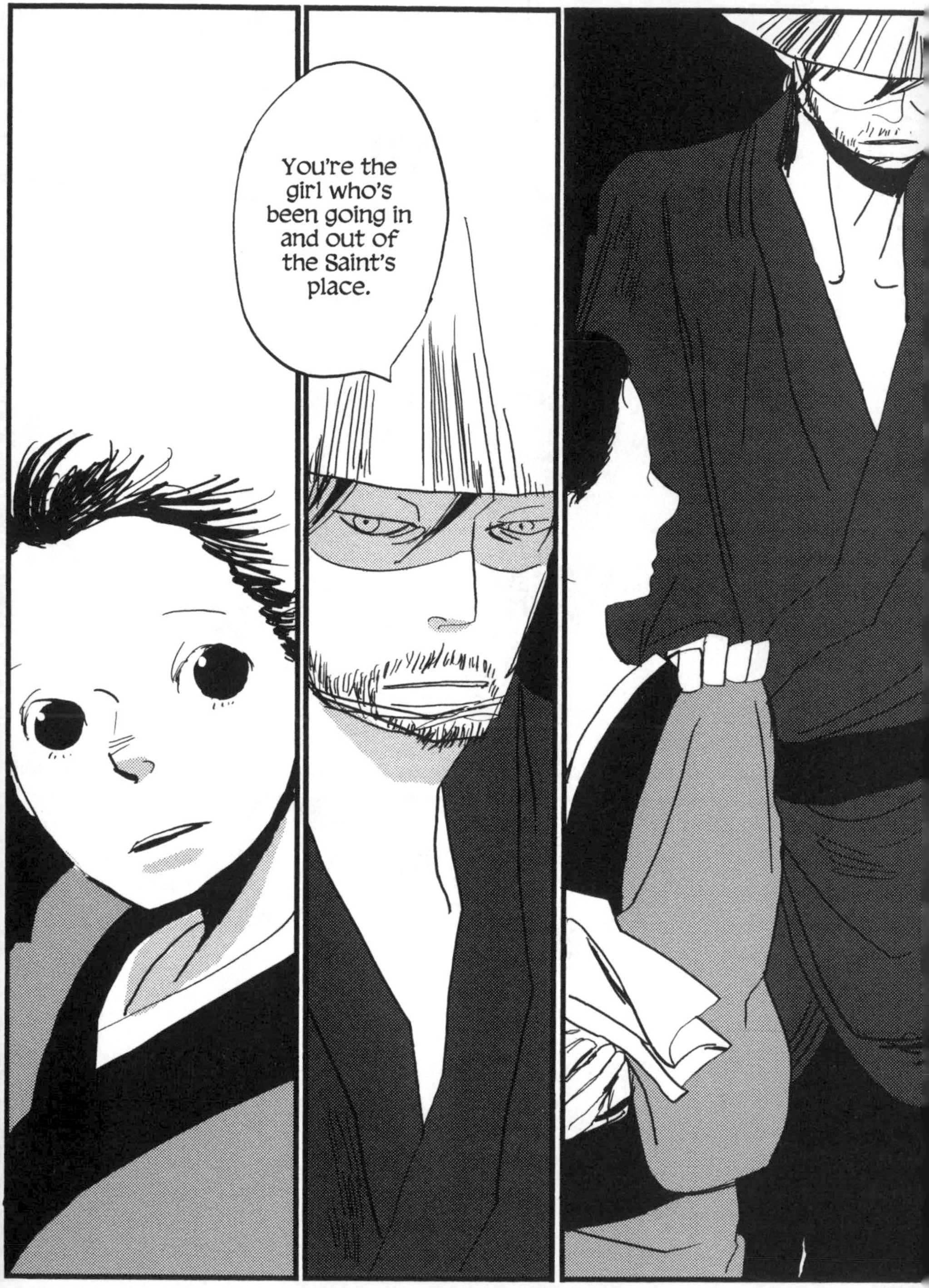
You're the girl who's been going in and out of the Saint's place.

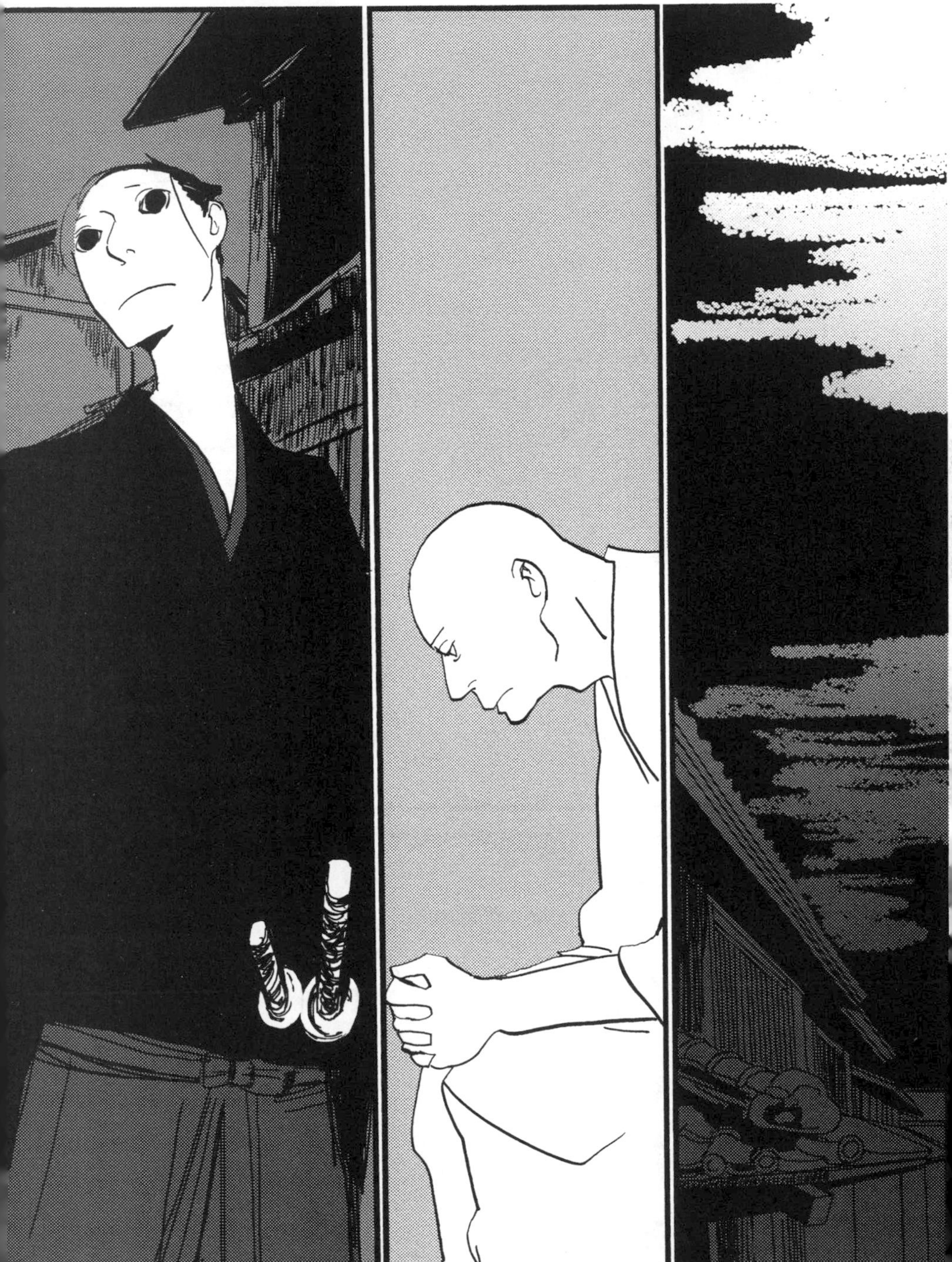

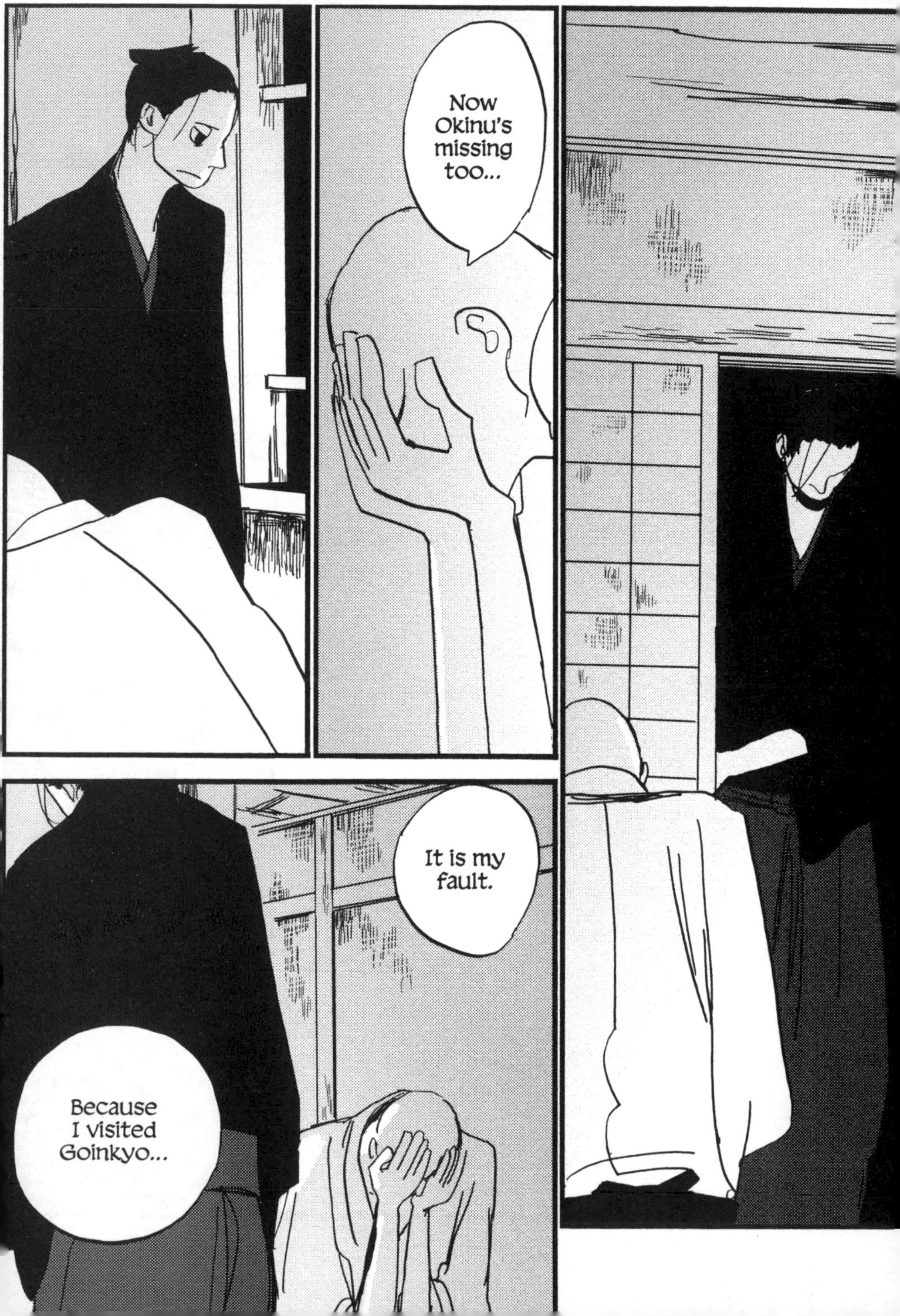
Now Okinu's missing too...
It is my fault.
Because I visited Goinkyo...

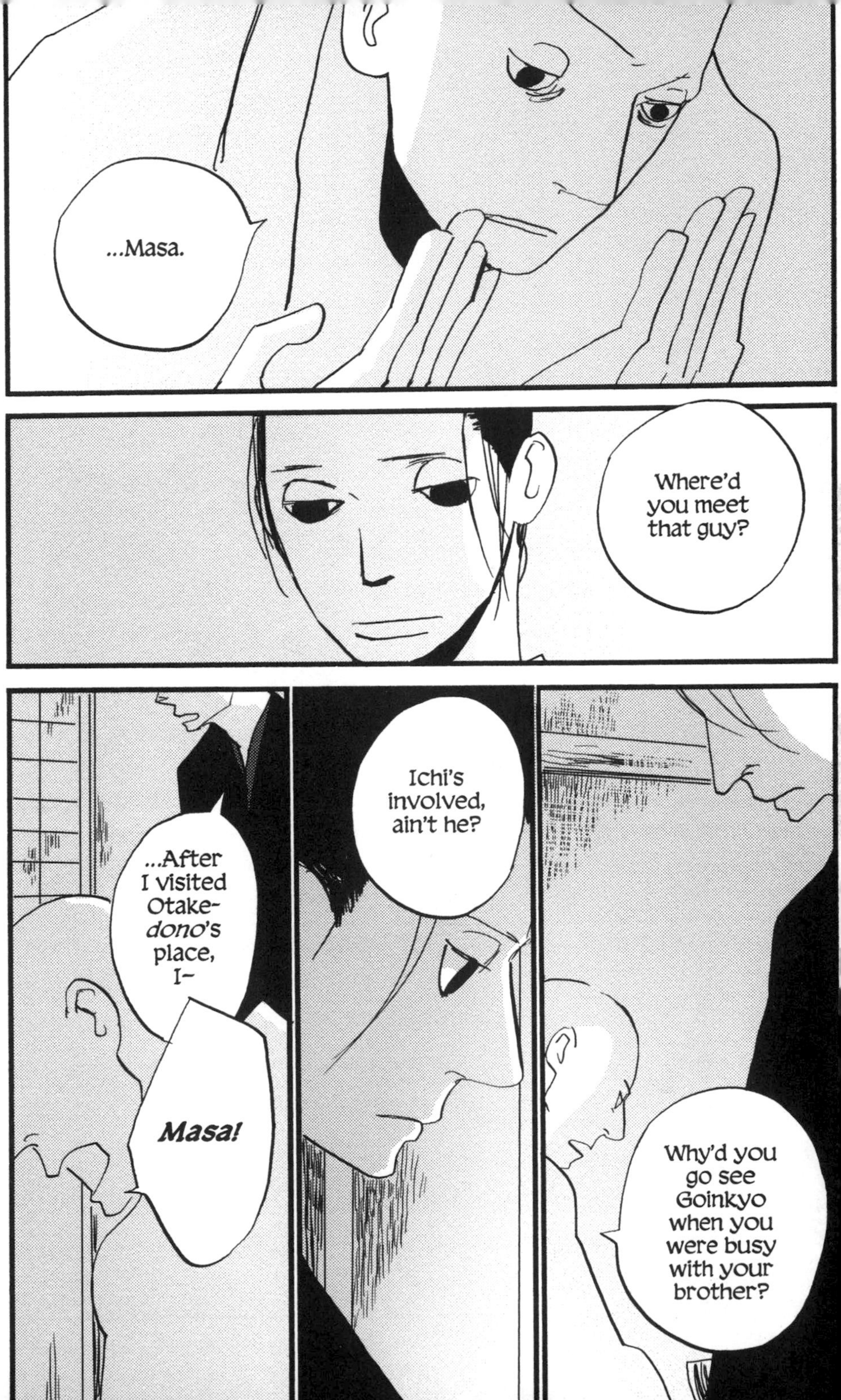
...Masa.
Where'd you meet that guy?
Why'd you go see Goinkyo when you were busy with your brother?
Ichi's involved, ain't he?
...After I visited Otake-*dono*'s place, I–
Masa!

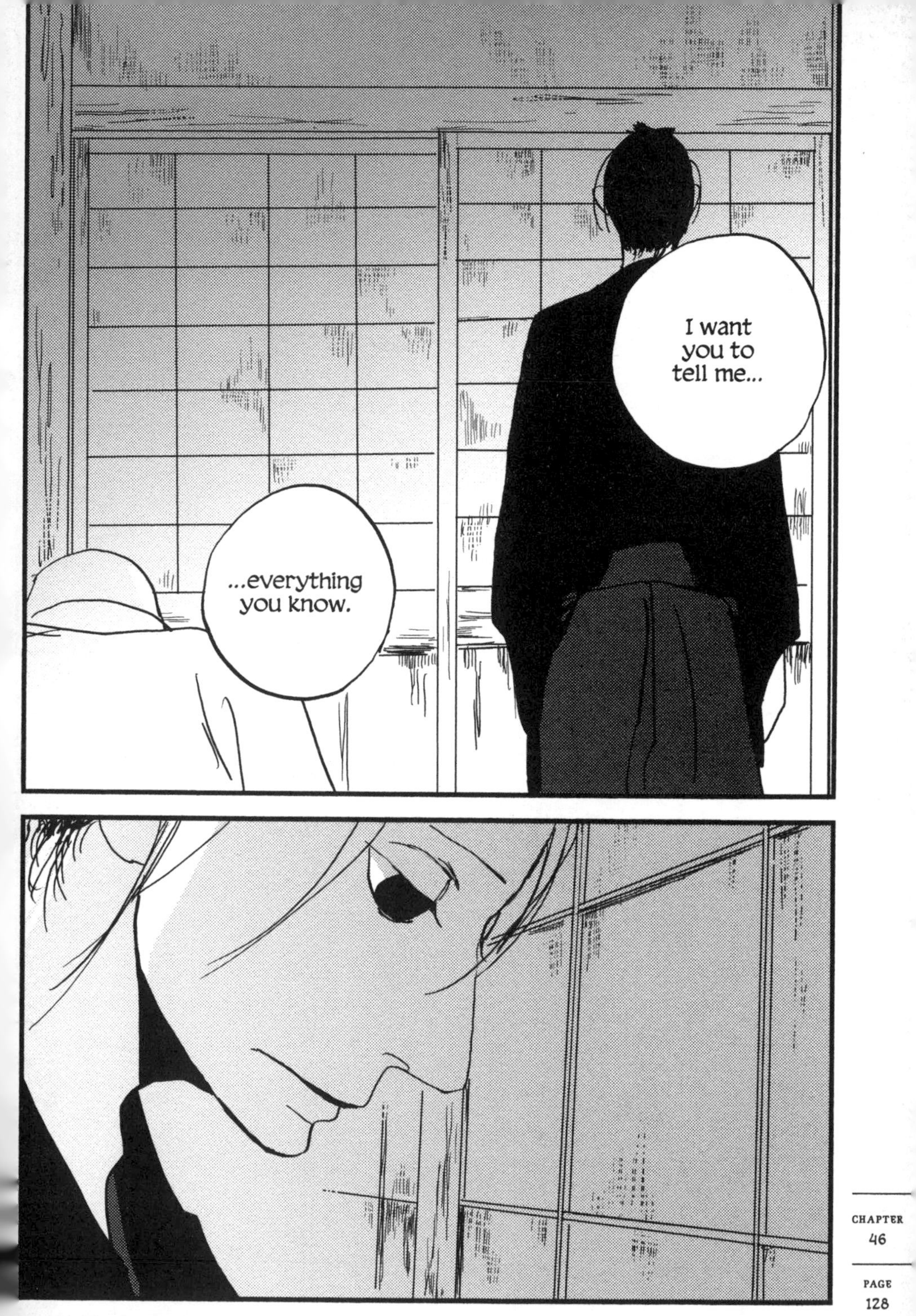
I want you to tell me...
...everything you know.

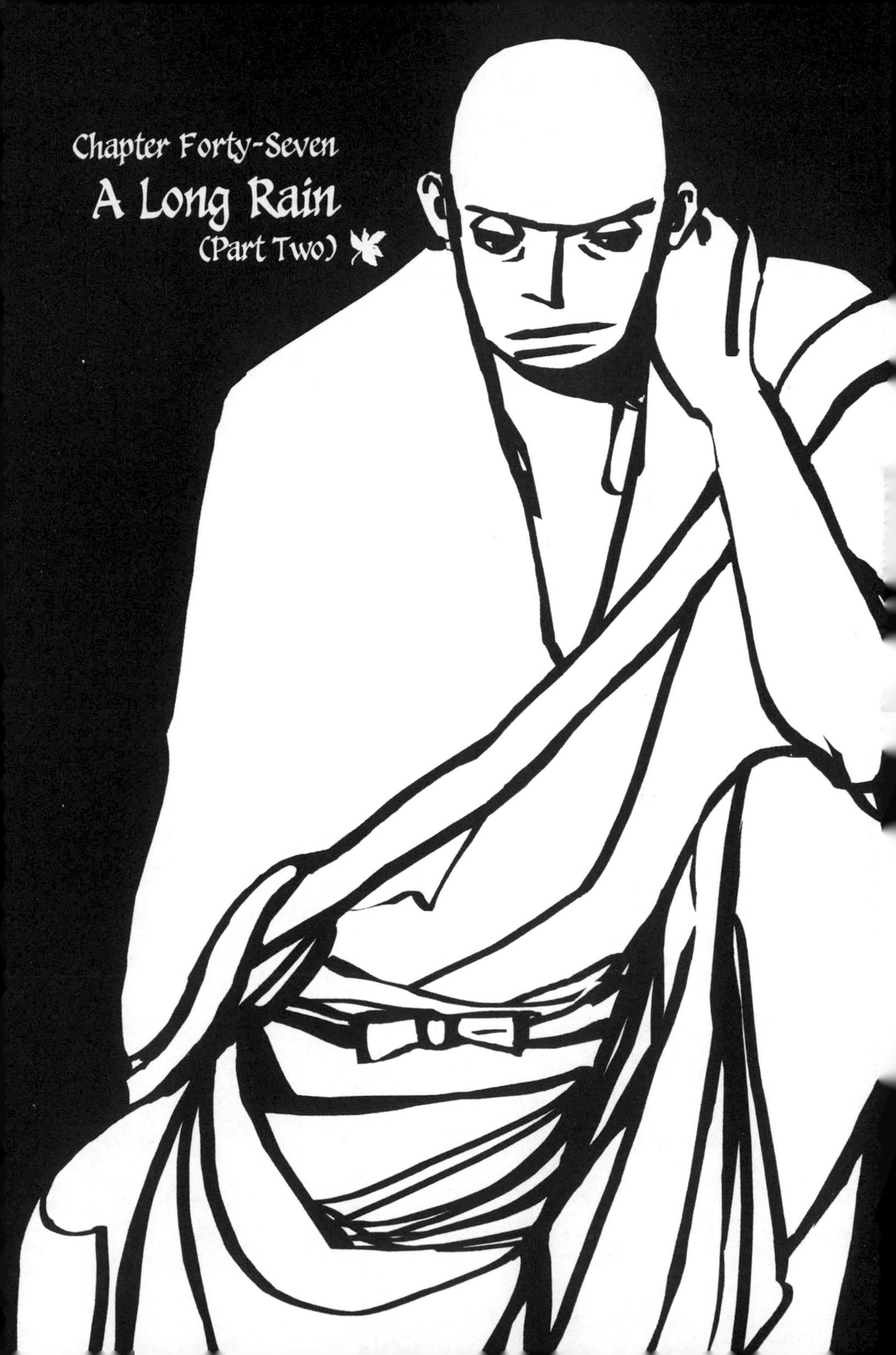
Chapter Forty-Seven
A Long Rain
(Part Two)

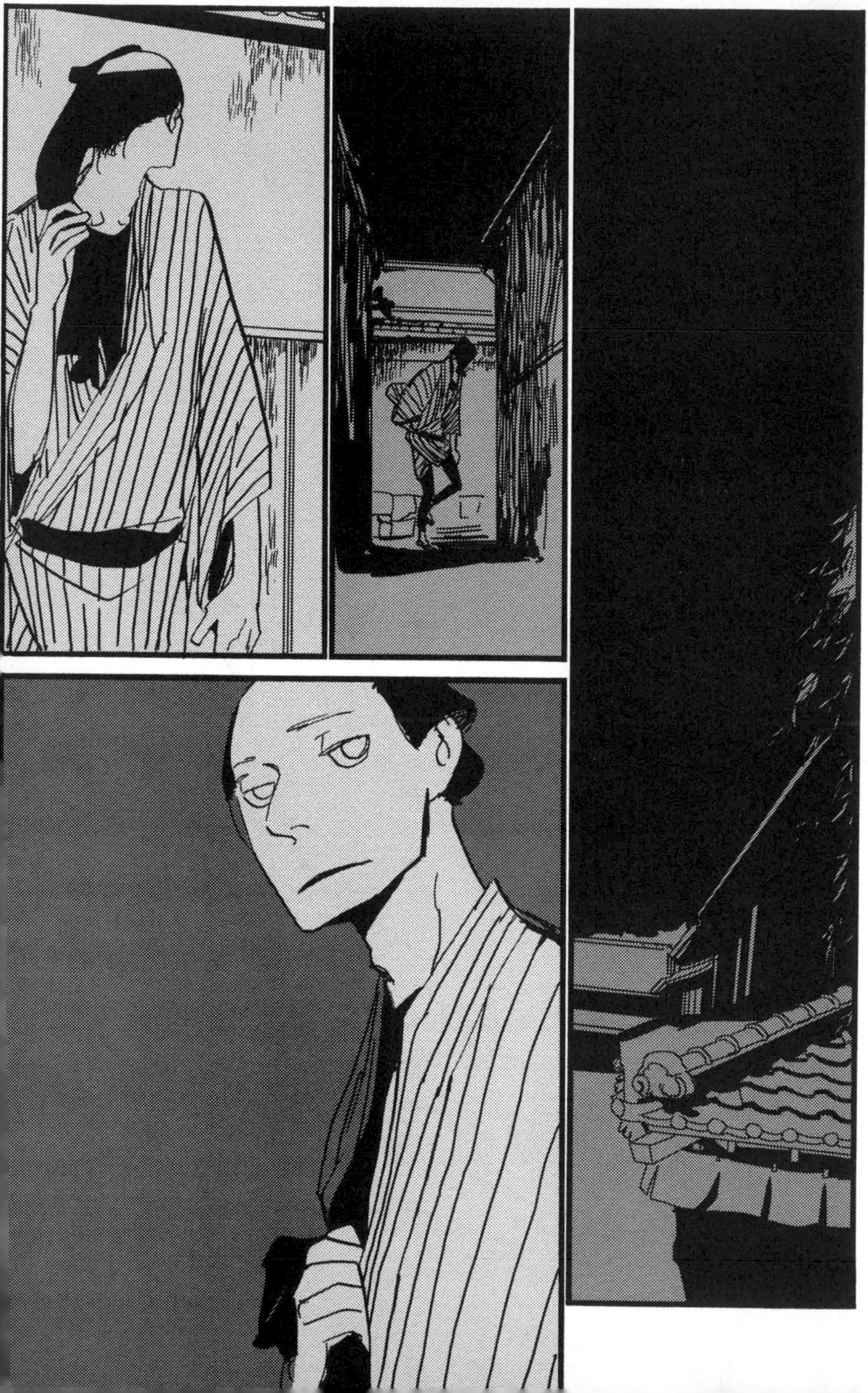

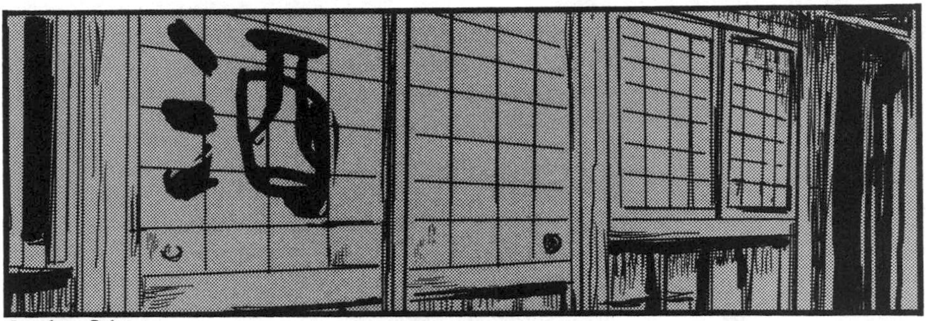

On sign: Sake

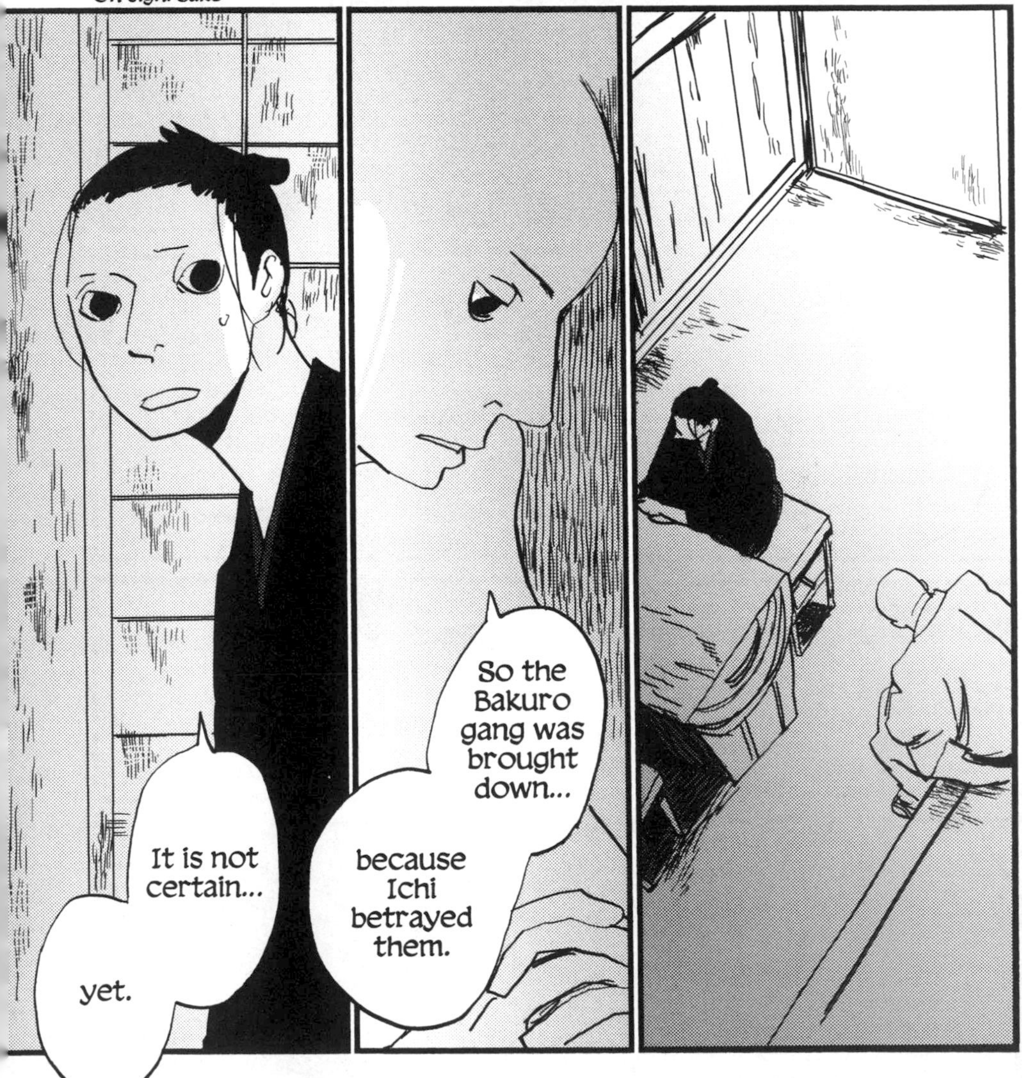
So the Bakuro gang was brought down...
because Ichi betrayed them.
It is not certain...
yet.

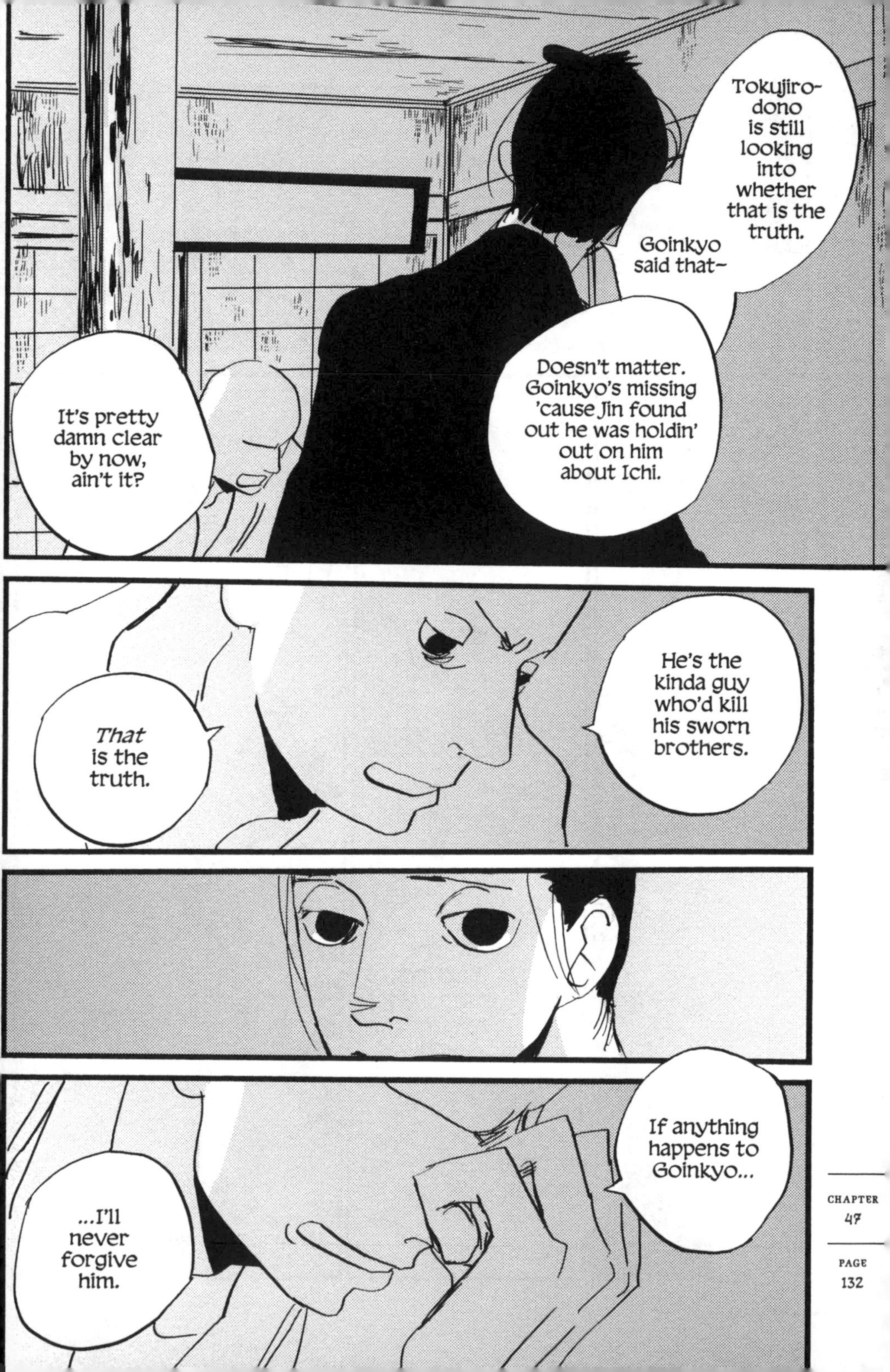
Tokujiro-dono is still looking into whether that is the truth.
Goinkyo said that~
Doesn't matter. Goinkyo's missing 'cause Jin found out he was holdin' out on him about Ichi.
It's pretty damn clear by now, ain't it?
He's the kinda guy who'd kill his sworn brothers.
That is the truth.
If anything happens to Goinkyo...
...I'll never forgive him.

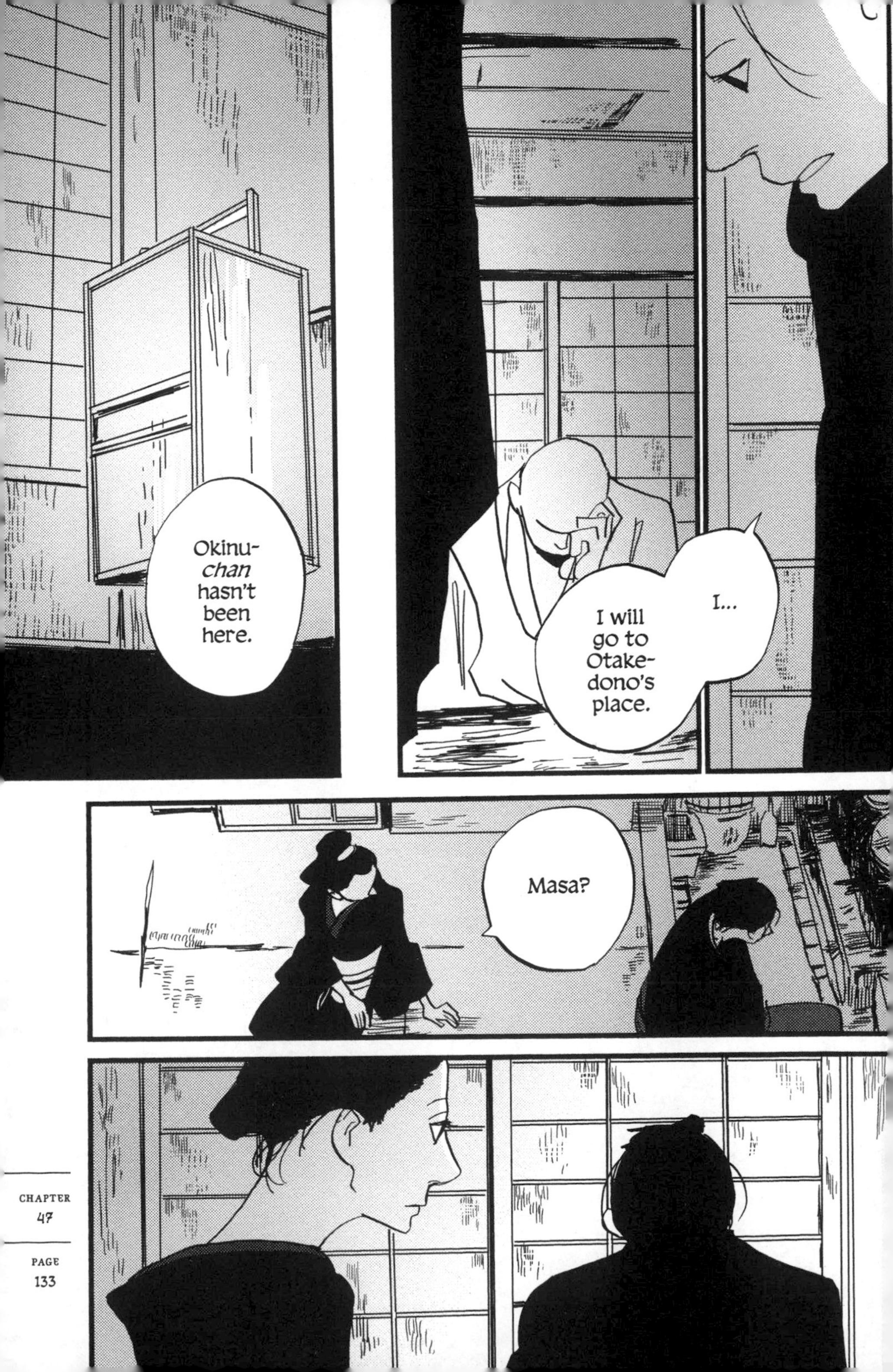
I...
I will go to Otake-dono's place.
Okinu-*chan* hasn't been here.
Masa?

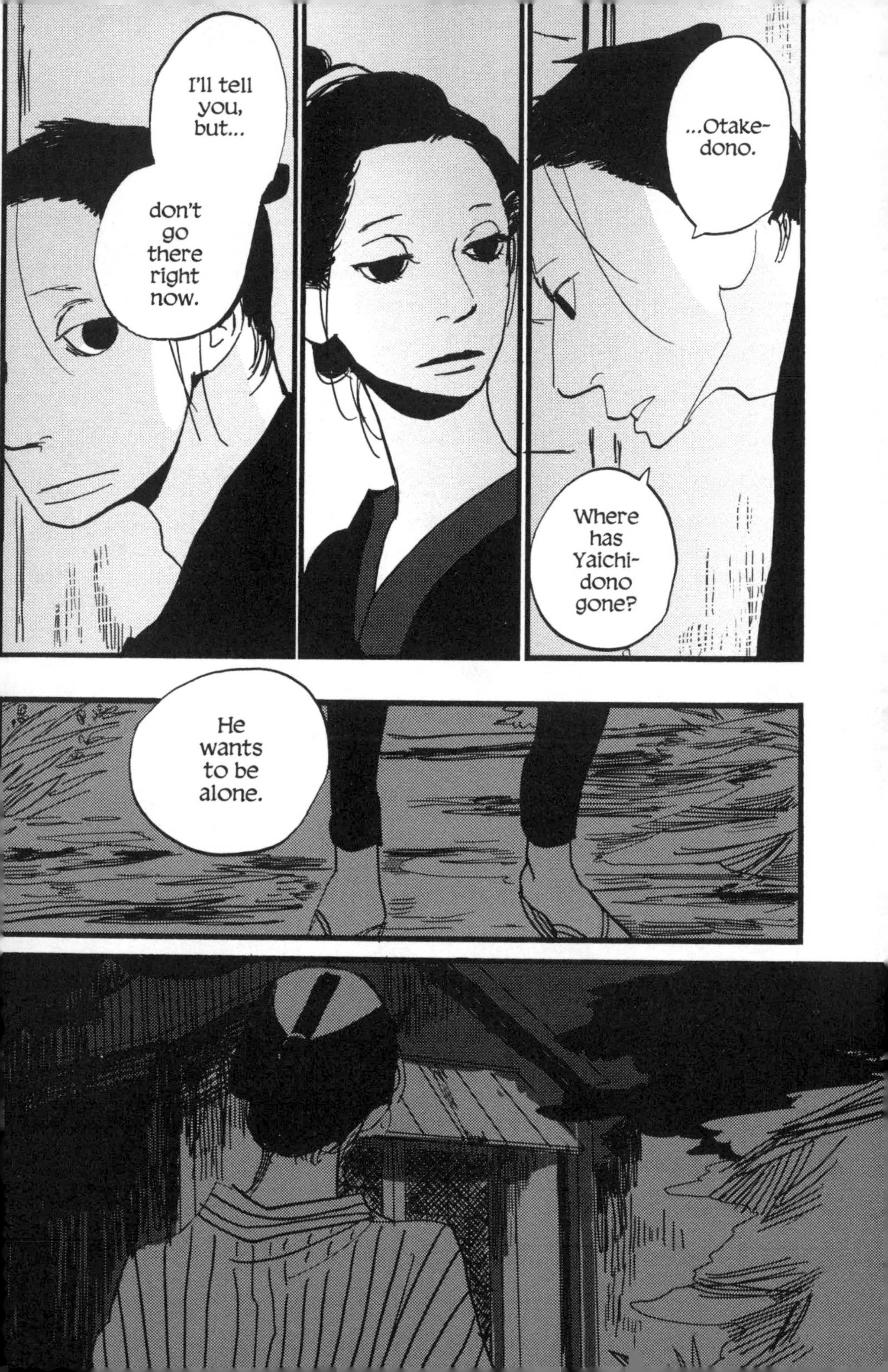
...Otake-dono.
Where has Yaichi-dono gone?
I'll tell you, but...
don't go there right now.
He wants to be alone.

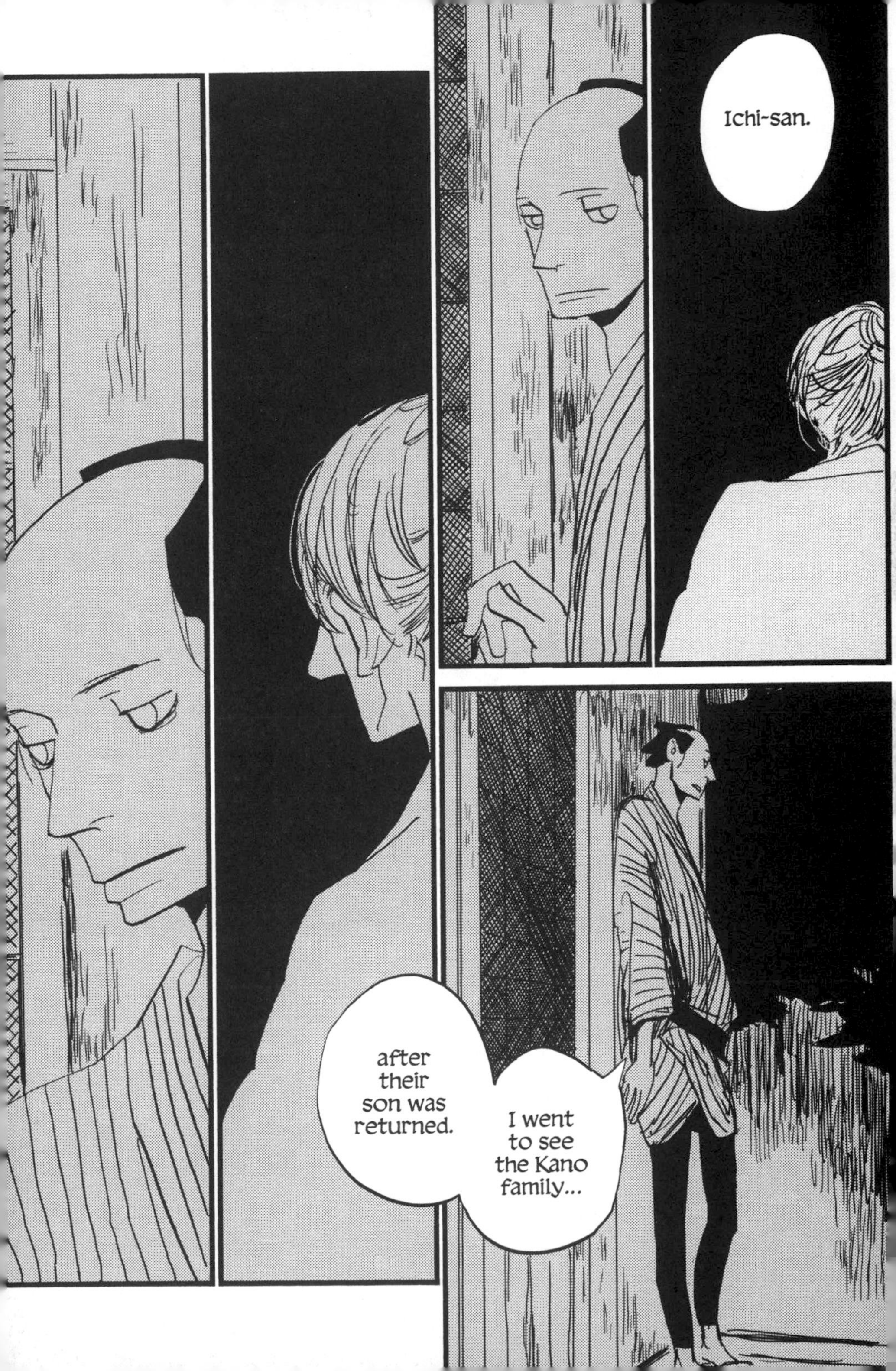
Ichi-san.
I went to see the Kano family...
after their son was returned.

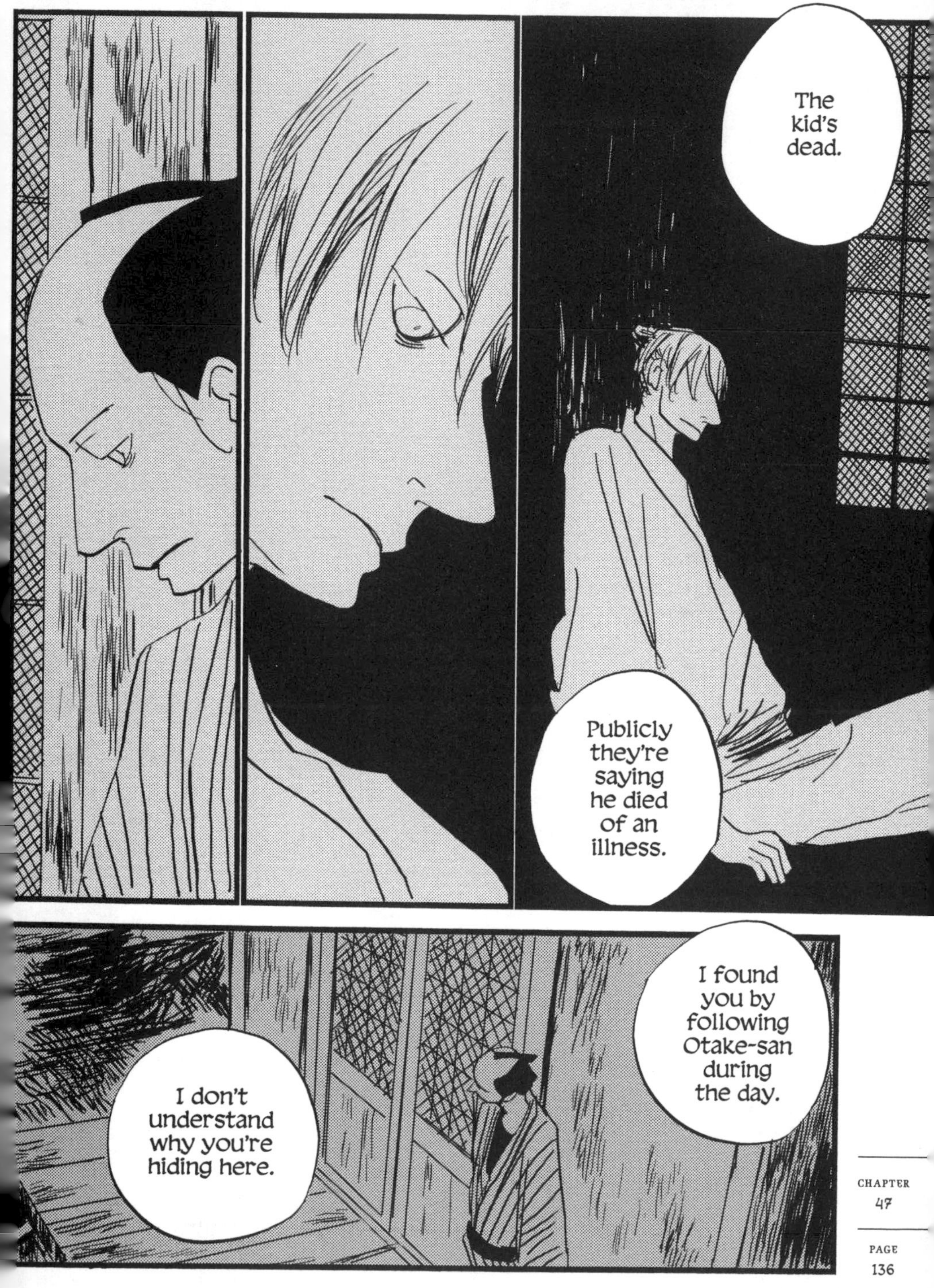
The kid's dead.
Publicly they're saying he died of an illness.
I found you by following Otake-san during the day.
I don't understand why you're hiding here.

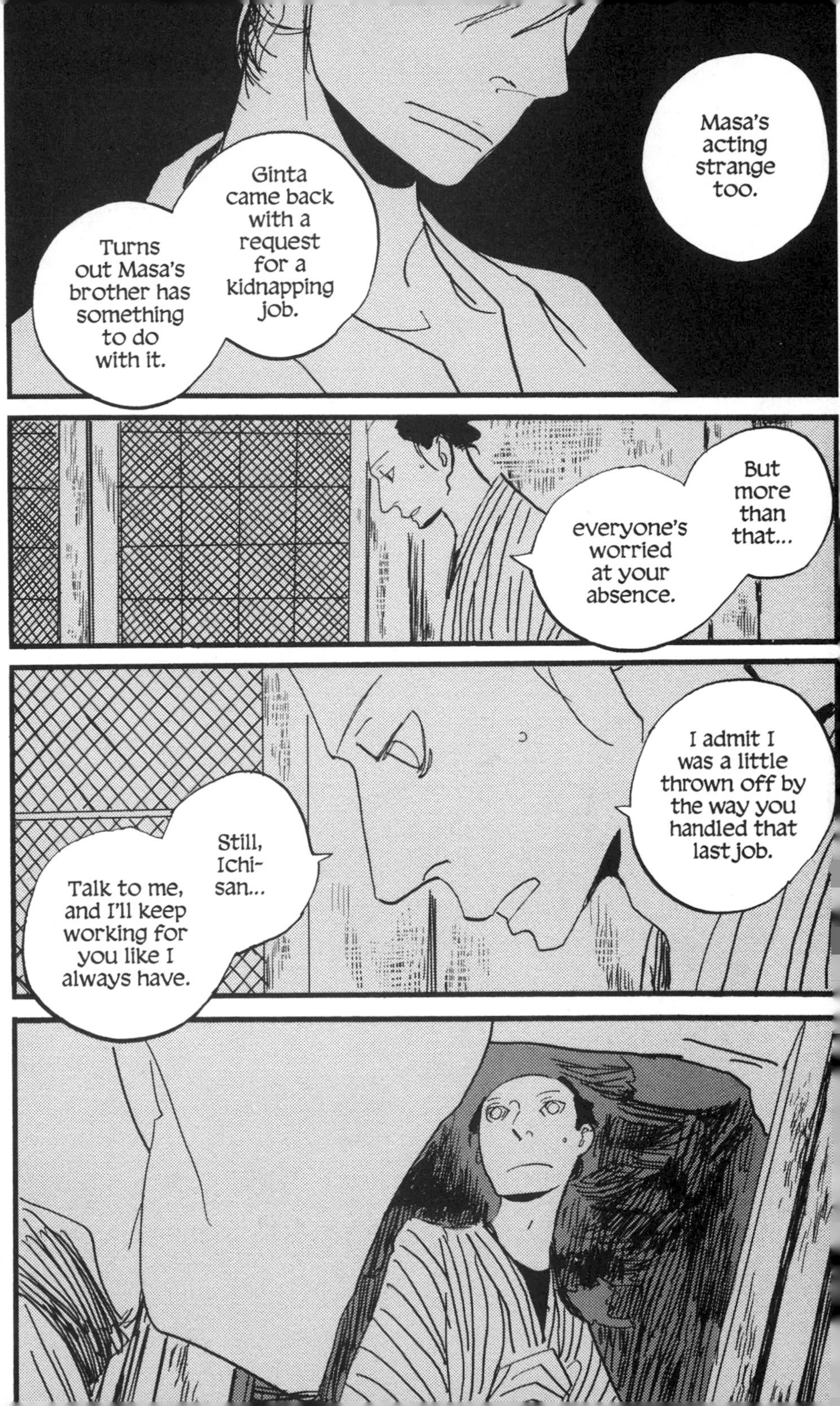
Masa's acting strange too.
Ginta came back with a request for a kidnapping job.
Turns out Masa's brother has something to do with it.
But more than that...
everyone's worried at your absence.
I admit I was a little thrown off by the way you handled that last job.
Still, Ichi-san...
Talk to me, and I'll keep working for you like I always have.

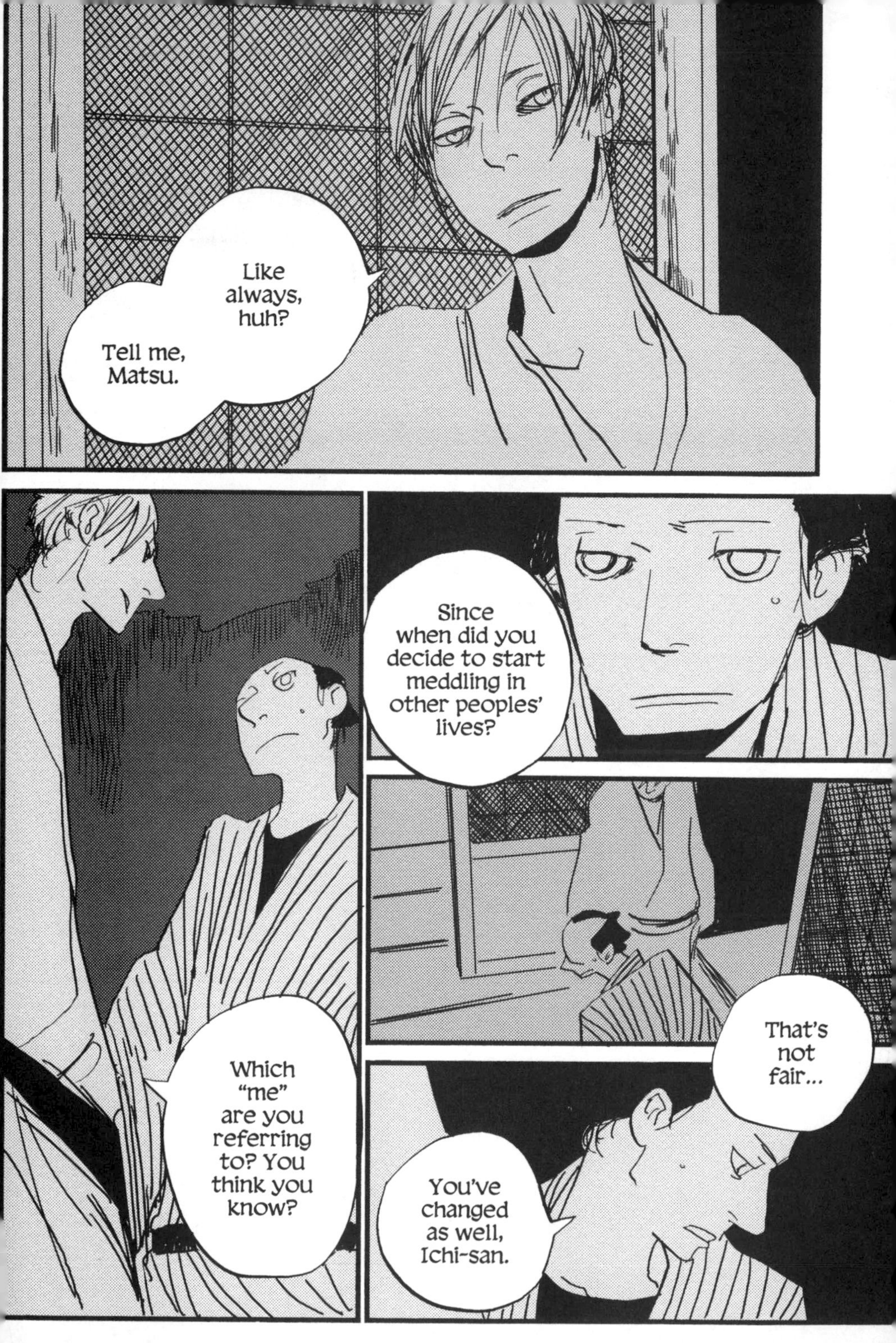
Like always, huh?
Tell me, Matsu.
Since when did you decide to start meddling in other peoples' lives?
That's not fair...
You've changed as well, Ichi-san.
Which "me" are you referring to? You think you know?

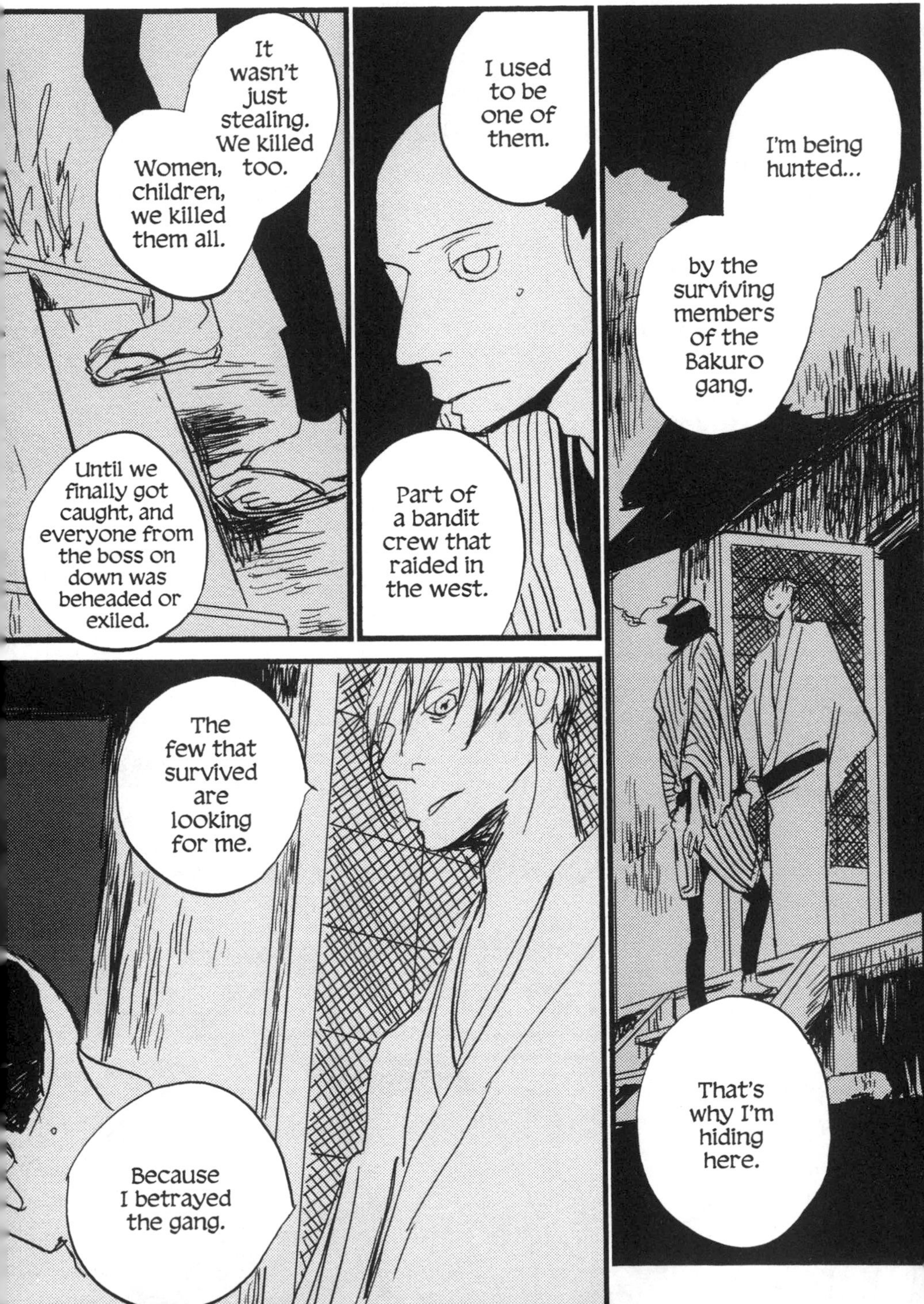
I'm being hunted...
by the surviving members of the Bakuro gang.
That's why I'm hiding here.
I used to be one of them.
Part of a bandit crew that raided in the west.
It wasn't just stealing. We killed too.
Women, children, we killed them all.
Until we finally got caught, and everyone from the boss on down was beheaded or exiled.
The few that survived are looking for me.
Because I betrayed the gang.

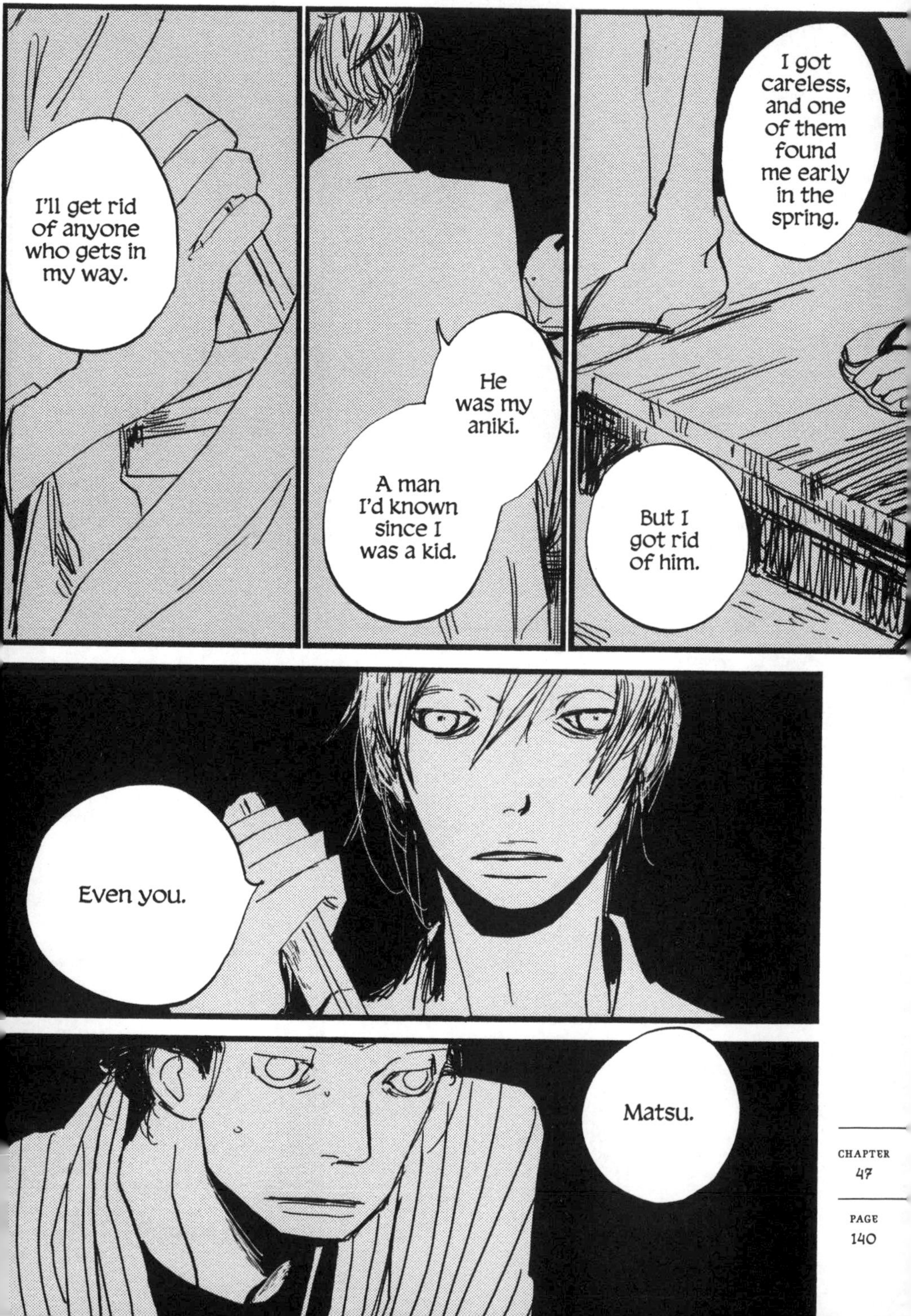
I got careless, and one of them found me early in the spring.
But I got rid of him.
He was my aniki.
A man I'd known since I was a kid.
I'll get rid of anyone who gets in my way.
Even you.
Matsu.

That's why I started the Five Leaves.

In other words...

...you're all useful to me only as long as you help me get my hands on enough money to protect myself.

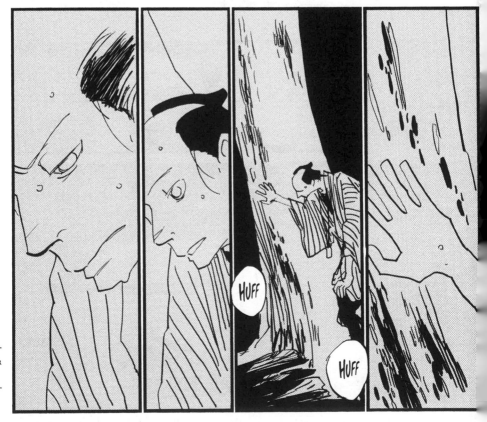

HUFF

HUFF

That's not the man...

I fell in love with...

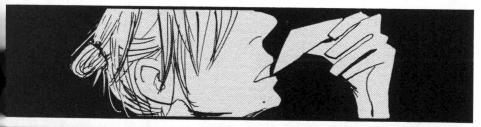

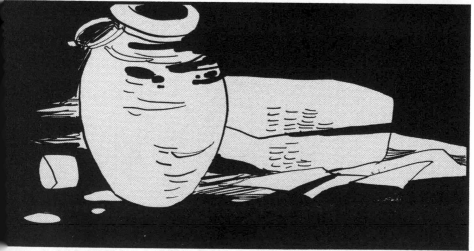

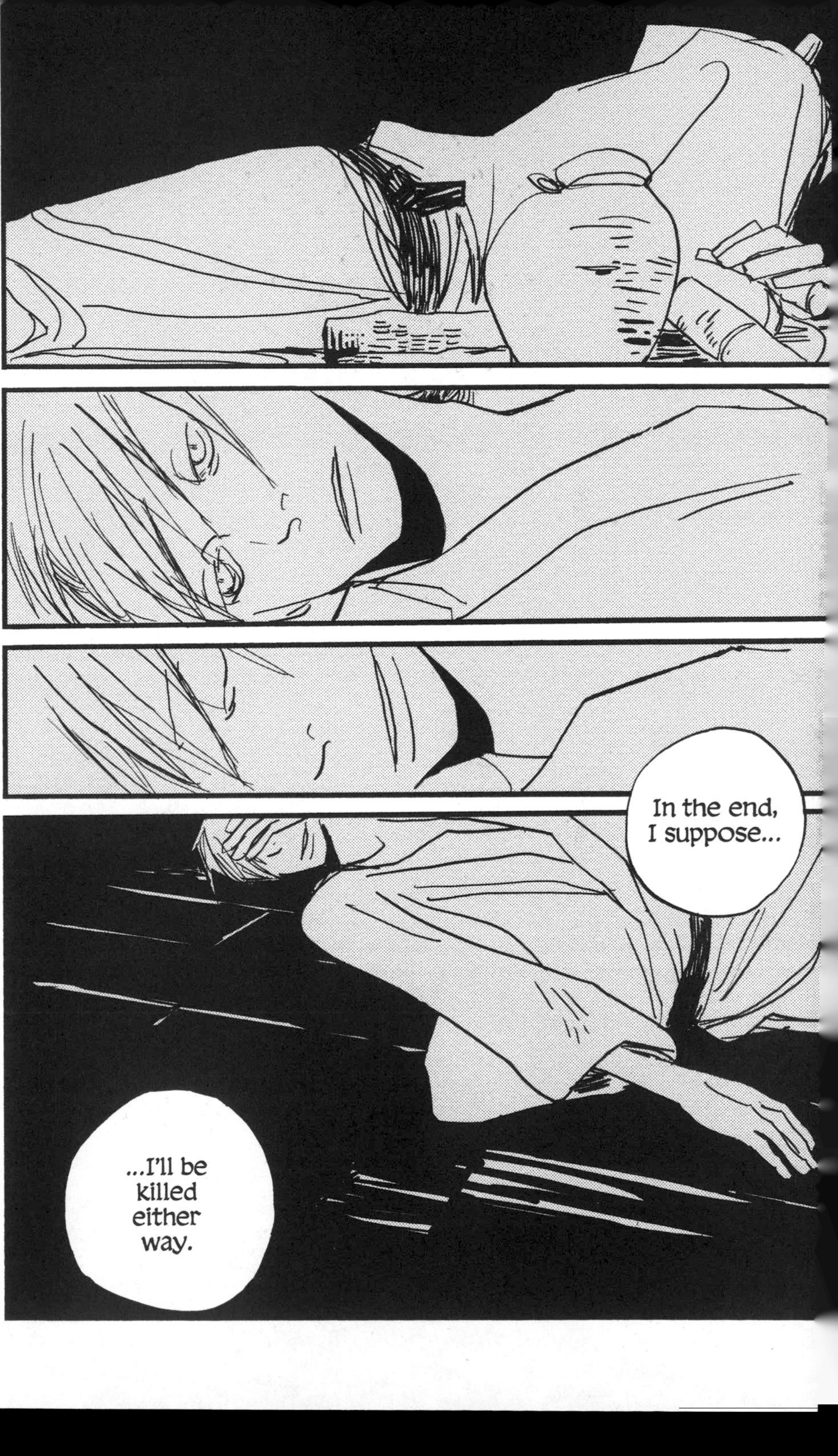
In the end, I suppose...
...I'll be killed either way.

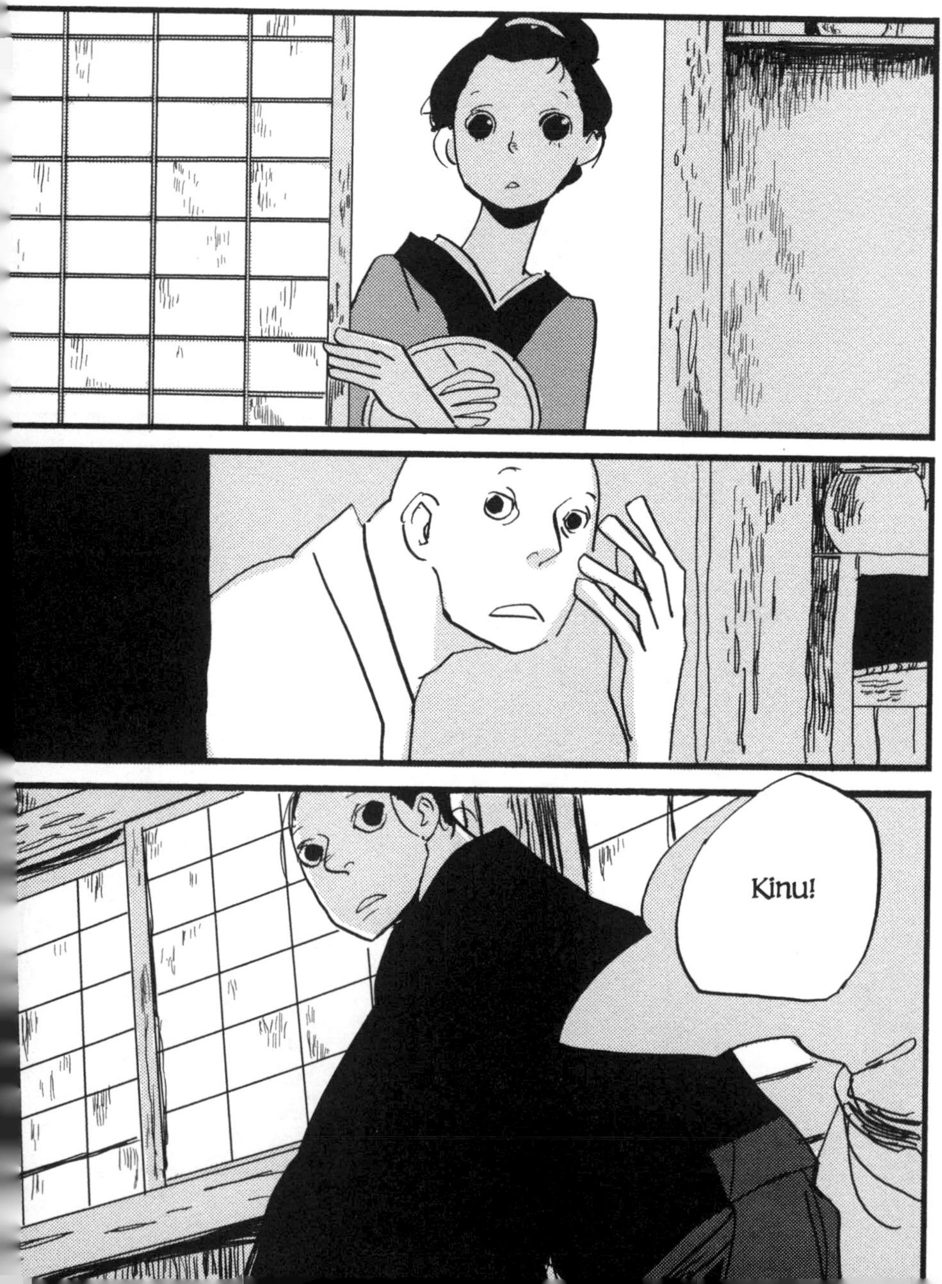
Kinu!

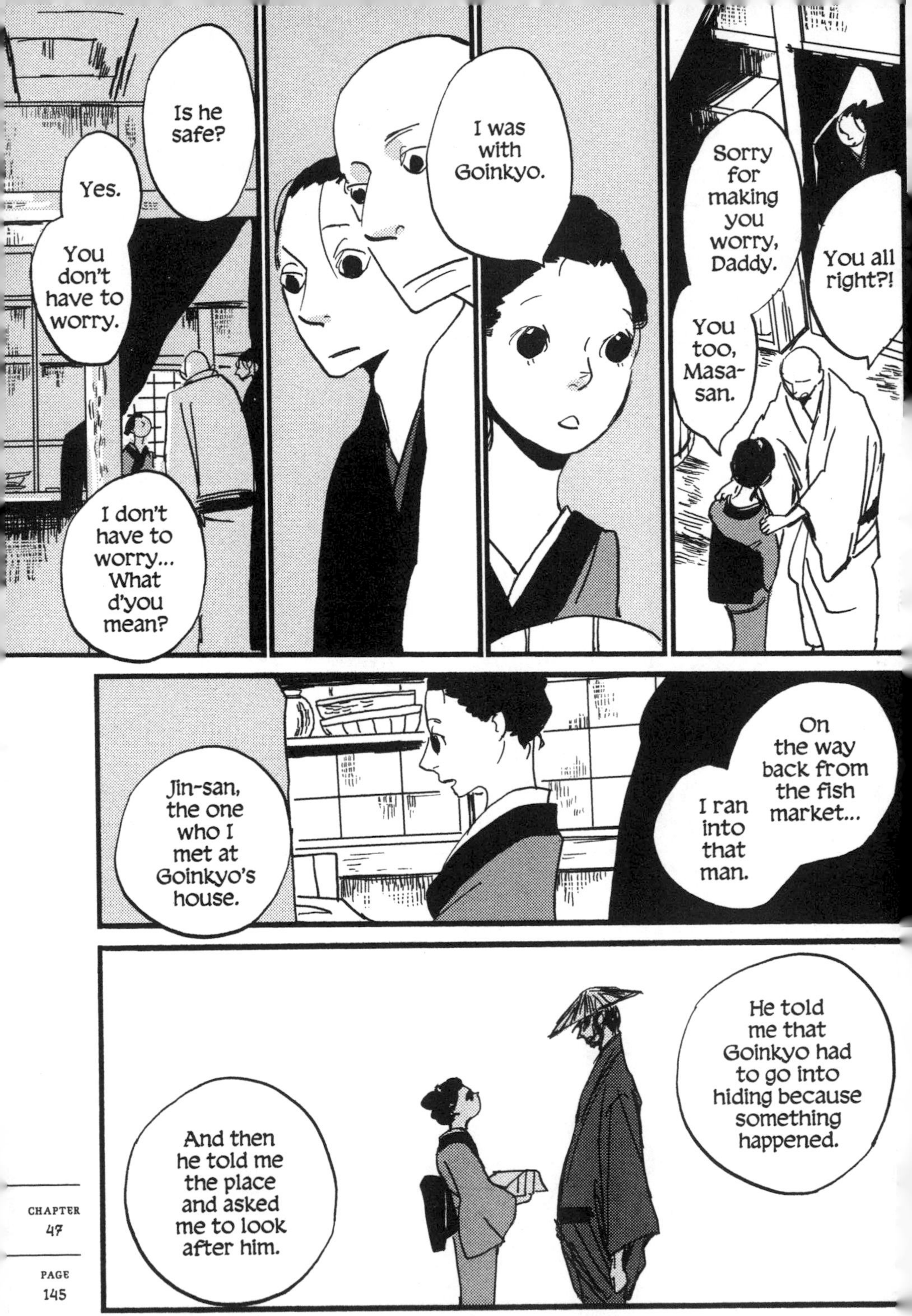
You all right?!
Sorry for making you worry, Daddy.
You too, Masa-san.
I was with Goinkyo.
Is he safe?
Yes.
You don't have to worry.
I don't have to worry... What d'you mean?
On the way back from the fish market...
I ran into that man.
Jin-san, the one who I met at Goinkyo's house.
He told me that Goinkyo had to go into hiding because something happened.
And then he told me the place and asked me to look after him.

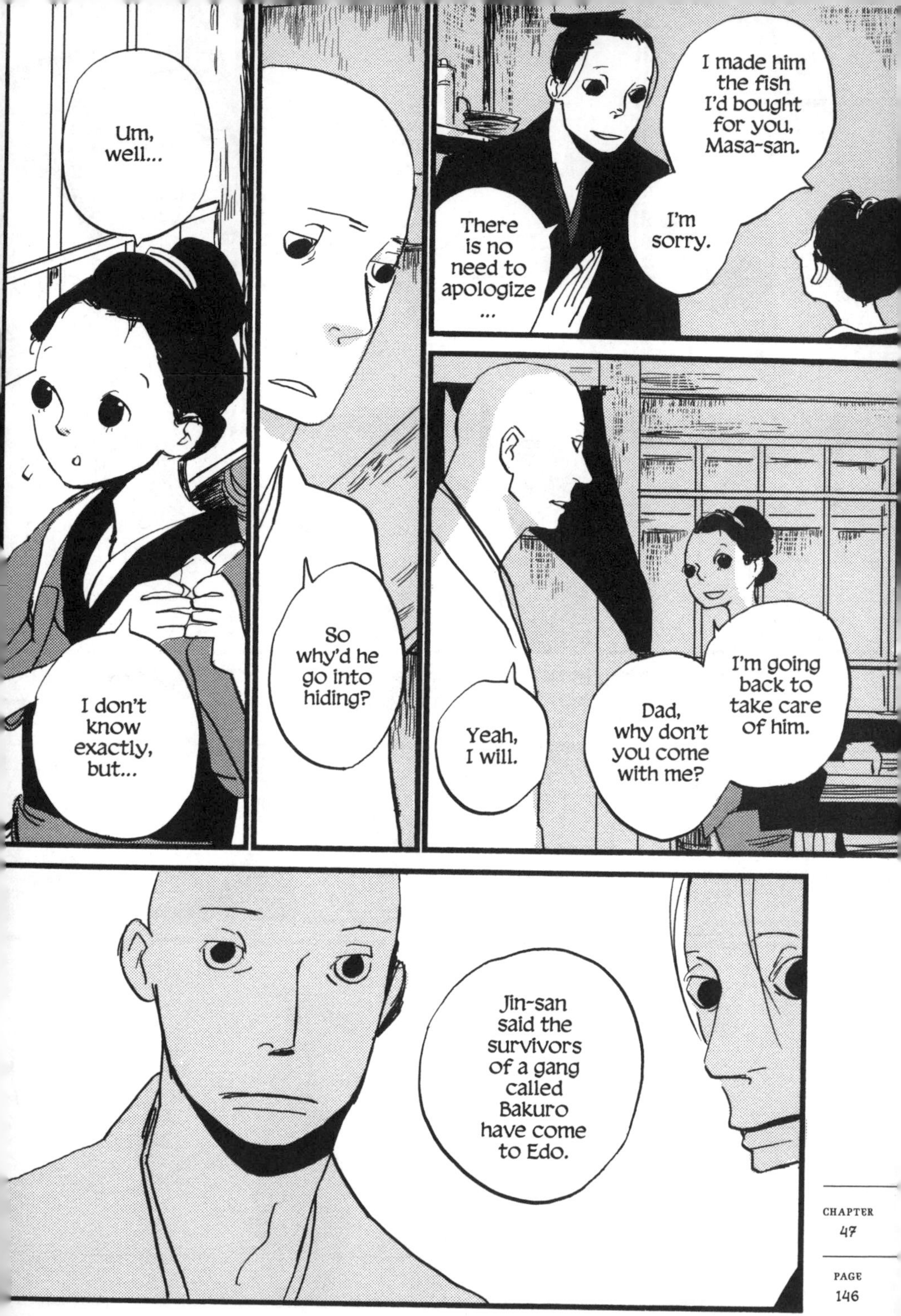
I made him the fish I'd bought for you, Masa-san.
I'm sorry.
There is no need to apologize ...
I'm going back to take care of him.
Dad, why don't you come with me?
Yeah, I will.
So why'd he go into hiding?
Um, well...
I don't know exactly, but...
Jin-san said the survivors of a gang called Bakuro have come to Edo.

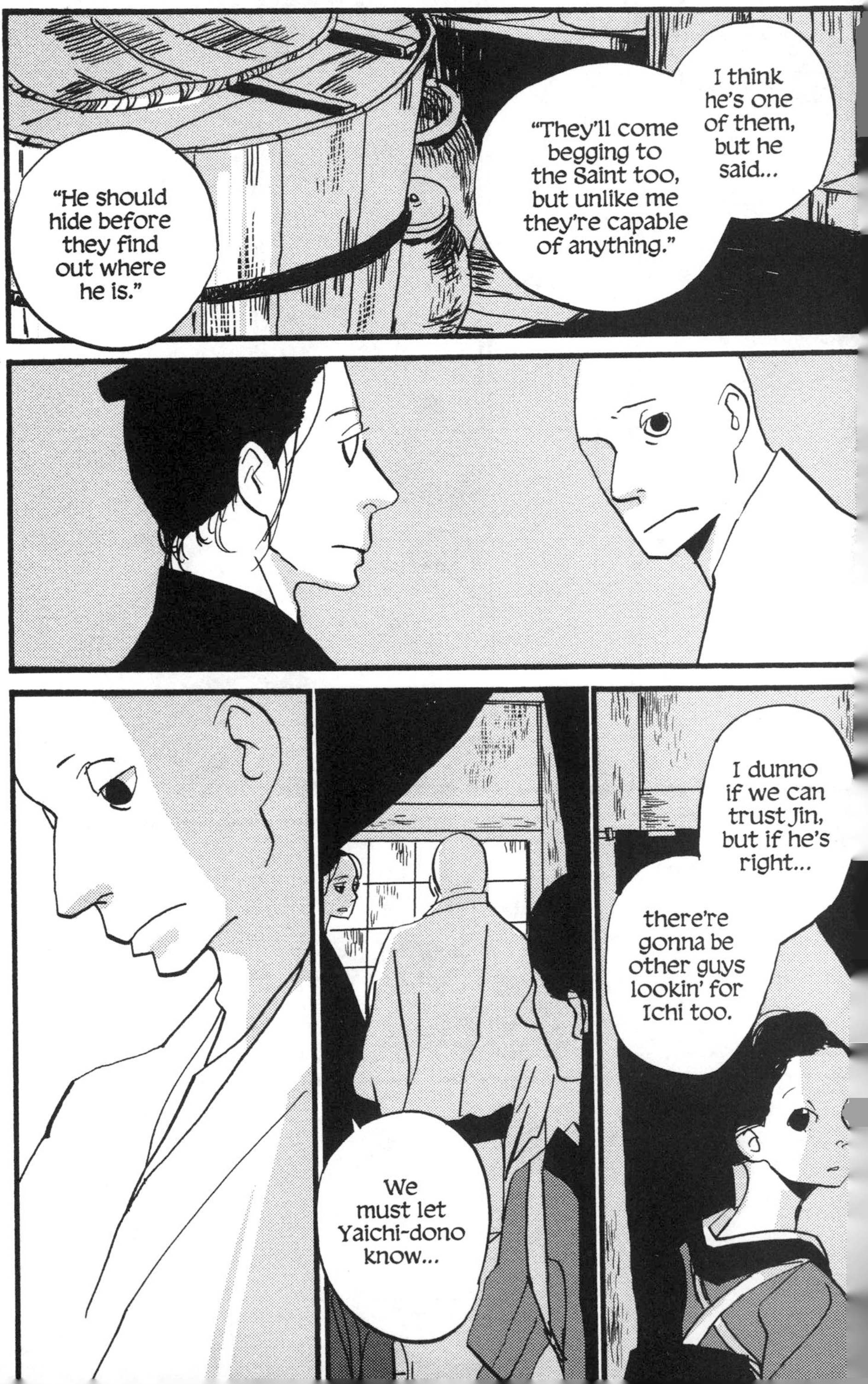
I think he's one of them, but he said...
"They'll come begging to the Saint too, but unlike me they're capable of anything."
"He should hide before they find out where he is."
I dunno if we can trust Jin, but if he's right...
there're gonna be other guys lookin' for Ichi too.
We must let Yaichi-dono know...

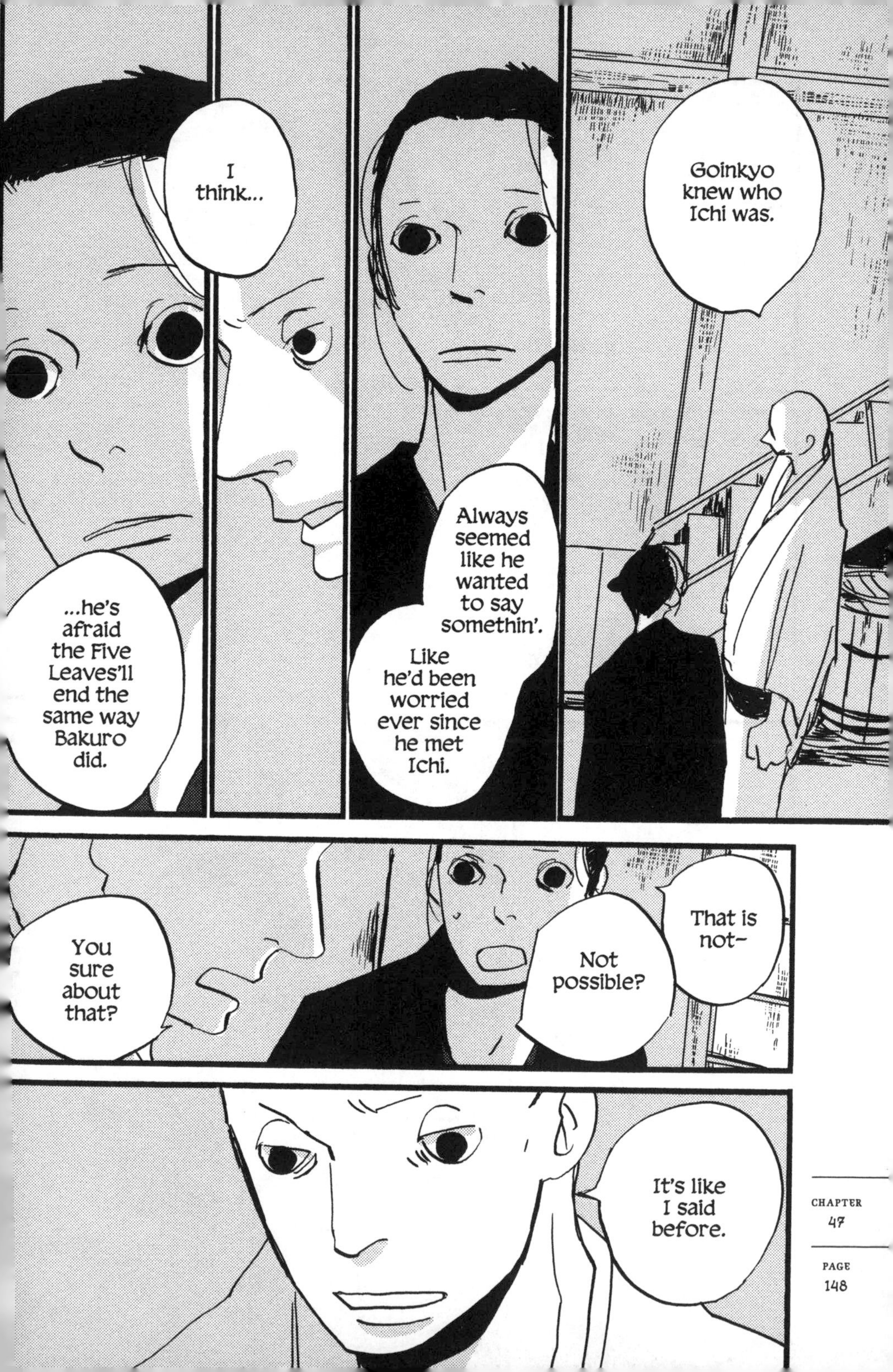
Goinkyo knew who Ichi was.
Always seemed like he wanted to say somethin'.
Like he'd been worried ever since he met Ichi.
I think...
...he's afraid the Five Leaves'll end the same way Bakuro did.
That is not-
Not possible?
You sure about that?
It's like I said before.

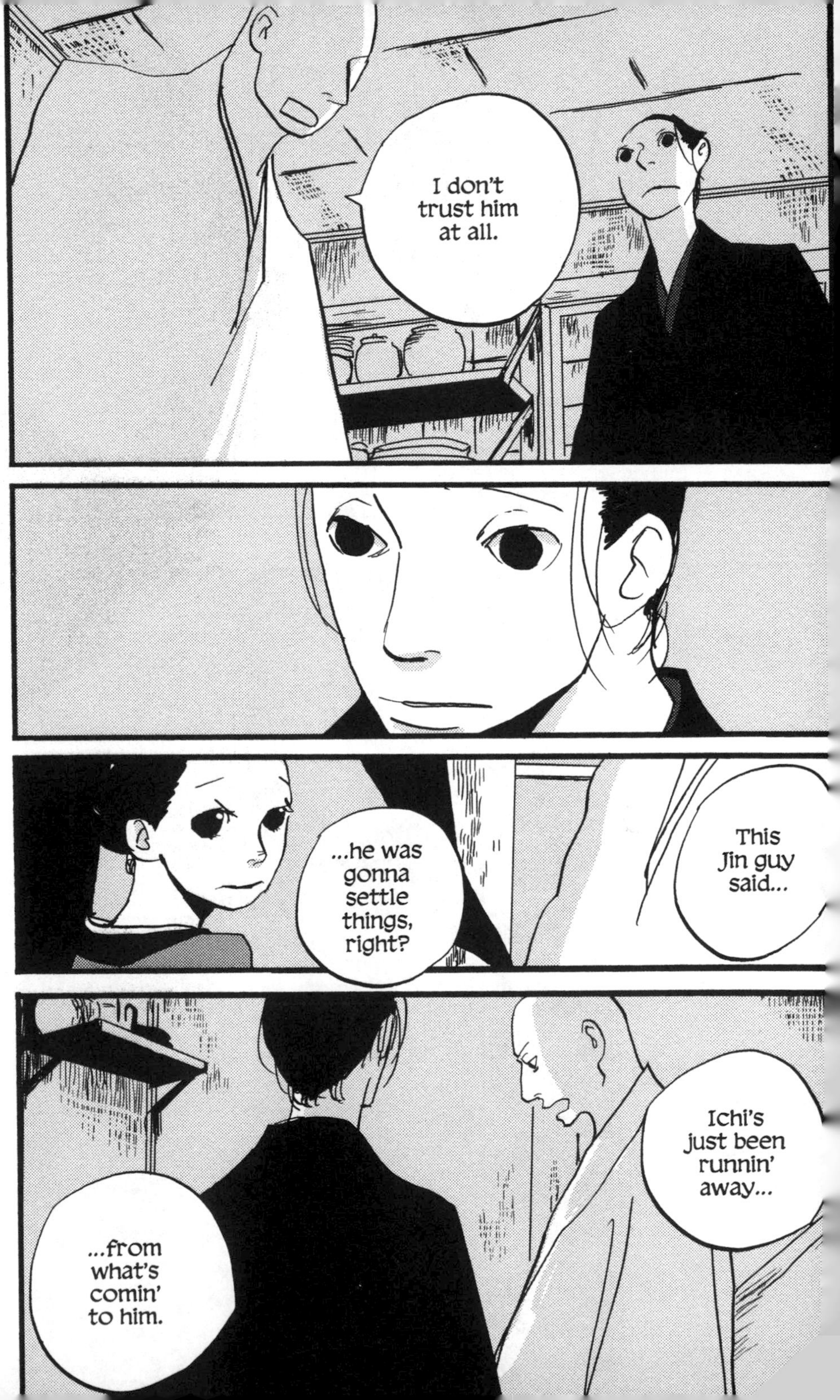
I don't trust him at all.
This Jin guy said...
...he was gonna settle things, right?
Ichi's just been runnin' away...
...from what's comin' to him.

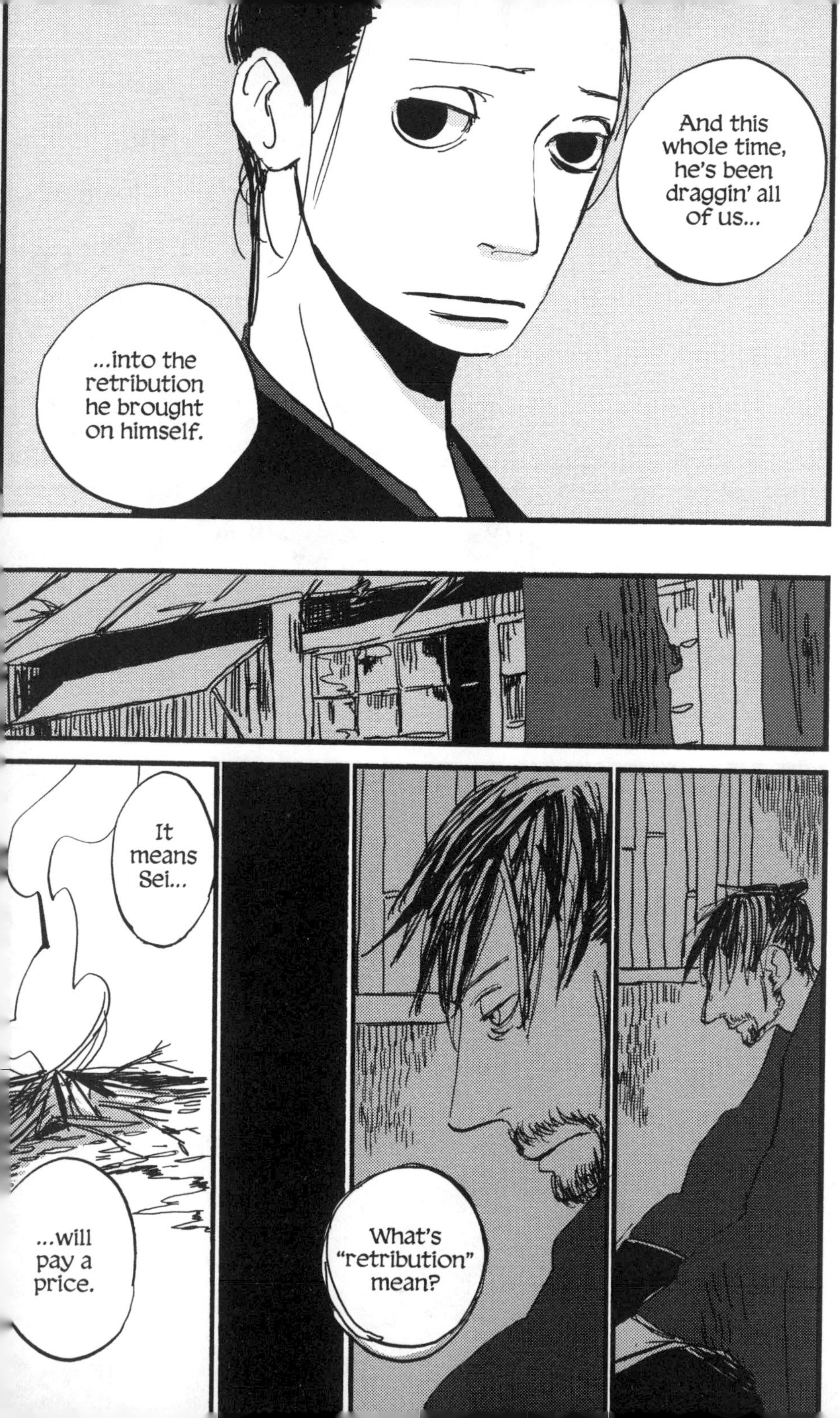

And this whole time, he's been draggin' all of us...
...into the retribution he brought on himself.
What's "retribution" mean?
It means Sei...
...will pay a price.

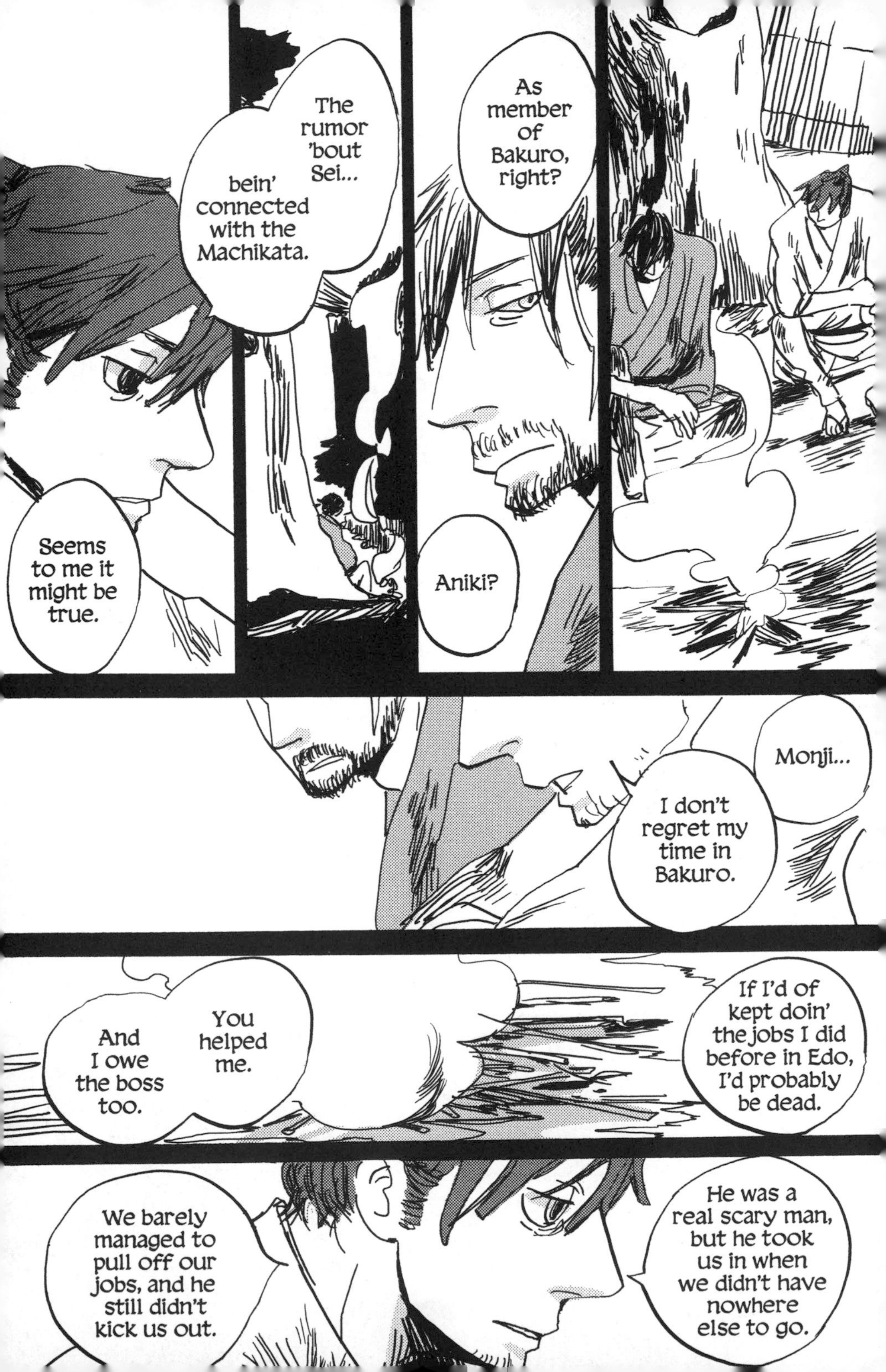
As member of Bakuro, right?
Aniki?
The rumor 'bout Sei...
bein' connected with the Machikata.
Seems to me it might be true.
Monji...
I don't regret my time in Bakuro.
If I'd of kept doin' the jobs I did before in Edo, I'd probably be dead.
You helped me.
And I owe the boss too.
He was a real scary man, but he took us in when we didn't have nowhere else to go.
We barely managed to pull off our jobs, and he still didn't kick us out.

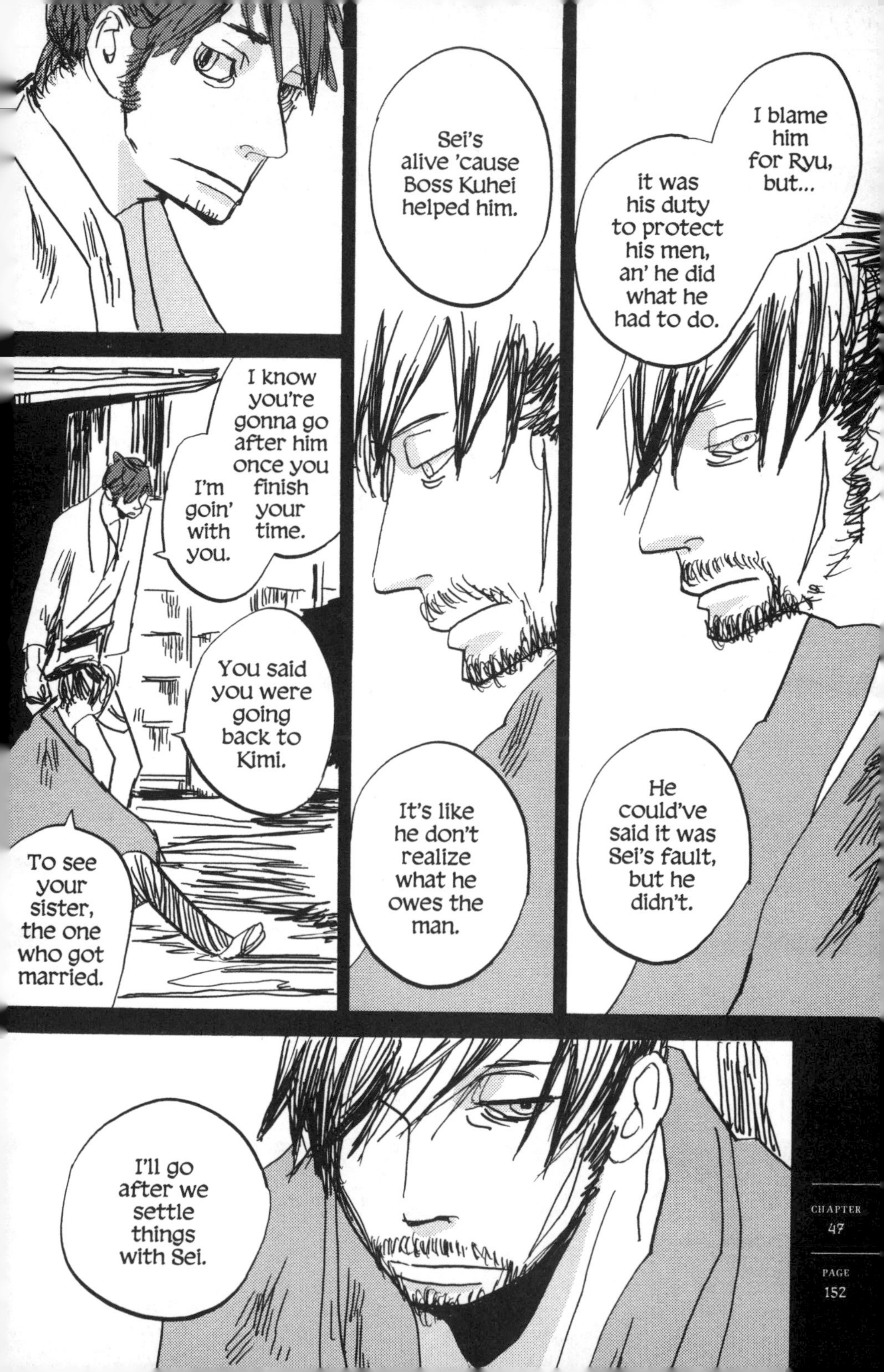
I blame him for Ryu, but...
it was his duty to protect his men, an' he did what he had to do.
He could've said it was Sei's fault, but he didn't.
Sei's alive 'cause Boss Kuhei helped him.
It's like he don't realize what he owes the man.
I know you're gonna go after him once you finish your time.
I'm goin' with you.
You said you were going back to Kimi.
To see your sister, the one who got married.
I'll go after we settle things with Sei.

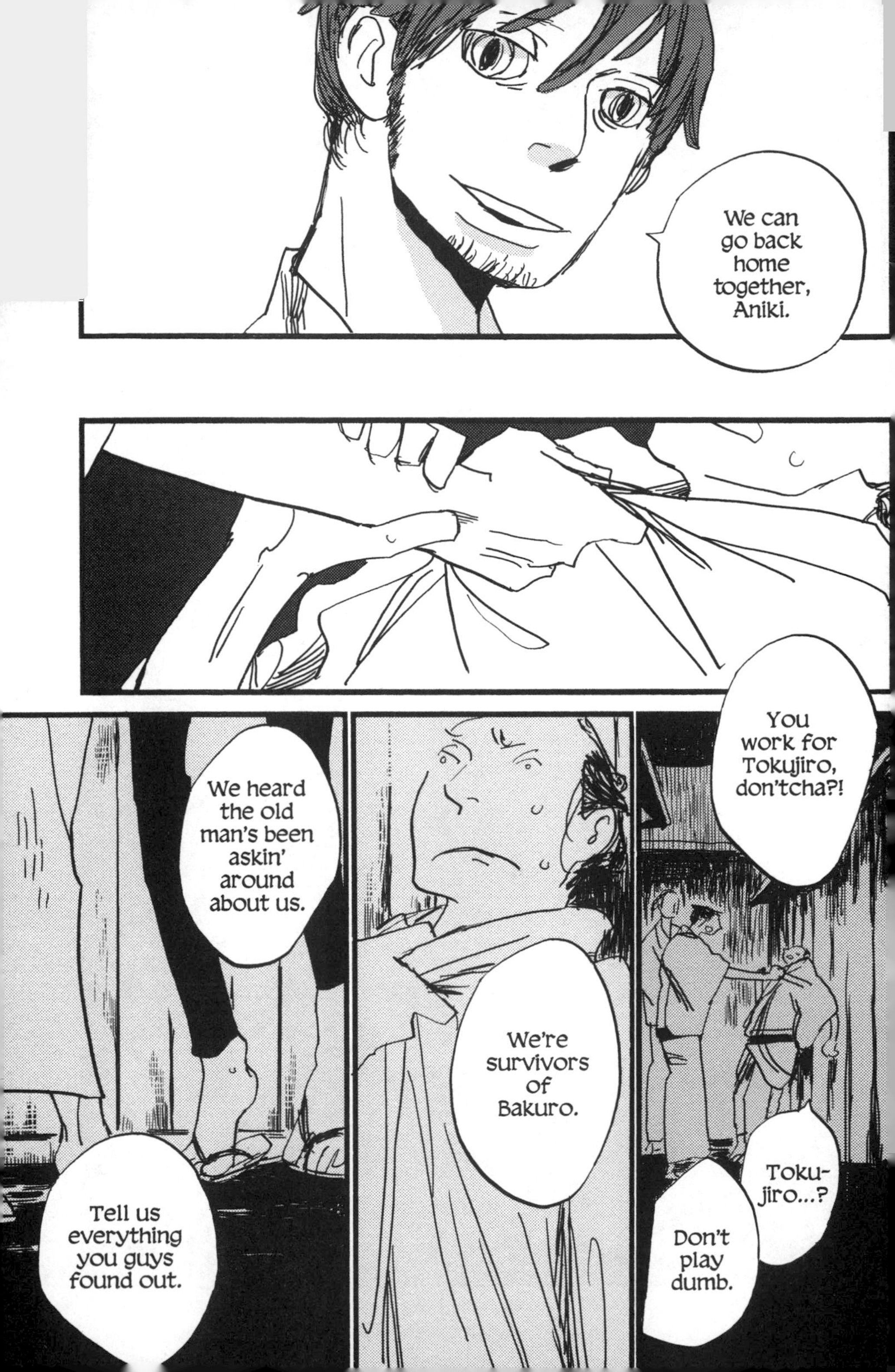
We can go back home together, Aniki.
You work for Tokujiro, don'tcha?!
Toku-jiro...?
Don't play dumb.
We're survivors of Bakuro.
We heard the old man's been askin' around about us.
Tell us everything you guys found out.

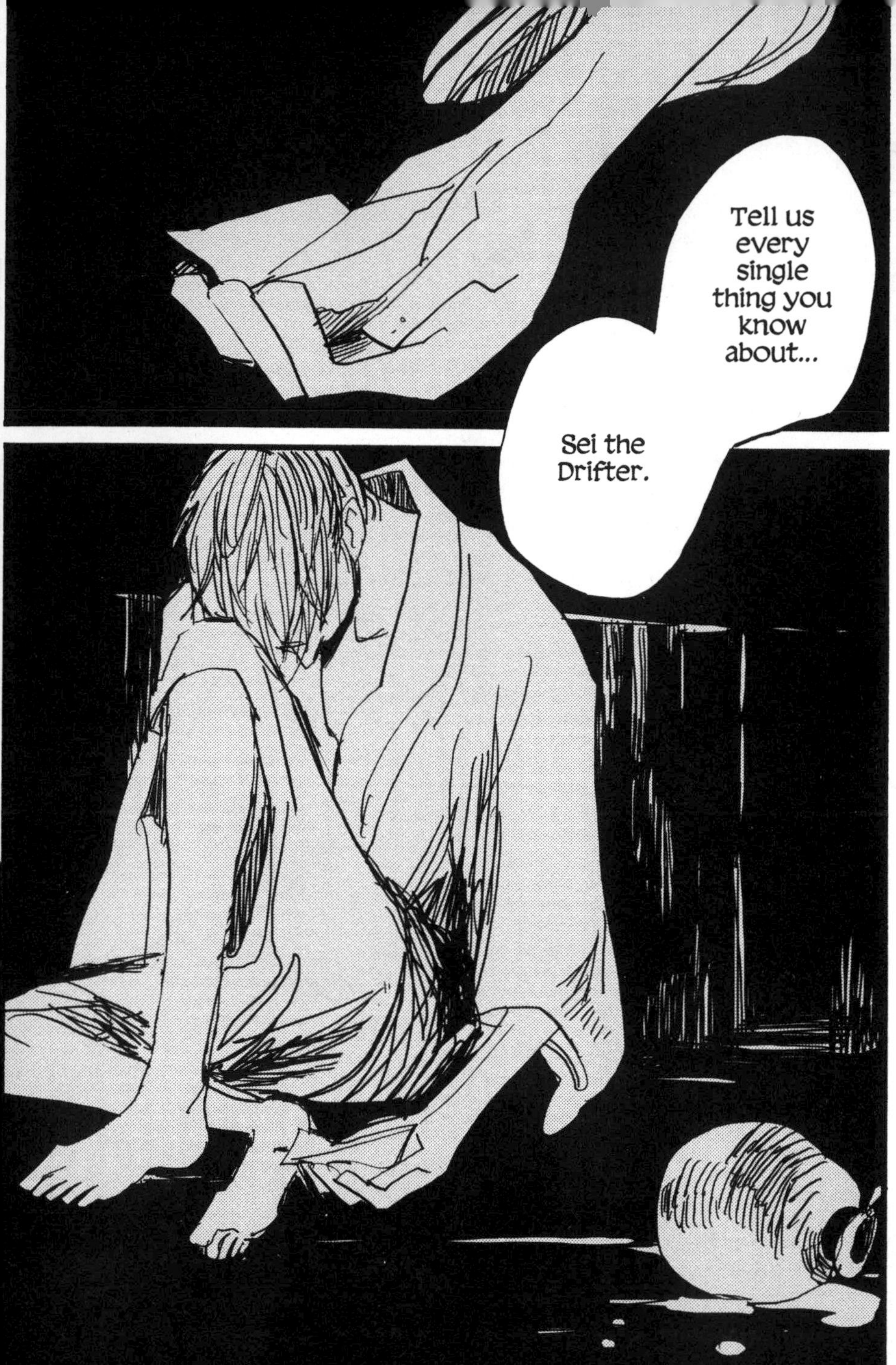
Tell us every single thing you know about...
Sei the Drifter.

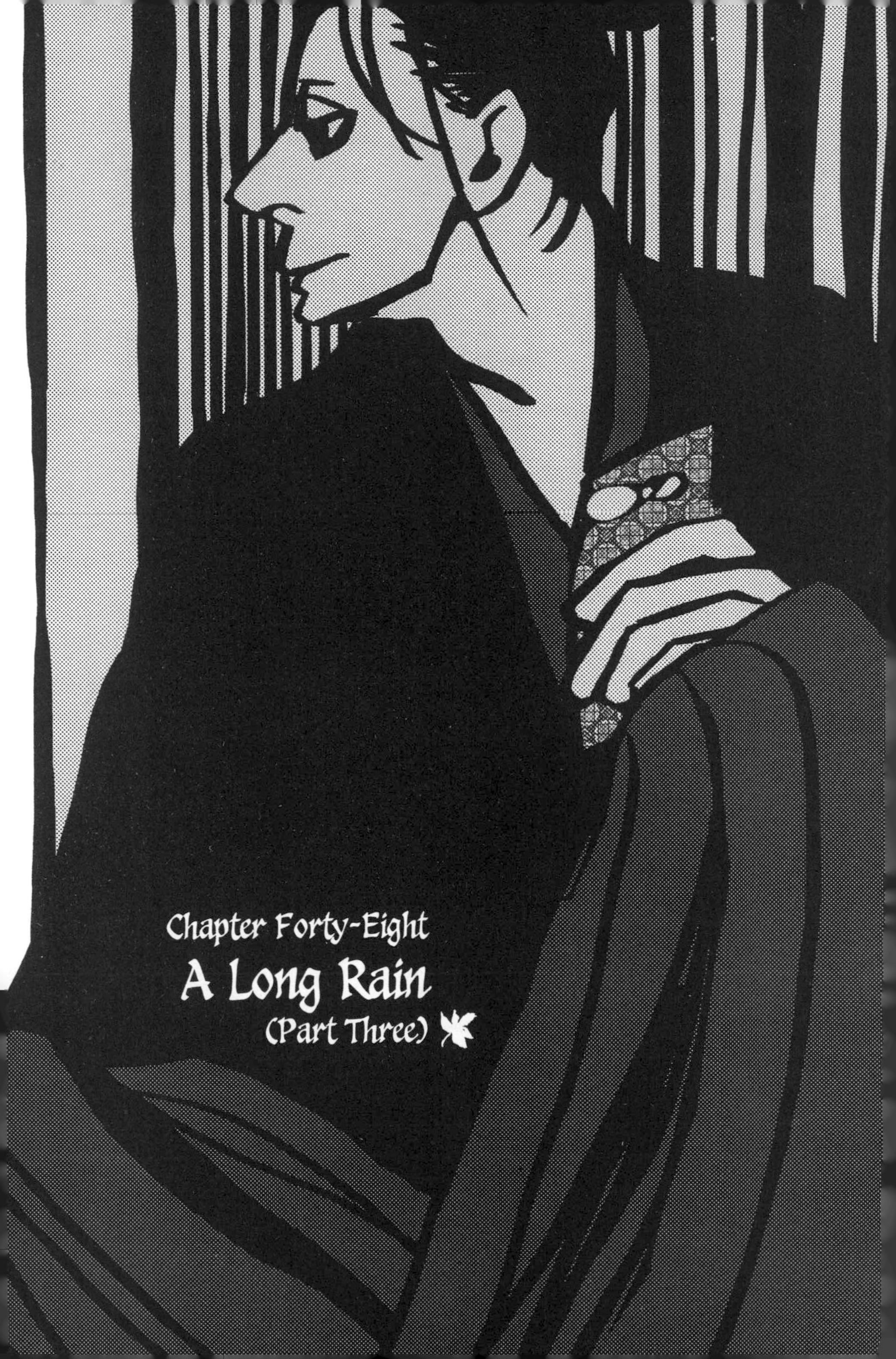
Chapter Forty-Eight
A Long Rain
(Part Three)

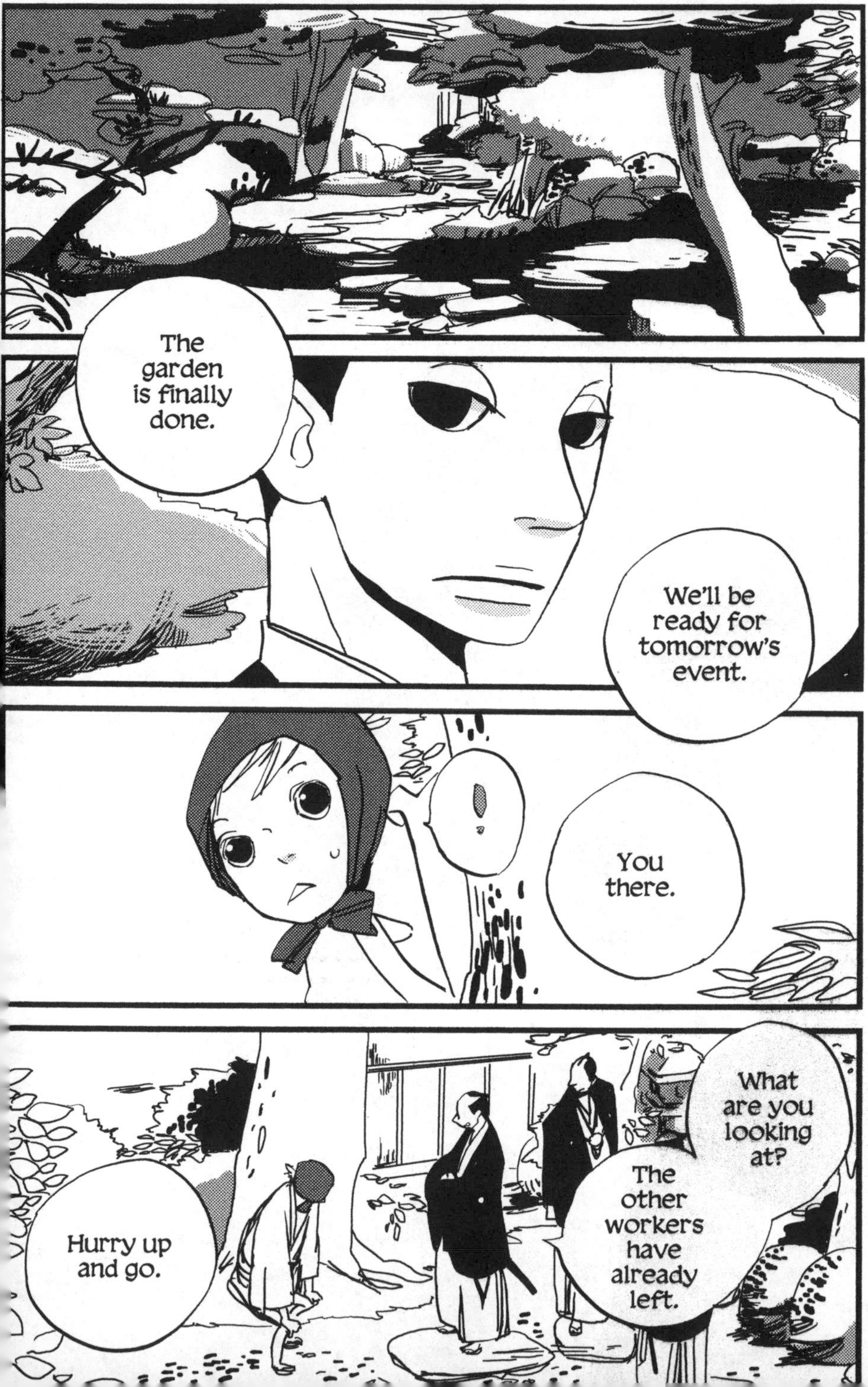
The garden is finally done.
We'll be ready for tomorrow's event.
You there.
What are you looking at?
The other workers have already left.
Hurry up and go.

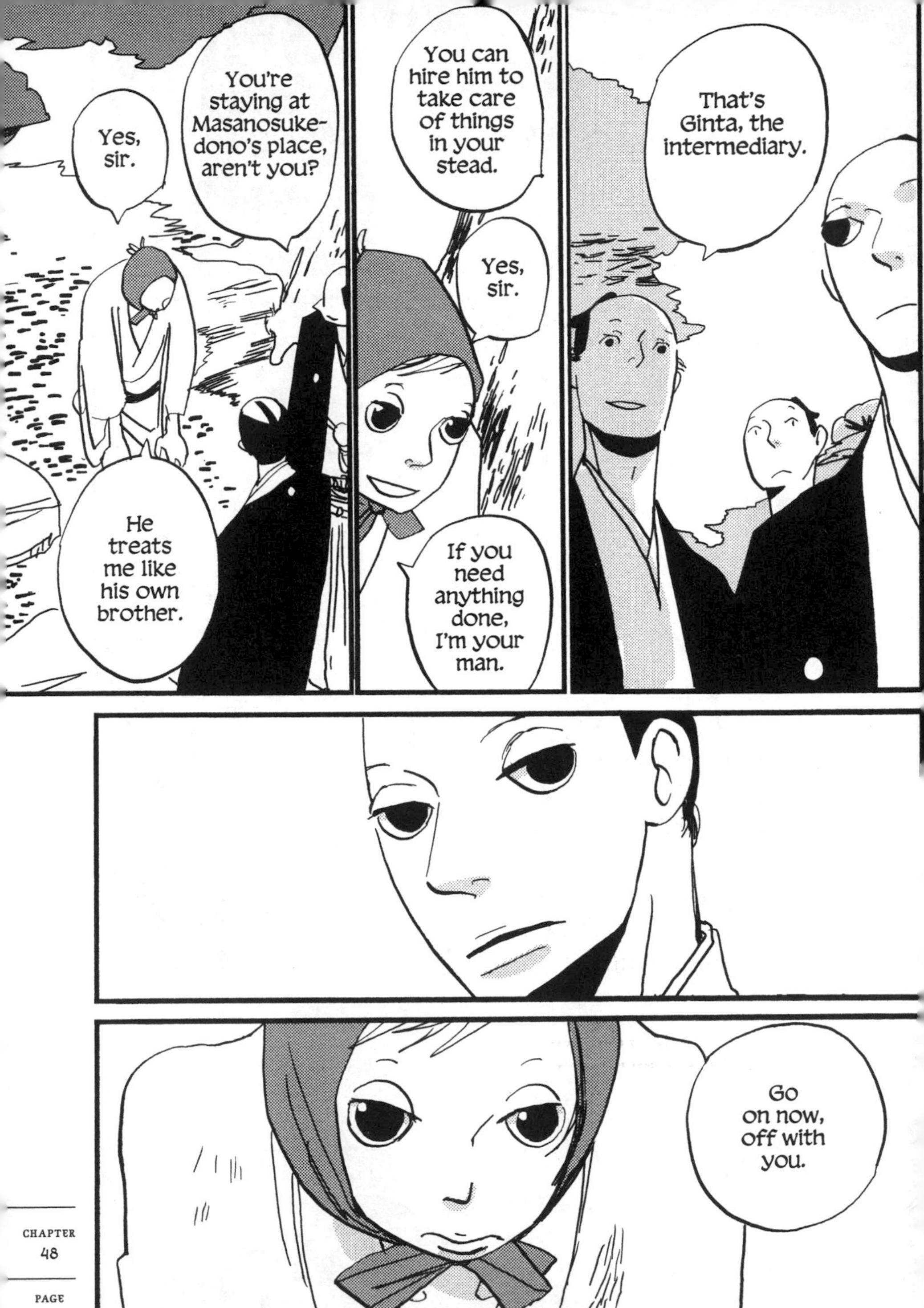
That's Ginta, the intermediary.
You can hire him to take care of things in your stead.
Yes, sir.
If you need anything done, I'm your man.
You're staying at Masanosuke-dono's place, aren't you?
Yes, sir.
He treats me like his own brother.
Go on now, off with you.

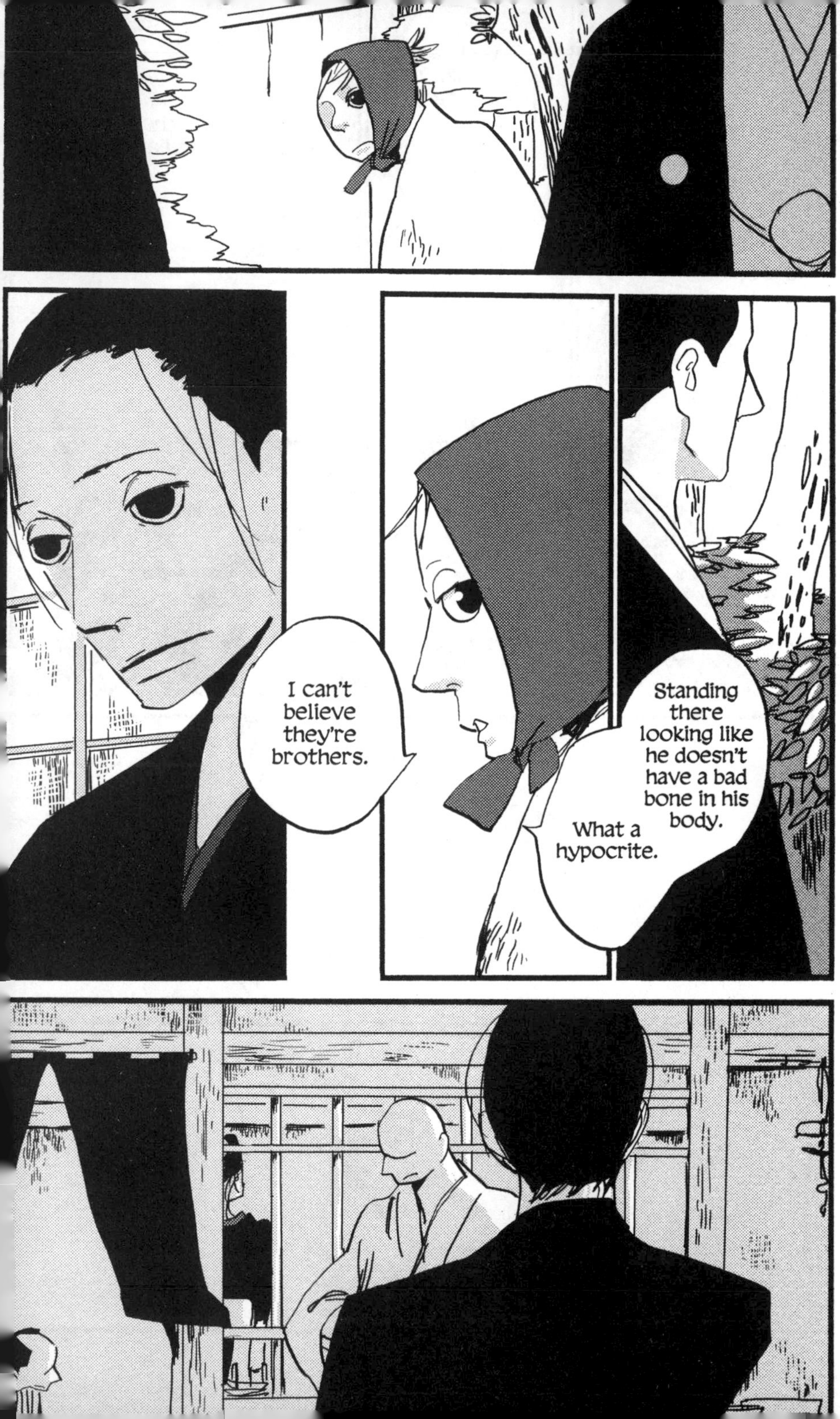
Standing there looking like he doesn't have a bad bone in his body.
What a hypocrite.
I can't believe they're brothers.

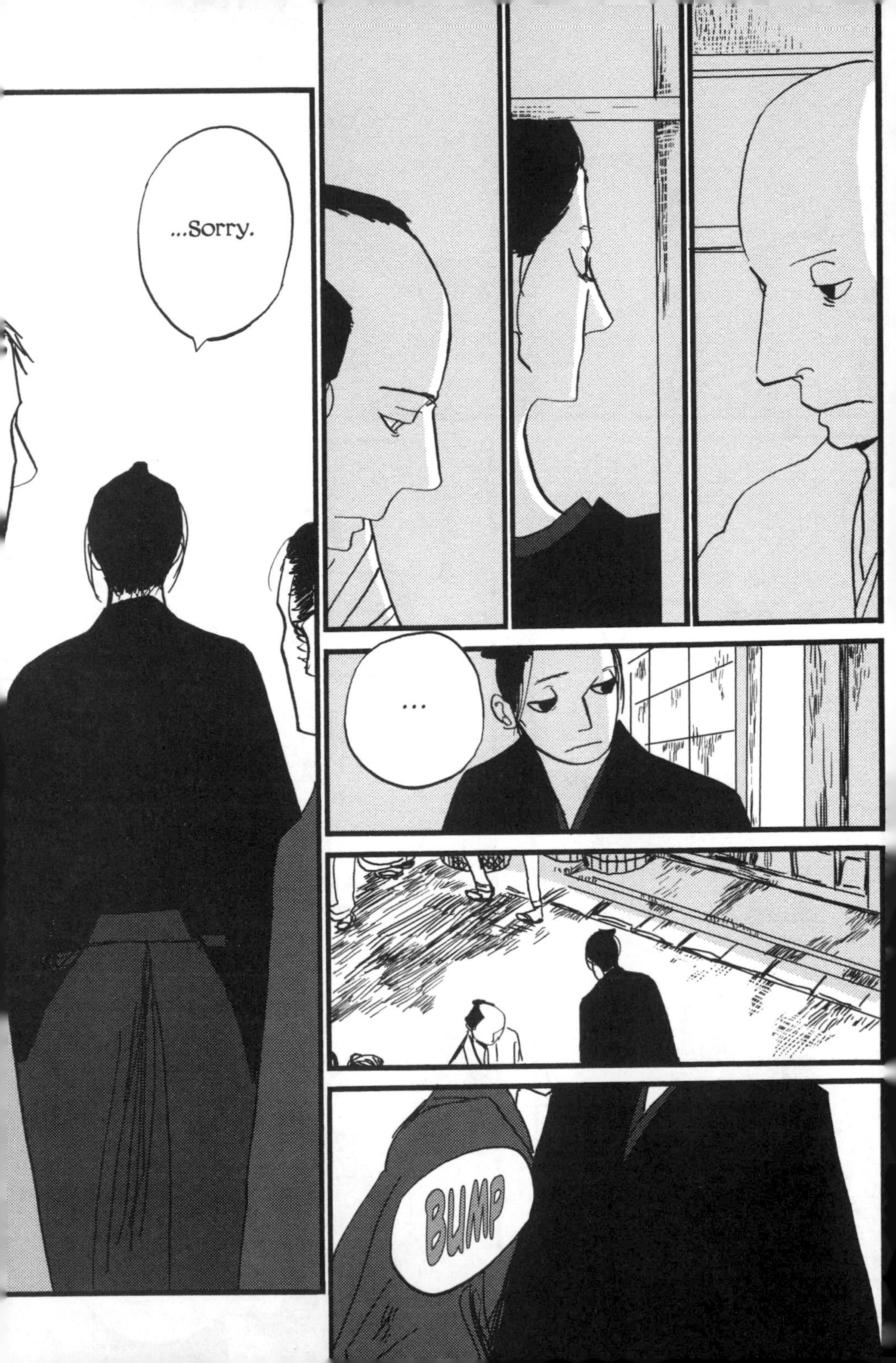
...
BUMP
...Sorry.

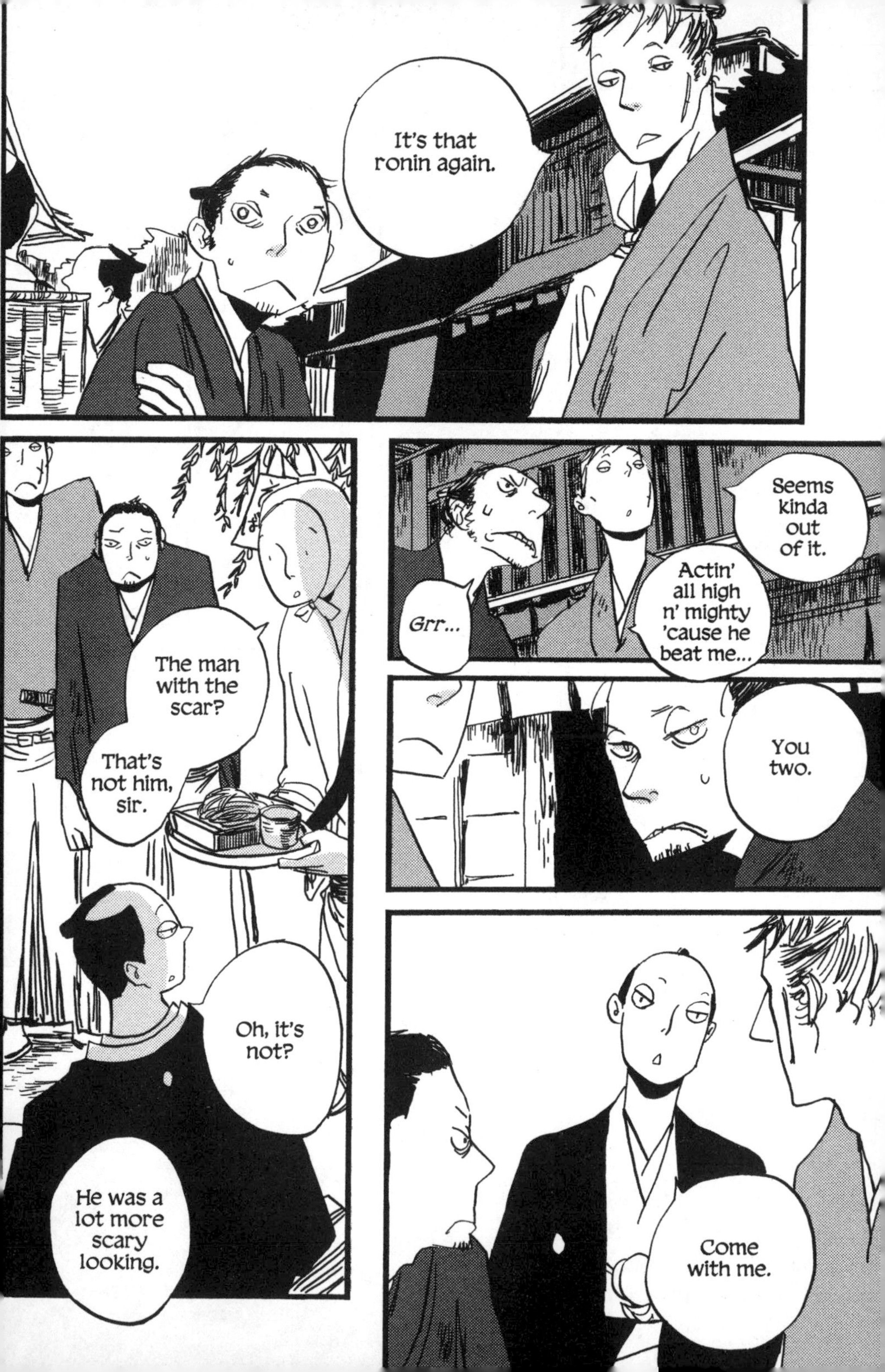
It's that ronin again.
Seems kinda out of it.
Actin' all high n' mighty 'cause he beat me...
Grr...
You two.
Come with me.
The man with the scar?
That's not him, sir.
Oh, it's not?
He was a lot more scary looking.

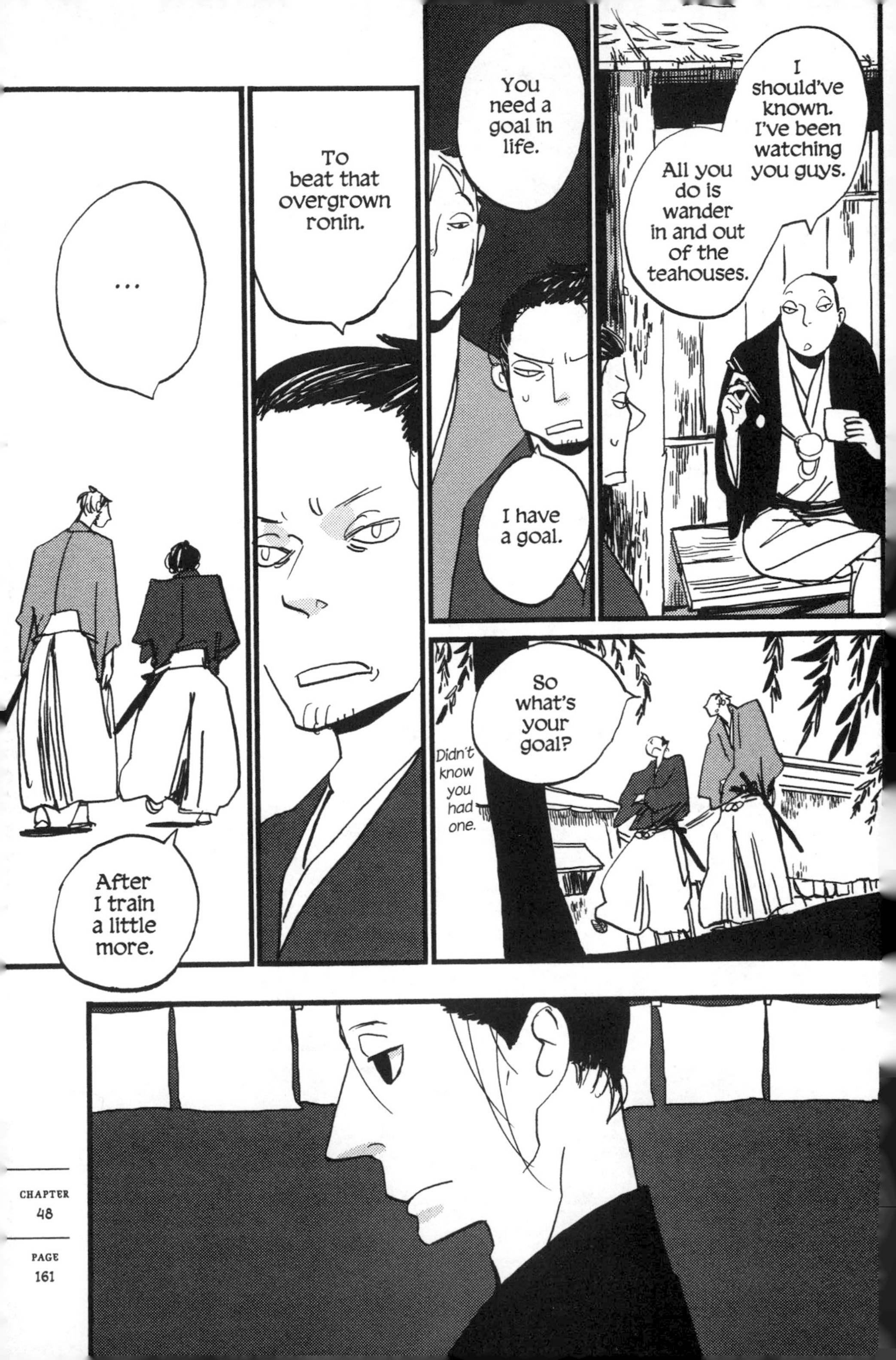
I should've known. I've been watching you guys.
All you do is wander in and out of the teahouses.
You need a goal in life.
I have a goal.
So what's your goal?
Didn't know you had one.
To beat that overgrown ronin.
...
After I train a little more.

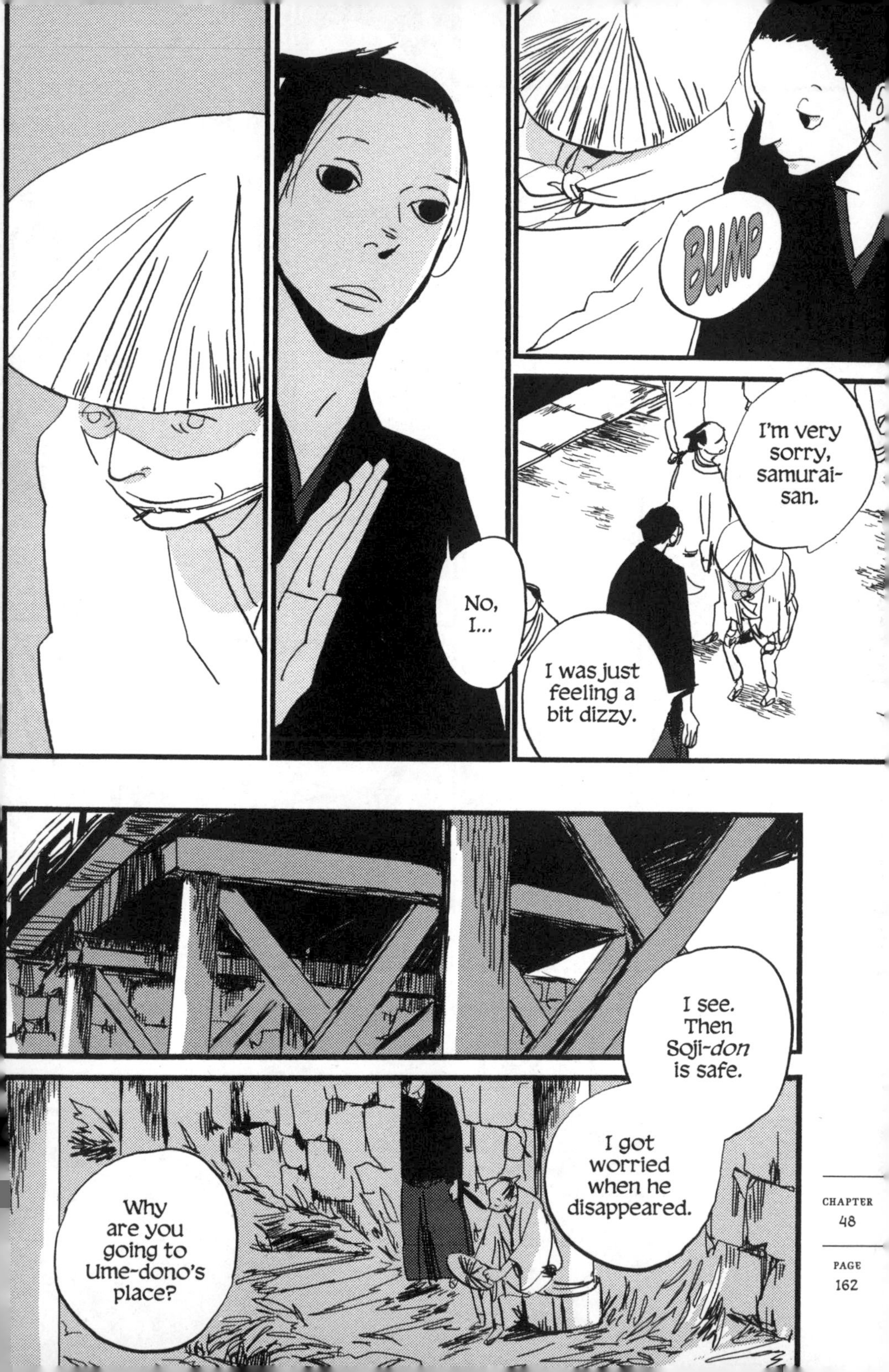
BUMP
I'm very sorry, samurai-san.
No, I...
I was just feeling a bit dizzy.
I see. Then Soji-*don* is safe.
I got worried when he disappeared.
Why are you going to Ume-dono's place?

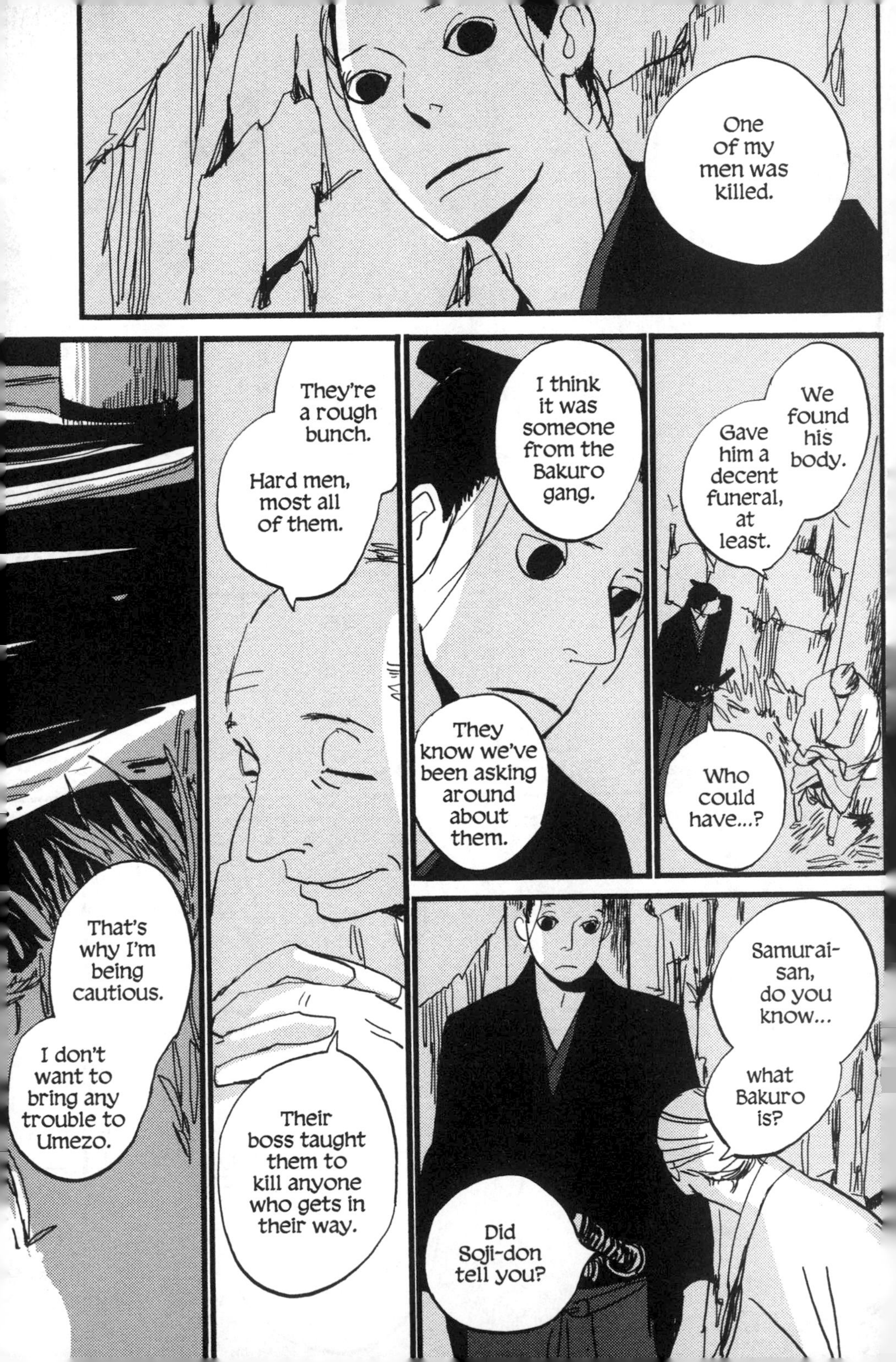
One of my men was killed.
We found his body.
Gave him a decent funeral, at least.
Who could have...?
I think it was someone from the Bakuro gang.
They know we've been asking around about them.
Samurai-san, do you know...
what Bakuro is?
Did Soji-don tell you?
They're a rough bunch.
Hard men, most all of them.
Their boss taught them to kill anyone who gets in their way.
That's why I'm being cautious.
I don't want to bring any trouble to Umezo.

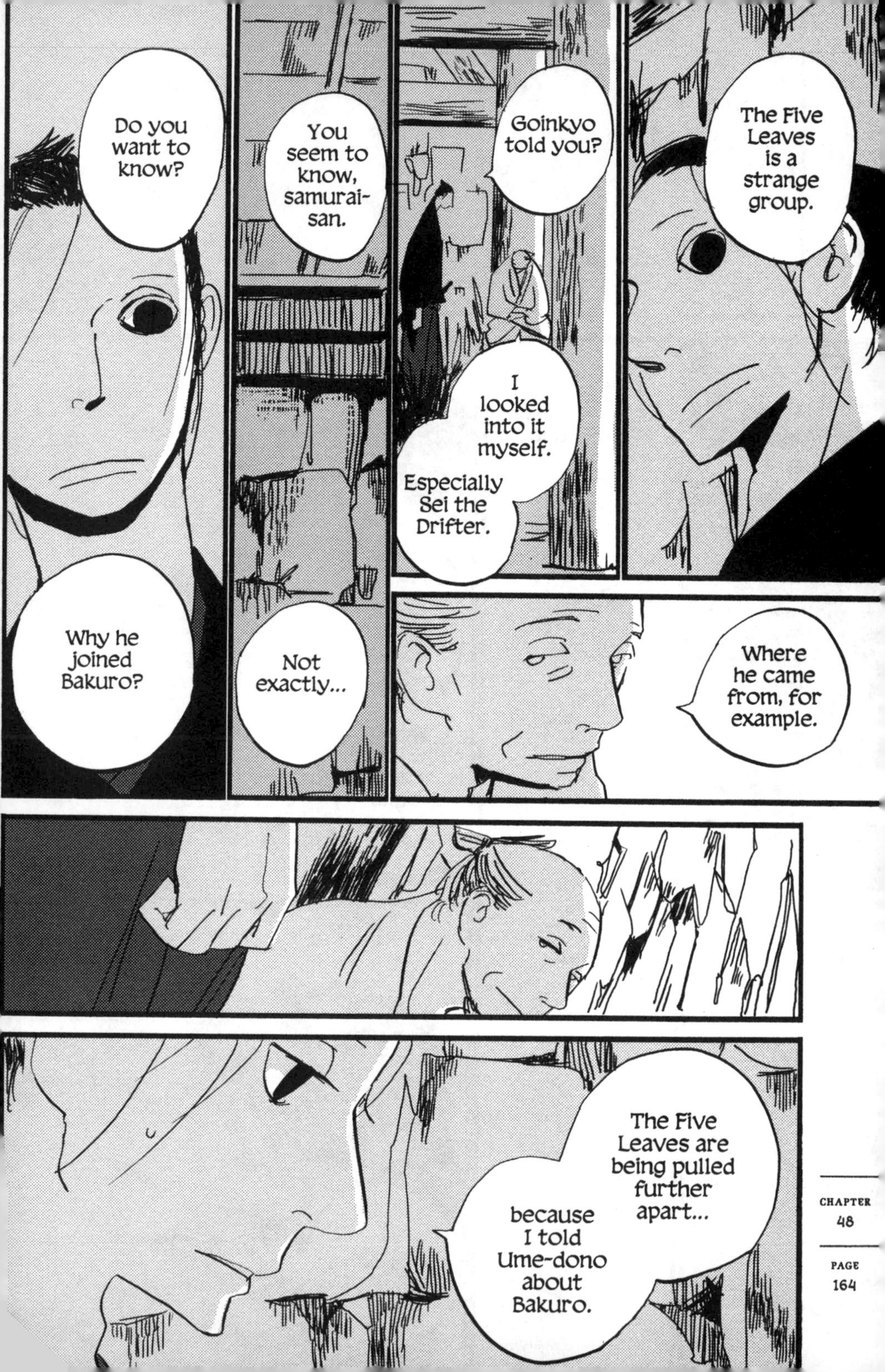
The Five Leaves is a strange group.
Goinkyo told you?
I looked into it myself.
Especially Sei the Drifter.
Where he came from, for example.
You seem to know, samurai-san.
Not exactly...
Do you want to know?
Why he joined Bakuro?
The Five Leaves are being pulled further apart...
because I told Ume-dono about Bakuro.

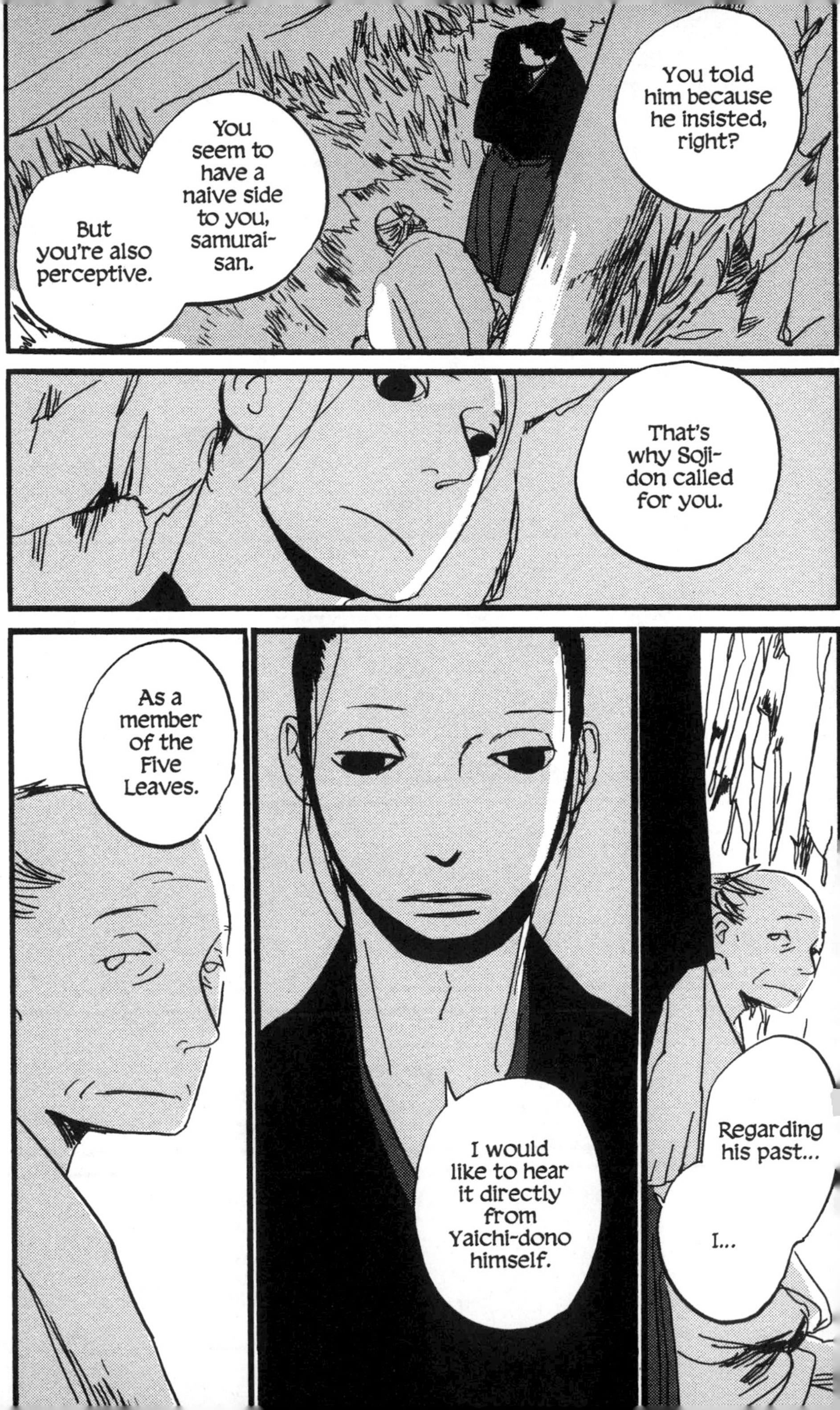
You told him because he insisted, right?
You seem to have a naive side to you, samurai-san.
But you're also perceptive.
That's why Soji-don called for you.
Regarding his past...
I...
I would like to hear it directly from Yaichi-dono himself.
As a member of the Five Leaves.

When he trusts me enough to tell me...

...at a time when he feels it is right to do so.

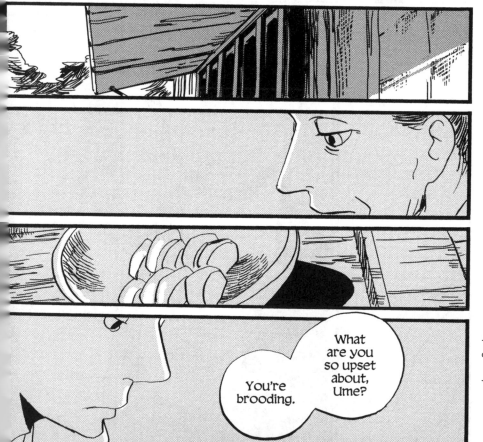

What are you so upset about, Ume?

You're brooding.

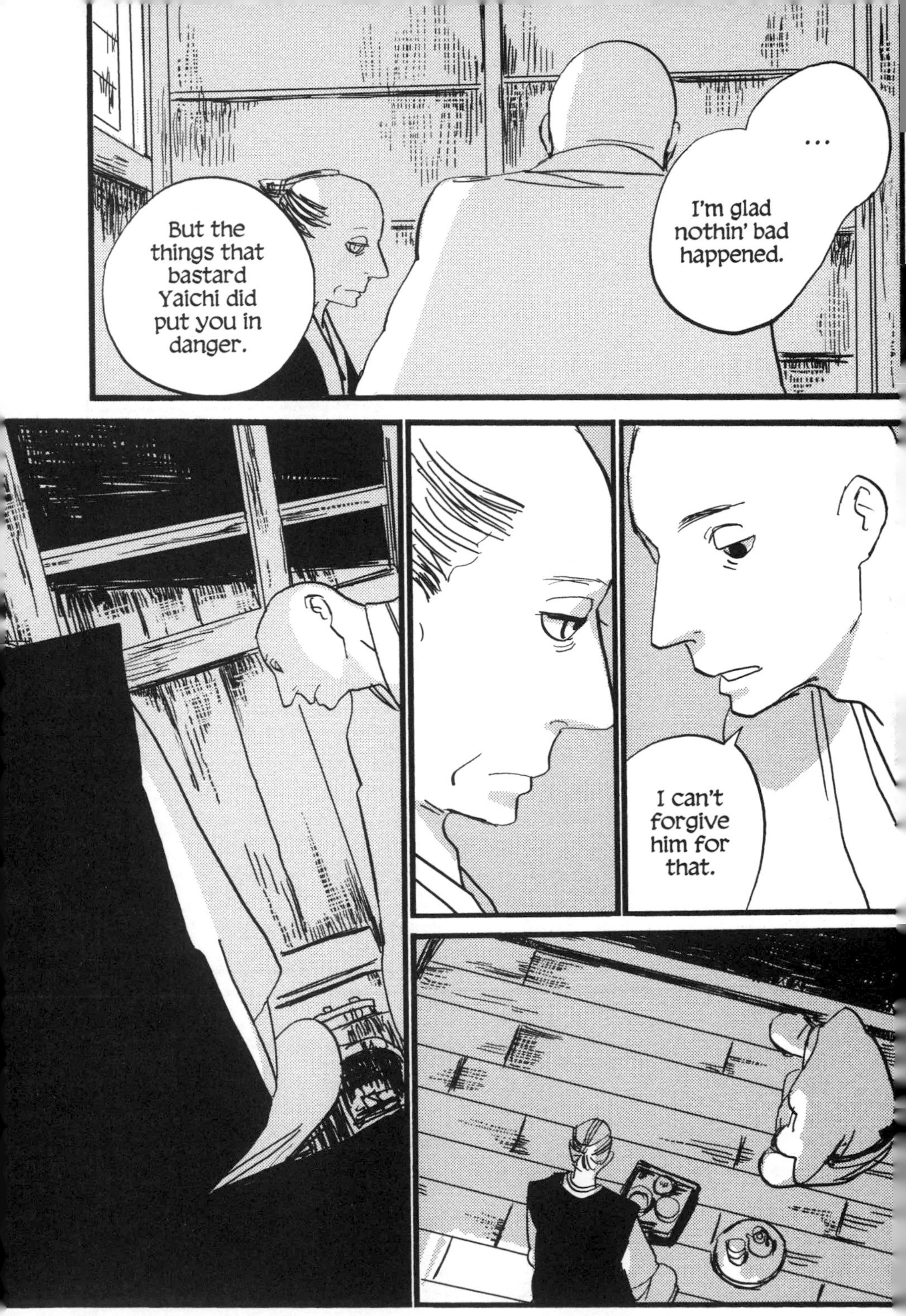
...
I'm glad nothin' bad happened.
But the things that bastard Yaichi did put you in danger.
I can't forgive him for that.

Why didn't you tell me?

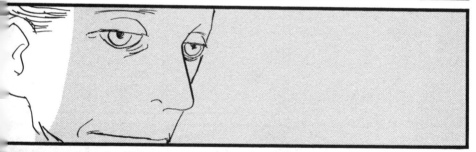

Because I know you well.

Ume.

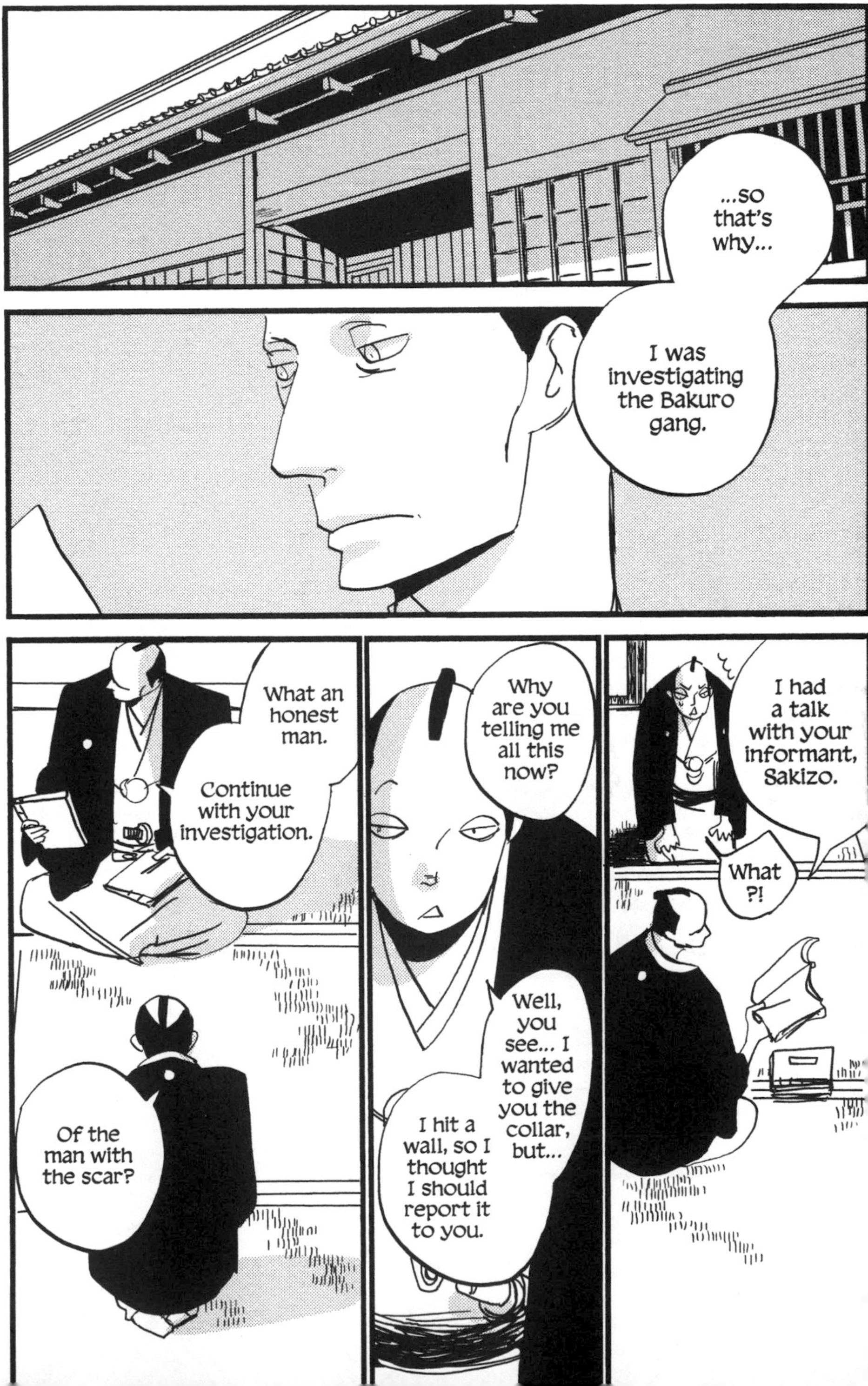
...so that's why...
I was investigating the Bakuro gang.
I had a talk with your informant, Sakizo.
What ?!
Why are you telling me all this now?
Well, you see... I wanted to give you the collar, but...
I hit a wall, so I thought I should report it to you.
What an honest man.
Continue with your investigation.
Of the man with the scar?

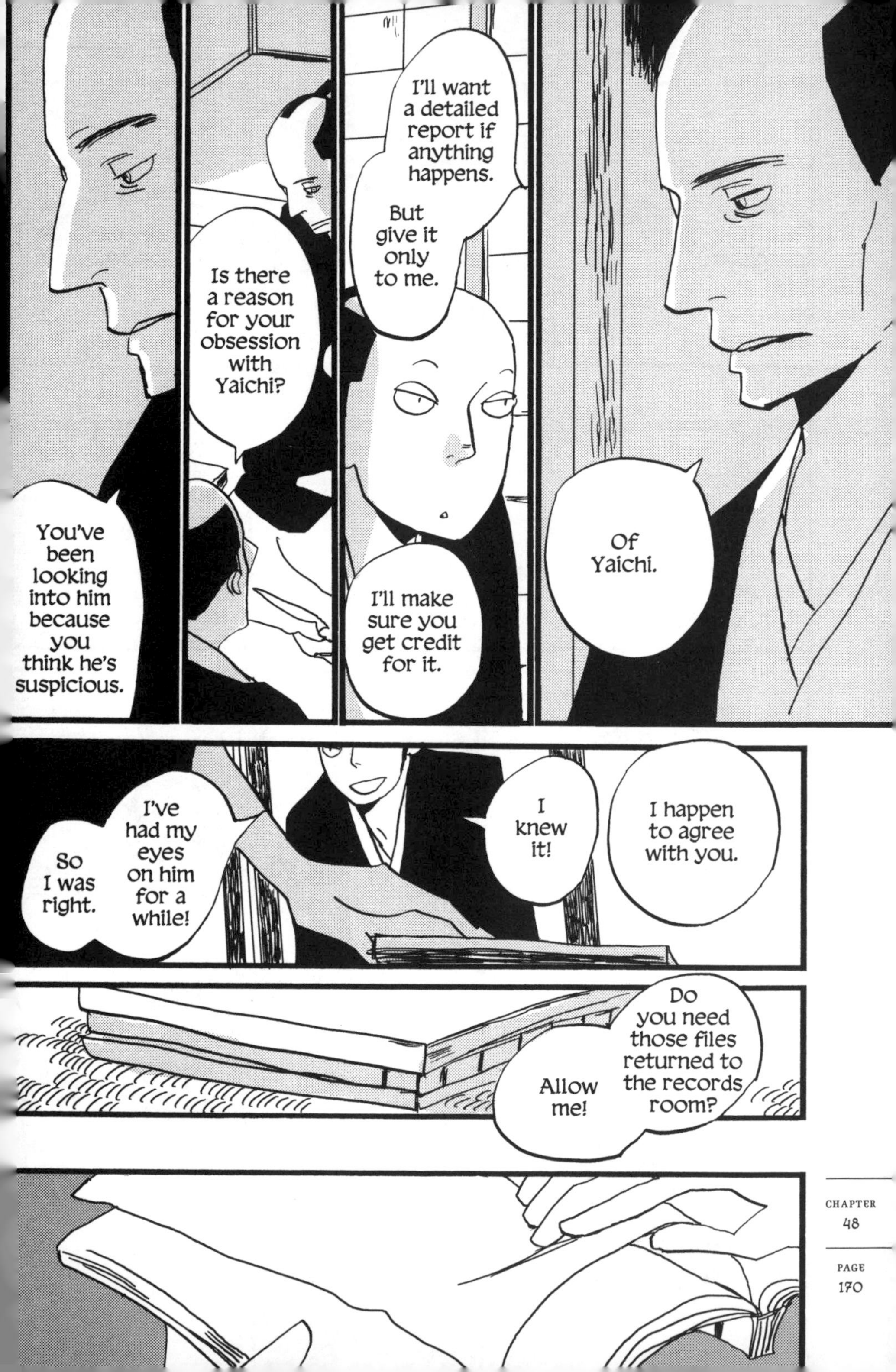
Of Yaichi.
I'll want a detailed report if anything happens.
But give it only to me.
I'll make sure you get credit for it.
Is there a reason for your obsession with Yaichi?
You've been looking into him because you think he's suspicious.
I happen to agree with you.
I knew it!
I've had my eyes on him for a while!
So I was right.
Do you need those files returned to the records room?
Allow me!

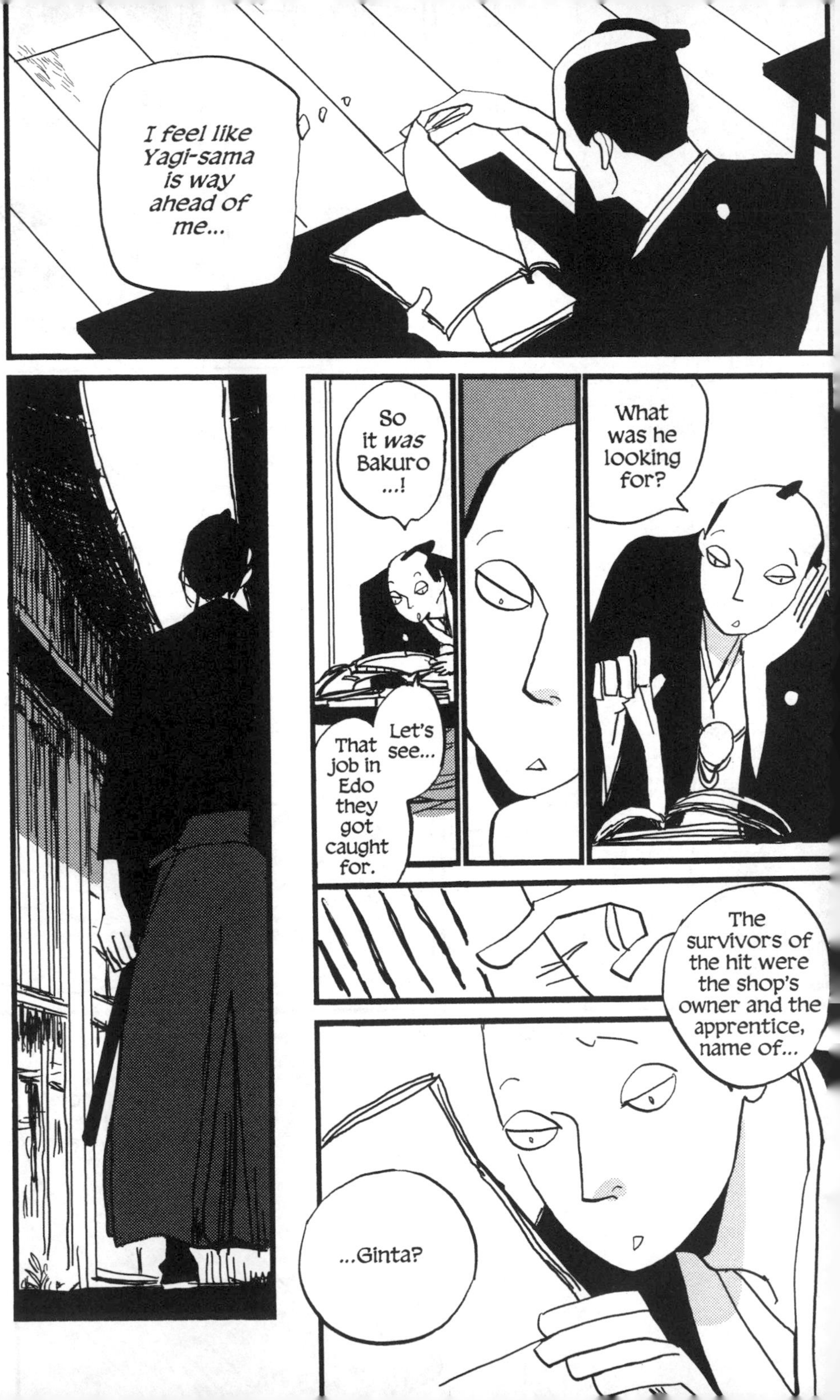
I feel like Yagi-sama is way ahead of me...
What was he looking for?
So it *was* Bakuro ...!
Let's see...
That job in Edo they got caught for.
The survivors of the hit were the shop's owner and the apprentice, name of...
...Ginta?

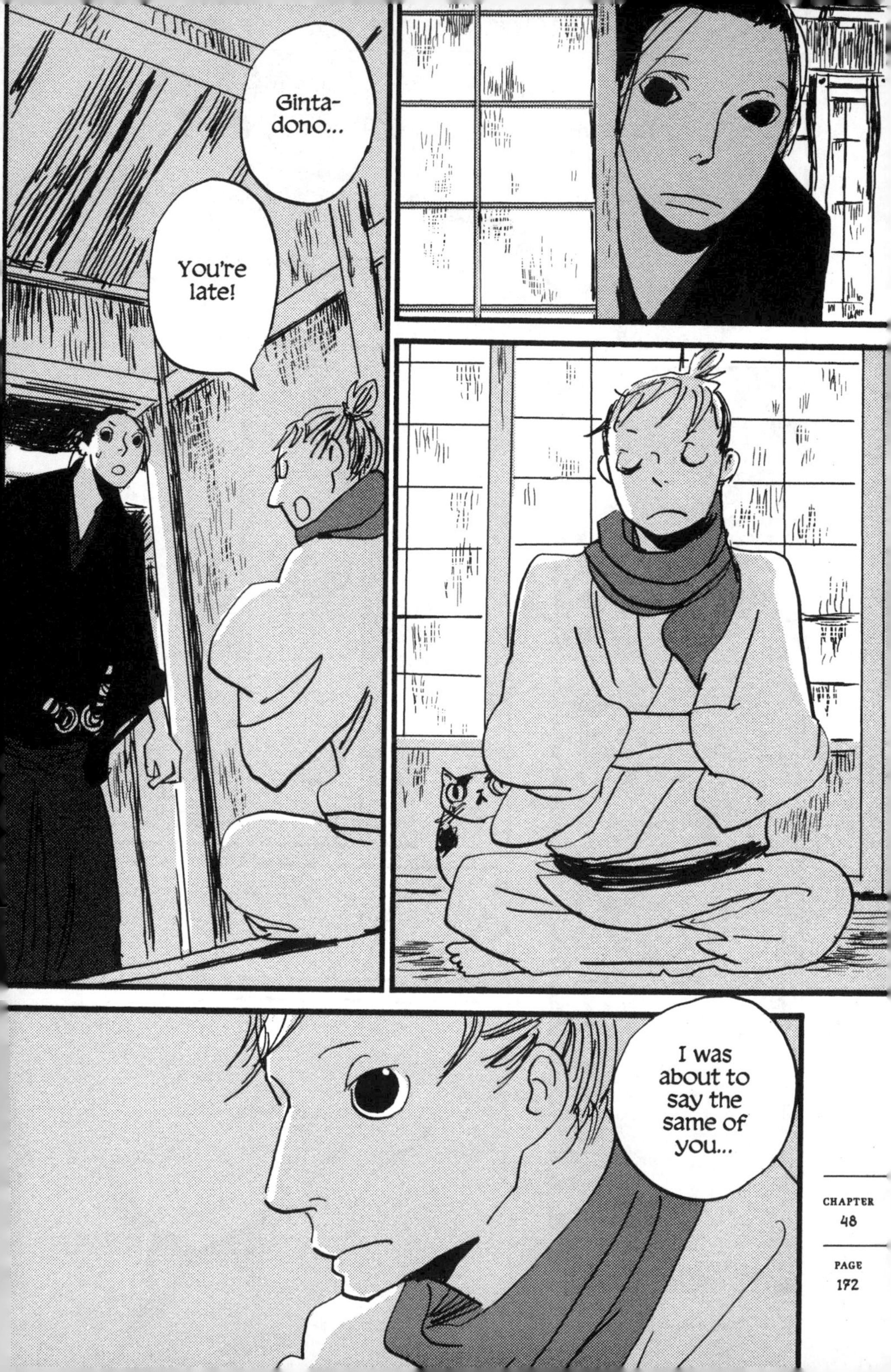
Ginta-dono...
You're late!
I was about to say the same of you...

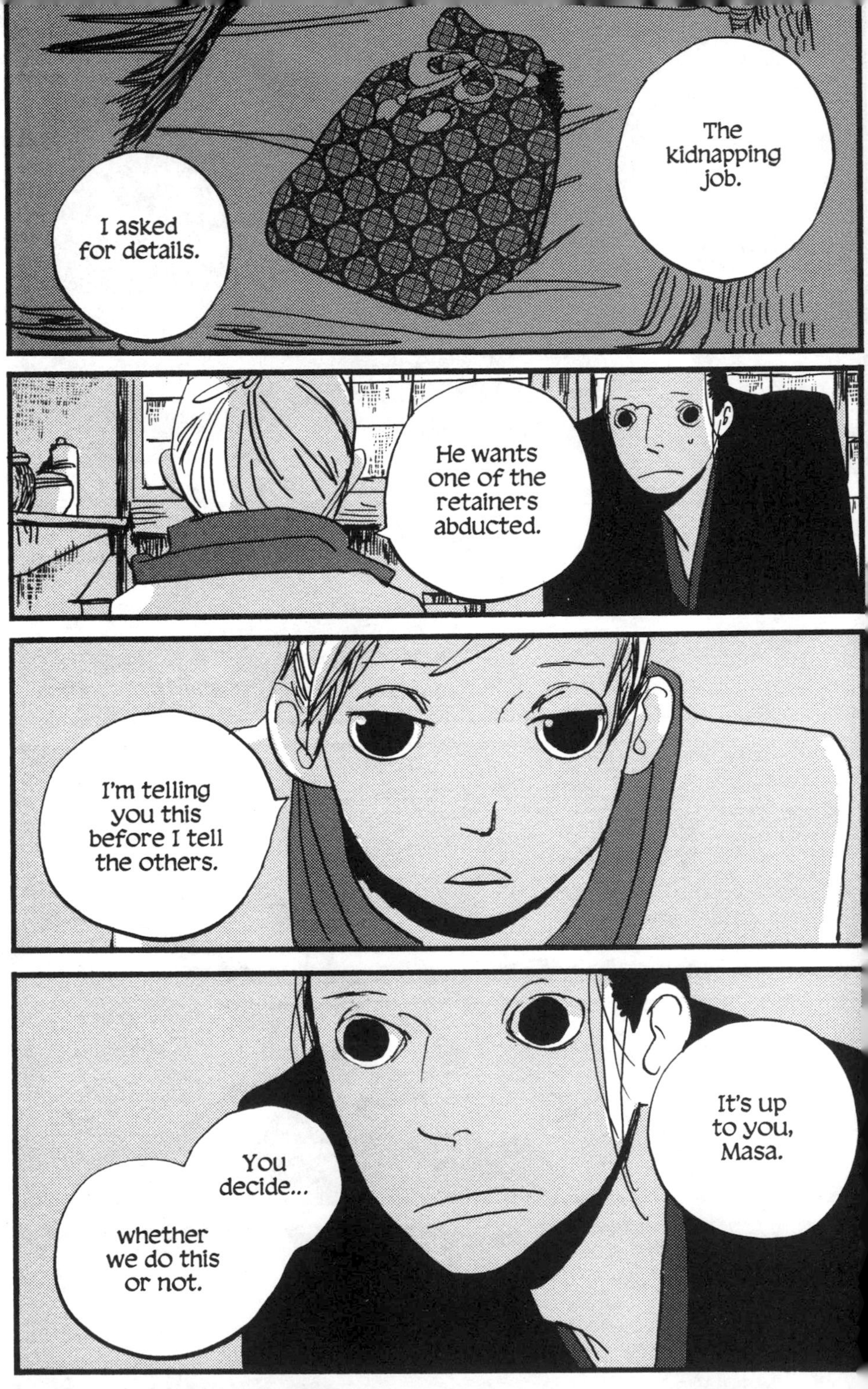
The kidnapping job.
I asked for details.
He wants one of the retainers abducted.
I'm telling you this before I tell the others.
It's up to you, Masa.
You decide... whether we do this or not.

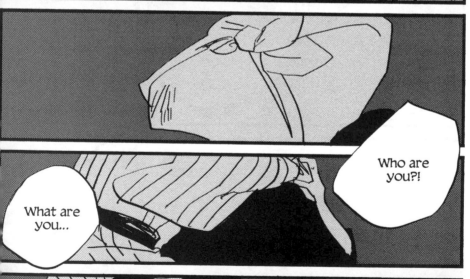

Who are
you?!

What are
you...

You're gettin' sloppy.
He saw our faces.
Doesn't matter for this one.

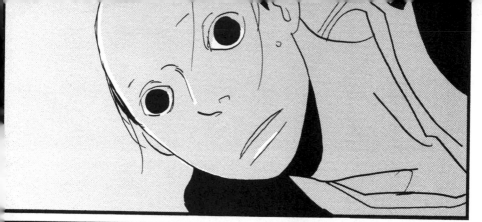

Aniue...

...

What... What is this?

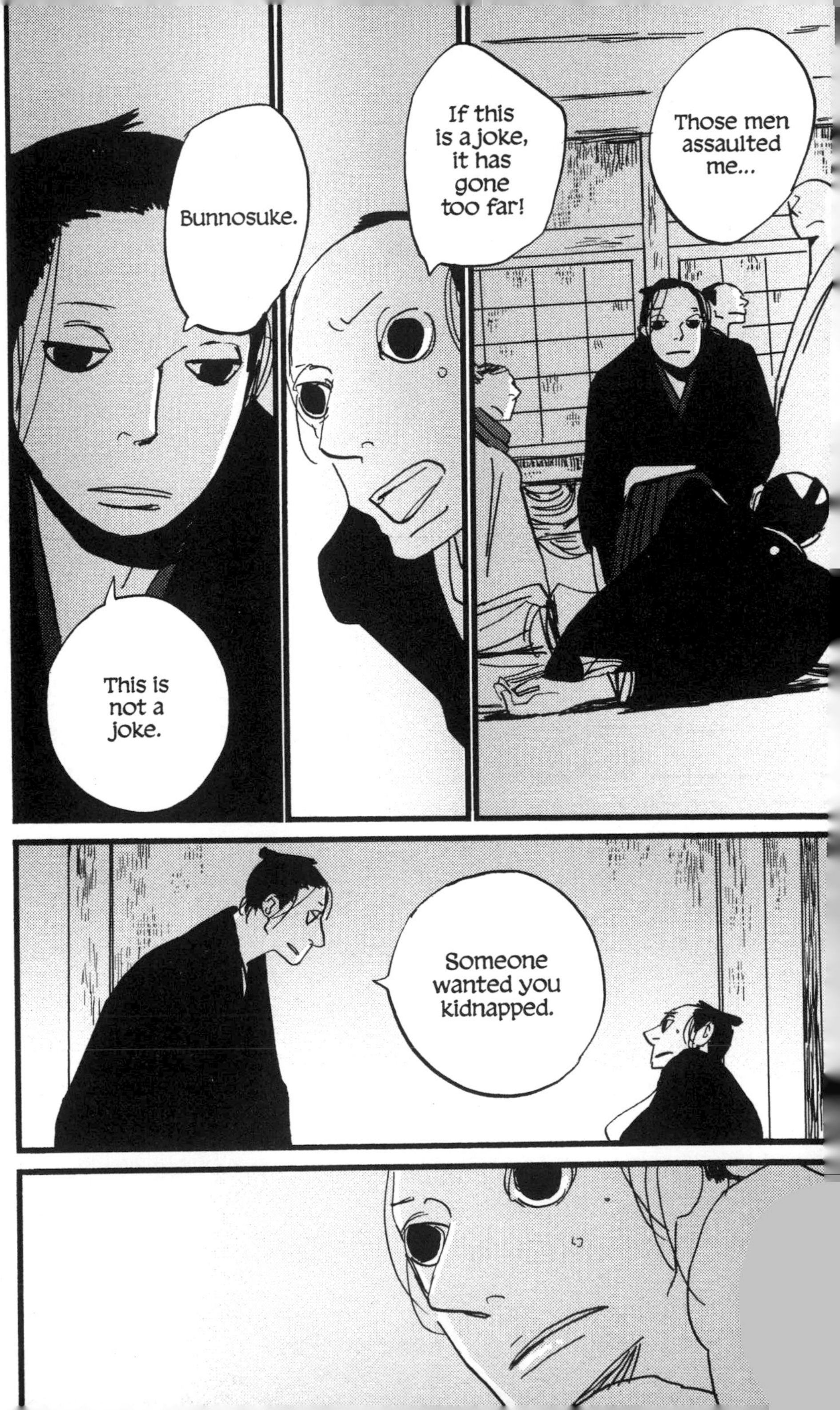
Those men assaulted me...
If this is a joke, it has gone too far!
Bunnosuke.
This is not a joke.
Someone wanted you kidnapped.

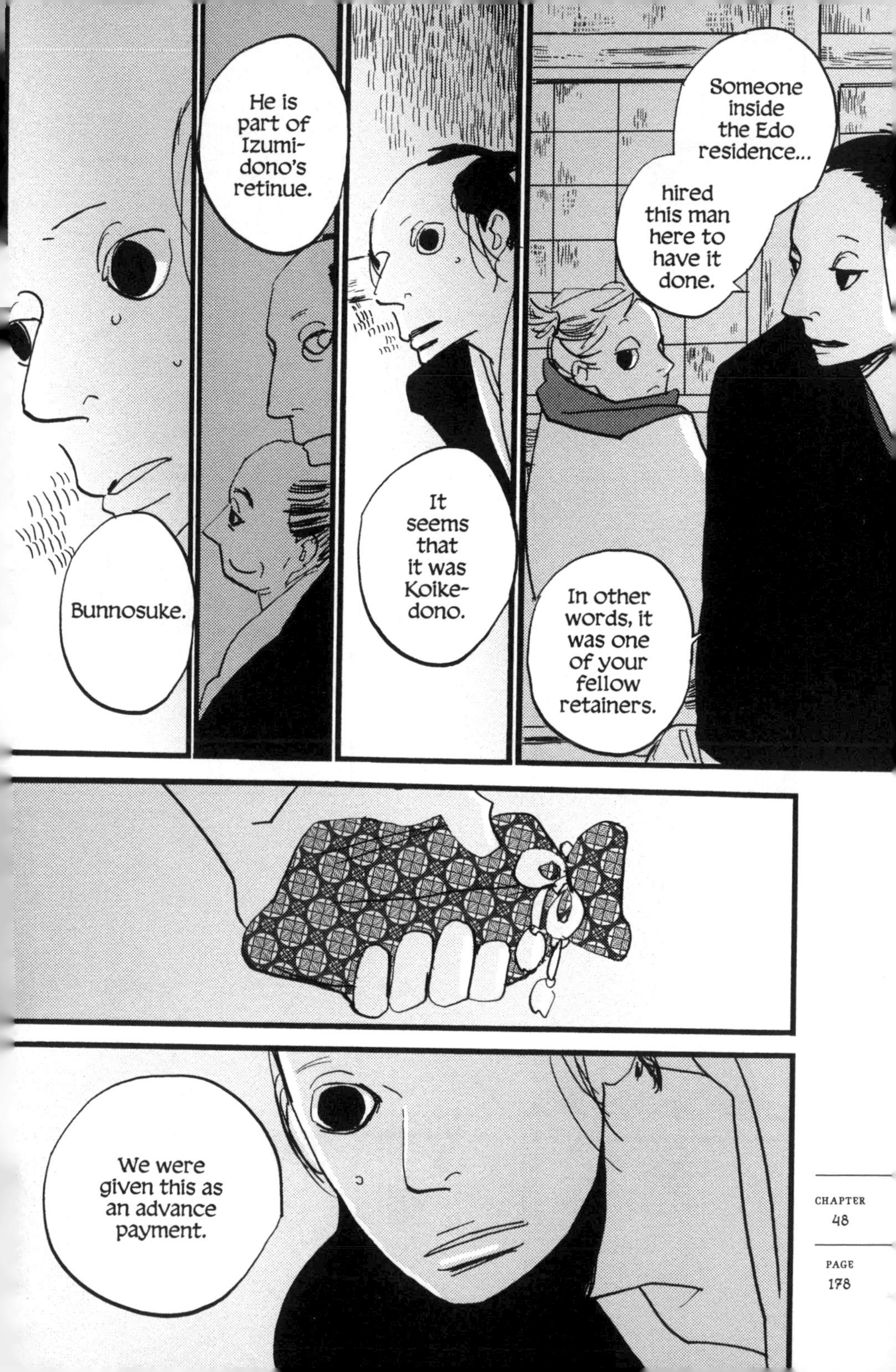
Someone inside the Edo residence...
hired this man here to have it done.
In other words, it was one of your fellow retainers.
It seems that it was Koike-dono.
He is part of Izumi-dono's retinue.
Bunnosuke.
We were given this as an advance payment.

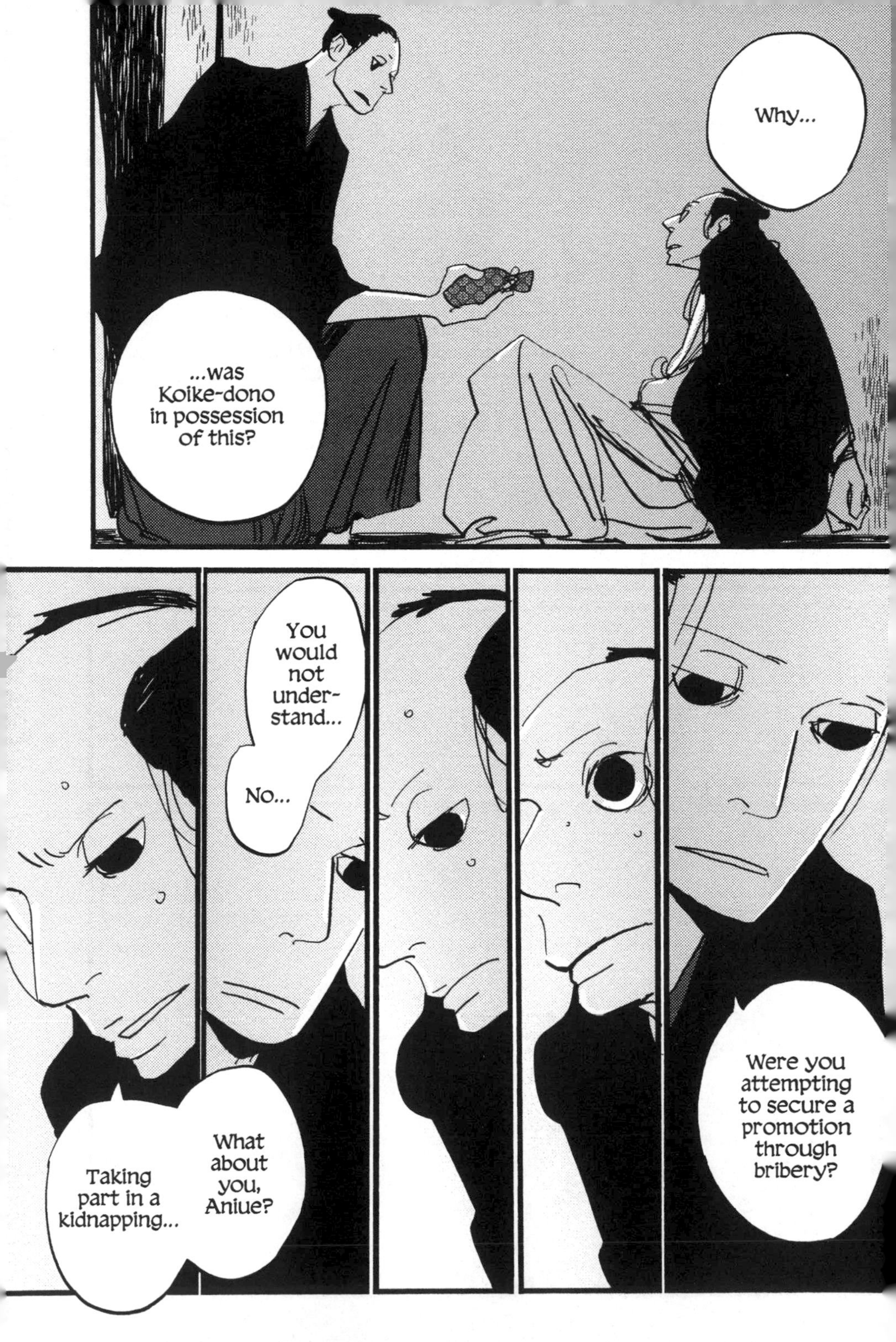
Why...
...was Koike-dono in possession of this?
Were you attempting to secure a promotion through bribery?
You would not understand...
No...
What about you, Aniue?
Taking part in a kidnapping...

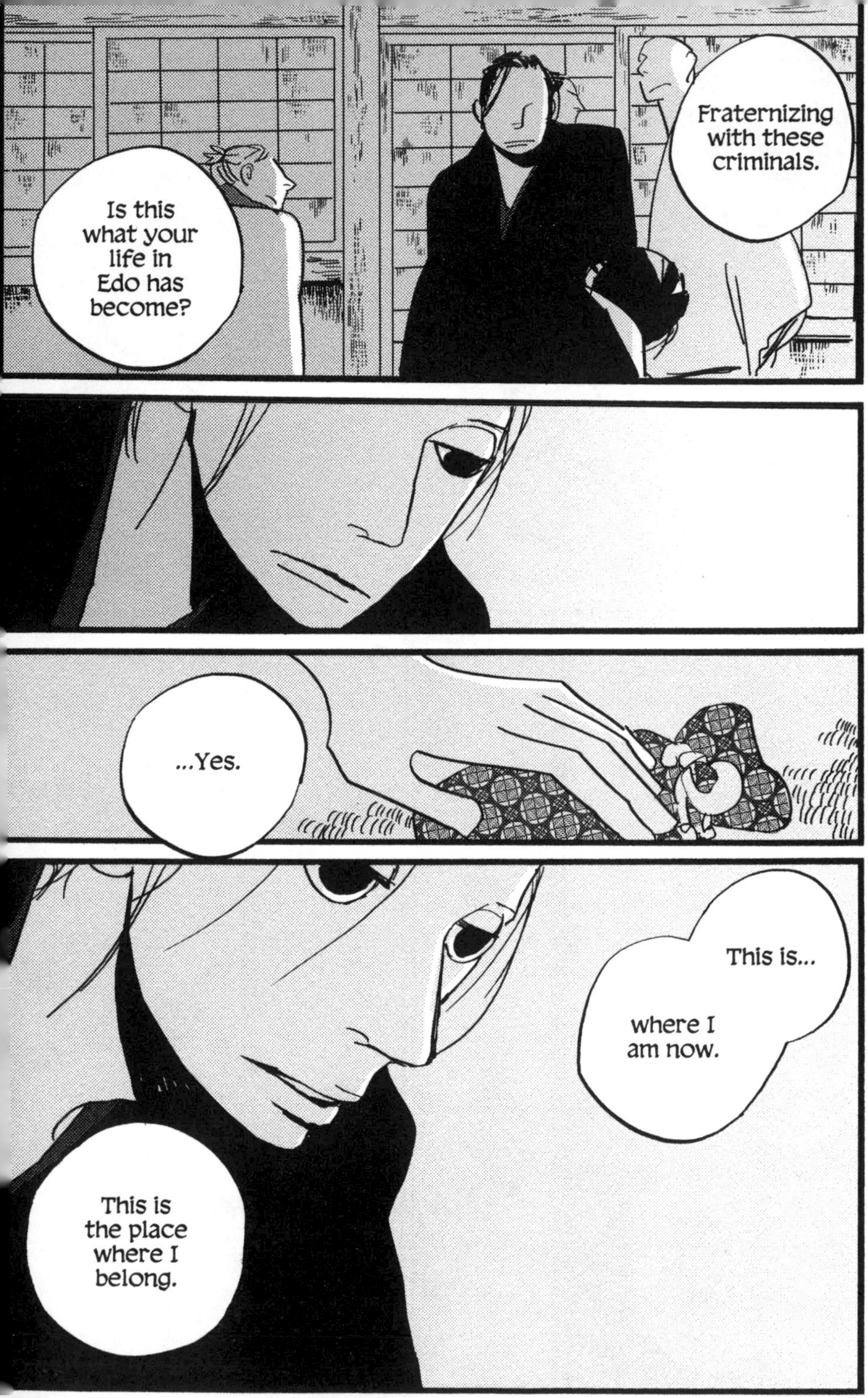
Fraternizing with these criminals.
Is this what your life in Edo has become?
...Yes.
This is... where I am now.
This is the place where I belong.

Chapter Forty-Nine

A Long Rain

(Part Four)

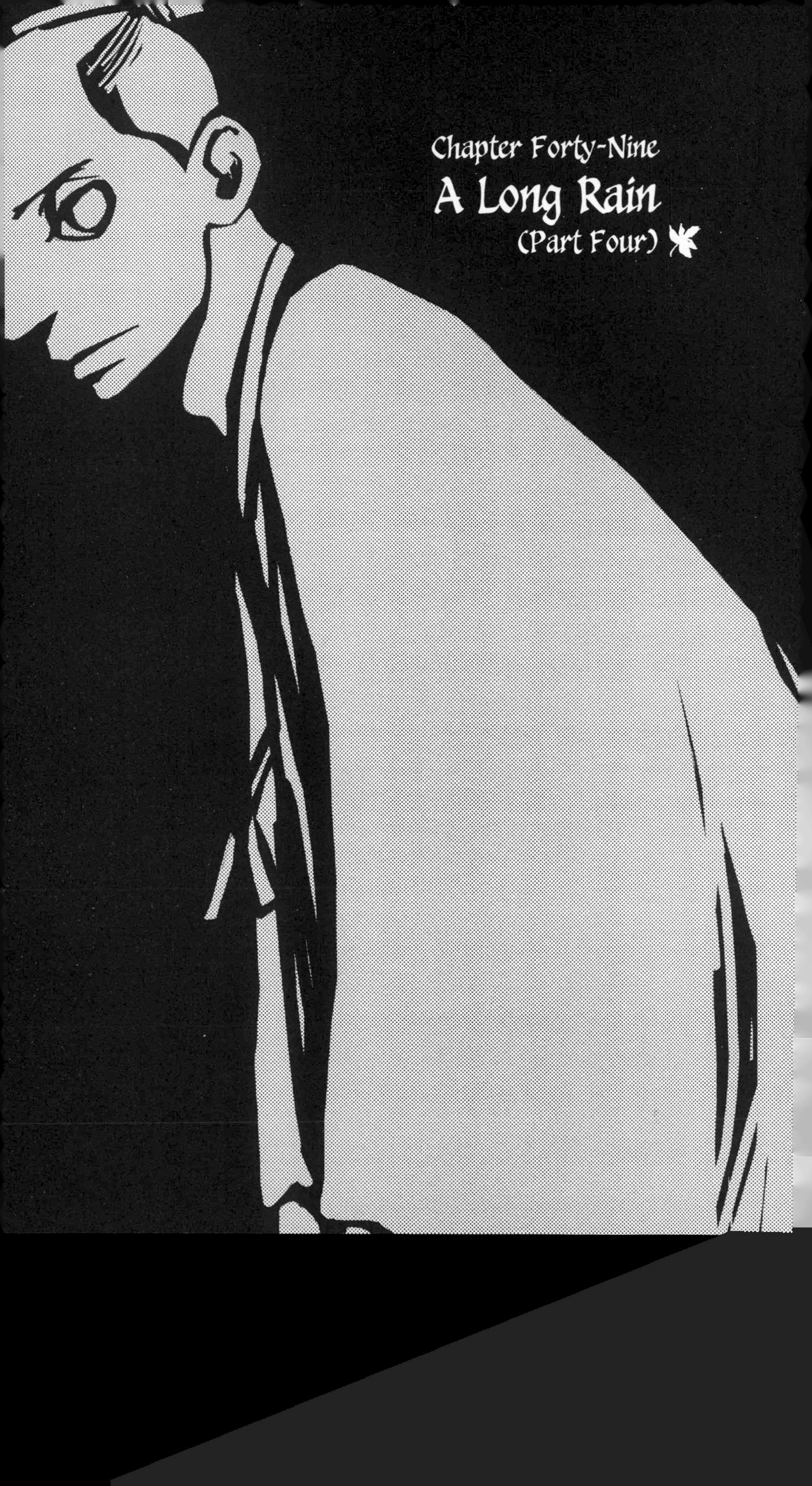

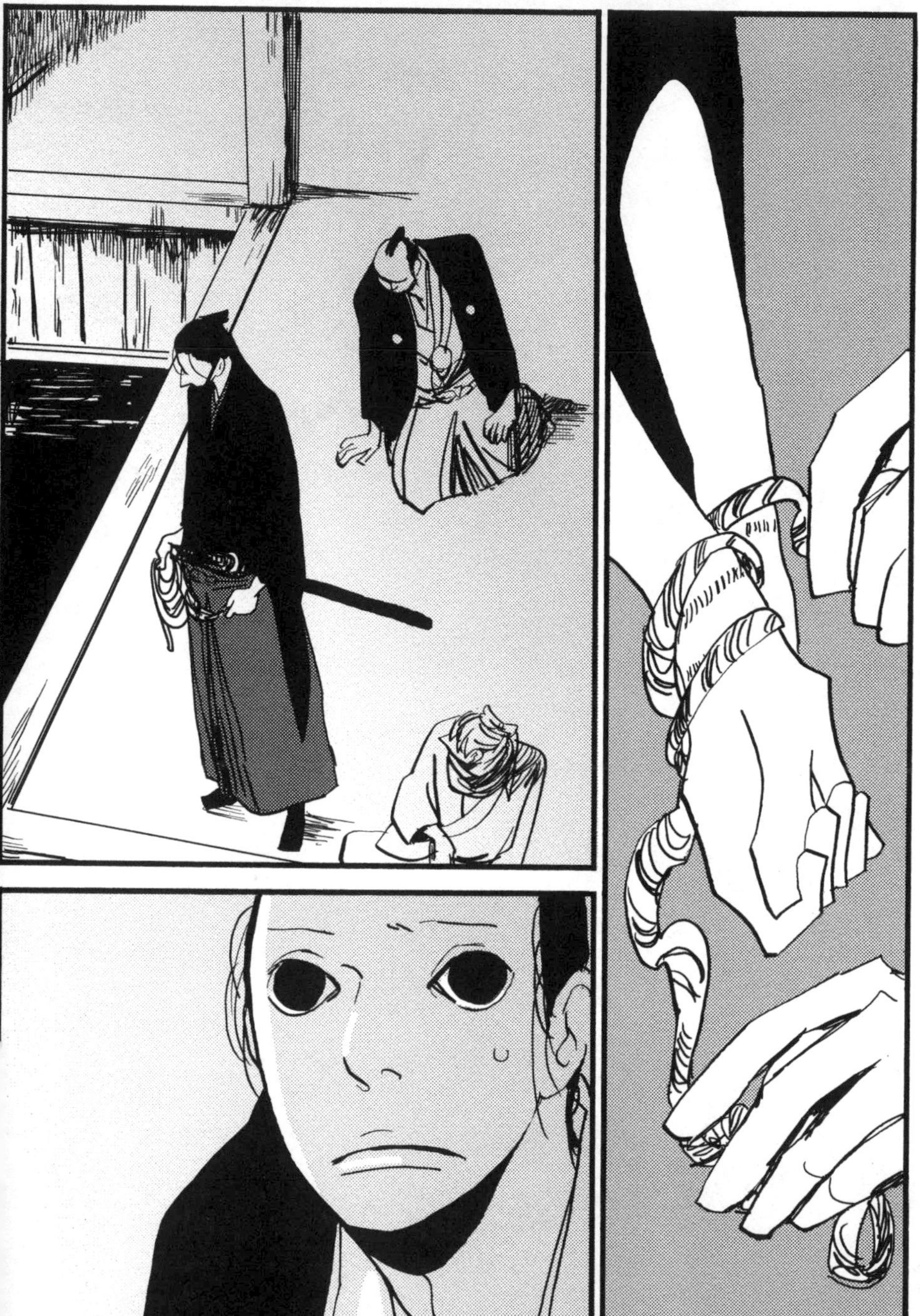

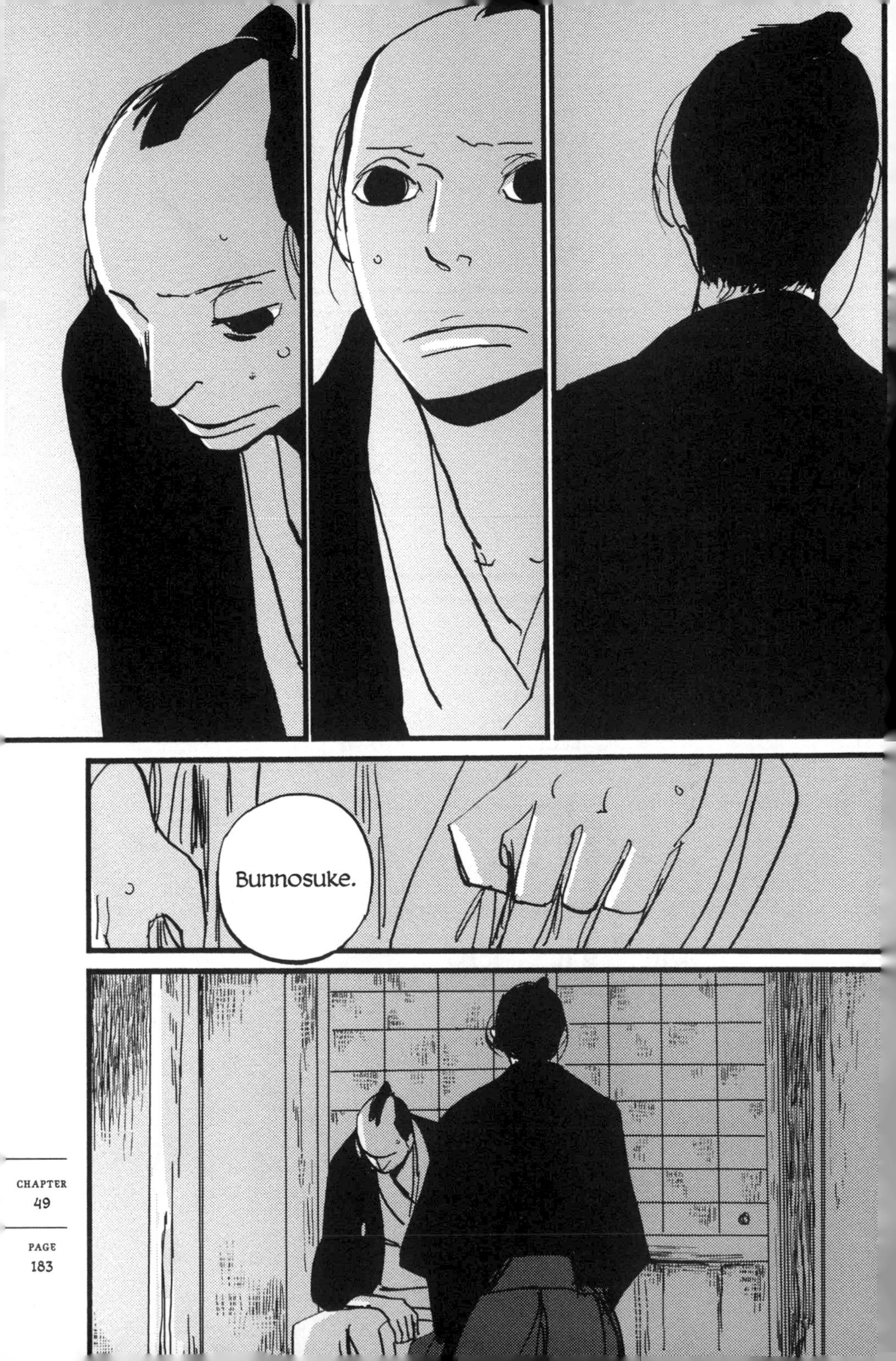
Bunnosuke.

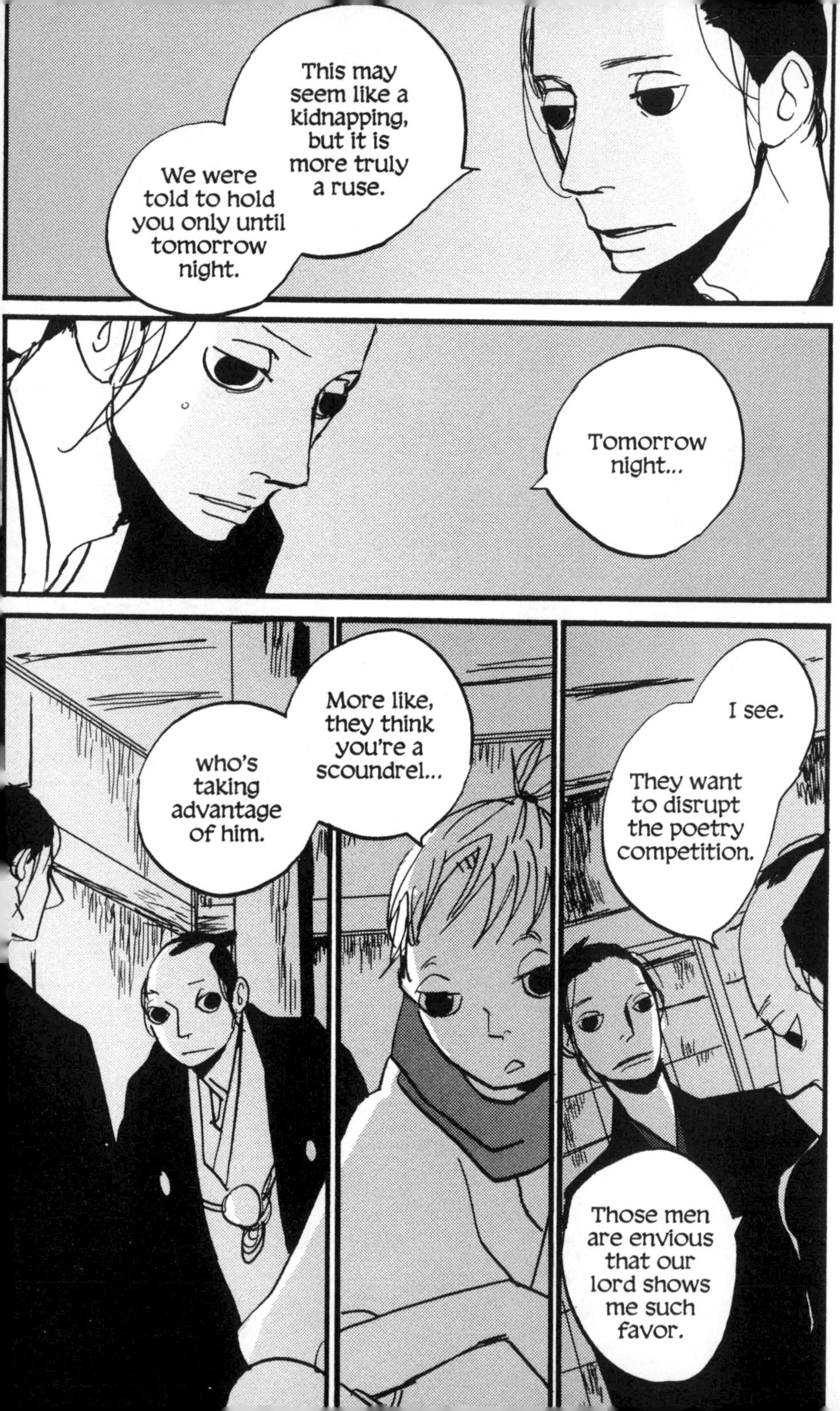
This may seem like a kidnapping, but it is more truly a ruse.
We were told to hold you only until tomorrow night.
Tomorrow night...
I see.
They want to disrupt the poetry competition.
Those men are envious that our lord shows me such favor.
More like, they think you're a scoundrel...
who's taking advantage of him.

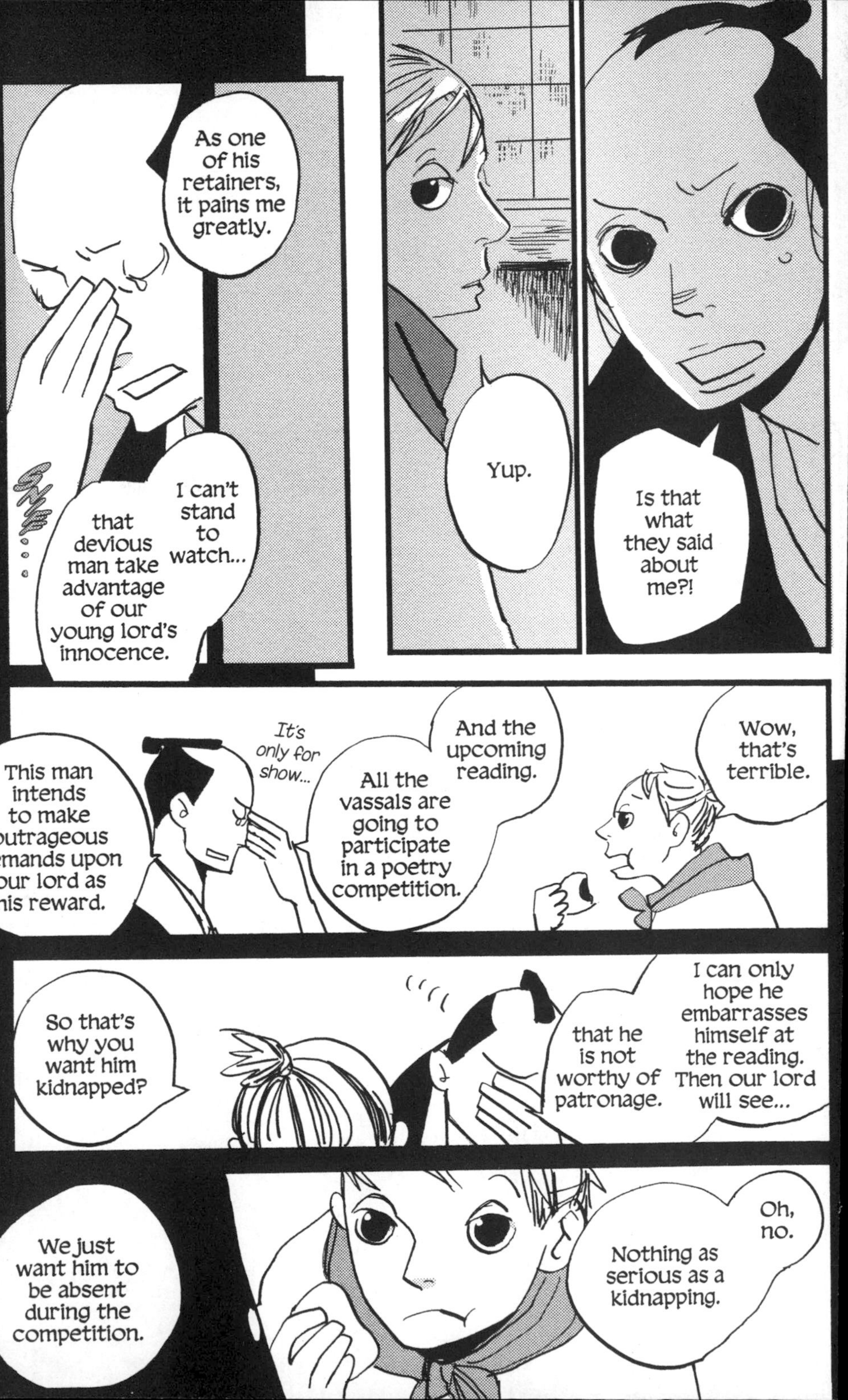
Is that what they said about me?!
Yup.
As one of his retainers, it pains me greatly.
I can't stand to watch...
that devious man take advantage of our young lord's innocence.
Wow, that's terrible.
And the upcoming reading.
All the vassals are going to participate in a poetry competition.
It's only for show...
This man intends to make outrageous demands upon our lord as his reward.
I can only hope he embarrasses himself at the reading. Then our lord will see...
that he is not worthy of patronage.
So that's why you want him kidnapped?
Oh, no.
Nothing as serious as a kidnapping.
We just want him to be absent during the competition.

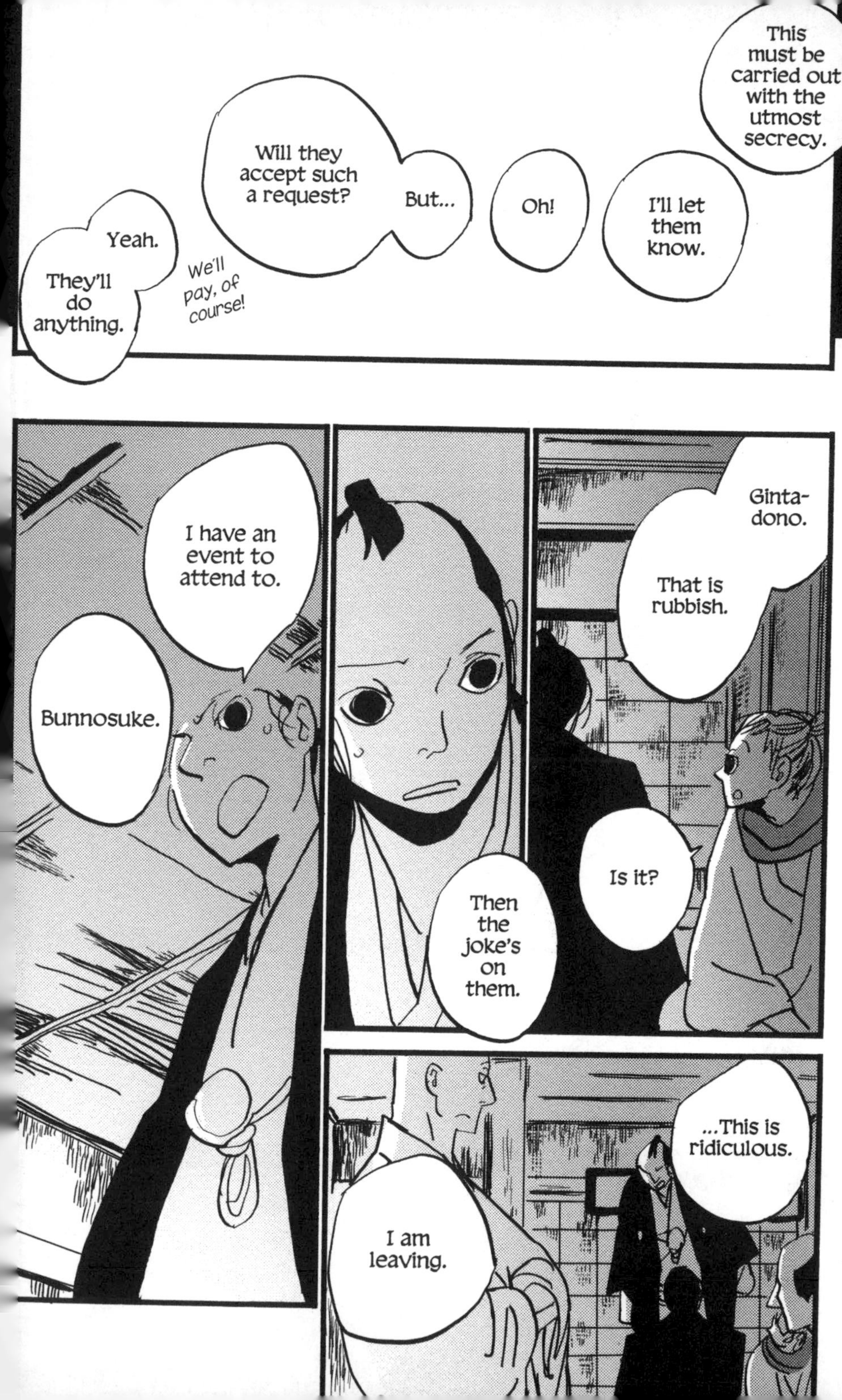
This must be carried out with the utmost secrecy.
I'll let them know.
Oh!
But...
Will they accept such a request?
We'll pay, of course!
Yeah.
They'll do anything.
Ginta-dono.
That is rubbish.
Is it?
Then the joke's on them.
I have an event to attend to.
Bunnosuke.
...This is ridiculous.
I am leaving.

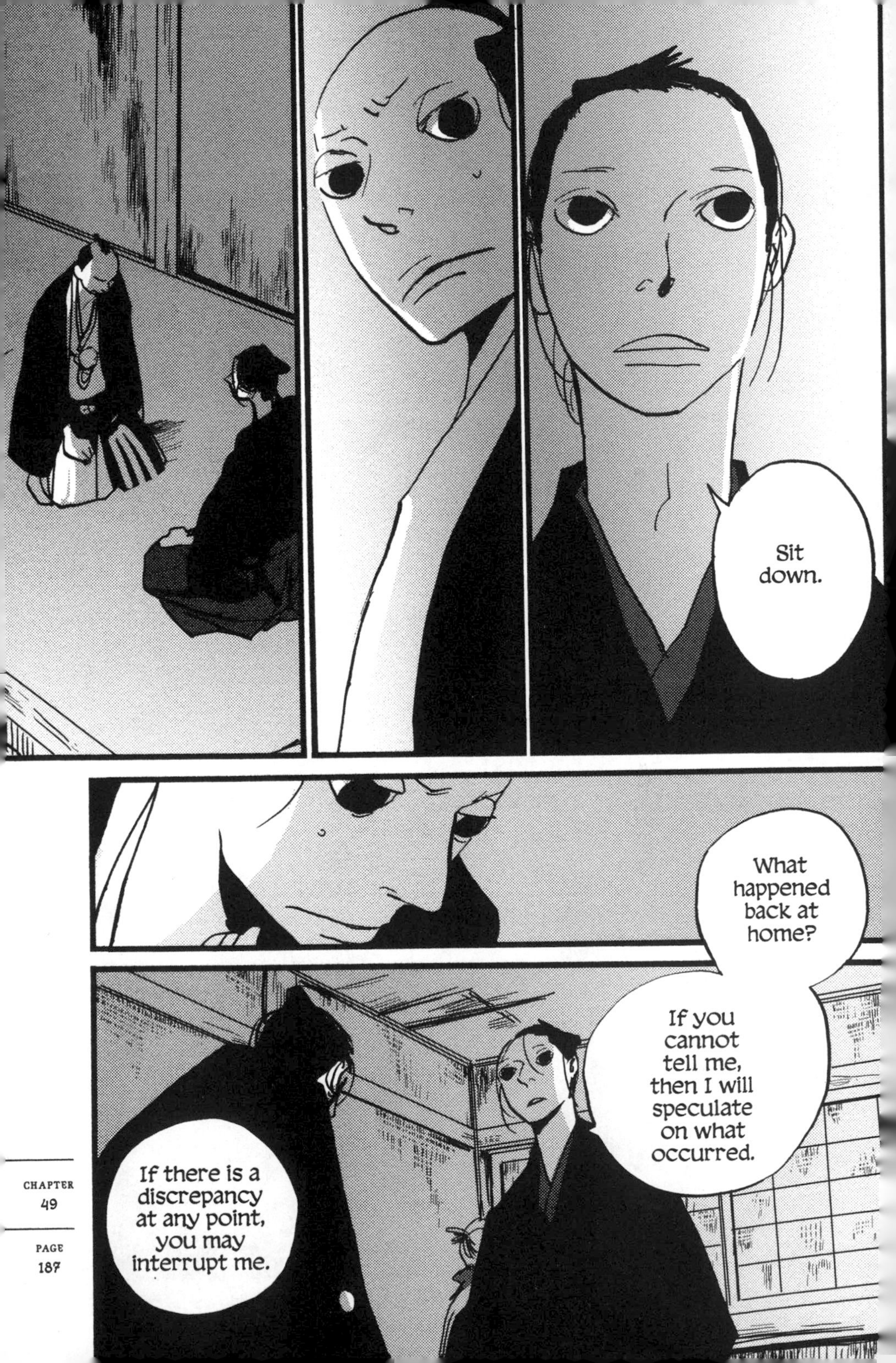
Sit down.
What happened back at home?
If you cannot tell me, then I will speculate on what occurred.
If there is a discrepancy at any point, you may interrupt me.

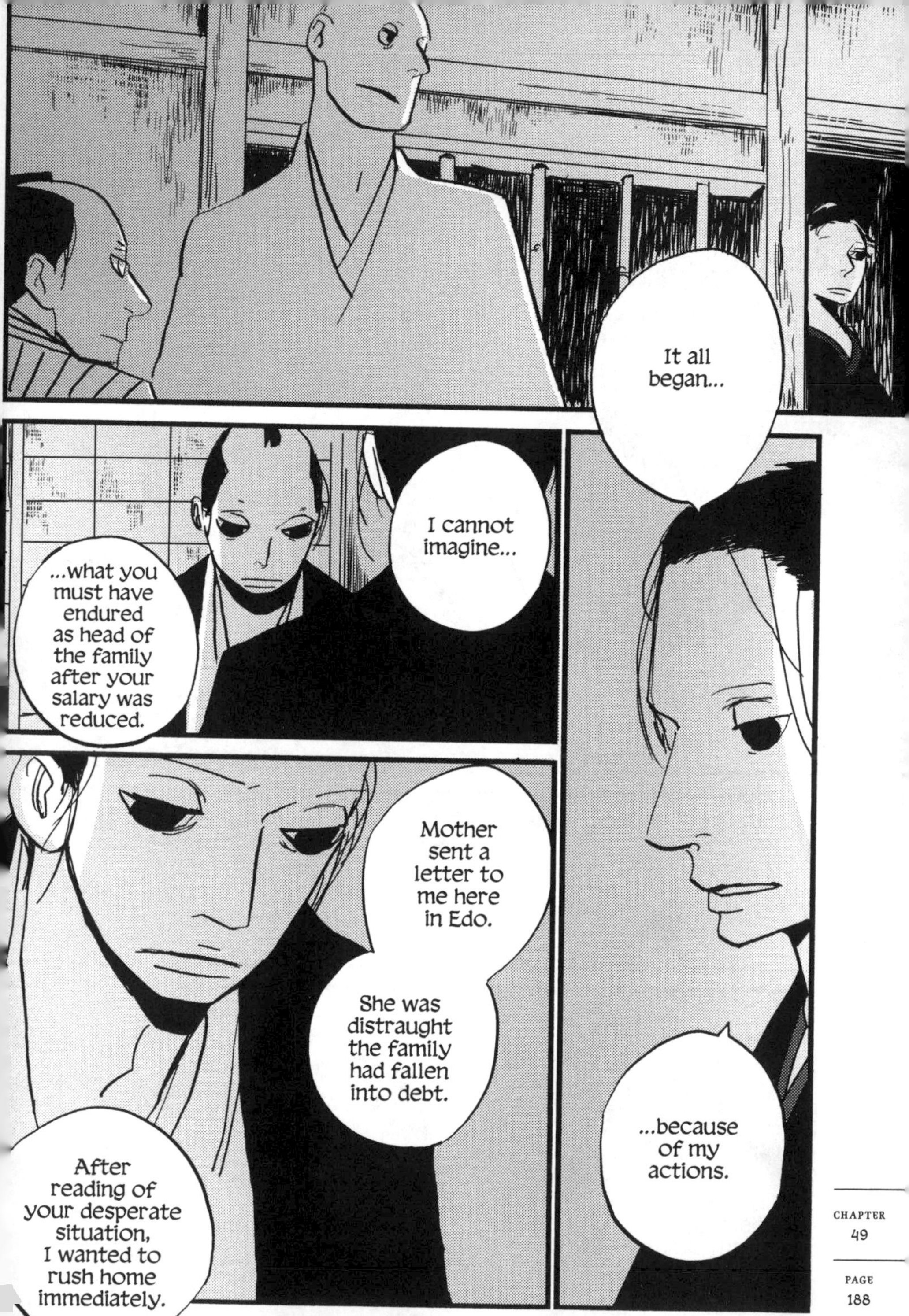
It all began...
...because of my actions.
I cannot imagine...
...what you must have endured as head of the family after your salary was reduced.
Mother sent a letter to me here in Edo.
She was distraught the family had fallen into debt.
After reading of your desperate situation, I wanted to rush home immediately.

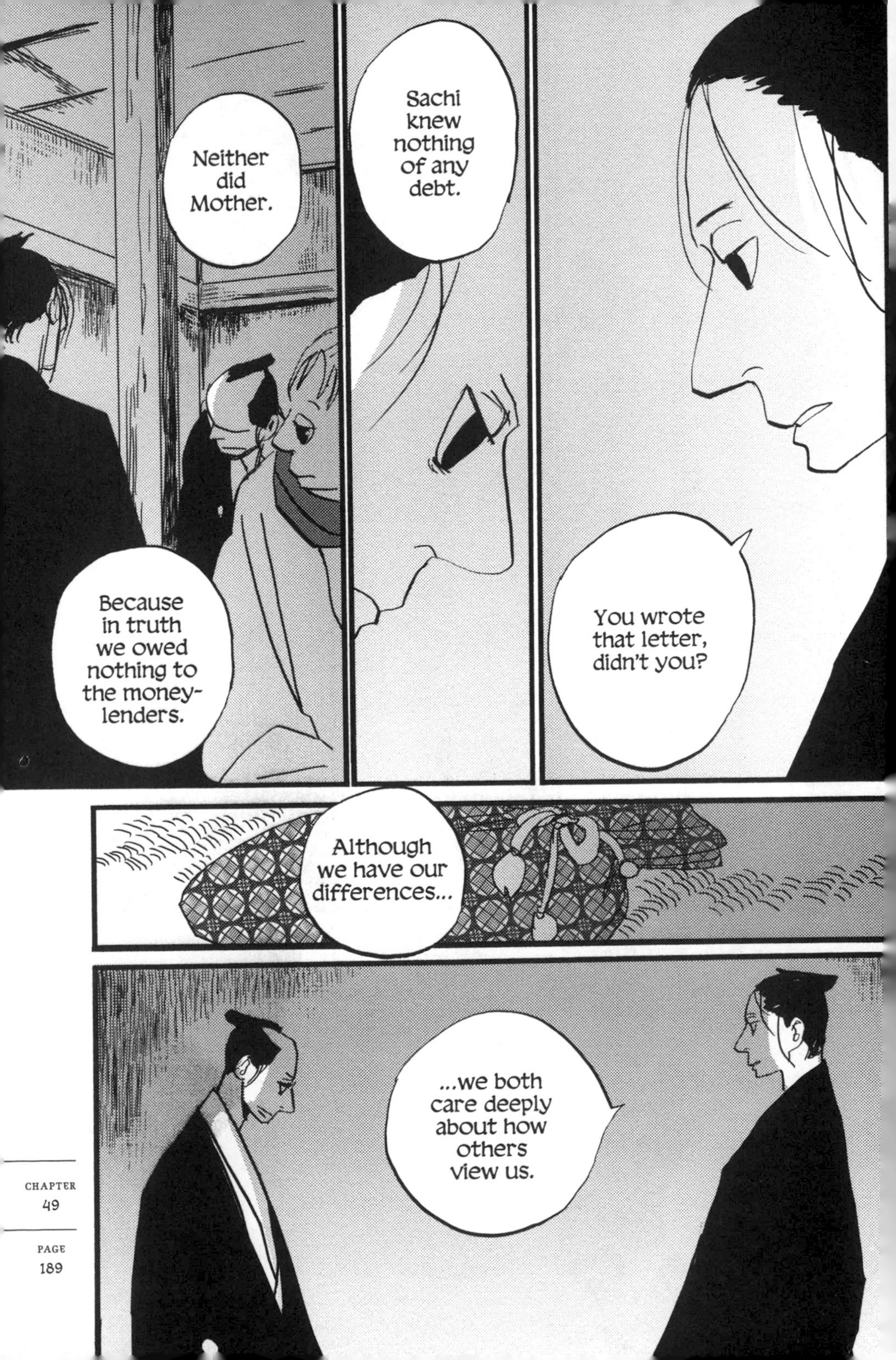
You wrote that letter, didn't you?
Sachi knew nothing of any debt.
Neither did Mother.
Because in truth we owed nothing to the money-lenders.
Although we have our differences...
...we both care deeply about how others view us.

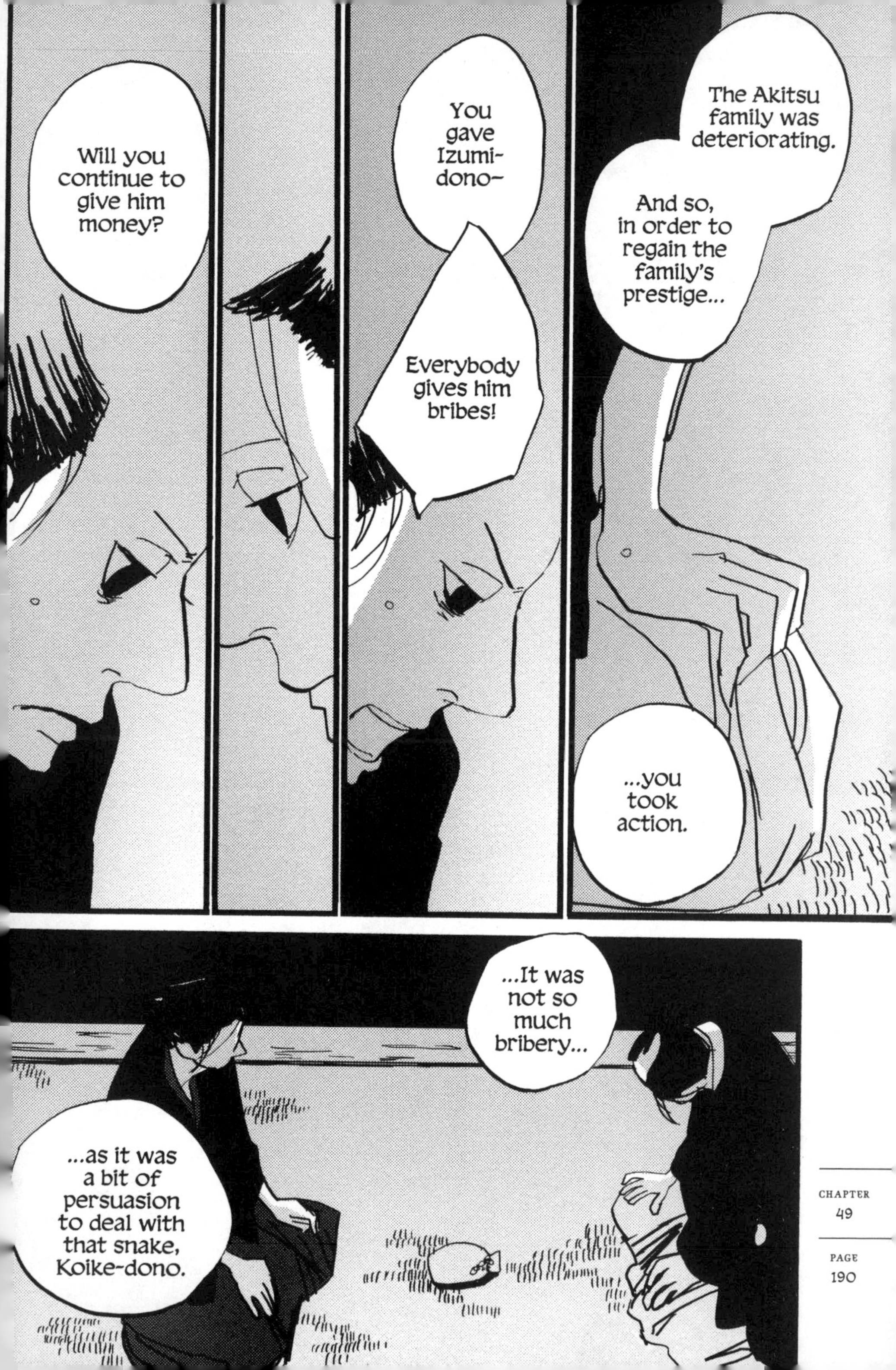
The Akitsu family was deteriorating.
And so, in order to regain the family's prestige...
...you took action.
You gave Izumi-dono—
Everybody gives him bribes!
Will you continue to give him money?
...It was not so much bribery...
...as it was a bit of persuasion to deal with that snake, Koike-dono.

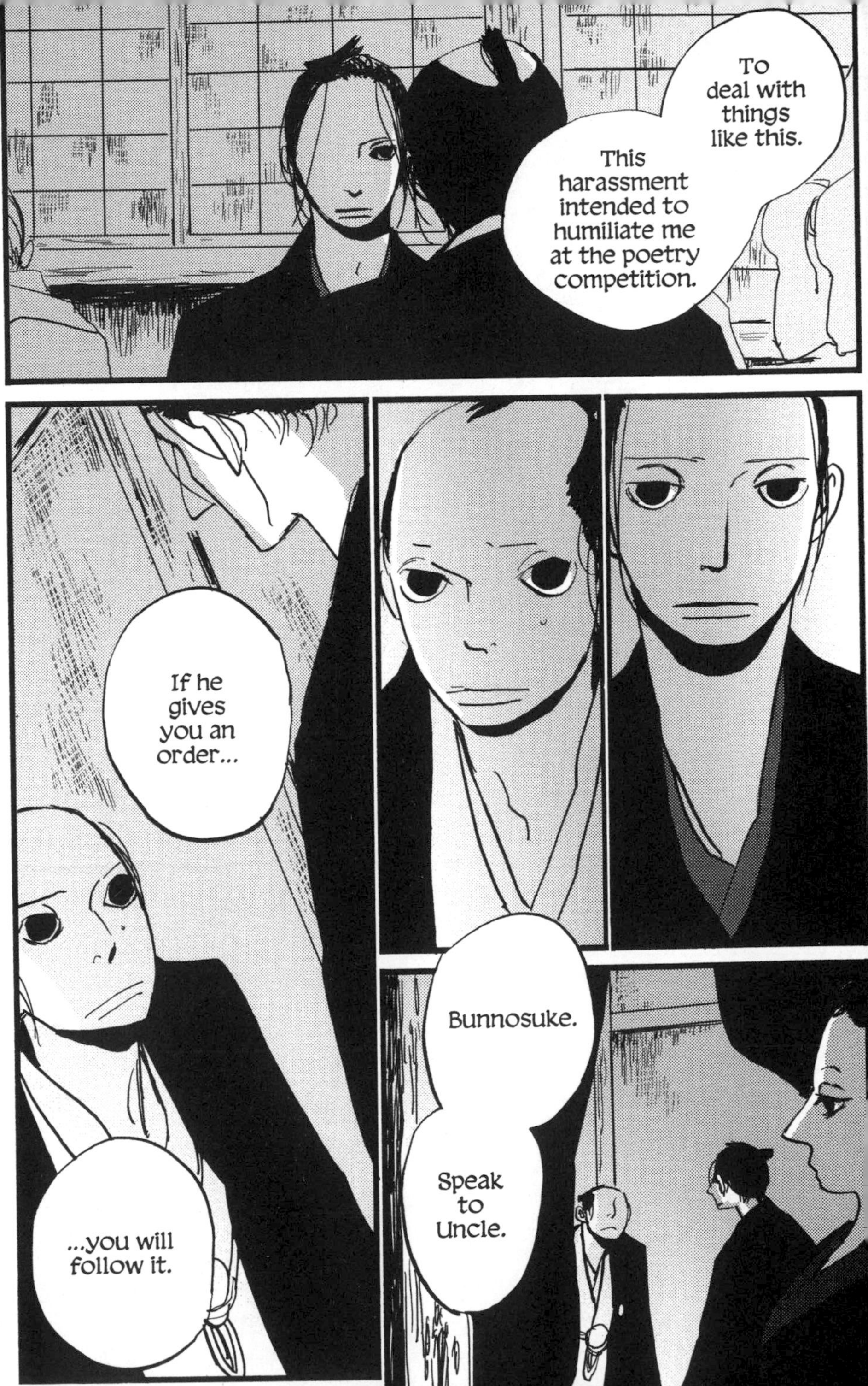
To deal with things like this.
This harassment intended to humiliate me at the poetry competition.
Bunnosuke.
Speak to Uncle.
If he gives you an order...
...you will follow it.

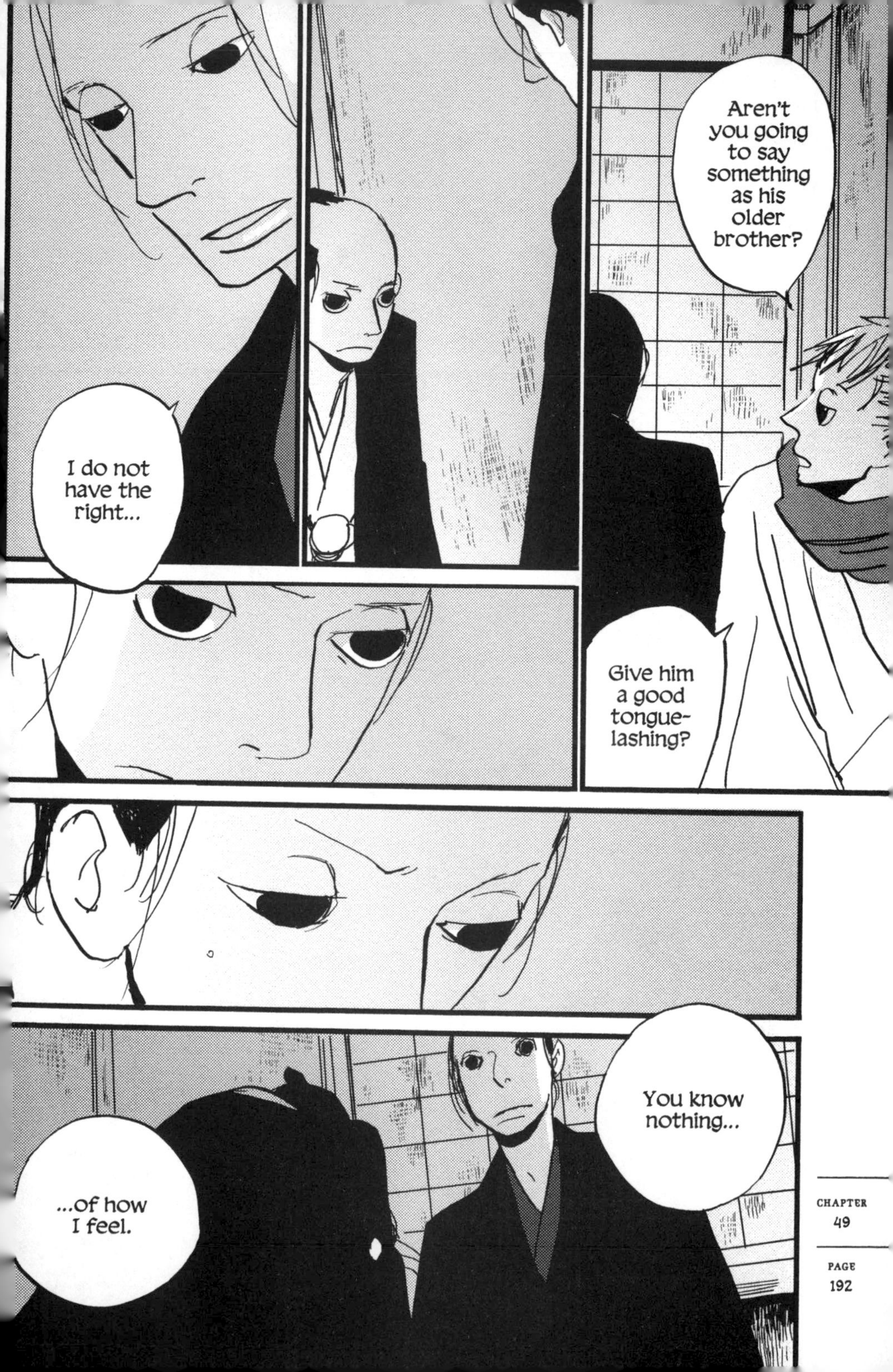
Aren't you going to say something as his older brother?
Give him a good tongue-lashing?
I do not have the right...
You know nothing...
...of how I feel.

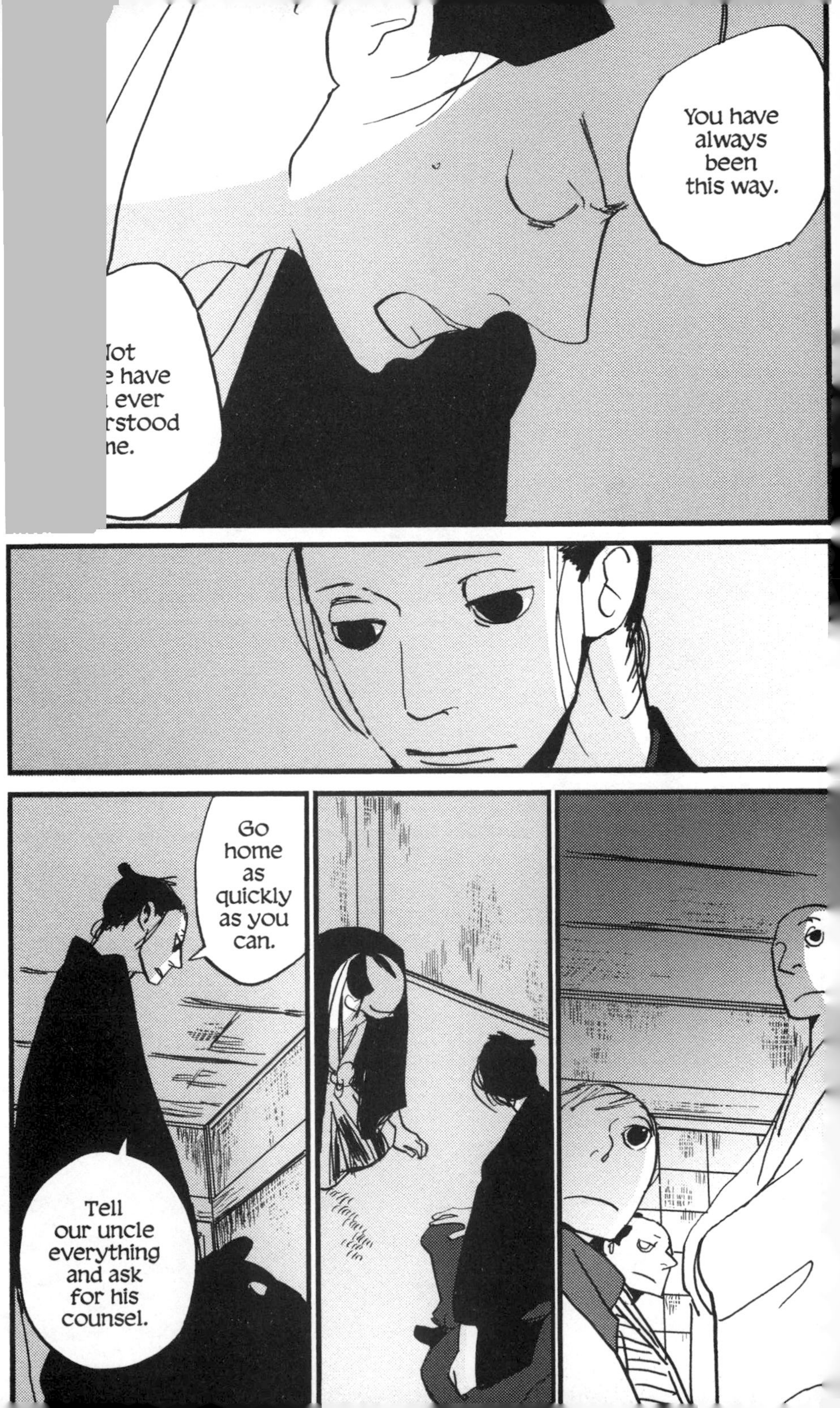
You have always been this way.
Not e have ever rstood ne.
Go home as quickly as you can.
Tell our uncle everything and ask for his counsel.

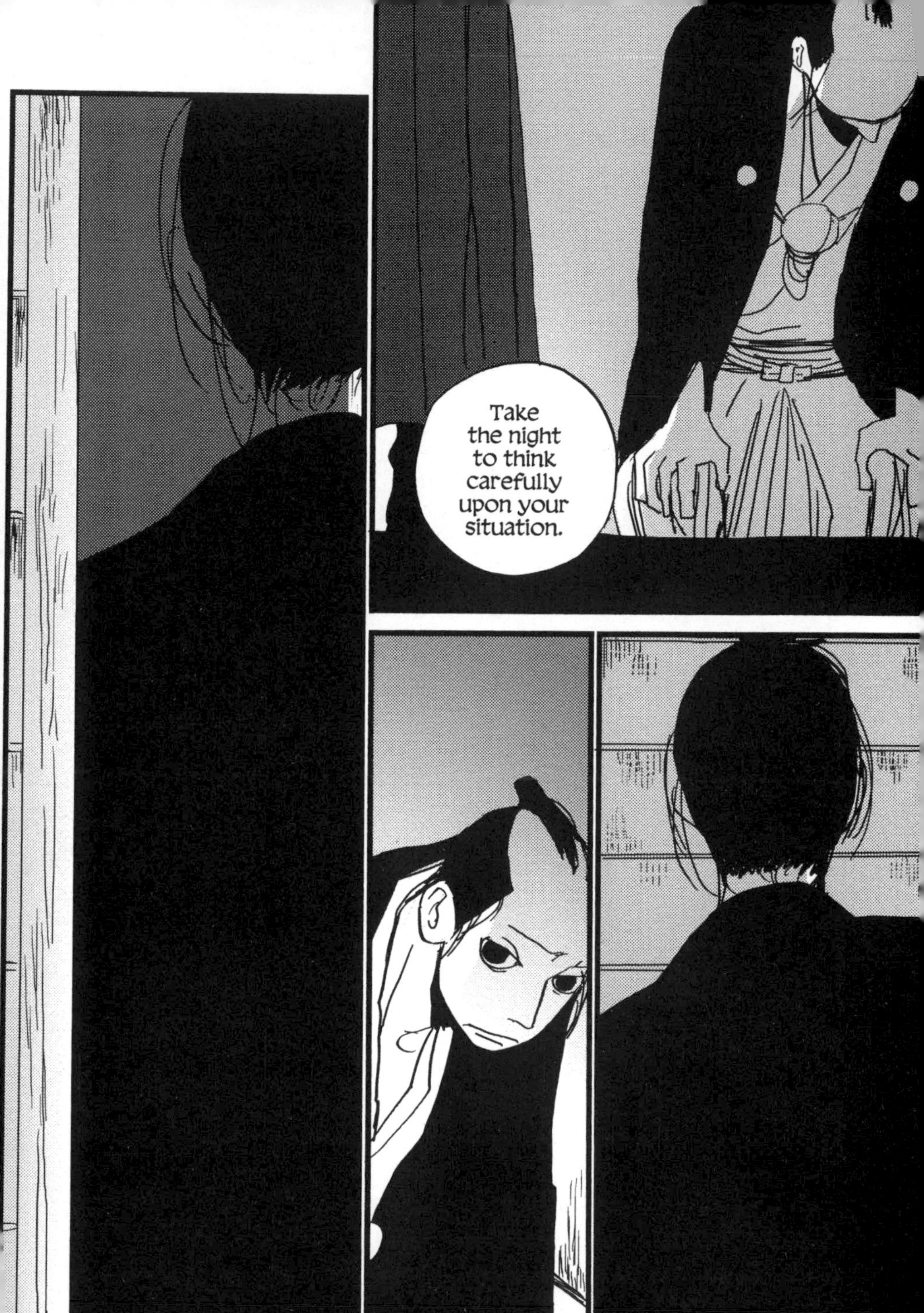
Take the night to think carefully upon your situation.

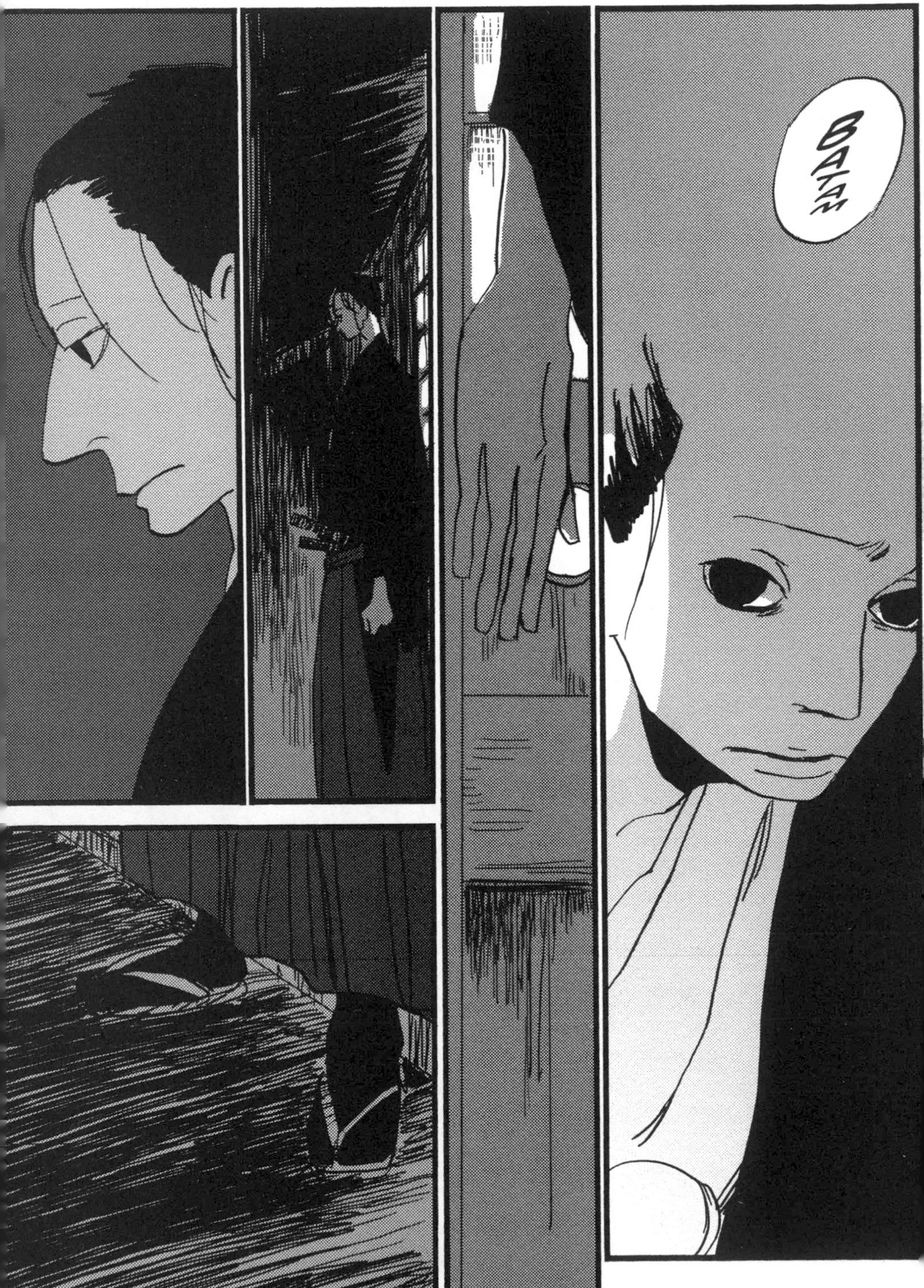
BATAM

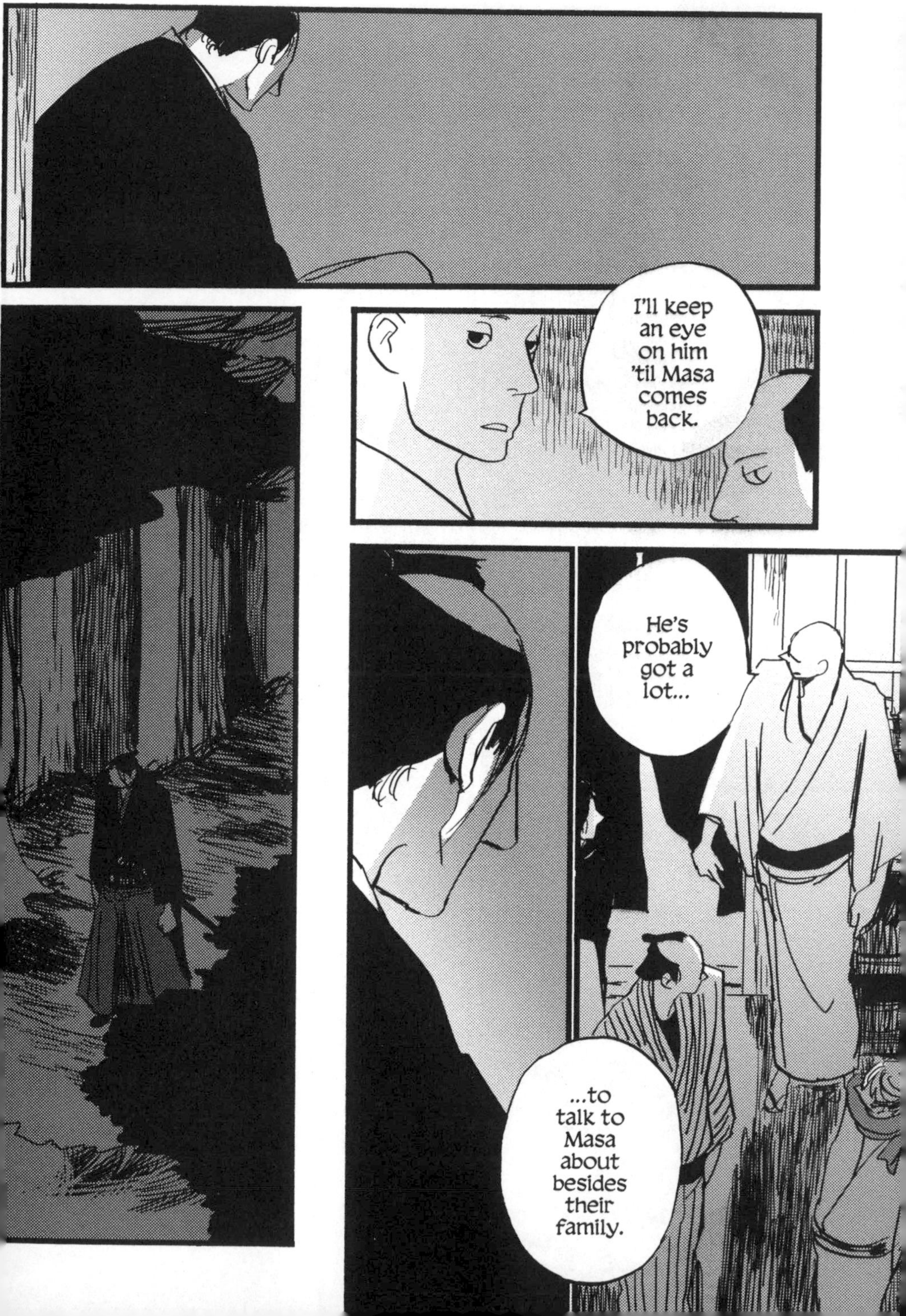
I'll keep an eye on him 'til Masa comes back.
He's probably got a lot...
...to talk to Masa about besides their family.

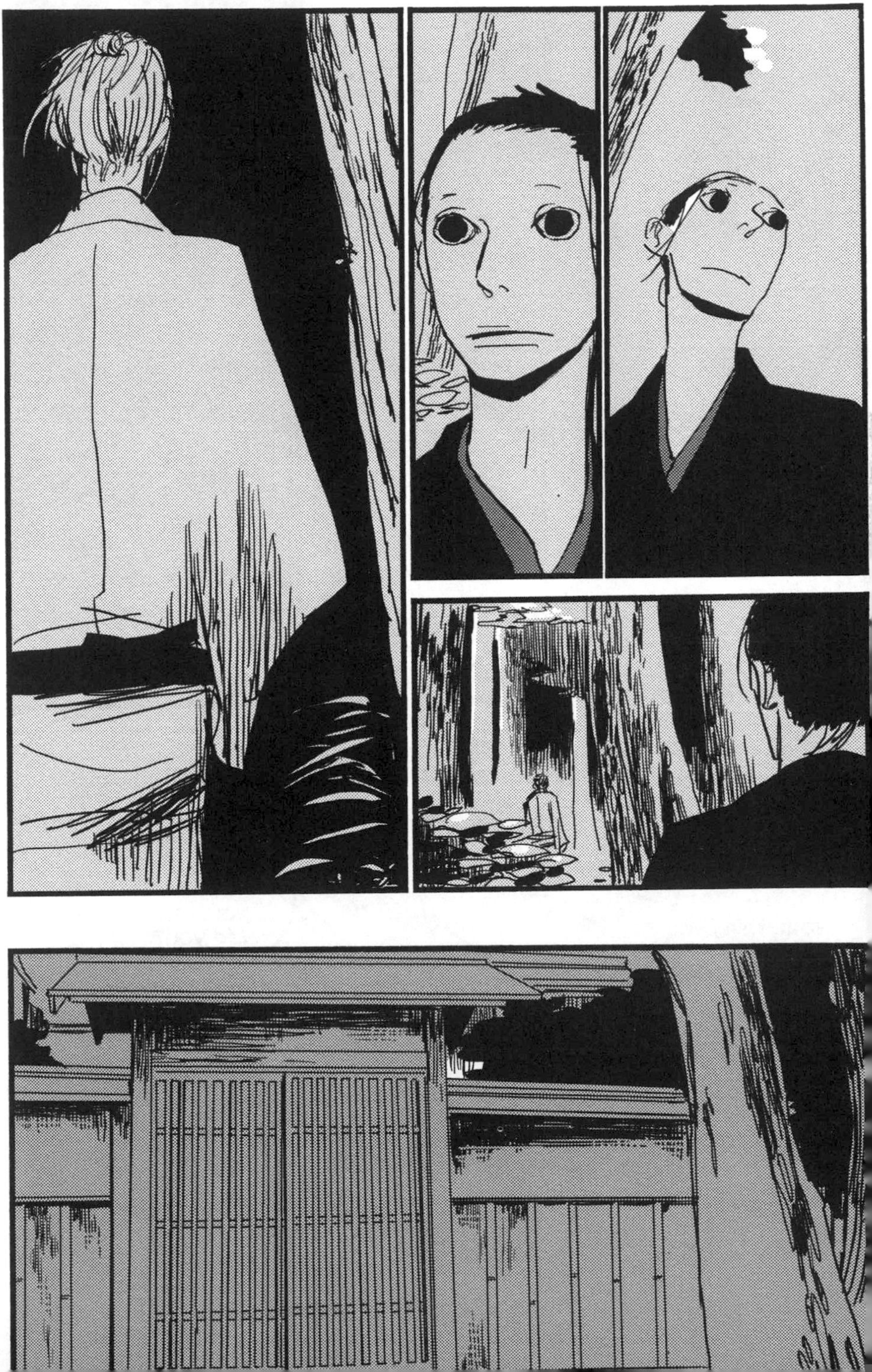

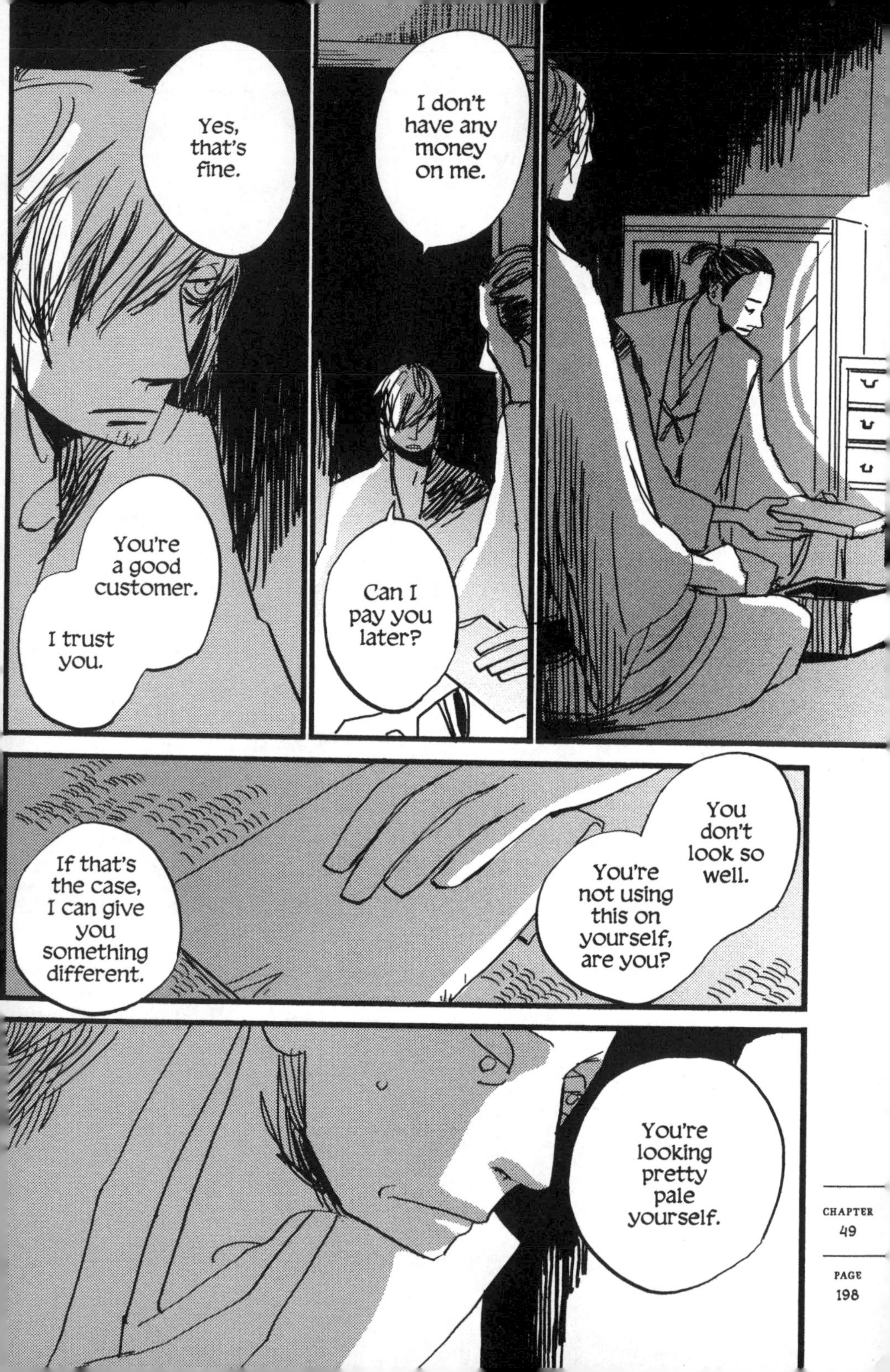
I don't have any money on me.
Can I pay you later?
Yes, that's fine.
You're a good customer.
I trust you.
You don't look so well.
You're not using this on yourself, are you?
If that's the case, I can give you something different.
You're looking pretty pale yourself.

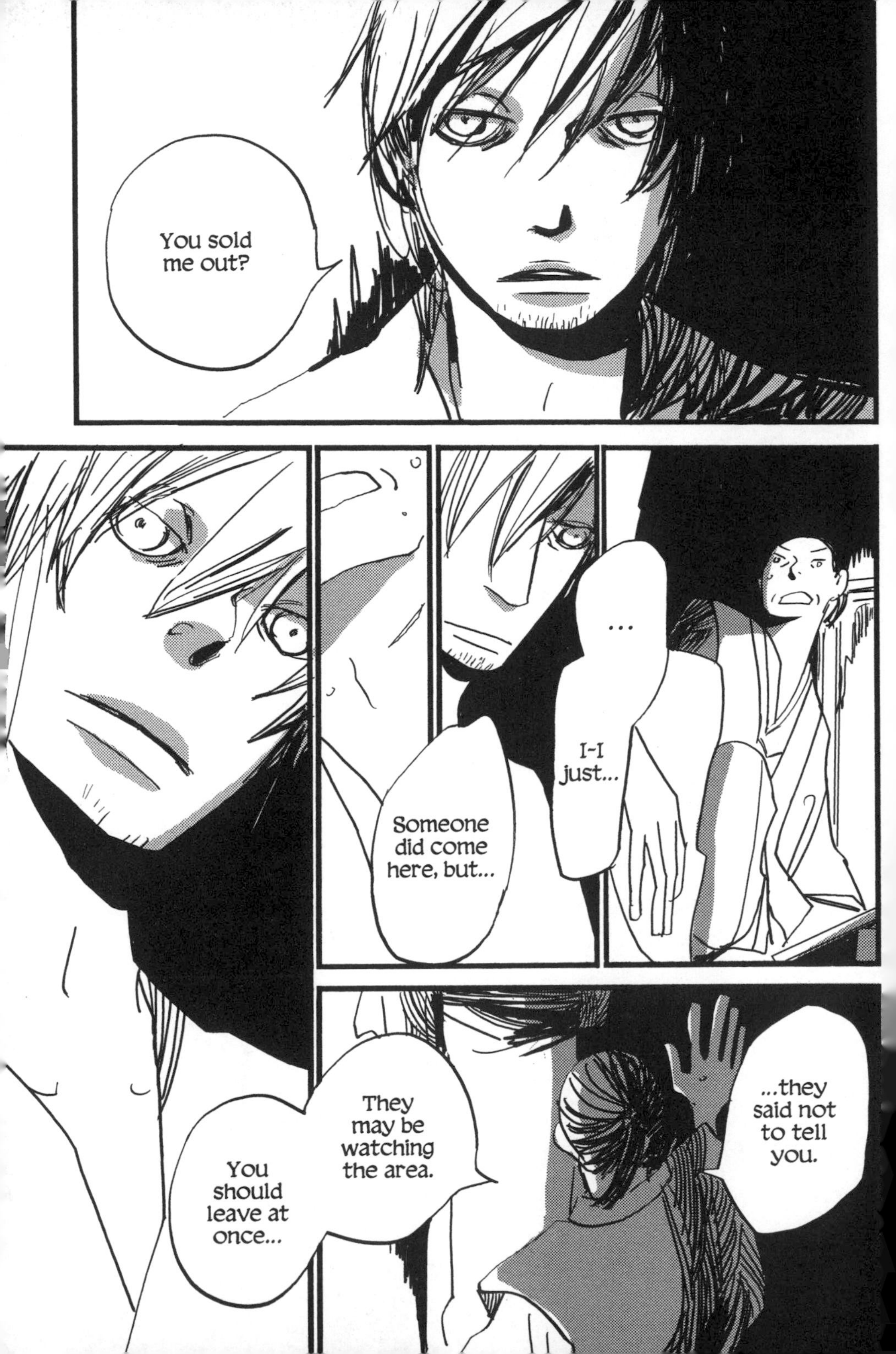
You sold me out?
...
I-I just...
Someone did come here, but...
...they said not to tell you.
They may be watching the area.
You should leave at once...

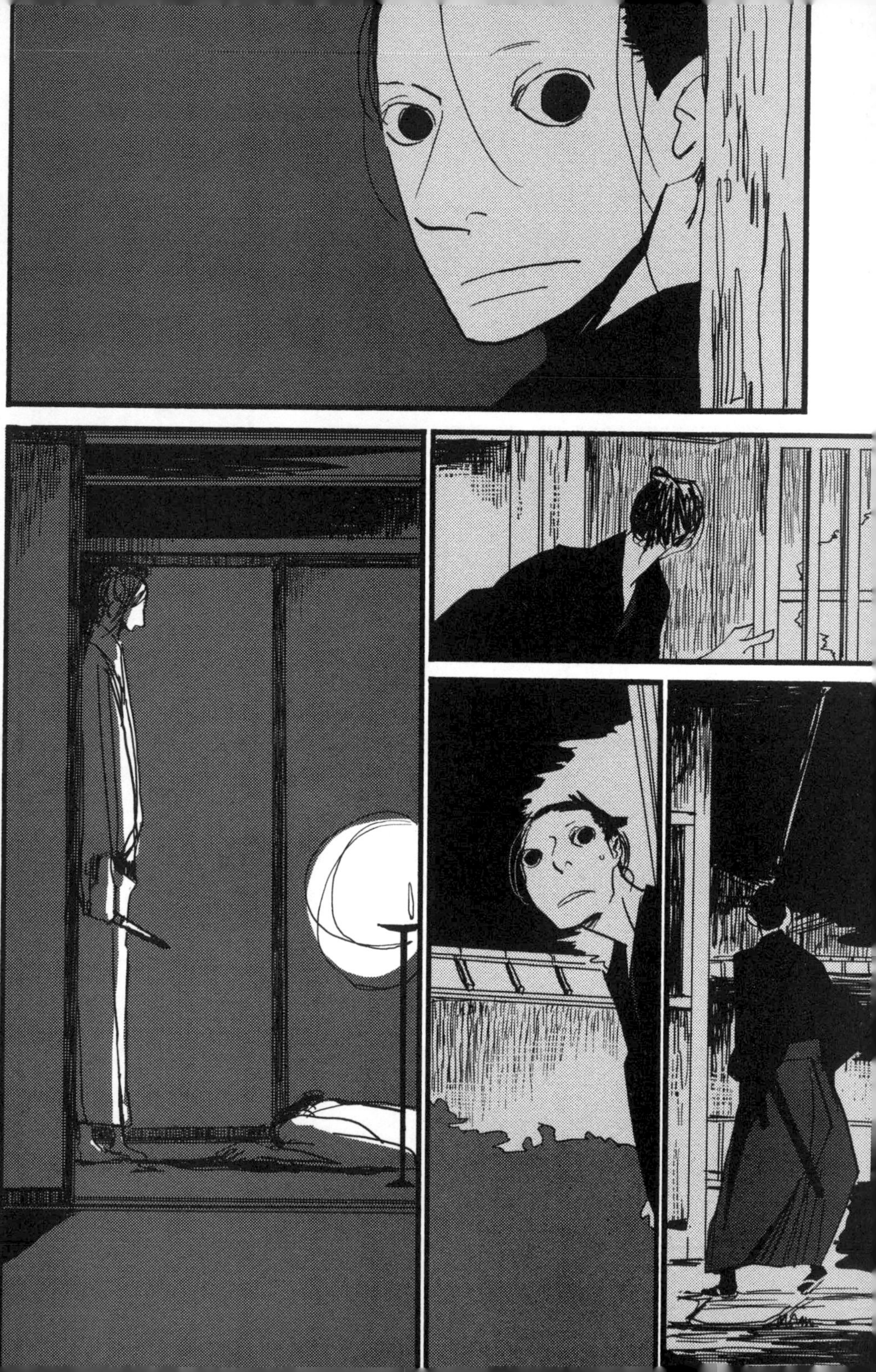

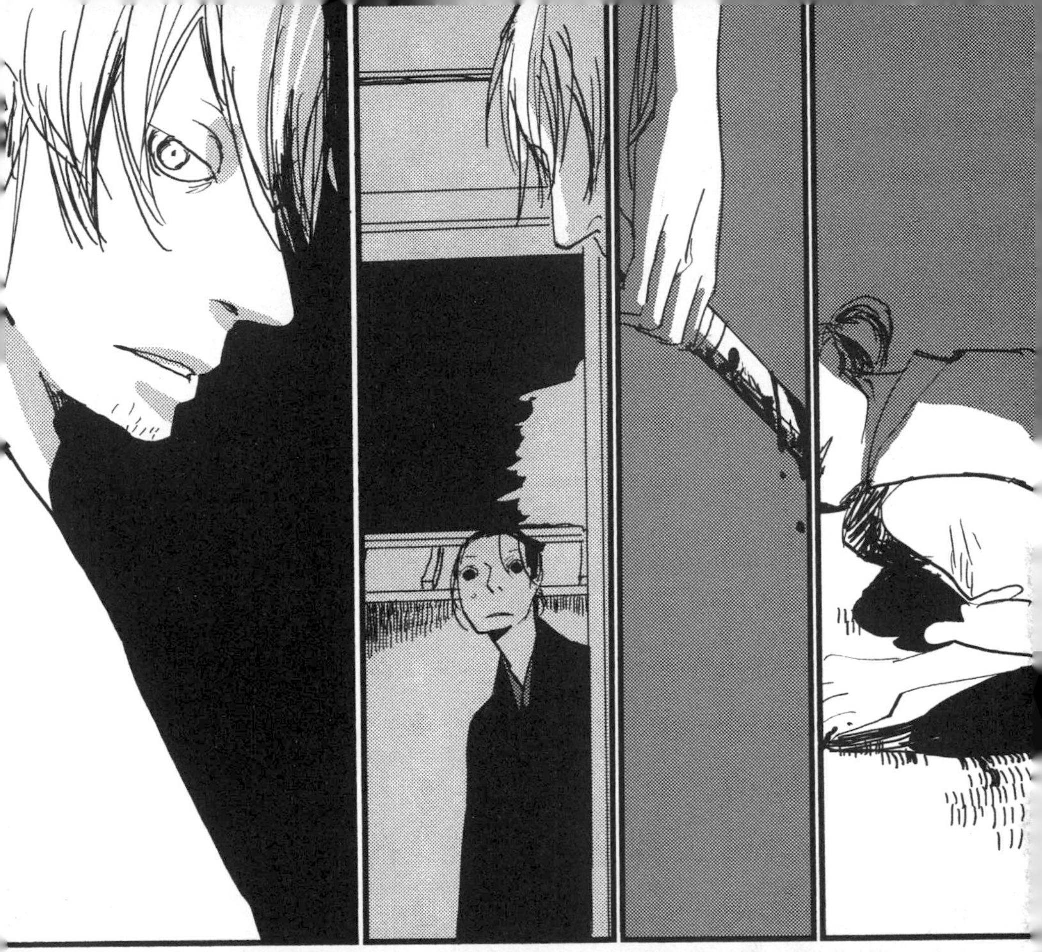

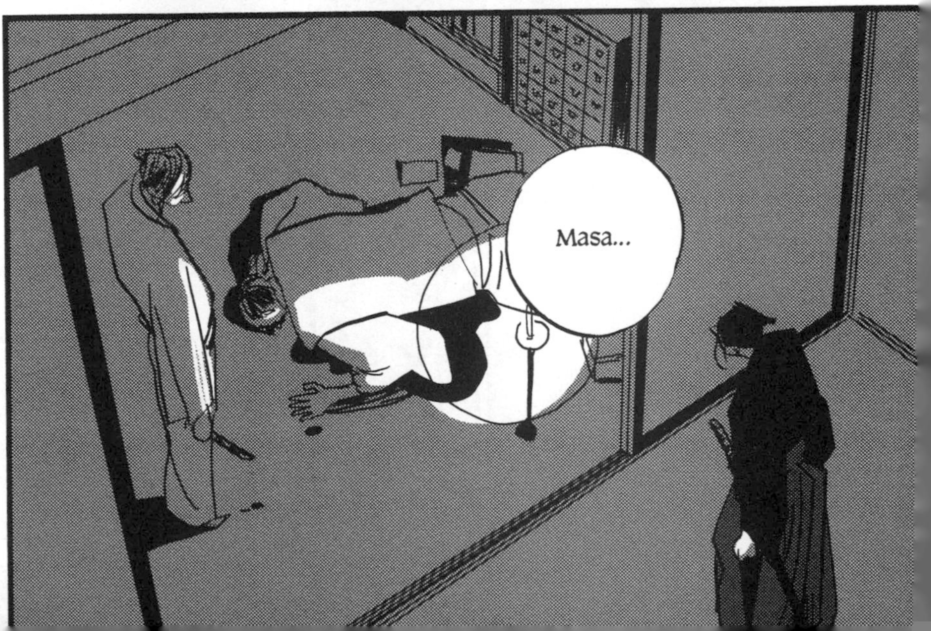
Masa...

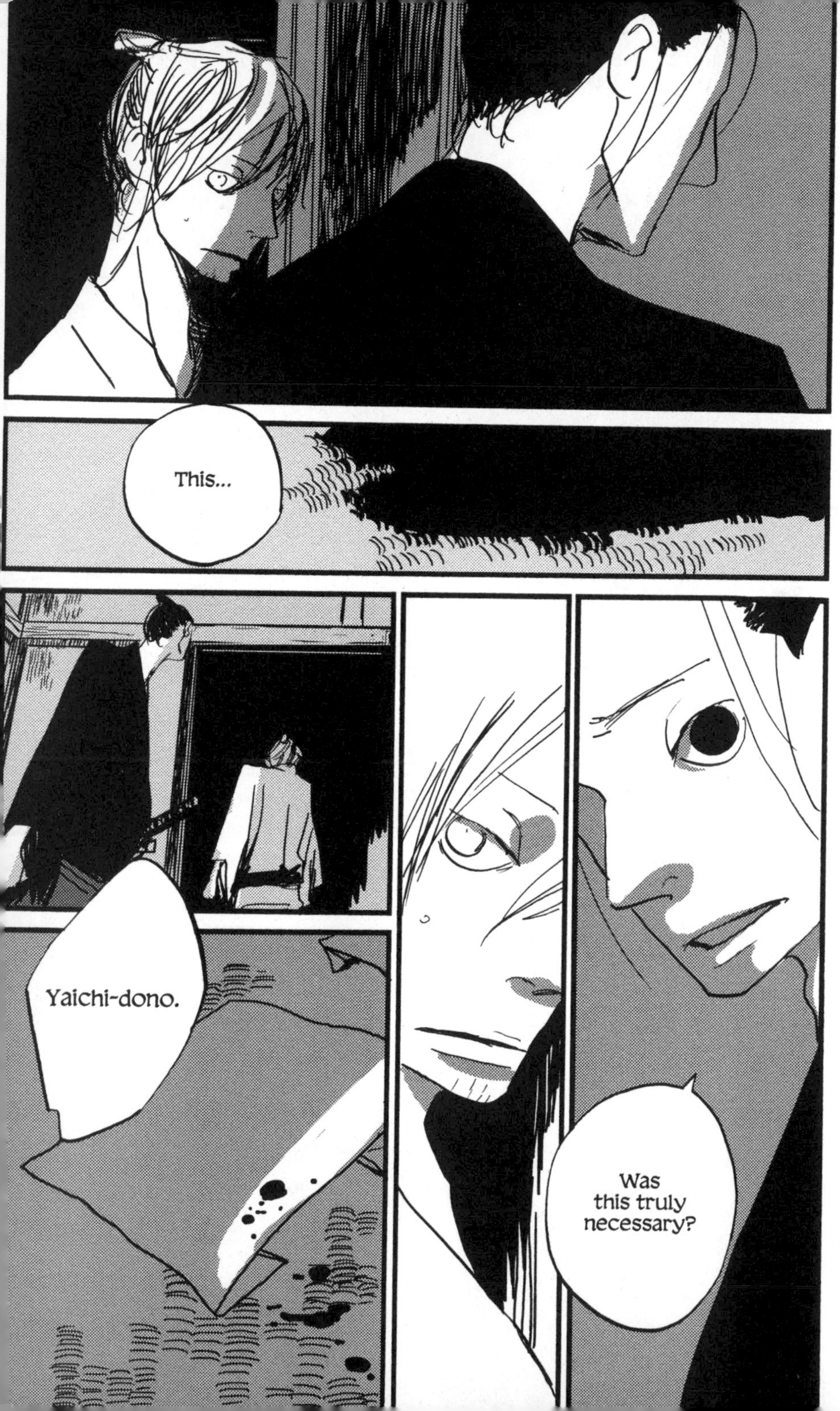
This...
Was this truly necessary?
Yaichi-dono.

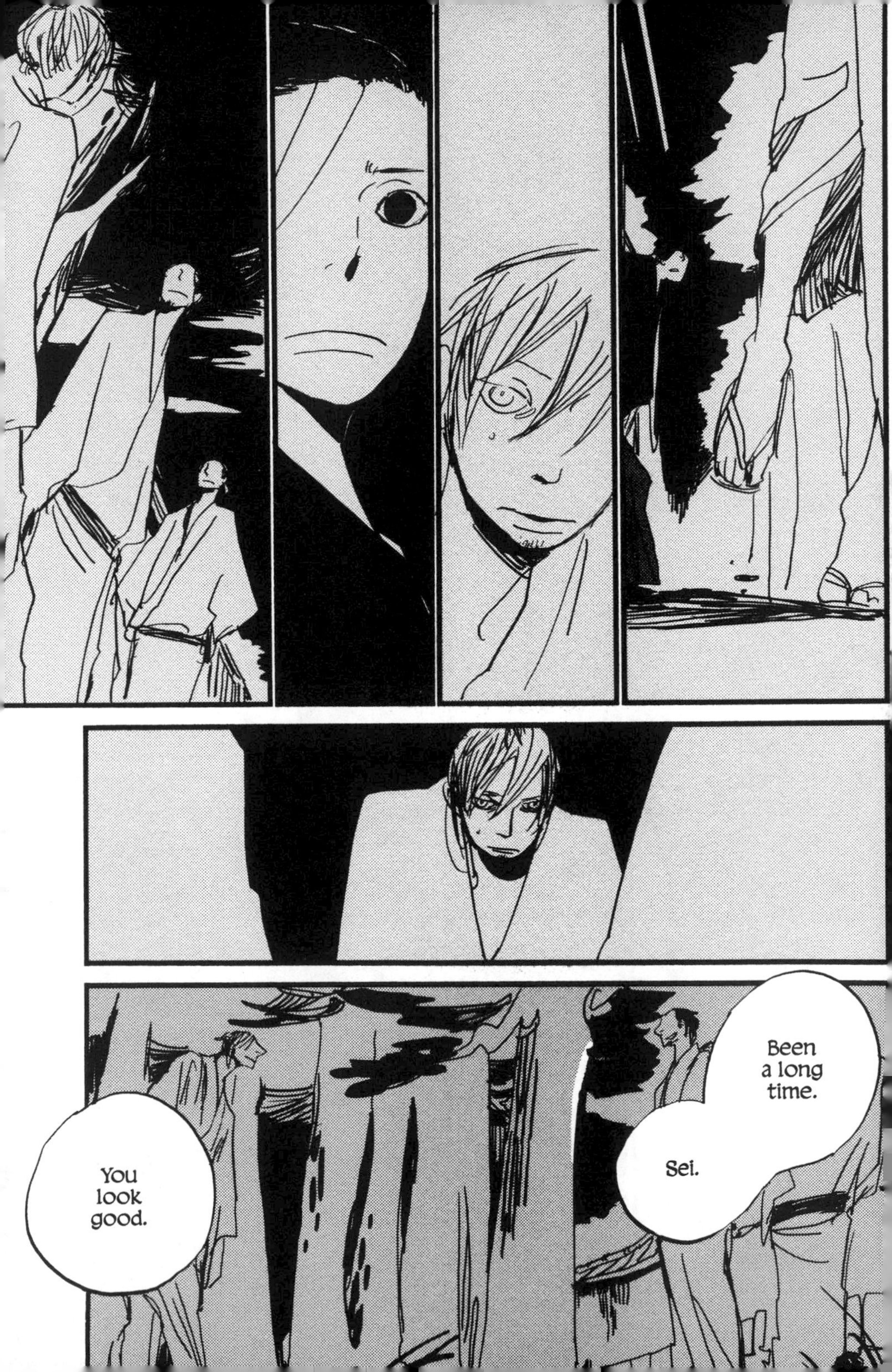
Been a long time.
Sei.
You look good.

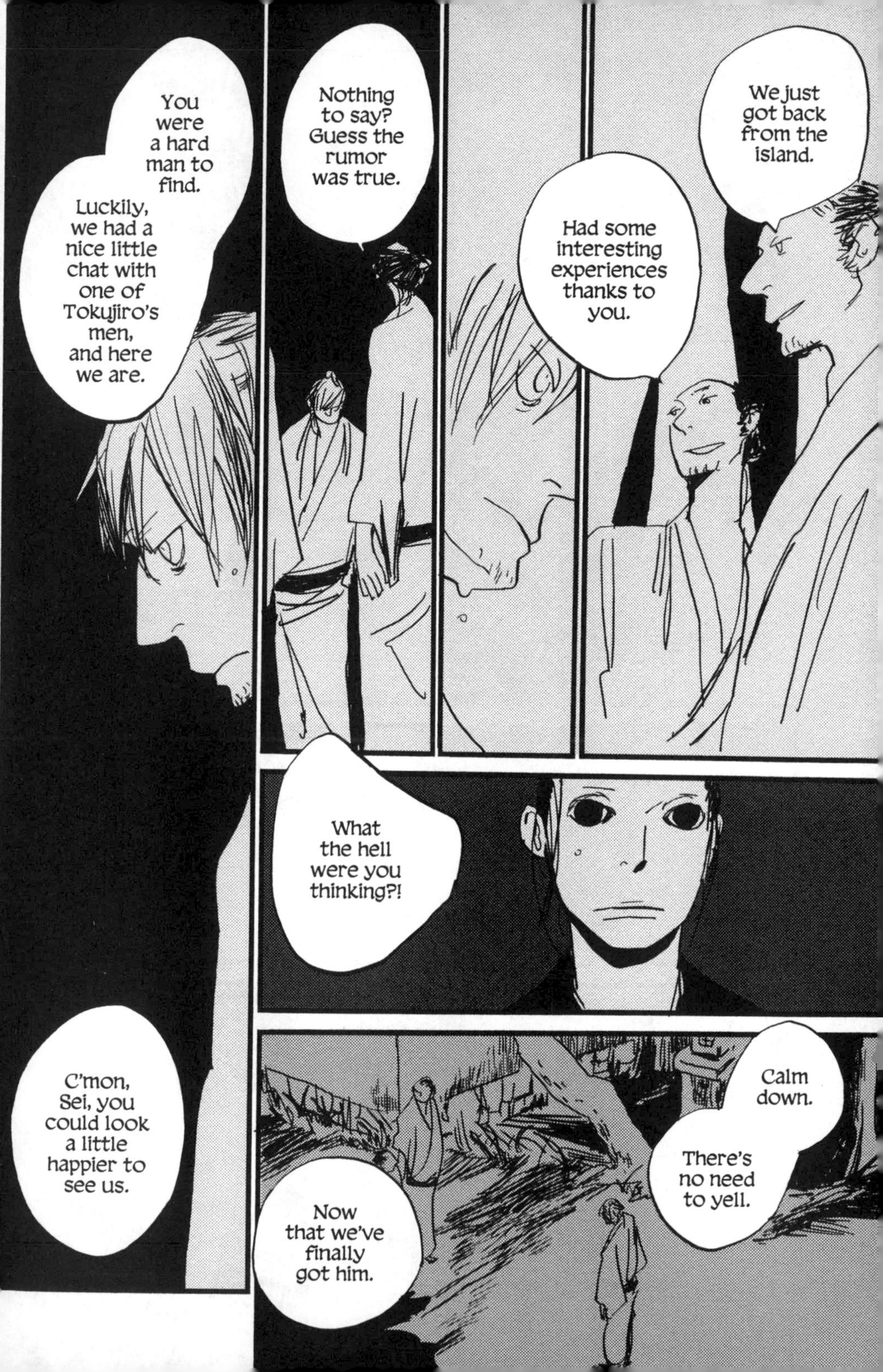
We just got back from the island.
Had some interesting experiences thanks to you.
Nothing to say? Guess the rumor was true.
What the hell were you thinking?!
Calm down.
There's no need to yell.
Now that we've finally got him.
You were a hard man to find.
Luckily, we had a nice little chat with one of Tokujiro's men, and here we are.
C'mon, Sei, you could look a little happier to see us.

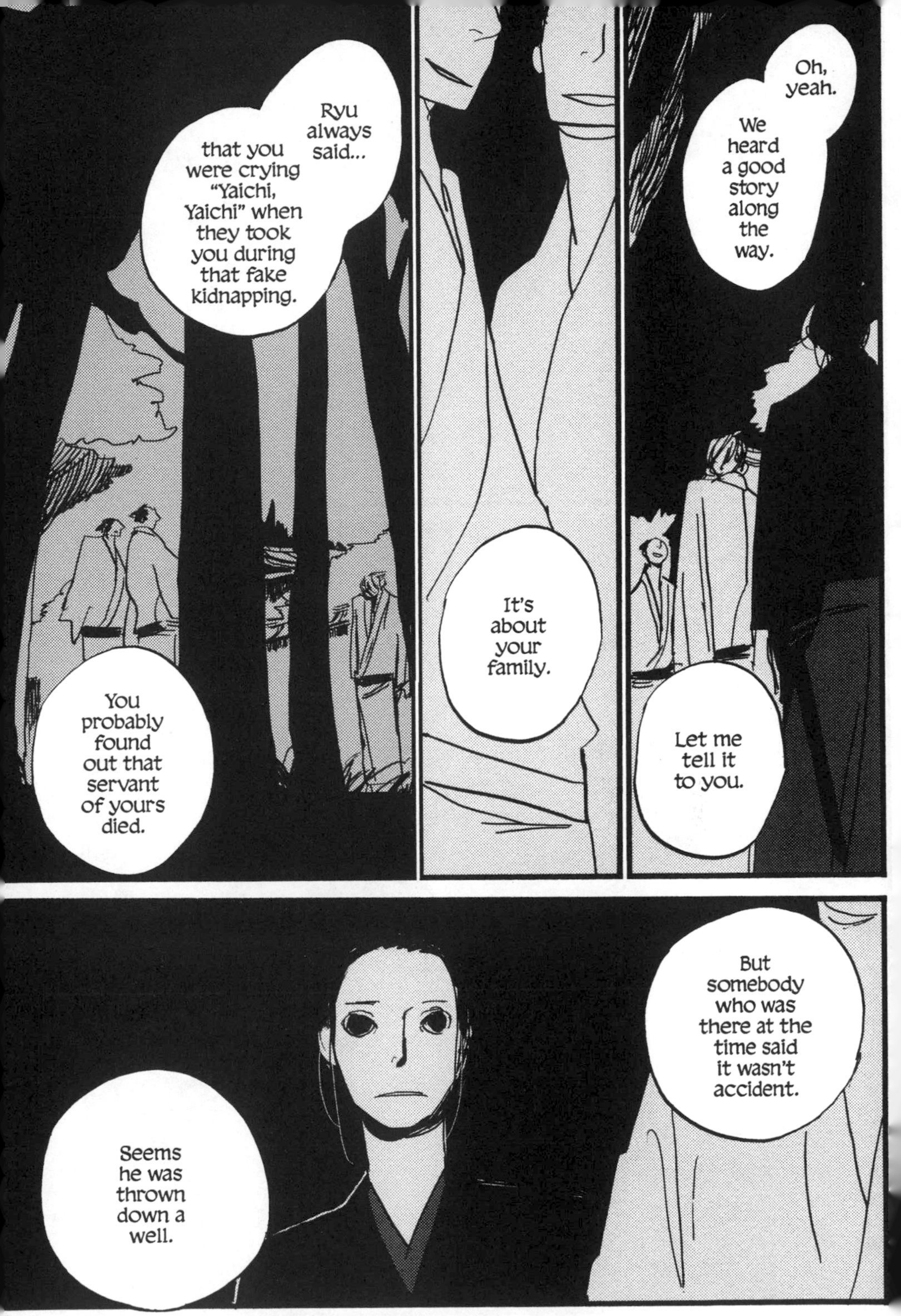
Oh, yeah.
We heard a good story along the way.
Let me tell it to you.
It's about your family.
Ryu always said...
that you were crying "Yaichi, Yaichi" when they took you during that fake kidnapping.
You probably found out that servant of yours died.
But somebody who was there at the time said it wasn't accident.
Seems he was thrown down a well.

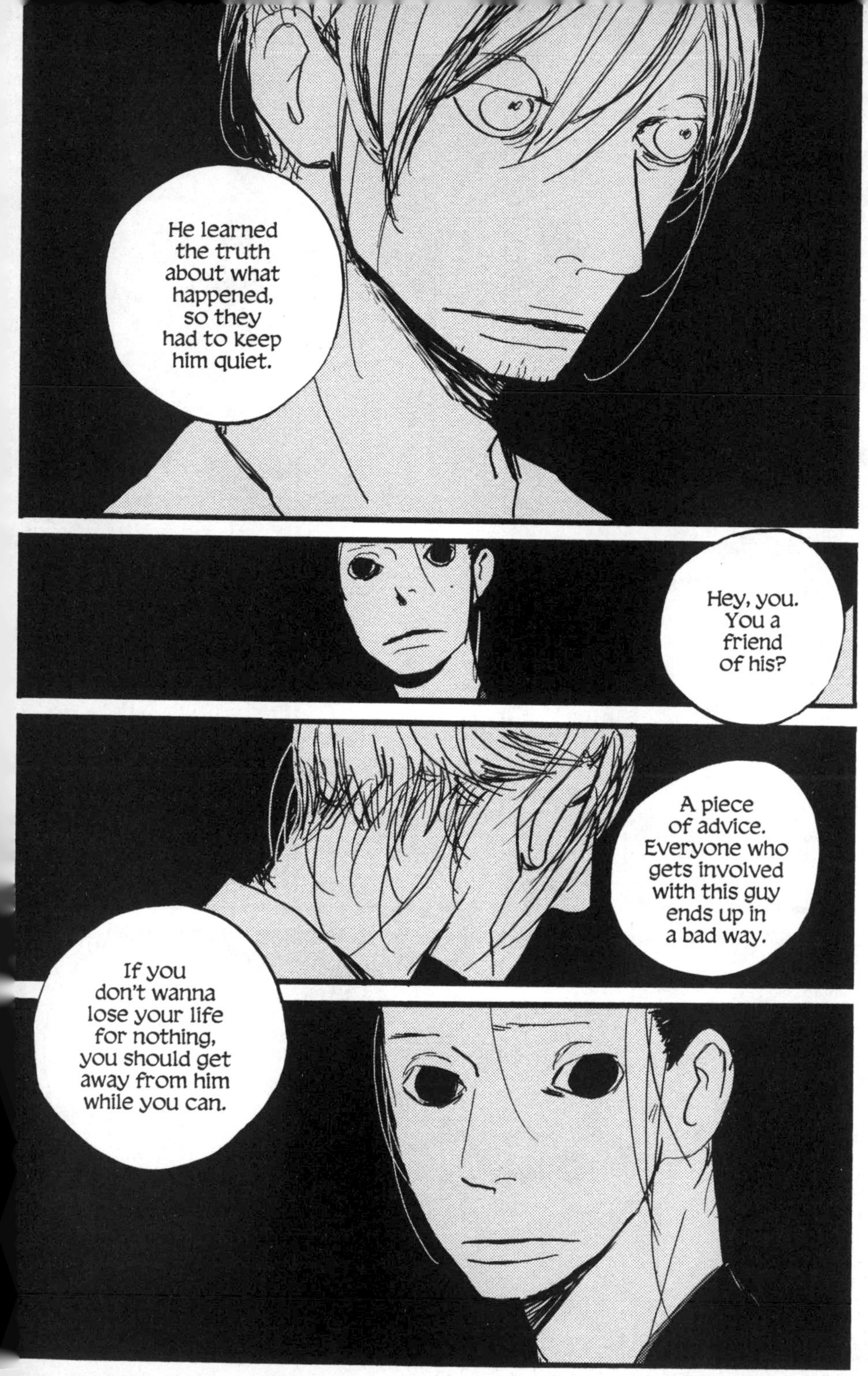
He learned the truth about what happened, so they had to keep him quiet.
Hey, you. You a friend of his?
A piece of advice. Everyone who gets involved with this guy ends up in a bad way.
If you don't wanna lose your life for nothing, you should get away from him while you can.

Chapter Fifty

A Long Rain

(Part Five)

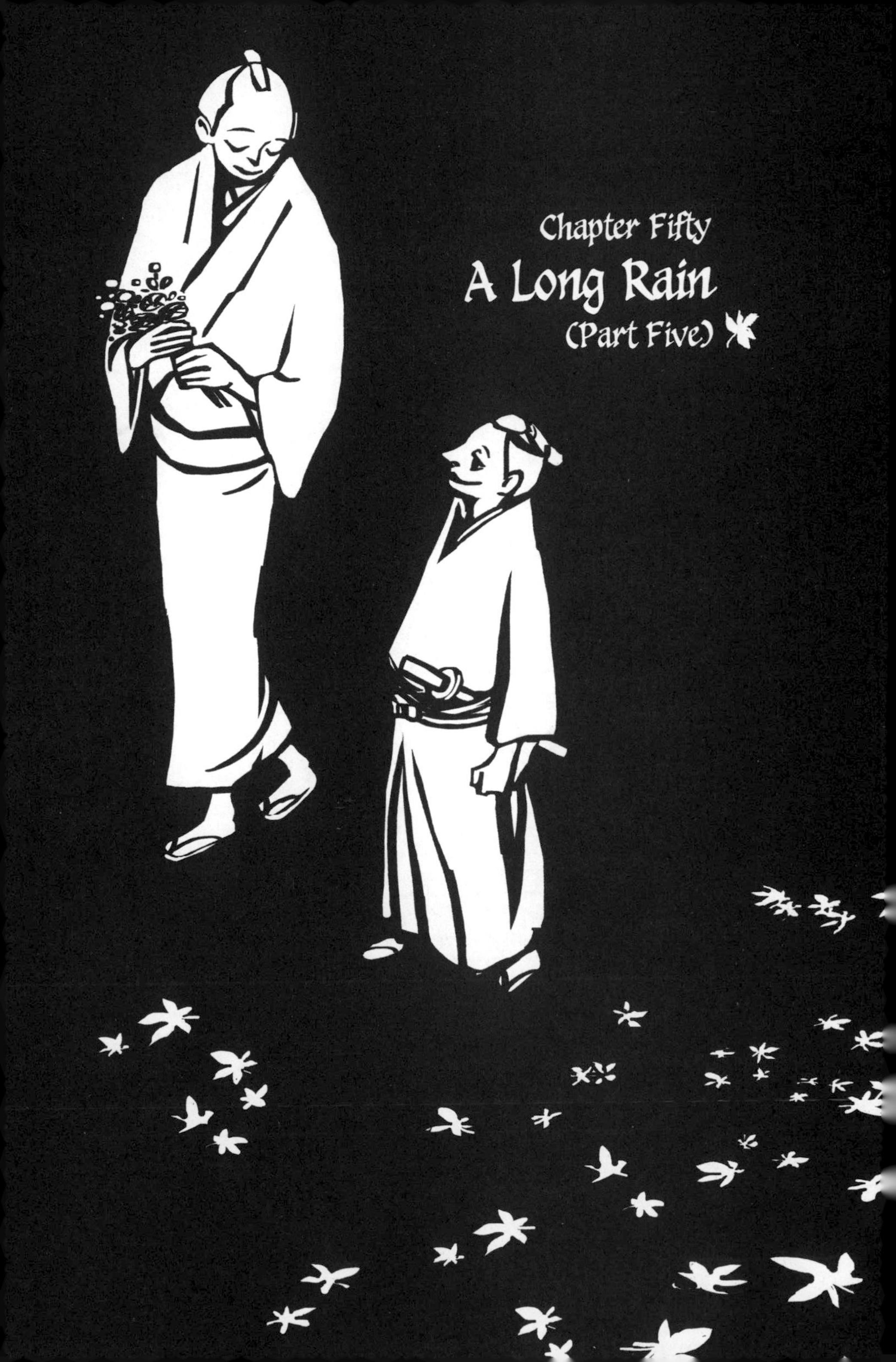

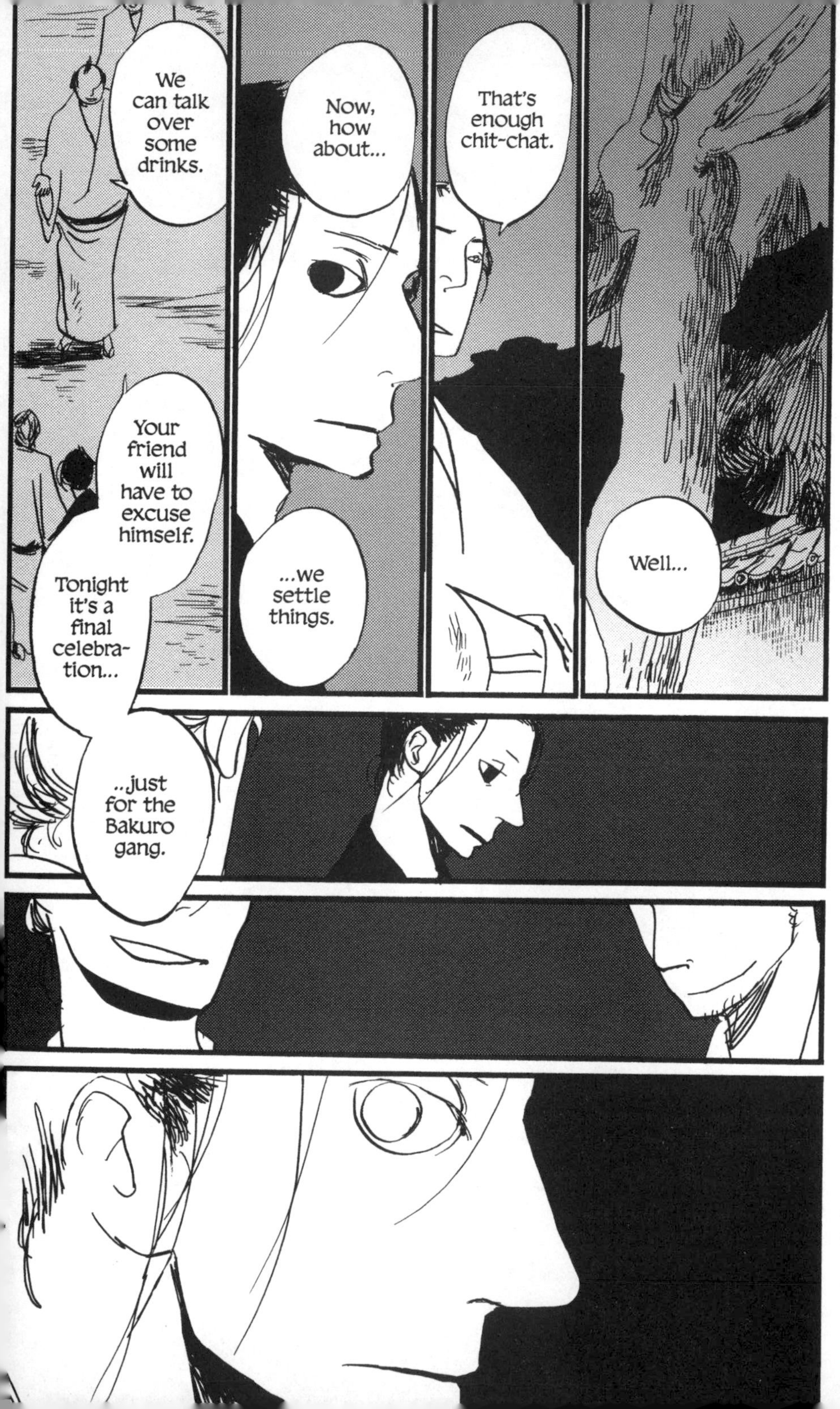
Well...
That's enough chit-chat.
Now, how about...
...we settle things.
We can talk over some drinks.
Your friend will have to excuse himself.
Tonight it's a final celebration...
...just for the Bakuro gang.

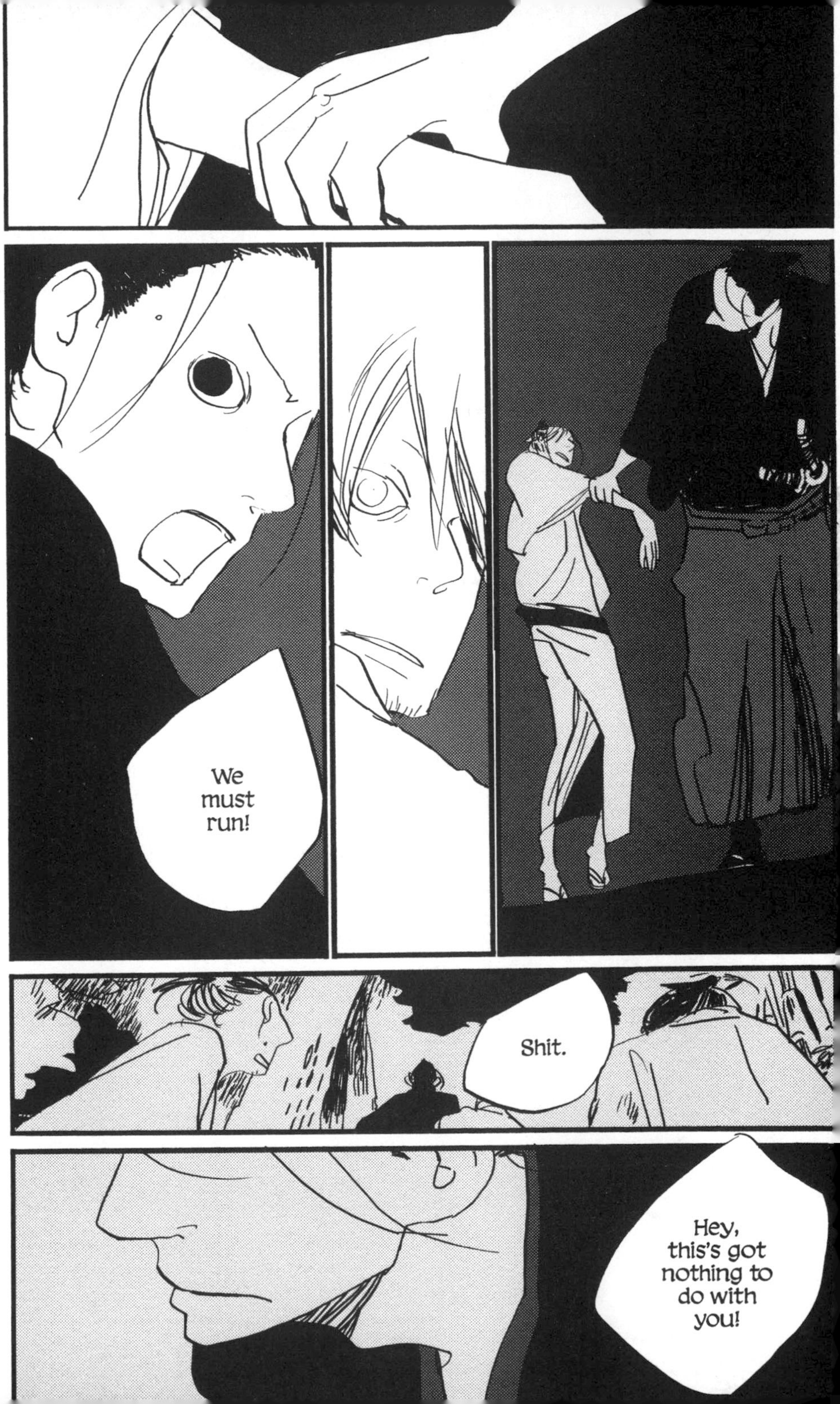
We must run!
Shit.
Hey, this's got nothing to do with you!

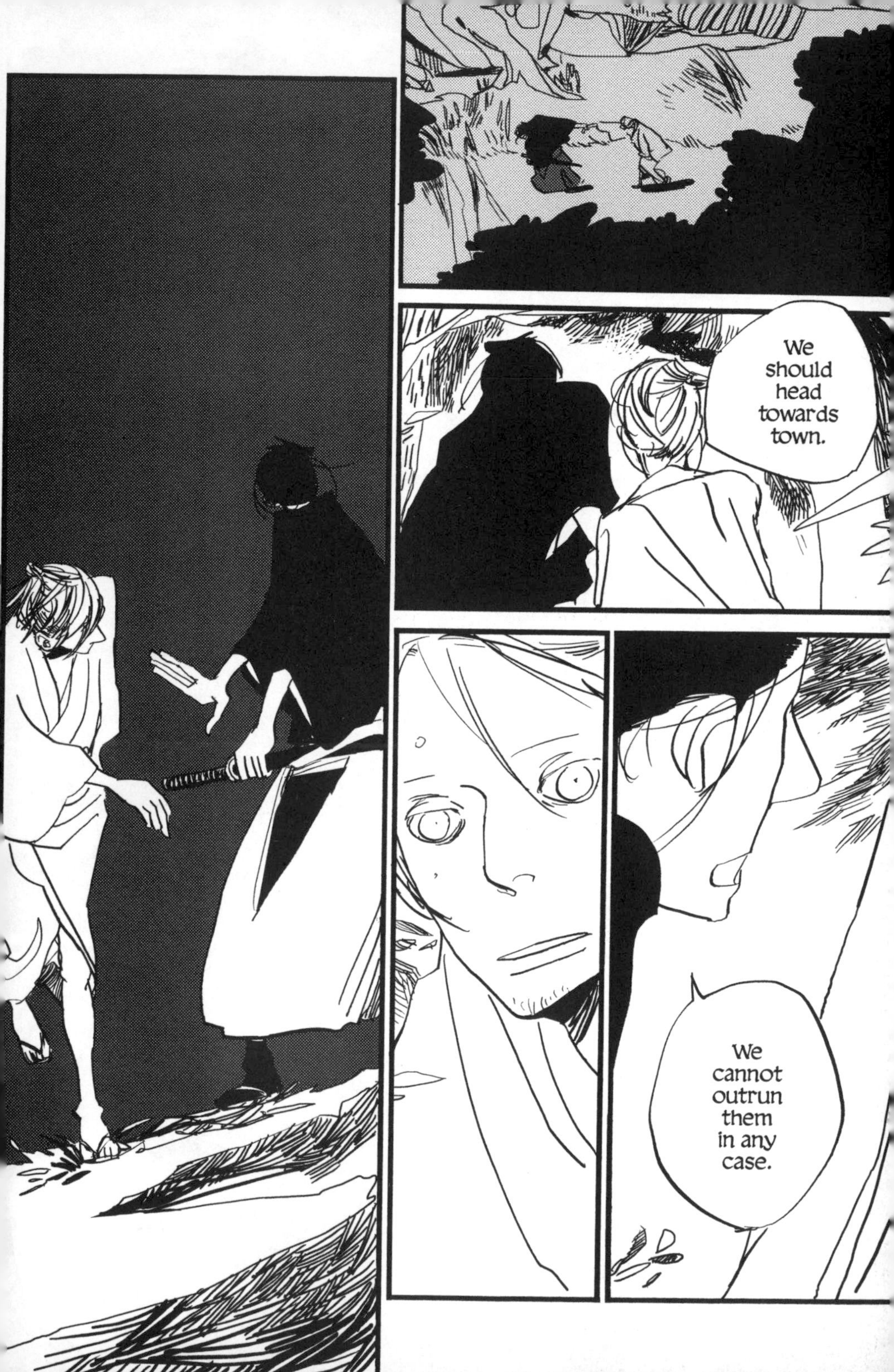
We should head towards town.
We cannot outrun them in any case.

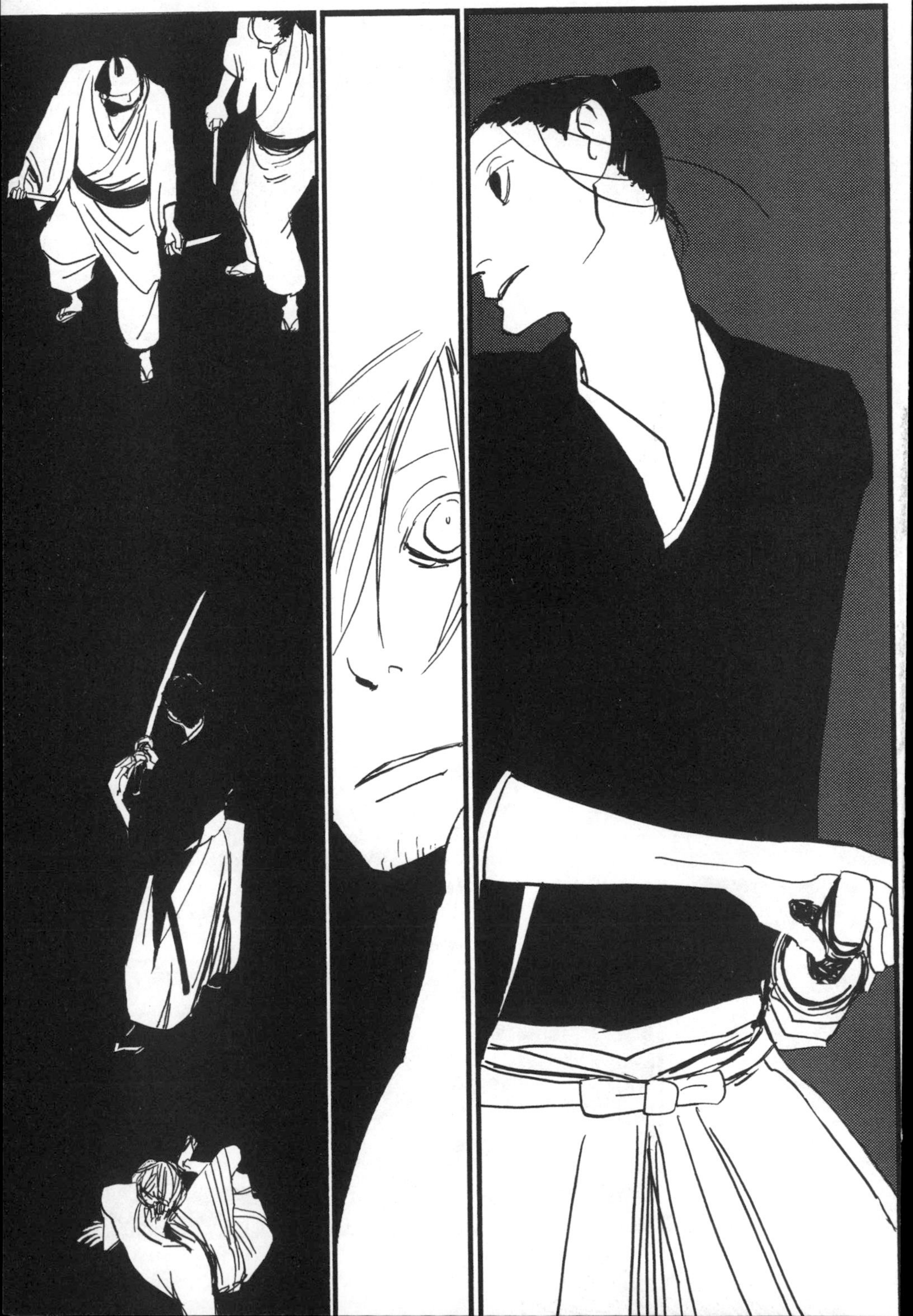

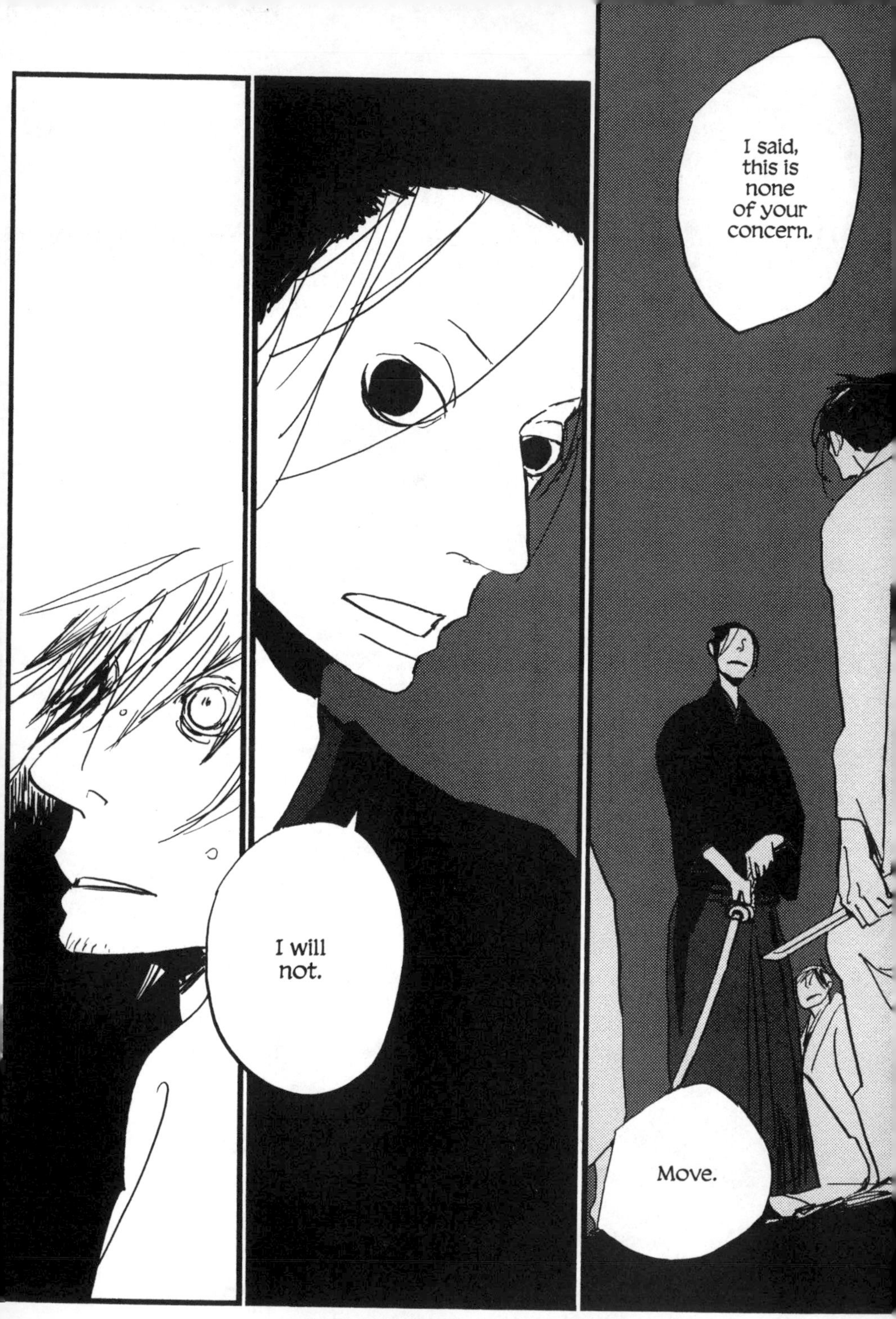
I said, this is none of your concern.
Move.
I will not.

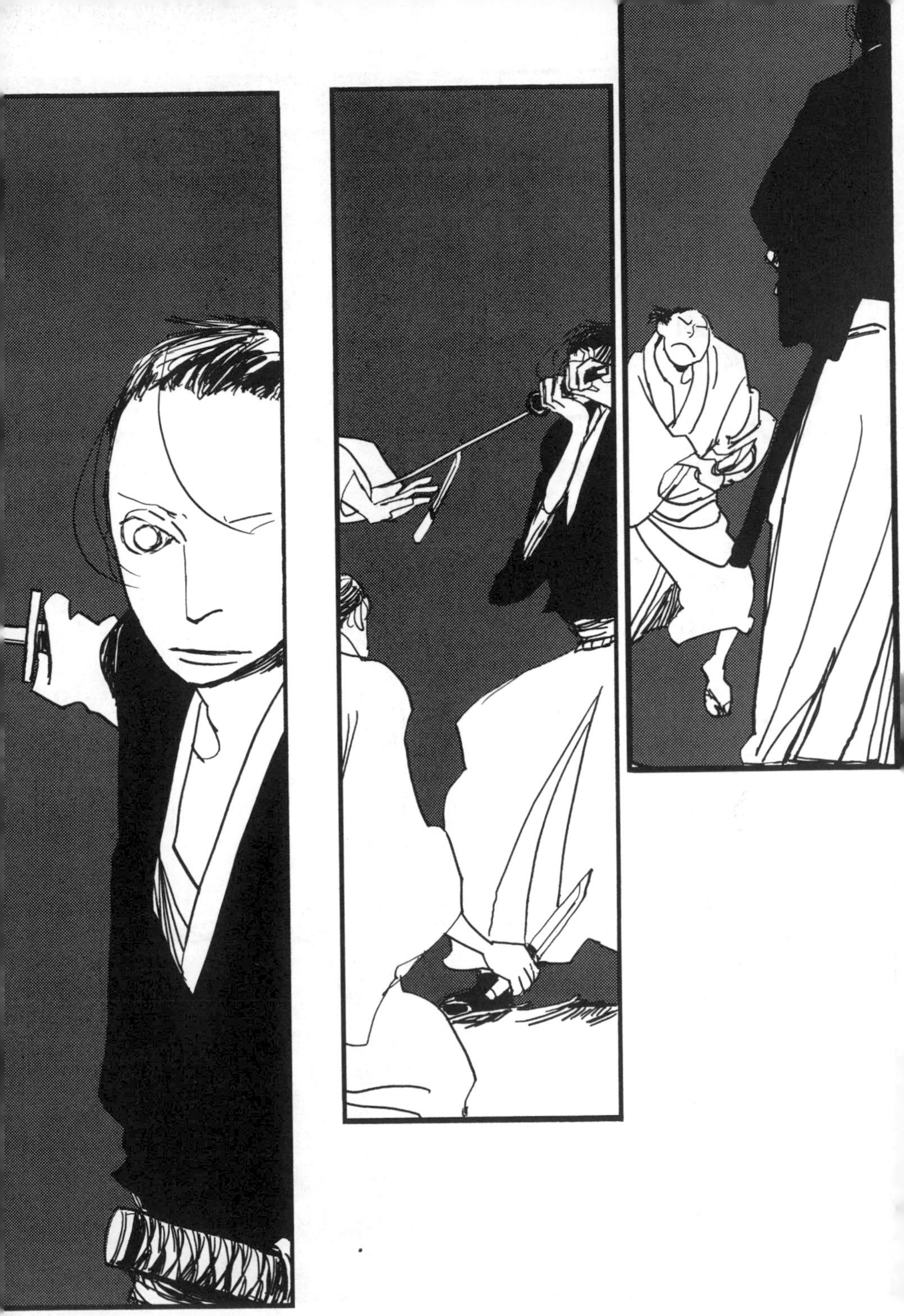

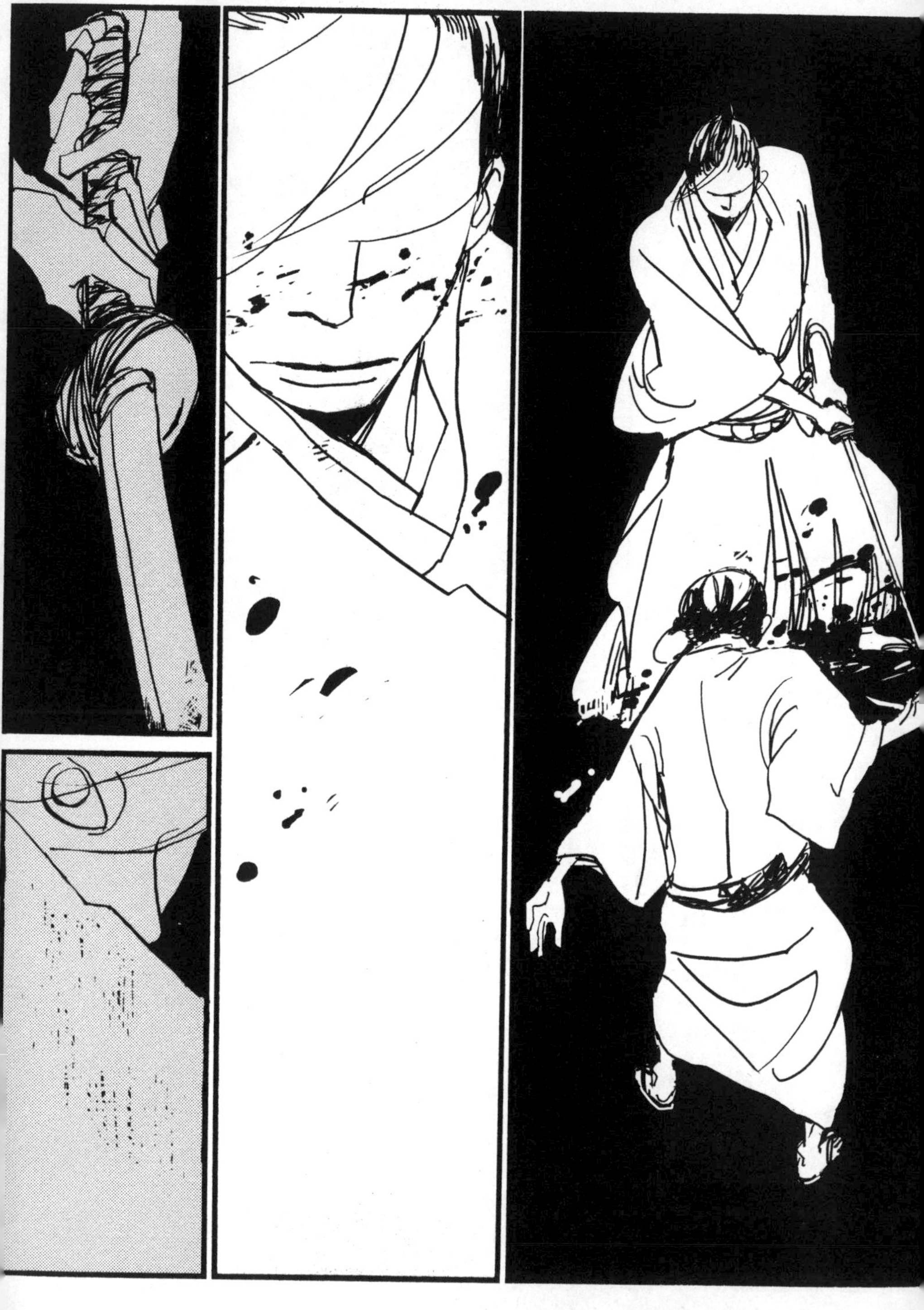

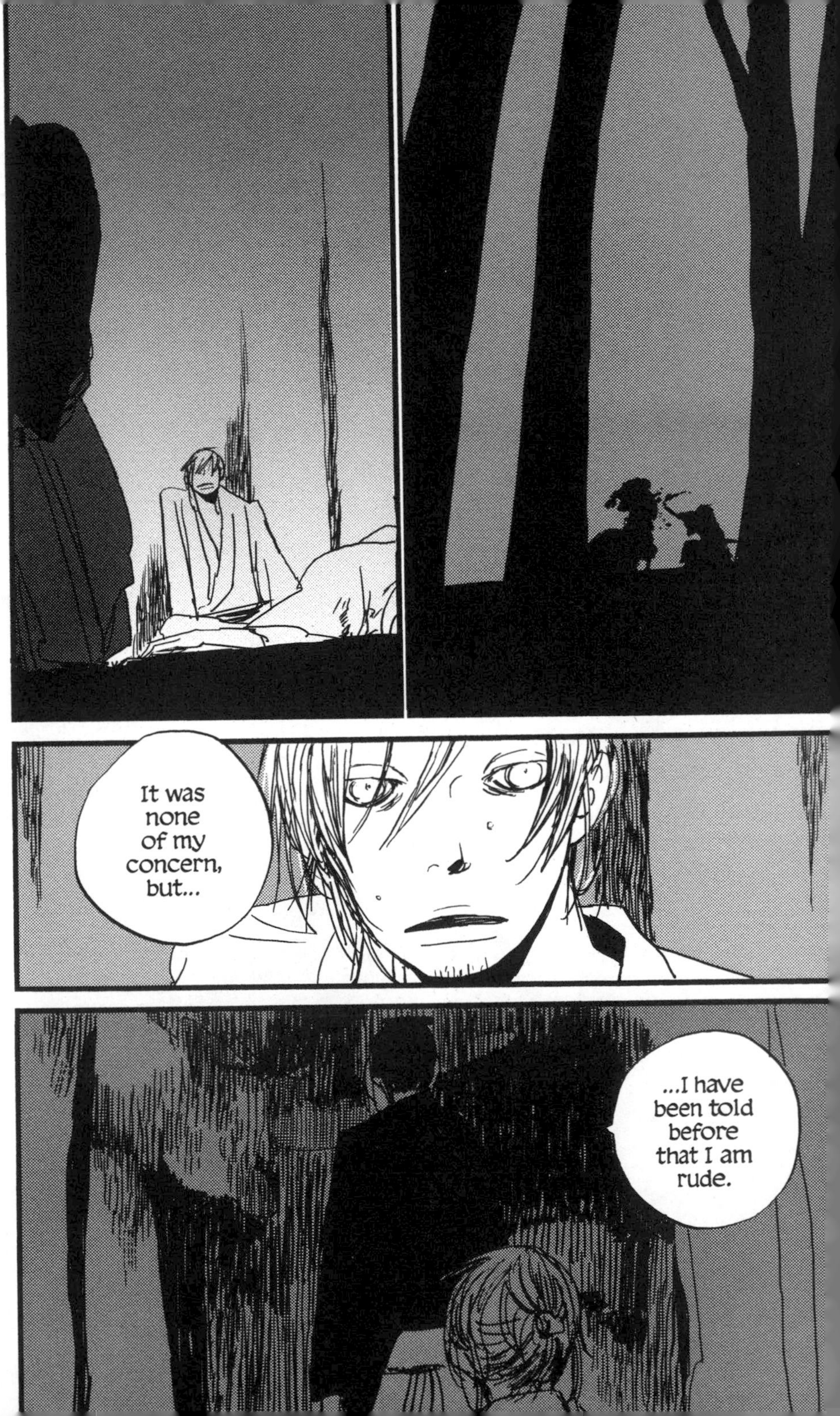
It was none of my concern, but...
...I have been told before that I am rude.

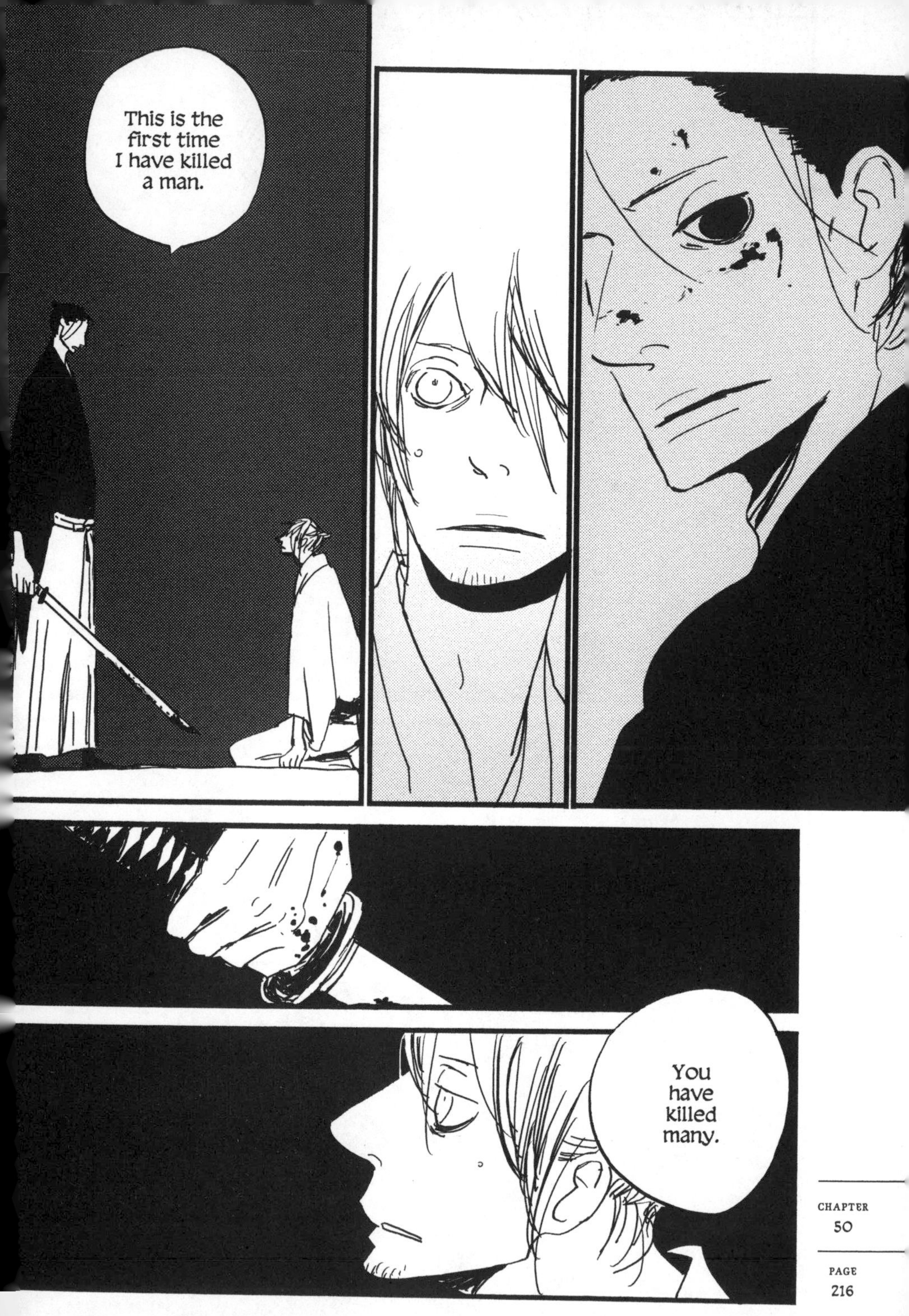
This is the first time I have killed a man.
You have killed many.

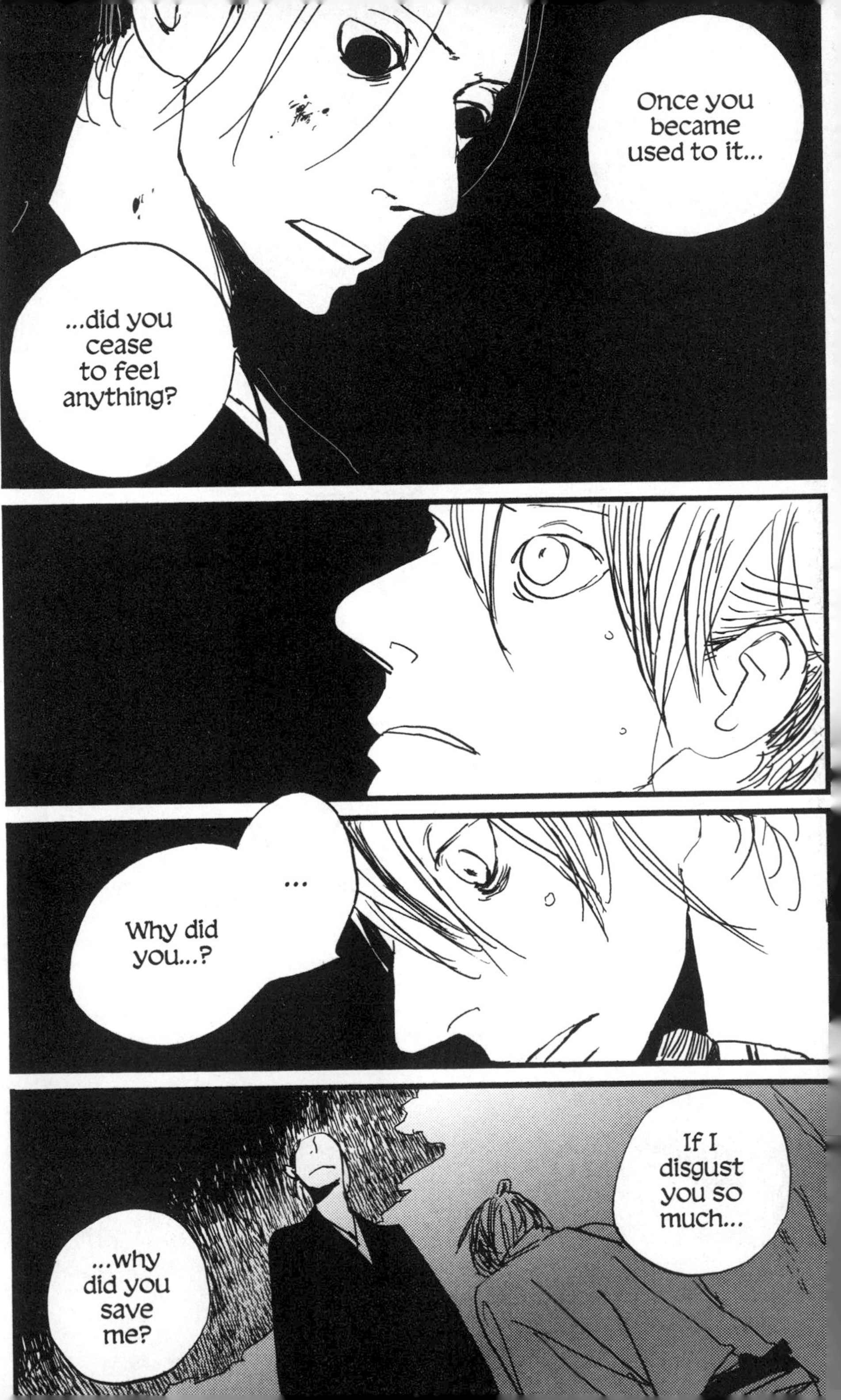
Once you became used to it...
...did you cease to feel anything?
...
Why did you...?
If I disgust you so much...
...why did you save me?

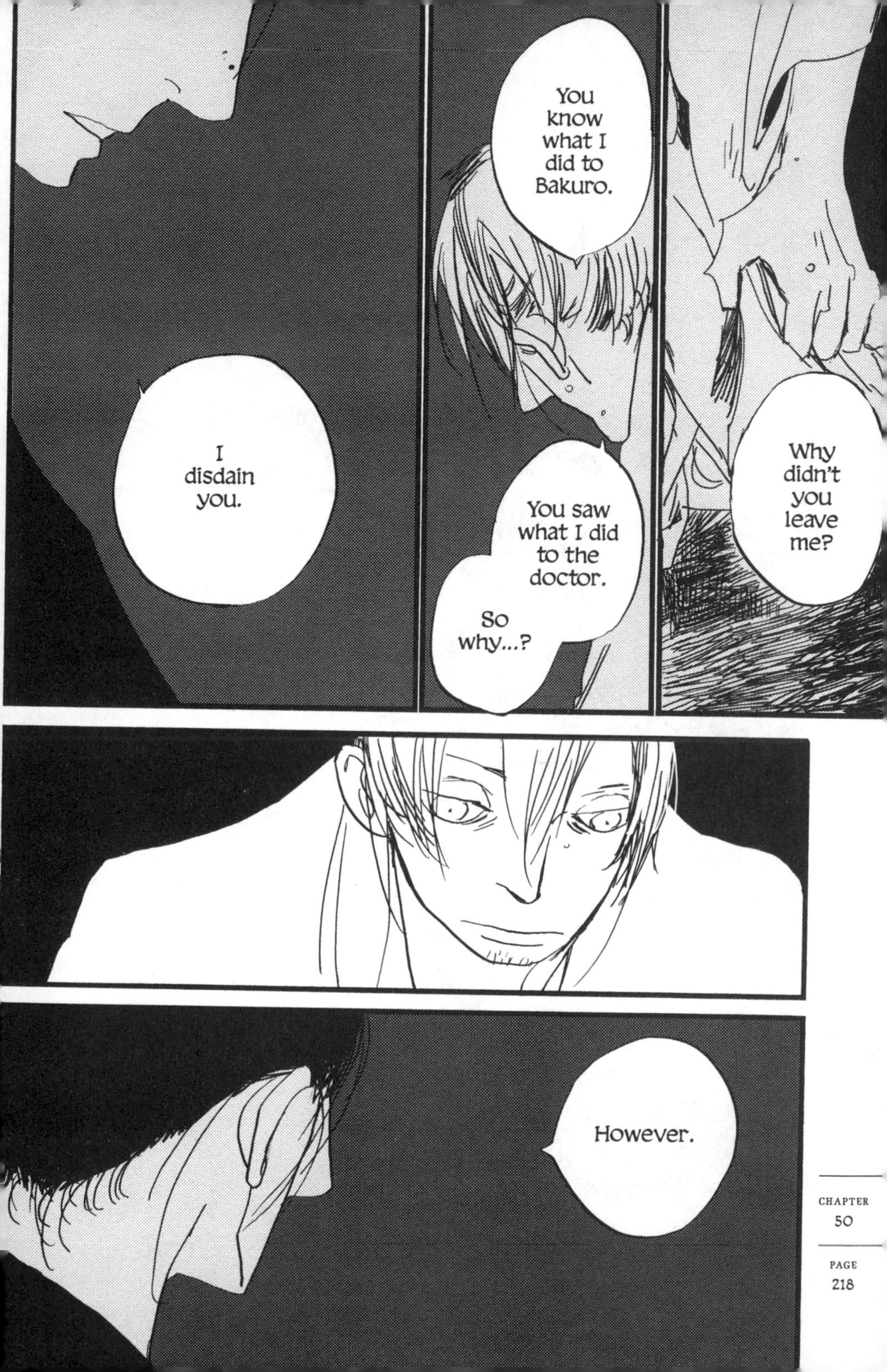
Why didn't you leave me?
You know what I did to Bakuro.
You saw what I did to the doctor.
So why...?
I disdain you.
However.

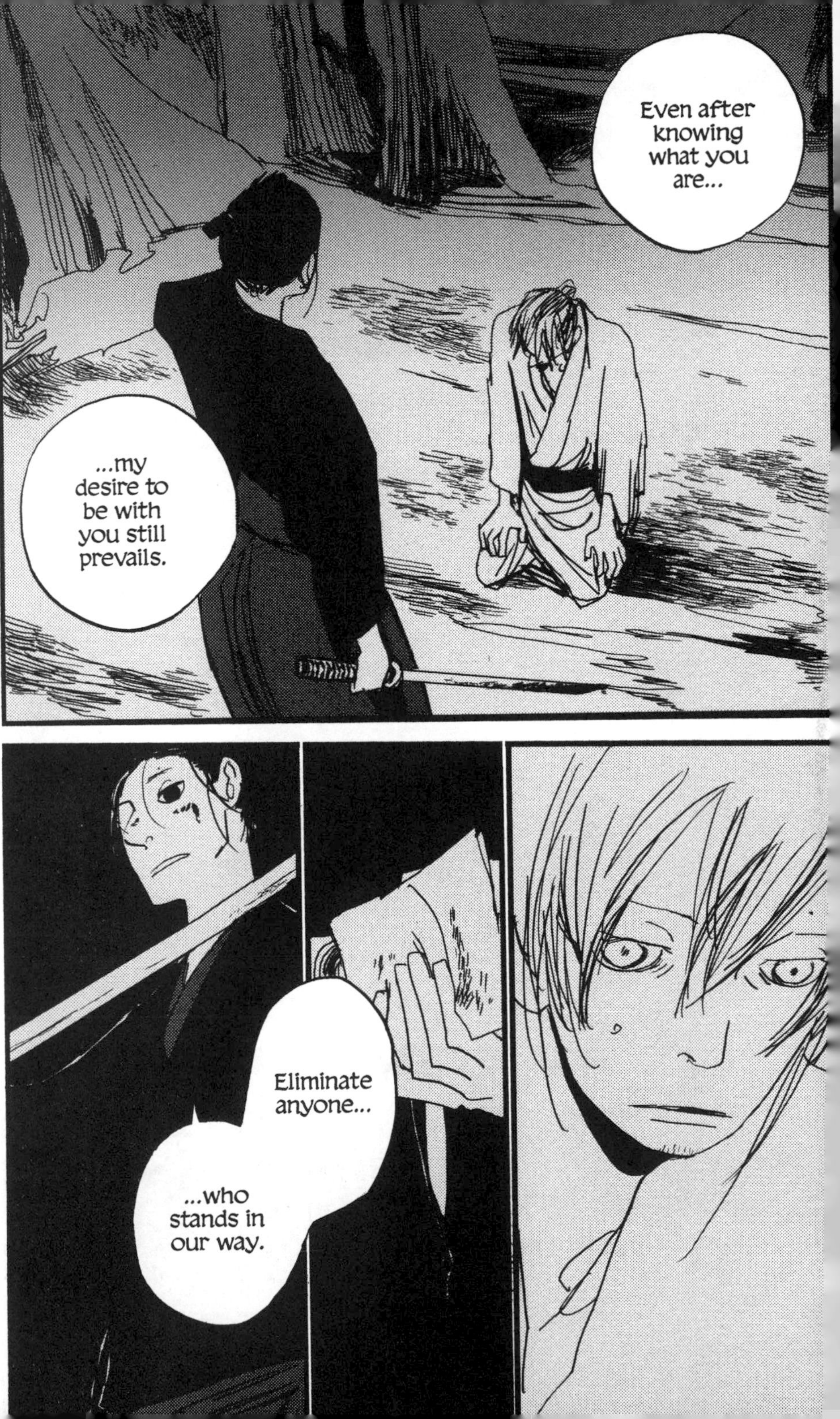
Even after knowing what you are...
...my desire to be with you still prevails.
Eliminate anyone...
...who stands in our way.

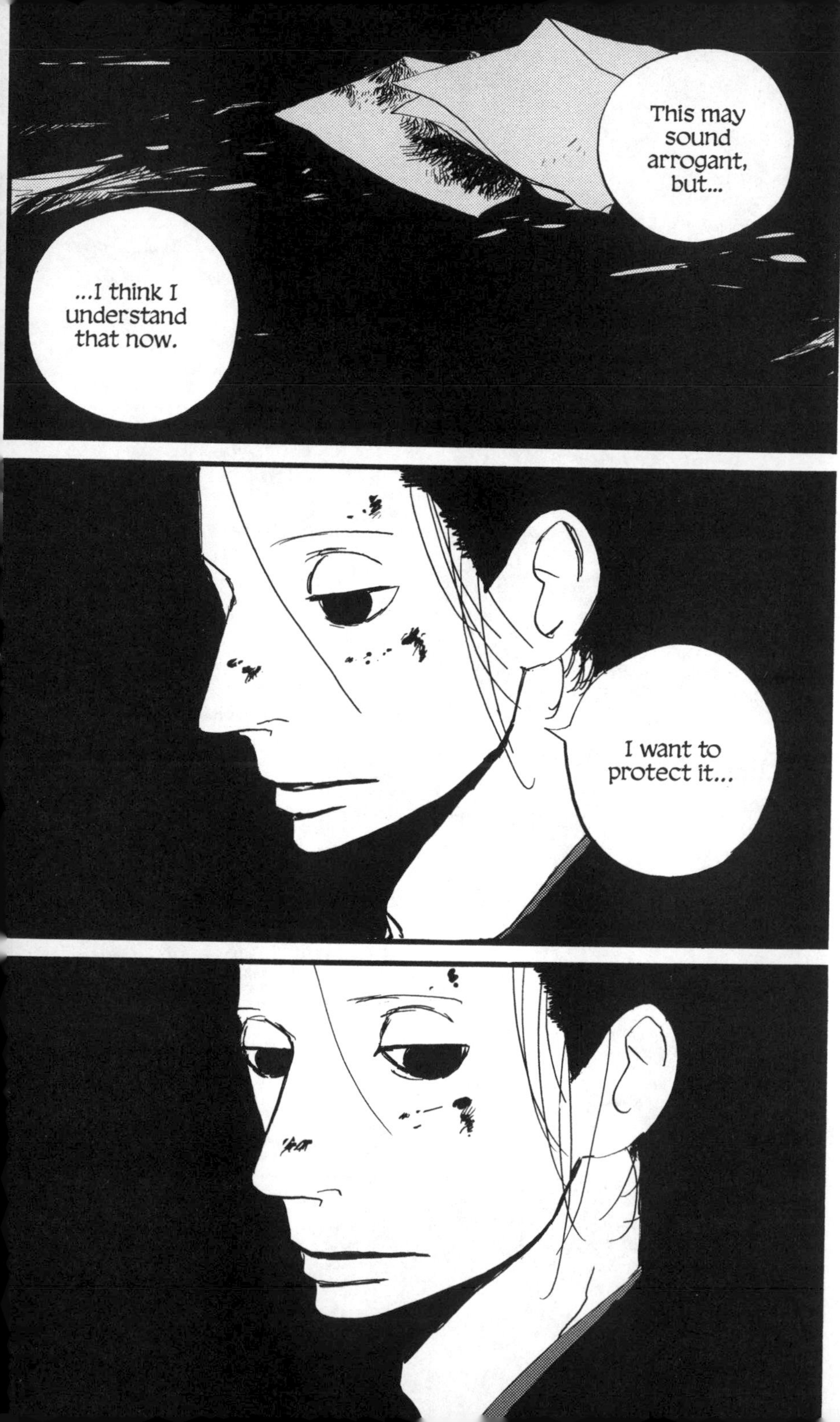
This may sound arrogant, but...
...I think I understand that now.
I want to protect it...

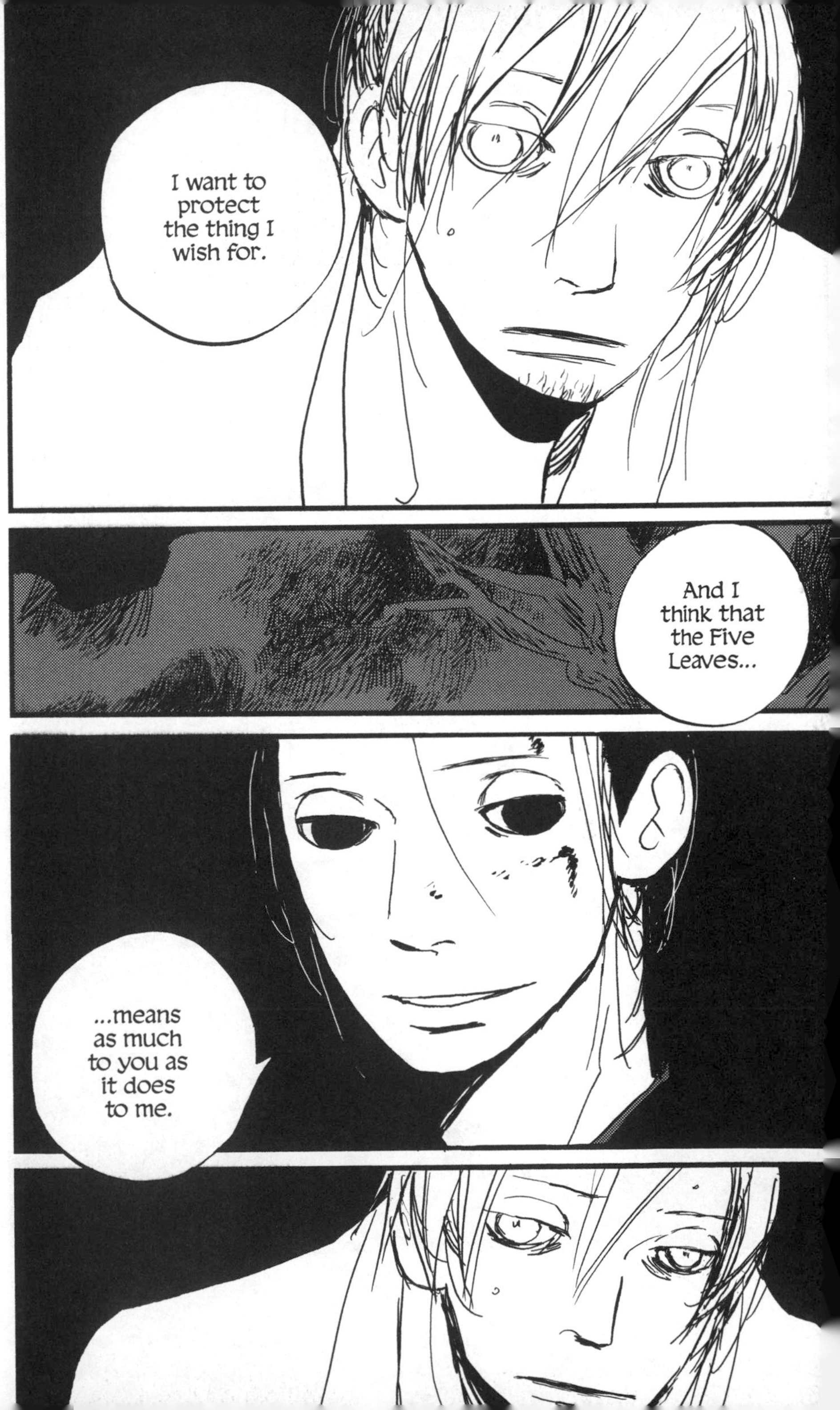
I want to protect the thing I wish for.
And I think that the Five Leaves...
...means as much to you as it does to me.

Let us return...

Yaichi-dono.

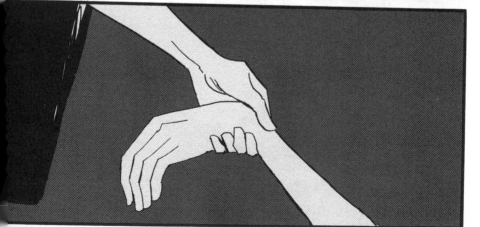

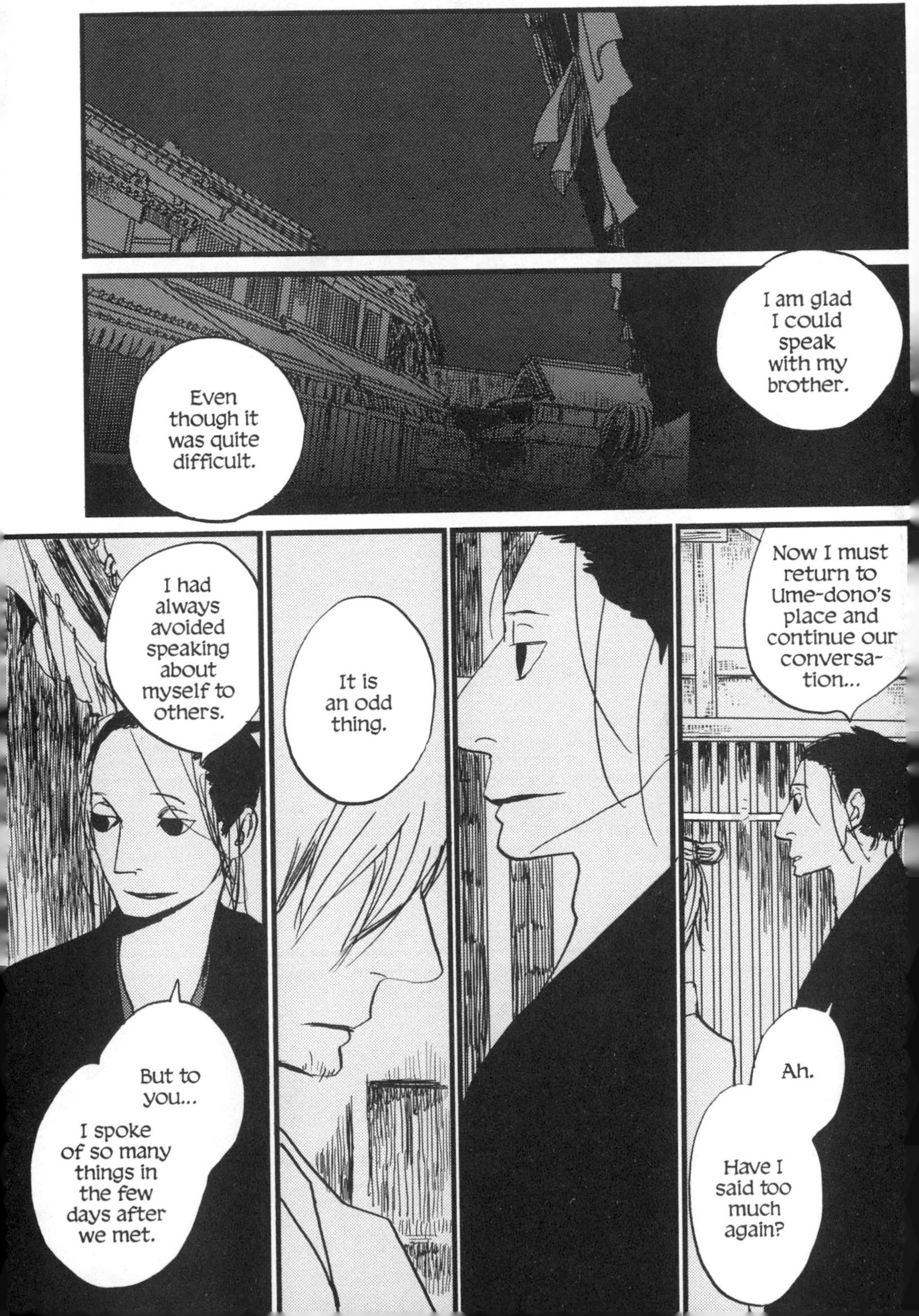
I am glad I could speak with my brother.
Even though it was quite difficult.
Now I must return to Ume-dono's place and continue our conversa-tion...
Ah.
Have I said too much again?
It is an odd thing.
I had always avoided speaking about myself to others.
But to you...
I spoke of so many things in the few days after we met.

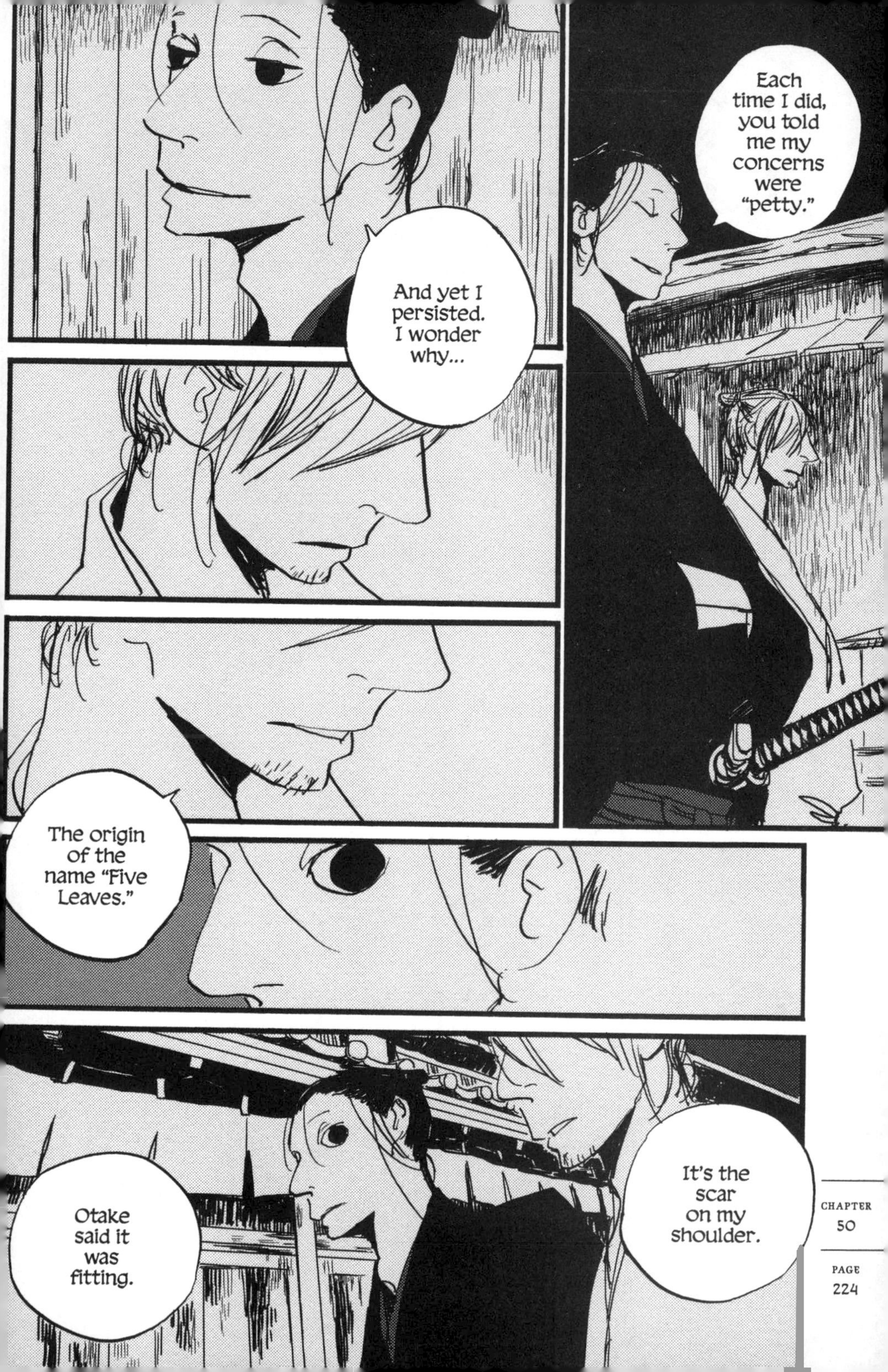
Each time I did, you told me my concerns were "petty."
And yet I persisted. I wonder why...
The origin of the name "Five Leaves."
It's the scar on my shoulder.
Otake said it was fitting.

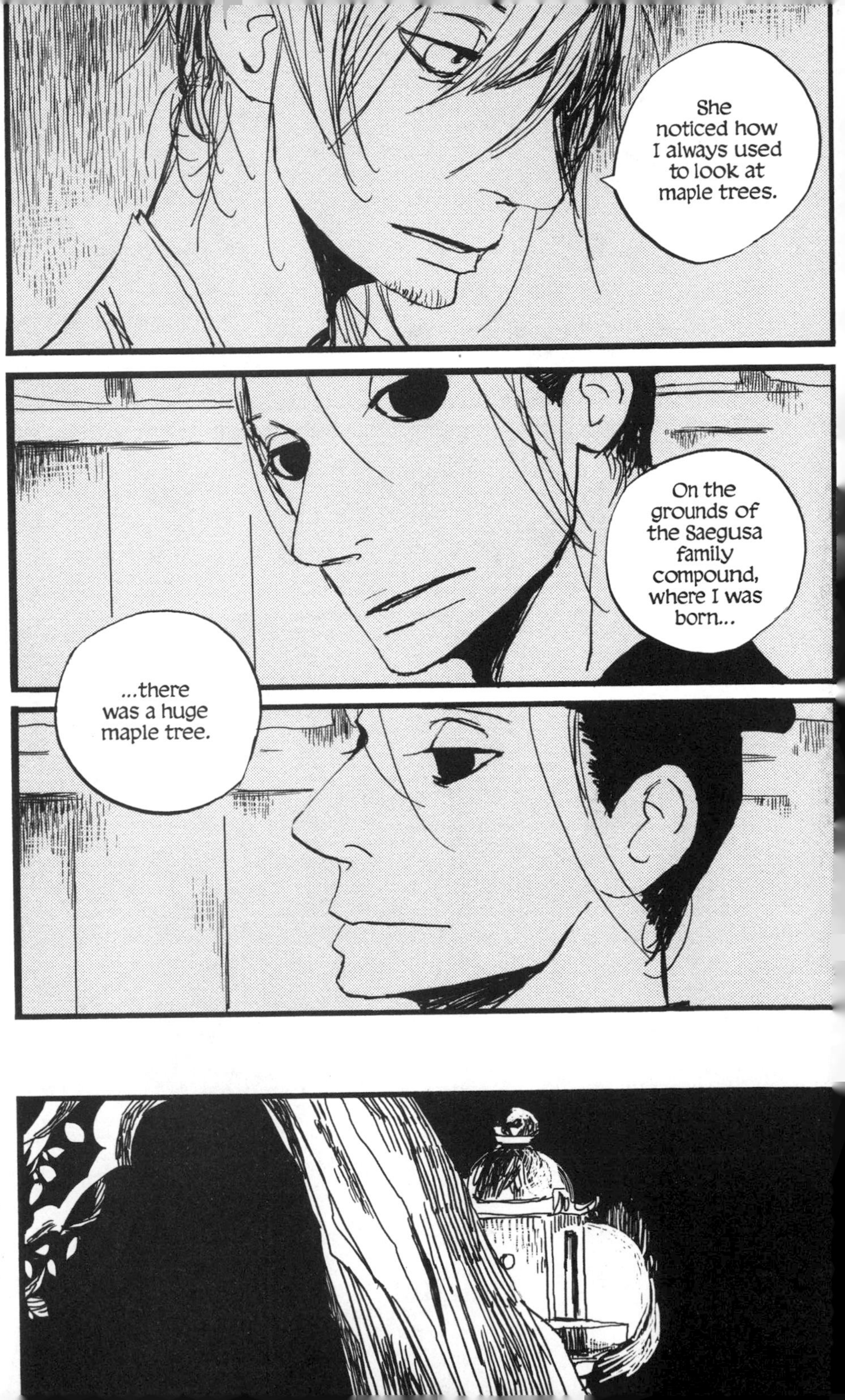
She noticed how I always used to look at maple trees.
On the grounds of the Saegusa family compound, where I was born...
...there was a huge maple tree.

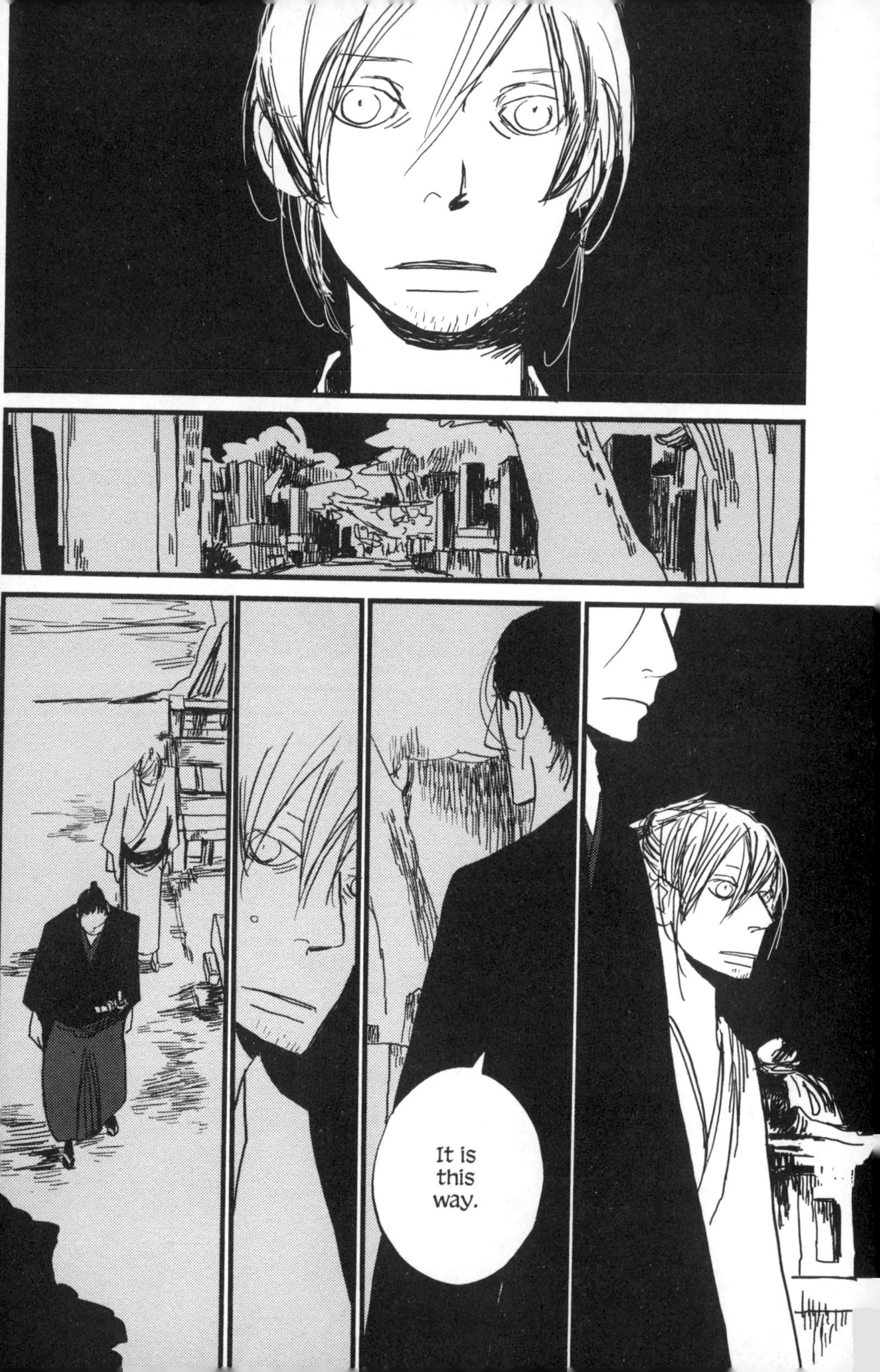
It is this way.

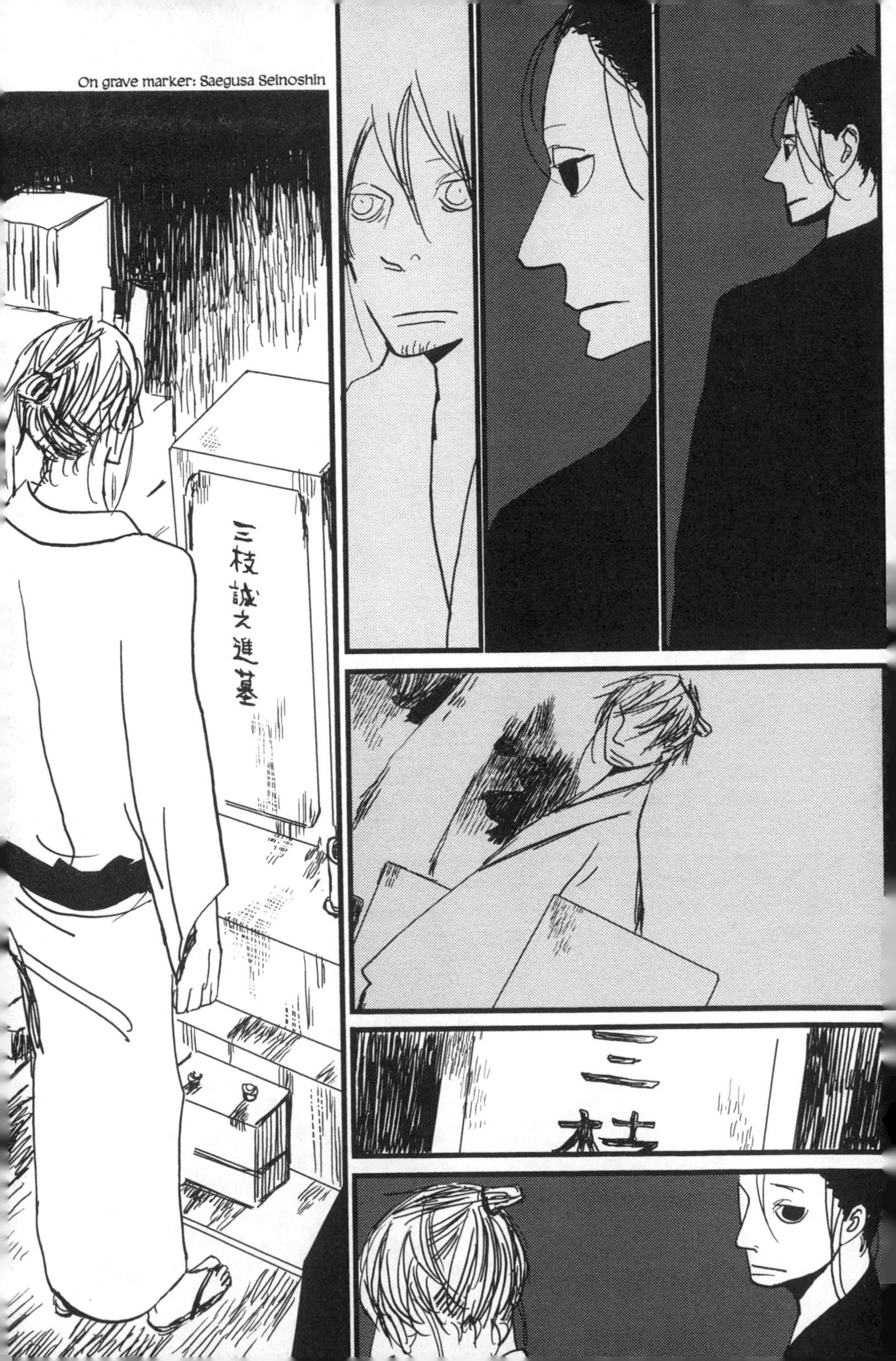
三枝誠之進墓

On grave marker: Saegusa Seinoshin

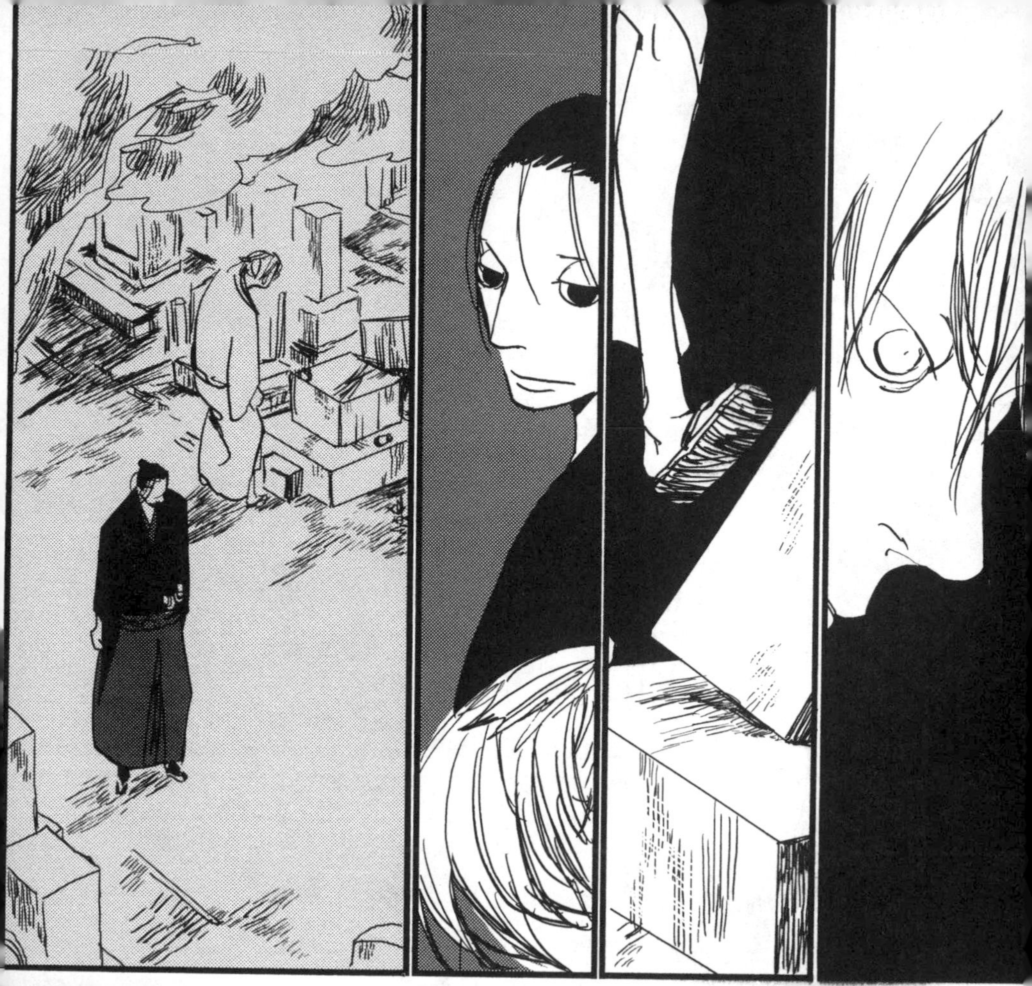

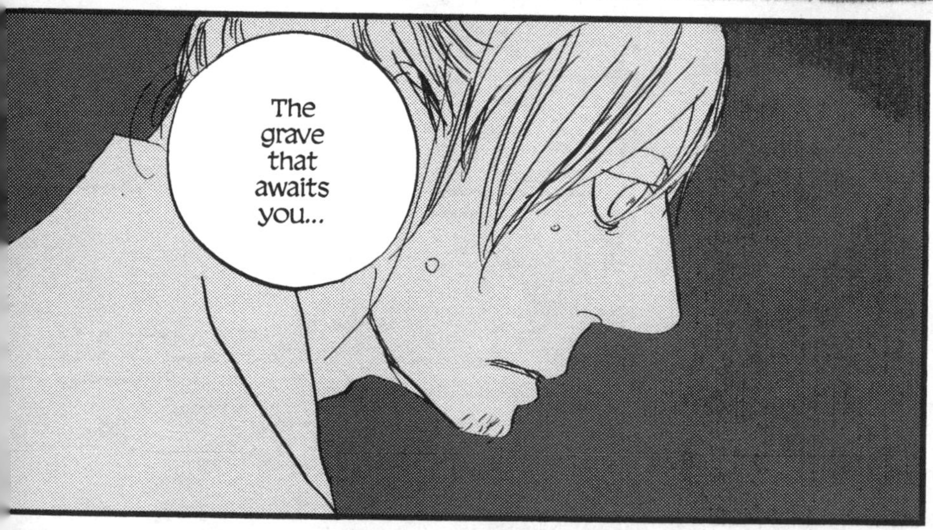
The grave that awaits you...

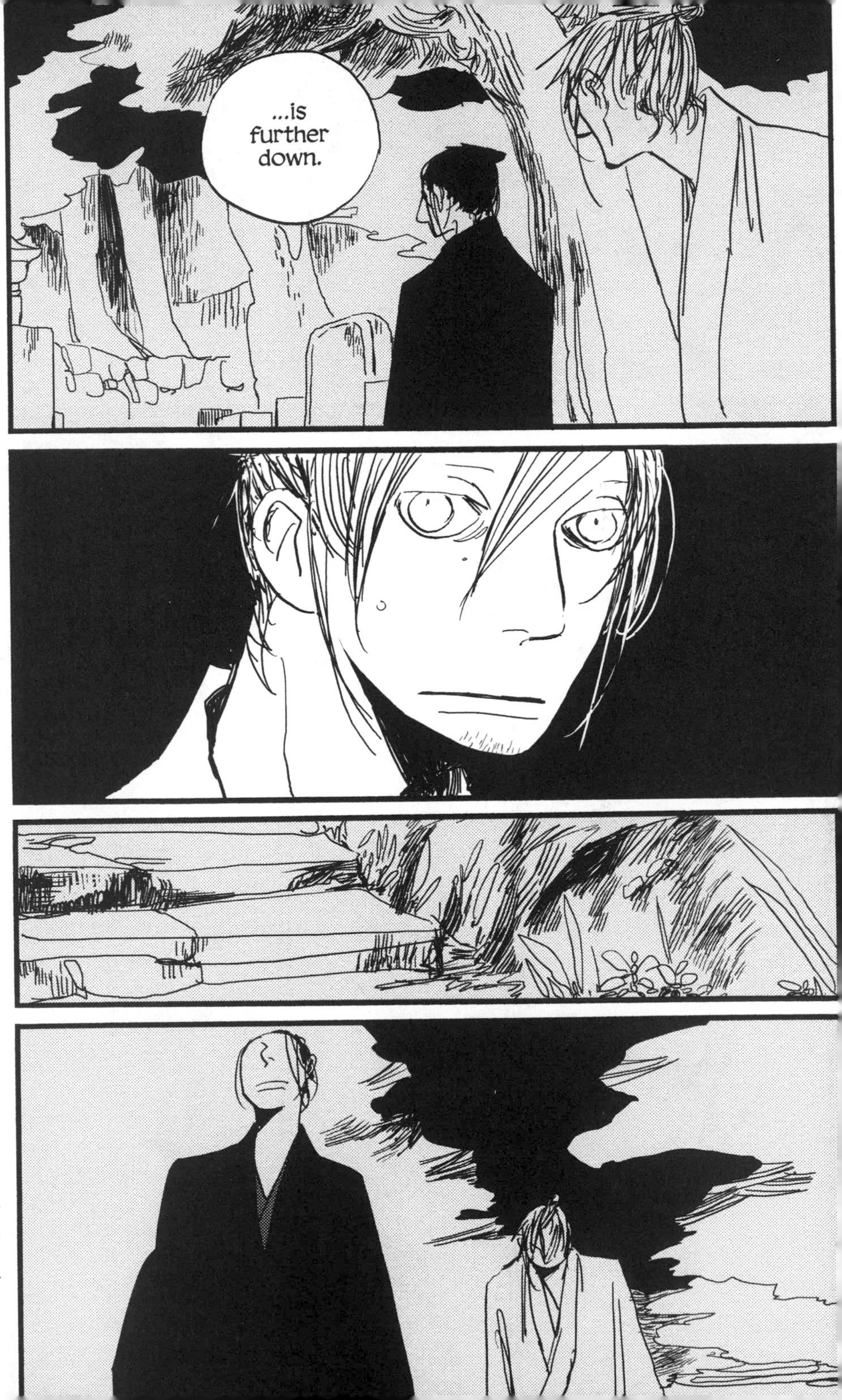
...is further down.

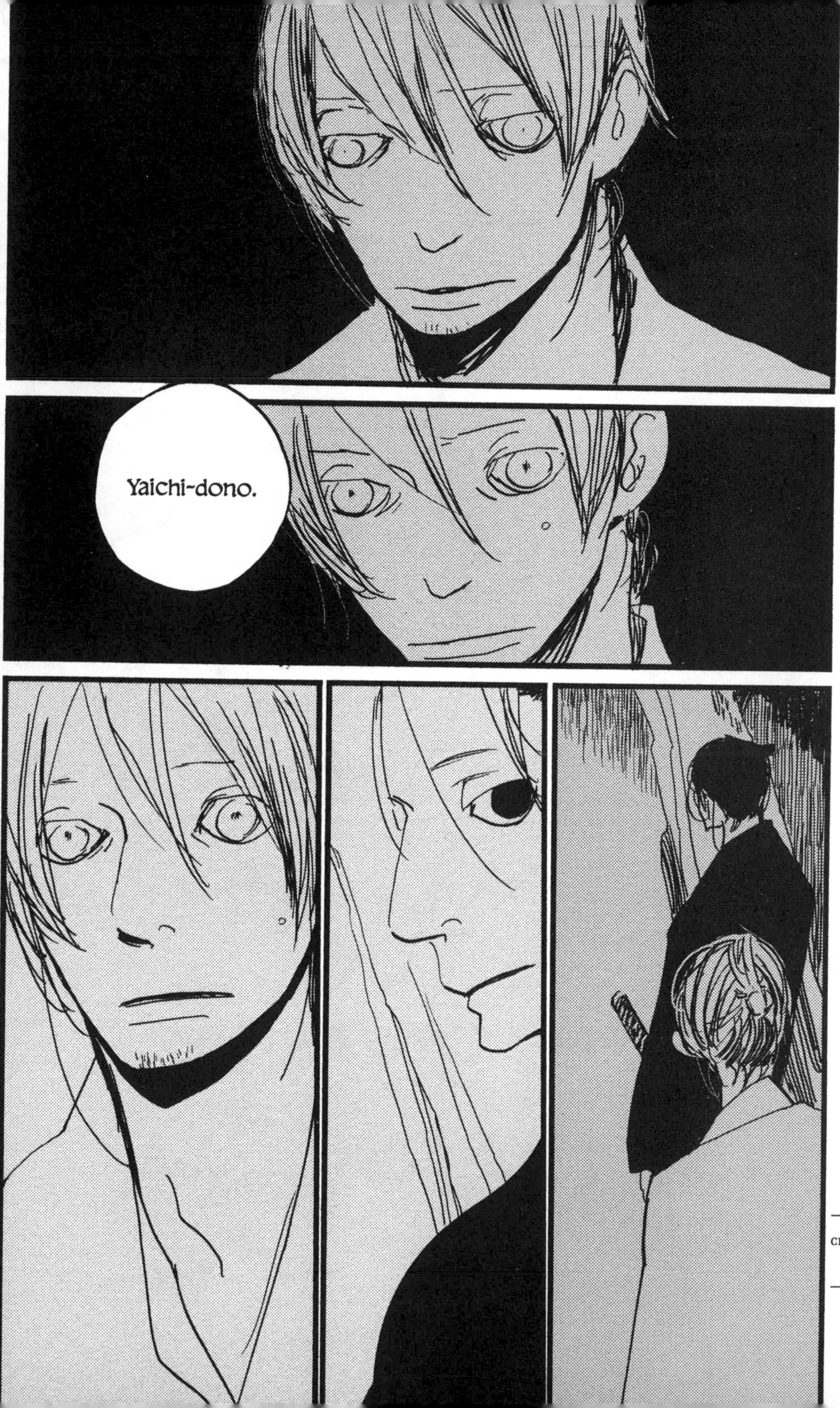
Yaichi-dono.

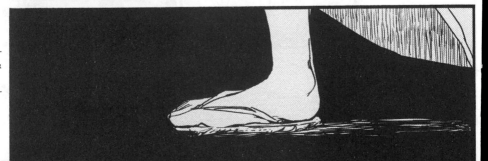

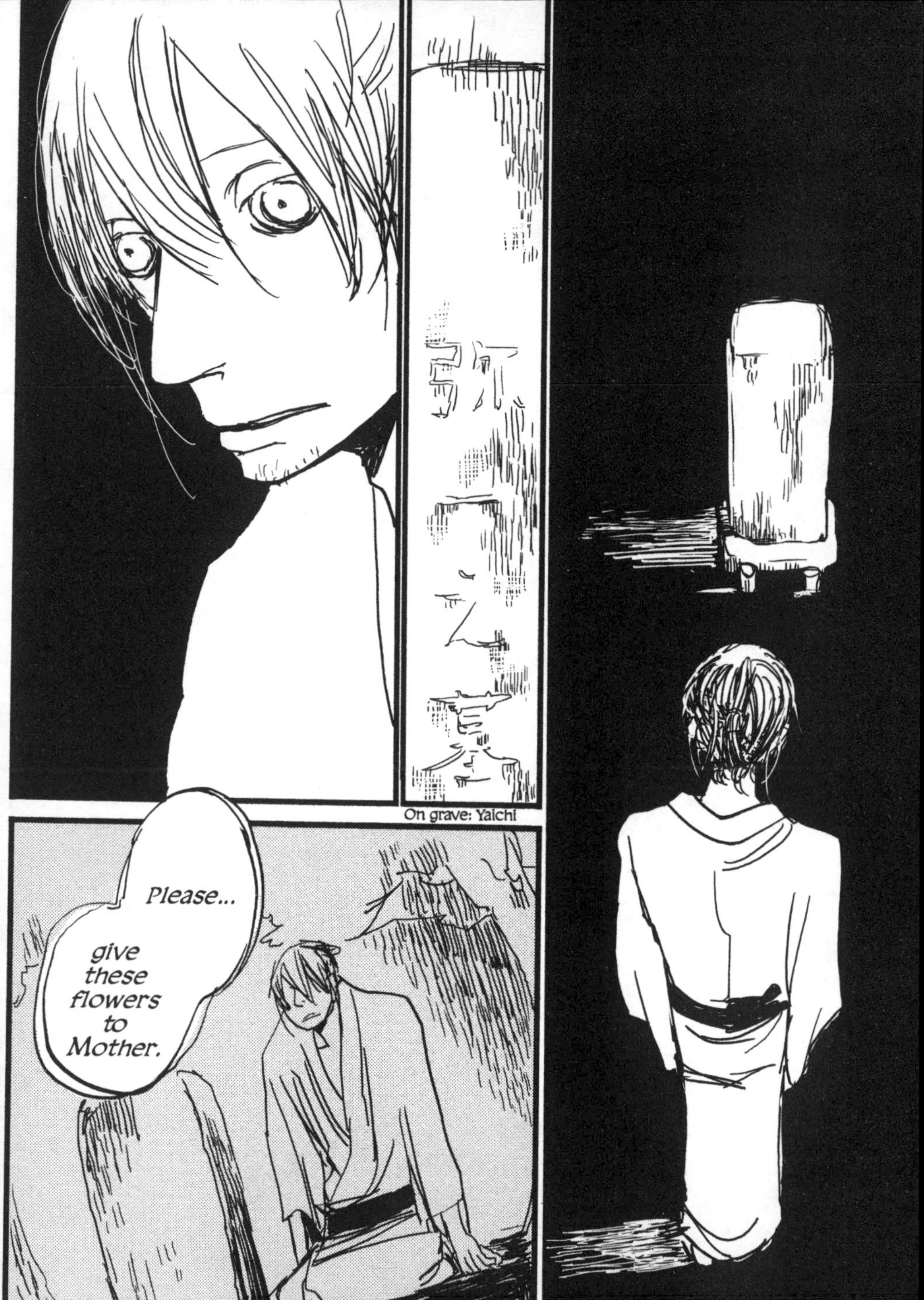
On grave: Yaichi
Please... give these flowers to Mother.

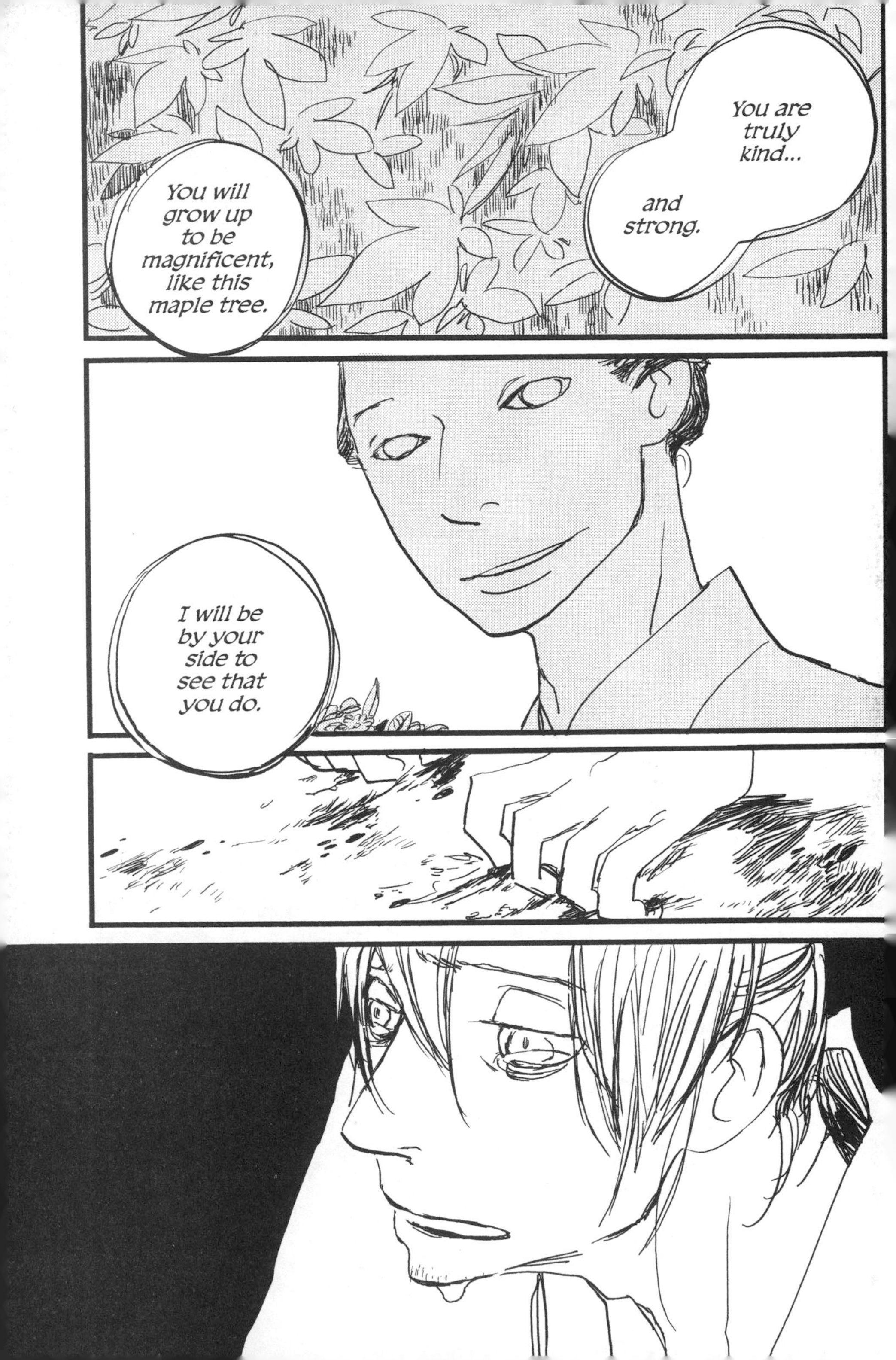
You are truly kind...
and strong.
You will grow up to be magnificent, like this maple tree.
I will be by your side to see that you do.

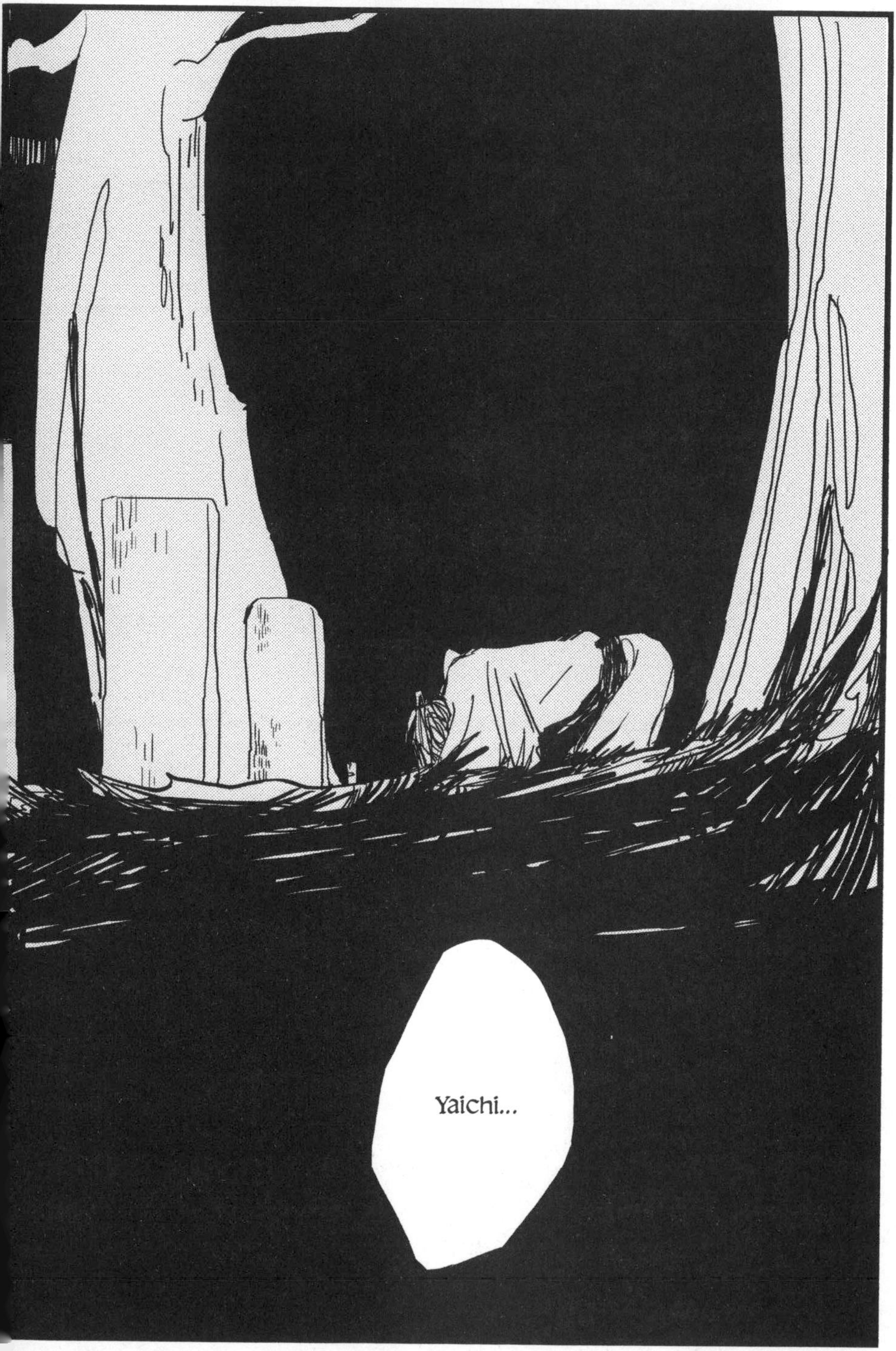
Yaichi...

END

House of Five Leaves

VOLUME **7**

GLOSSARY

ANIUE. A respectful term used by younger siblings when addressing the eldest brother in the family. A bit archaic in flavor, it is no longer commonly used. PAGE 176

ANIKI. Literally means "big brother" but is also used by gang members to refer to the boss of their crew. PAGE 4

CHAN. An honorific suffix used as an endearment when the speaker is talking to a person (usually a girl) younger and lower in status. PAGE 133

DAIMYO. A feudal lord, the ruler of a domain (or *han*, in Japanese) under the shogunate. PAGE 108

DON. A shortened, more casual form of *dono*. PAGE 162

DONO. An honorific suffix that's the equivalent of "sir" or "lady." A very formal term, it's not commonly used these days. PAGE 127

HATAMOTO. In the Edo period, men bearing the title of *hatamoto* served directly under the shogun. PAGE 40

IZAKAYA. A traditional Japanese pub that serves liquor and simple dishes. PAGE 5

MACHIKATA. The Edo-era analogue of a uniformed municipal police force, it was staffed mainly by low-ranking samurai. PAGE 5

RAKUGAN. Sweets made of a rice flour and sugar base, they are usually tinted with pastel colors and shaped into decorative forms. PAGE 15

RONIN. A masterless or unemployed samurai. PAGE 4

SAKAYAKI. A feudal-era men's hairstyle. The crown of the head was shaved and the remaining hair bound into a topknot. PAGE 79

SAMA. An honorific suffix used when addressing someone higher in status, or when the speaker wants to emphasize the respect in which he or she holds the person being addressed. PAGE 15

SAN. An honorific suffix that functions roughly like "Mr." or "Ms." in English. It is the most status-neutral and common way of addressing others in Japanese. PAGE 56

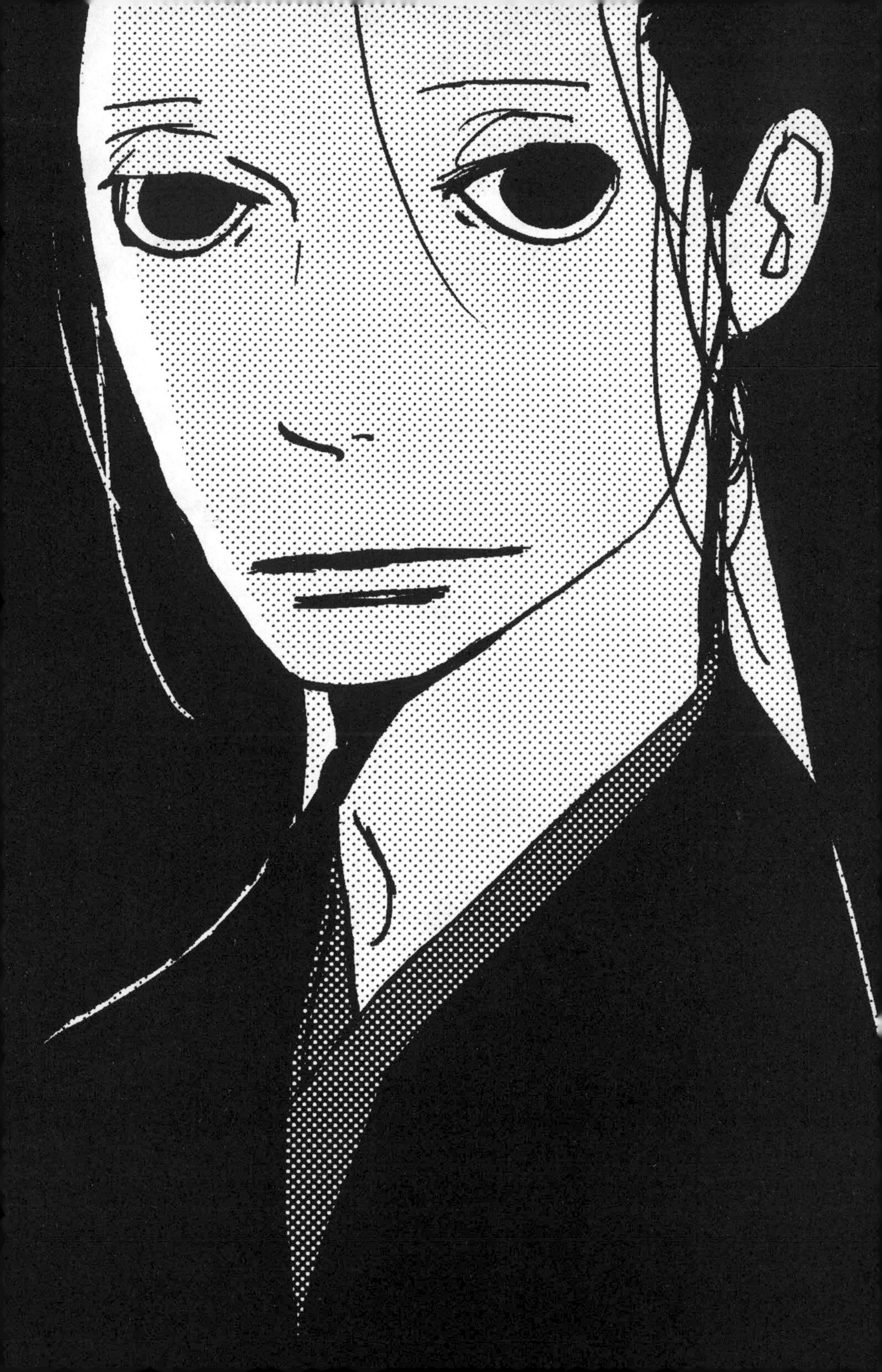

THE FINAL VOLUME...

Masanosuke gives Bunnosuke one last piece of advice as his older brother. Rumors about the Five Leaves are spreading around town, leaving the members of the crew plagued with suspicion as to who is responsible. Meanwhile, Yaichi is finally run to ground by Jin, his former superior, at the same time that his past is uncovered by the superintendent Yagi. With the House of Five Leaves coming to an end, will the precious bonds of their friendships survive?

AVAILABLE SEPTEMBER 2012

House
of Five
Leaves

Five Leaves
Complete Series Premium Edition

This beautiful box set features the complete two-volume, twelve-episode DVD set of the acclaimed anime series and features the original Japanese audio with English subtitles, as well as a sturdy slipcase and full-color hardcover art book.

House of Five Leaves Complete Series Premium Edition comes with a hardcover art book (full-color, 30+ pages), featuring character information, episode guides, artwork, behind-the-scenes storyboards, draft designs, concept art, and even a glossary of terms for insight on the culture of feudal Japan.

House of Five Leaves
Complete Series Premium Edition
12 episodes • approx. 274 minutes • color
Bonus Content:
Clean Opening and Ending, Japanese Trailer

House of

from groundbreaking manga creator

Natsume Ono!

The ronin Akitsu Masanosuke was working as a bodyguard in Edo, but due to his shy personality, he kept being let go from his bodyguard jobs despite his magnificent sword skills. Unable to find new work, he wanders around town and meets a man, the playboy who calls himself Yaichi. Even though Yaichi and Masanosuke had just met for the first time, Yaichi treats Masanosuke to a meal and offers to hire him as a bodyguard. Despite the mysteries that surround Yaichi, Masanosuke takes the job. He soon finds out that Yaichi is the leader of a group of kidnappers who call themselves the "Five Leaves." Now Masanosuke is faced with the dilemma of whether to join the Five Leaves and share in the profits of kidnapping, or to resist becoming a criminal.

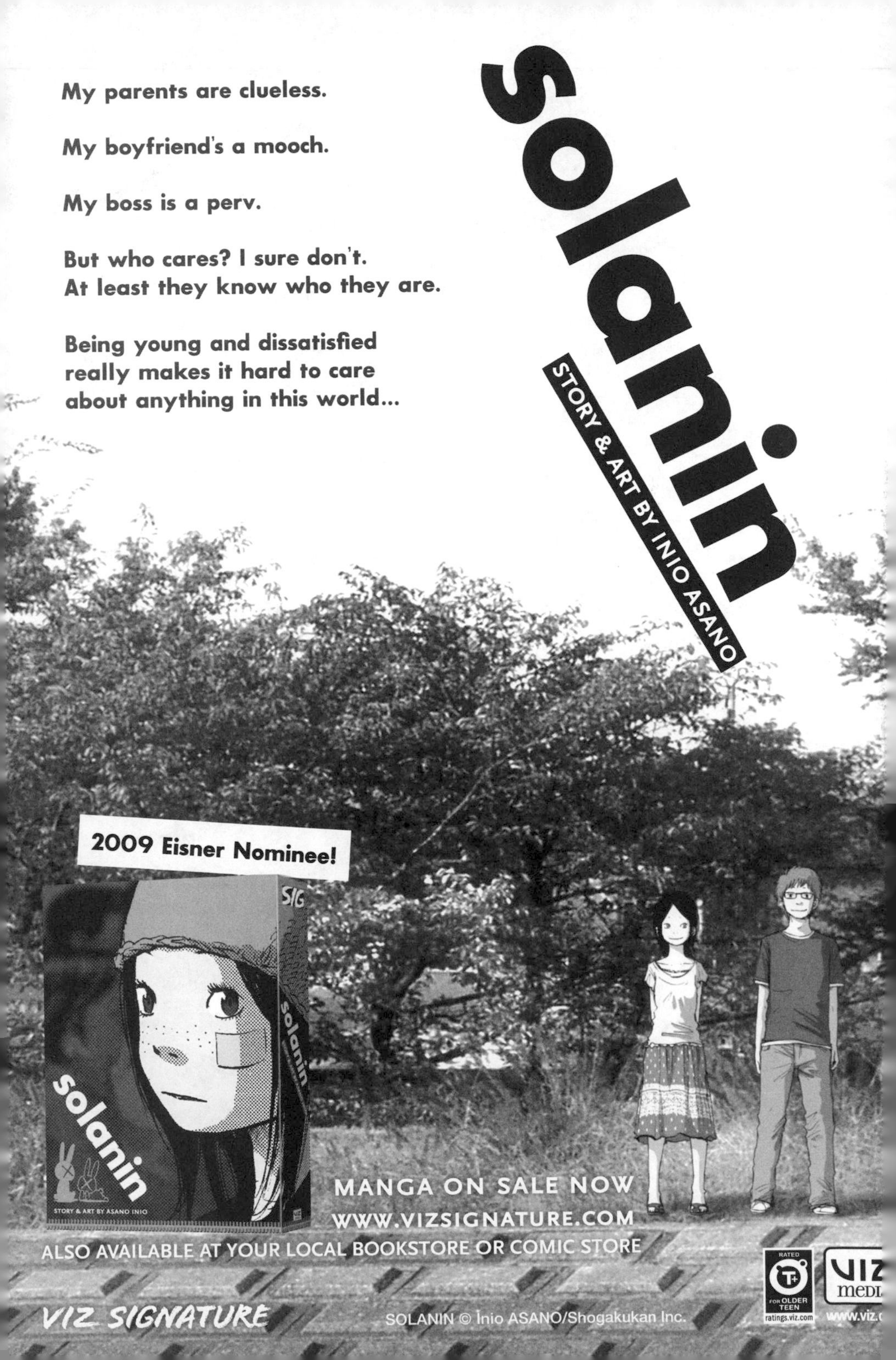

HOUSE OF FIVE LEAVES
Volume Seven

VIZ Signature Edition

STORY & ART BY NATSUME ONO

© 2006 Natsume ONO/Shogakukan
All rights reserved.
Original Japanese edition "SARAIYA GOYOU" published by SHOGAKUKAN Inc.

Original Japanese cover design by Atsuhiro YAMAMOTO

TRANSLATION Joe Yamazaki
TOUCH-UP ART & LETTERING Gia Cam Luc
DESIGN Fawn Lau
EDITOR Leyla Aker

Printed in the U.S.A.

Published by VIZ Media, LLC
P.O. Box 77010
San Francisco, CA 94107

10 9 8 7 6 5 4 3 2 1
First printing, June 2012

VIZ SIGNATURE
WWW.SIGIKKI.COM

PARENTAL ADVISORY
HOUSE OF FIVE LEAVES is rated T+ for Older Teen and is recommended for ages 16 and up.

RATED
T+
FOR OLDER TEEN
ratings.viz.com

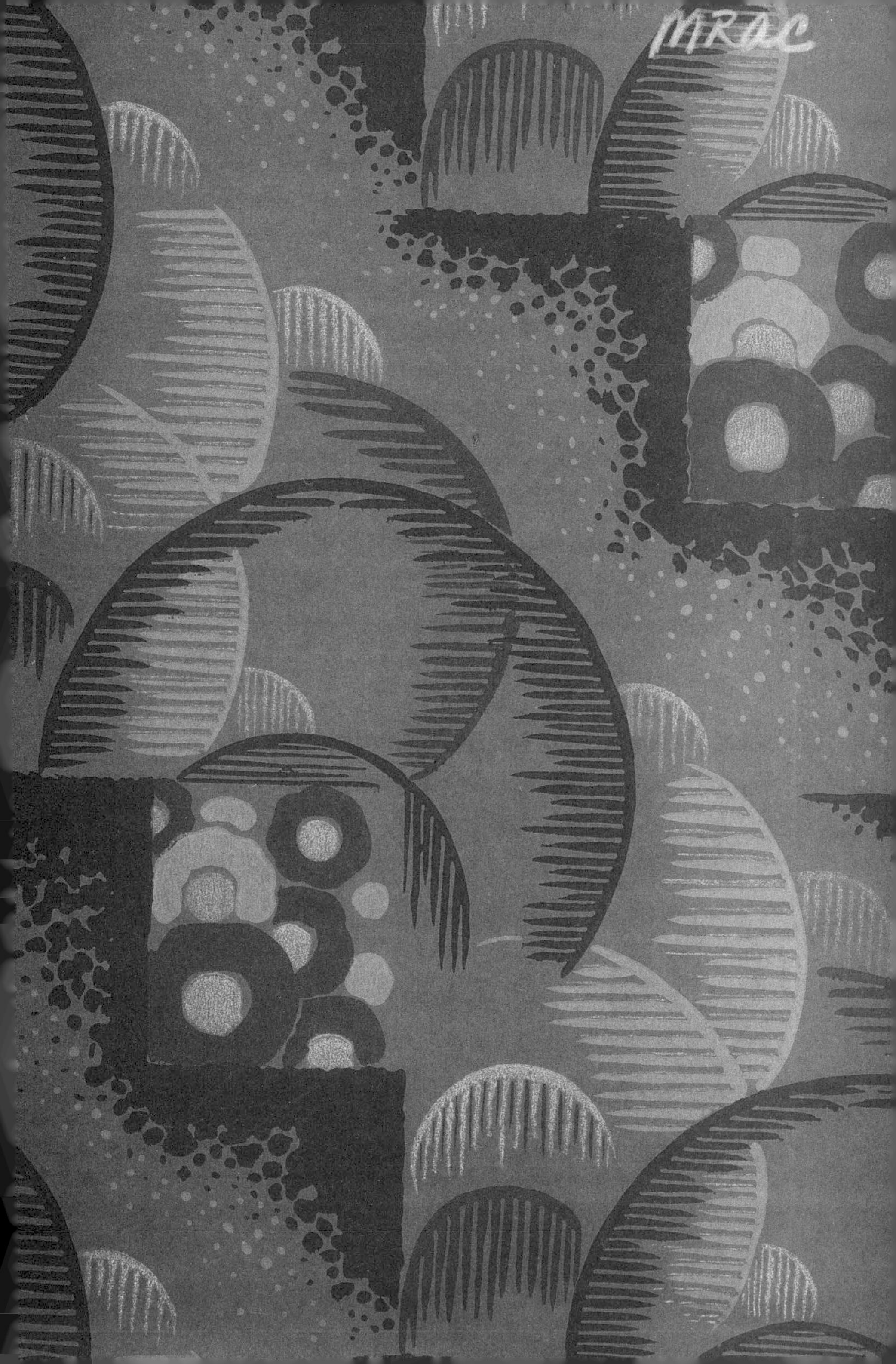
MRAC